# Sexuality Education

**Recent Titles in**
**Sex, Love, and Psychology**
*Judy Kuriansky, Series Editor*

Sexual Health (4 volumes)
*Mitchell S. Tepper and Annette Fuglsang Owens, editors*

Relationship Sabotage: Unconscious Factors that Destroy Couples, Marriages, and Family
*William J. Matta*

The Praeger Handbook of Transsexuality: Changing Gender to Match Mindset
*Rachel Ann Heath*

America's War on Sex
*Marty Klein*

Teenagers, HIV, and AIDS: Insights from Youths Living with the Virus
*Maureen E. Lyon and Lawrence J. D'Angelo, editors*

Rock 'n' Roll Wisdom: What Psychologically Astute Lyrics Teach about Life and Love
*Barry A. Farber*

Sixty, Sexy, and Successful: A Guide for Aging Male Baby Boomers
*Robert Schwalbe, PhD*

Managing Menopause Beautifully: Physically, Emotionally, and Sexually
*Dona Caine-Francis*

New Frontiers in Men's Sexual Health: Understanding Erectile Dysfunction and the
Revolutionary New Treatments
*Kamal A. Hanash, M.D.*

# SEXUALITY EDUCATION

## Past, Present, and Future

Volume 1
History and Foundations

Edited by Elizabeth Schroeder, EdD and Judy Kuriansky, PhD

*Praeger Perspectives*

Sex, Love, and Psychology

Westport, Connecticut
London

**Library of Congress Cataloging-in-Publication Data**

Sexuality education : past, present, and future / edited by Elizabeth Schroeder and Judy Kuriansky.
   v. ; cm. — (Sex, love, and psychology, ISSN 1554–222X)
   Includes bibliographical references and index.
   Contents: v. 1. — History and Foundations.
   ISBN 978–0–275–99794–6 (set : alk. paper) — ISBN 978–0–275–99796–0 (v.1 : alk. paper) — ISBN 978–0–275–99798–4 (v.2 : alk. paper) — ISBN 978–0–275–99800–4 (v.3 : alk. paper) — ISBN 978–0–275–99802–8 (v.4 : alk. paper)
   1. Sex instruction—History. I. Schroeder, Elizabeth. II. Kuriansky, Judith.
HQ56.S38634 2009
613.9071'273—dc22          2008051469

British Library Cataloguing in Publication Data is available.

Library of Congress Catalog Card Number: 2008051469
ISBN: 978–0–275–99794–6 (set)
         978–0–275–99796–0 (Vol. 1)
         978–0–275–99798–4 (Vol. 2)
         978–0–275–99800–4 (Vol. 3)
         978–0–275–99802–8 (Vol. 4)
ISSN: 1554–222X

First published in 2009

Praeger Publishers, 88 Post Road West, Westport, CT 06881
An imprint of Greenwood Publishing Group, Inc.
www.praeger.com

Printed in the United States of America

The paper used in this book complies with the
Permanent Paper Standard issued by the National
Information Standards Organization (Z39.48–1984).

10 9 8 7 6 5 4 3 2 1

Every reasonable effort has been made to trace the owners of copyright materials in this book, but in some instances this has proven impossible. The editors and publisher will be glad to receive information leading to more complete acknowledgments in subsequent printings of the book and in the meantime extend their apologies for any omissions.

# CONTENTS

# FOREWORD

For more than two generations, sexuality educators have been championing the cause for understanding the importance of healthy sexuality and sexual expression in human development. It has been a rocky road, still under construction, filled with numerous detours, challenges and fraught with significant controversy due to powerful social and political forces. The continuation of this effort is essential as recent data at this writing, especially about young people, is extraordinarily alarming:

- 100 young people become pregnant every hour of every day in America;
- 50 young people give birth every hour of every day in America;
- 25 young people have a pregnancy termination every hour of every day in America;
- 425 young people contract a sexually transmitted infection every hour of every day in America;
- 2 young people become infected with HIV every hour of every day in America.

So as you can see, this is not some vague social problem floating around in our culture. What kind of society allows this to occur? Shouldn't we question ourselves? Shouldn't this make us tremble? Shockingly, our best thinking and our best doing in this great country of ours got us where we are today. We simply must do better. For these reasons I am grateful for the opportunity to write this foreword for *Sexuality Education: Past, Present, and Future*. This is a formidable set of volumes and will provide essential tools in meeting the enormous challenges facing us as we move through the twenty-first century.

As I began to write the foreword for this important set of books, I was encouraged by the possibility of change. The United States has elected a new president and congressional leadership on the promise of change. Specific to the themes in this four book set, our new president Barack Obama is the first candidate in our lifetime who has openly supported comprehensive sexuality education throughout his campaign. He has consistently embraced research and reason and has resisted strong conservative attempts to restrain scientific public discourse on sexuality issues through the life cycle. While the extent to which the new administration will support comprehensive sexuality education is yet to be seen, dialogue about this critical issue has already begun at important senior levels of government. I believe this essential dialogue will be informed by this rich and vital resource of books with contributions from national leaders in the sexuality field.

*Sexuality Education: Past, Present, and Future* covers a vast range of issues of great value to educators, student's, policymakers, researchers, and the general public. All of these groups now have access to a unique overview that has never before been presented together in this fashion, from tracing the early development of the field to bringing it forward toward the most progressive possibilities for the future. I am honored that my own work of 25 years on adolescent pregnancy prevention with the Children's Aid Society in New York is discussed in various chapters in this series. No other resource I have seen has made a more thorough and intensive examination of the evolution of sexuality education—allowing us to see what has existed, what has changed or remains the same, and what holds promise for the future. This deep and rich four volume set also addresses the invaluable yet often overlooked need for educational intervention which is evident in the voices of learners themselves. Whether we reach people through a formal classroom setting, or teach eager persons in a remote rural areas willing to walk miles and sit on a dirt floor to learn about these topics, or educate individuals through one-on-one interventions via the Internet or over the air waves—a key component is understanding what learners *need* and also *want*—to know about sexuality.

Volume 1 sets the stage for the issues and context of this valuable process. Volume 2 is an invaluable resource for all sexuality educators, researchers, health professionals, policymakers and legislators, as it offers diverse and provocative reports of what different populations in the United States—and around the world—seek to learn about sexuality and sexual expression and how they face similar issues about access to acquiring such life-enhancing education. Equally important are the contributions that help us distinguish differences in approach for diverse cultural populations, and knowing what is appropriate to teach learners of different ages in such groups. Volume 3 of this resource addresses this issue by describing programs with children and unique approaches with adolescents engaged in peer education efforts, while also highlighting the need for parents to receive support in their roles as sexuality educators of their own children. Also included in this volume is the recognition that age is not the only issue about which sexuality education initiatives must remain cognizant. Diversity, including learning style, age, developmental level, sexual orientation, and gender and relationship status, all affect the way in which sexuality information is conveyed and heard. Accordingly, this volume provides invaluable perspectives on the best practices to effectively reach the many diverse audiences sexuality educators serve.

What does the future of sexuality education hold? Answers will reveal themselves over time, but volume 4 presents readers with cutting edge information, programs, approaches, techniques, and resources that enable us to think about best practices and how sexuality education can—and should—take place. My own view on this is that orthodoxy has failed, so we must continue to develop nontraditional ways of teaching about sexuality, and to push through the resistance that attempts to censor the public discussion of sexuality and sexual expression. Only then will we truly consider nontraditional topics or relationships and make a difference in the way all people, young and older, learn about their sexuality—which is an essential and not well understood fiber in the fabric of their wholeness. Volume 4 thoroughly captures these notions.

In my book, *Lessons for Lifeguards*, I suggest that "effective programs do not happen by spontaneous combustion; someone has got to light the fire. Be incendiary in your efforts." I believe this four-volume set provides the fuel and other combustible materials to enable you to make a difference in your role as a sexuality educator, however you may define that role and with whomever you engage. As of this writing, I have worked 50 years with young people and their families. These extraordinary volumes reinforce why I continue to try to press ahead in our field.

*Dr. Michael A. Carrera*

# ACKNOWLEDGMENTS

"Thank you, thank you. Appreciation is the thing to do. Thank him, thank her. For all the things you do for me, thank you."

These words came to Judy in the middle of yet another all-nighter while working on the Herculean task of putting together this set of books, and they represent the feelings of both of us. The phrase formed the basis of a song that Judy and her co-lyricist and fellow composer, Russell Daisey, wrote and then performed at peace charity concerts in Japan. The spirit of appreciation that inspired the song was so appropriate for the Japanese tradition of honoring—but also very appropriately inspired the process of putting together this set of volumes.

To say that putting together this four-volume set was tantamount to giving birth to quadruplets is an unbelievable understatement. True, it wasn't as painful, but the labor took a long time, many people contributed to and supported us throughout the process, and we are very proud of the outcome.

So, now, at this time of completion of this four-volume set with over 60 chapters and more then 100 authors, we are moved to recall that spirit of appreciation that was captured in Judy's song:

- Our appreciation goes to all the contributors to these volumes, some of whom are dear friends as well as colleagues. We honor the individuals they are and the work they are doing, which is contributing so much to others. Their hard work and commitment to educating professionals and the public about the need for sexuality education, and the wide range of what can be considered sexuality education, have been invaluable. Thank you so much.
- Our appreciation also extends to all those written about in these pages; may they be comforted and inspired by their contributions to the caring and hard work

reflected in these chapters, to ease—and prevent—sexually related problems and contribute to sexually well-educated and healthy lives for all.

- We are also deeply grateful to Praeger Publishing's Debbie Carvalko, Praeger Senior Acquisitions Editor, psychology and health, who championed this project and was always available with wise counsel, vision, and encouragement. We're also grateful to Elizabeth Potenza, Praeger Development Editor, and Apex CoVantage's Project Manager, Mary Cotofan, for their kindness, attention, and hard work, whom we e-mailed over the course of this project more, even on Sundays, than some members of our own families. We thank them all for their valued guidance, patience, and  support throughout this project. We also extend gratitude to all the staff at Praeger and Apex CoVantage, who worked so diligently on this project.

In addition, from Judy:

I have deep appreciation for my wonderful and wise, creative and caring, friend and musical collaborator Russell, who was constantly there for me through so many all-nighters while I was writing my own chapters and editing others. He is truly an angel and a shining example of a consummate talent, great listener and sage advisor rolled into one. The same wisdom and championing is true of my mom, Sylvia, whom I cherish and to whom I owe so much for her constant love and devotion. She is also truly an angel. No words can ever express the depth of my appreciation and affection for her, but *her* words, "one thing at a time," were such good counsel for her daughter who is compelled to multitask 10 things at once. Yet her confidence, "I know you will get it all done," was also reassuring. Equally inspiring is her profound respect for sexuality education, especially—as she'll even describe in her sweet way—having grown up in a generation less open about such things. And then, just when the work was reaching a fevered pitch, two other angels appeared in the form of my Smith College interns—Amanda Calvo and Jennifer Arias—with their warm hearts, devotion, trustworthiness, enthusiastic spirit, varied talents, and brilliance beyond their years, not to mention their keen editing skills and willingness to try any format for a table or look up any detail on the Internet. The chapters they each contributed to are favorites, as every word is infused with their love, hard work, and good humor, like when reminding me to sleep or eat. I adore them and I am filled with pride for who they are and for the professionals they will become.

Another angel was there from the start, my coeditor, Elizabeth Schroeder, who is indeed a dream come true as a colleague and friend with whom to share such a task. Her excellent judgment, steadfast reliability, warm heart, terrific good-humor and great team spirit—not to mention her brilliantly written e-mails, which always served to uplift and amuse—set a new standard for a collaborator with such a broad "skill set" in a woman with such a pleasant personality mixed with a smart and organized brain. I am very blessed—and now very spoiled—to have worked with her on this project and look forward to many more in the future.

And from Elizabeth:

I would not have been a part of this project had it not been for Bill Taverner, director of education at Planned Parenthood of Greater Northern New Jersey's Center for Family Life Education. You are a most generous, wonderful colleague, Bill, and I value you immensely.

I also wish to thank Nora Gelperin, director of education and training at Answer, who provided instrumental research assistance for the series. Nora, you are a consummate professional, colleague, and friend who I can also now refer to as my coworker. I am so lucky to know you.

I was also fortunate to have had a wonderful graduate student from Montclair State University, Holly Den Bleyker, helping me with obtaining permissions, inputting edits, and lending her keen eye to a good number of the chapters. Holly, I will miss being able to avail myself of your amazing work!

Above all, I need to thank Dr. Judy Kuriansky. Readers should know that Judy originally had a supervisory role as the series editor but became so excited by and committed to the project that she joined as an equal coeditor, both generating her own content and securing much of it as well. This four book set honestly would not have happened without her, and her contributions— as an author of so many compelling, eye-opening chapters; as an editor with a creative, analytical eye; and as a brilliant thinker and brainstormer whose humor and collegiality really kept me going throughout this project—truly made the set the unique resource it is. Judy, I am honored to have worked with you on this and to now be able to call you friend. So what's our next project?

Finally, we both want to thank all the sexuality educators in the field—those who have done the work in the past, those who are doing the work today, and those who will do the work in the future. Whatever your role—university professor, school teacher or administrator, community-based educator, researcher, advocate, therapist or clinician, parent or other adult with children or young people in your life, or anyone else who knows how vital it is to learn about sexuality in its broadest definition throughout the life cycle—know that you are so important. Thank you for reading this set about sexuality education and for all you do for individuals, communities, society, and the world.

*Judy Kuriansky and Elizabeth Schroeder*

# INTRODUCTION

*Elizabeth Schroeder*

And you may ask yourself, "well—how did I get here?"
—David Byrne, singer, Talking Heads

Teaching human sexuality has a long history that, like any aspect of history, is replete with both positive and negative experiences, and challenges as well as triumphs. In response to David Byrne's question, sexuality educators often have interesting stories about how they ended up in this field—many times prefacing this with, "I never imagined that I'd be doing this for a living!" Others, however, know from the time they are in high school or college that they wish to teach others about human sexuality.

The field of sexuality education has been, and continues to be, affected by various factors, including the culture of a given generation, the government in power at a particular time, the current health issues and challenges, and the allocation of federal and state funding. Social ills related to sexuality also have a considerable impact. These include negative health consequences such as sexually transmitted infections, too-early pregnancy and childbirth, sexual violence, and more. These social ills become complicated by the fact that they are often reported in the news media with responses rife with contradictions over how these problems should be addressed.

Even with all these trials, sexuality education is and should be about much more than preventing negative consequences. Such teaching should start early and set the basic framework for all human interactions. It should teach respect for others and for oneself. It should embrace the idea that sexual feelings and expressions are gifts that should be cherished, yet handled with care, rather than considered as simply animal instincts that are feared and considered out of control.

Teaching human sexuality is multifaceted. In many ways, teaching about sexuality takes place informally each and every day through interpersonal interactions. Messages about sexuality and teaching people how to use their sexuality happen when a mother holds her baby; when an adult tells a male child "only girls should have long hair"; when a television commercial advertises Bratz dolls dressed scantily; when a person tells a friend to flirt with a bartender or server at a restaurant in order to receive special treatment. Yet, with so many daily, informal messages and lessons about sexuality, the formal teaching of human sexuality is a discipline that requires training in content and skills in delivering information in effective ways depending on the audience. It also requires a clear sense of values and beliefs and how they influence teaching.

Volume 1 of this four-part set provides the reader with a historical look at sexuality education over the last century and examines some of the questions listed previously. The volume outlines and provides examples of different theoretical bases for sexuality education, and it describes how and why disagreement on teaching about sexuality began and why these disputes persist even into today's sexually saturated culture. Chapters in this volume present existing research on school- and community-based sexuality education programming and community controversies that have ensued as a result of these programs. Chapters also discuss criteria vital for an adult professional in order to be an effective sexuality educator and explore what *effectiveness* refers to within a given program or intervention. Other chapters explore issues of values and religions and suggest what the United States can learn from other countries where sexuality is not feared and is openly discussed with young people and, consequently, where rates of sexually transmitted infections (STIs) and teen pregnancy are lower.

David Byrne's question "well, how did I get here?" is appropriate for the sexuality education field and the rich history from which it has emerged. The questions addressed in this volume include: Why is it that sexuality education remains so controversial? Why is there a sense from some that teaching exclusively about abstinence is the only moral imperative and from others that spirituality and faith have no place in sexuality education? Why has the United States put such emphasis in school around academic achievement and test results without requiring that testing include health-related courses, including sexual health? Why is there insufficient support for doing what is necessary to create sexually healthy adolescents and adults when the world is faced with an HIV pandemic, millions of unplanned and unwanted pregnancies, unhealthy relationships, homophobia, and more? There are many possible answers to these questions, all of which involve, to some extent, politics, opinion, power struggles, overworked and underpaid sexuality professionals, frightened parents, and more. Regardless of the various answers, however, most people will agree that there have been many successes as a result of providing learners of all ages and developmental abilities with some form of sexuality education—along with failures, setbacks, and inconsistent messages for our learners.

The song quoted at the beginning of this foreword—a song first released in 1980—has another line repeated throughout, which is: "same as it ever was." This lyric also applies to sexuality education. Some of the issues of the early twentieth century are still issues faced today. The reader is invited, therefore, to explore all of these chapters with an eye toward noticing how history affects our present and our future (as discussed in volume 4 of this set)—to notice what was, what has changed, and what seems to be the "same as it ever was."

Sexuality education is a complex issue with no easy answers. However, by exploring the issues addressed in this volume, educators of all disciplines can have a perspective and foundation with which to form ways of integrating sexuality issues into their teaching efforts.

Part I

# SETTING THE STAGE

# Chapter One

# WHAT IS SEXUALITY EDUCATION? DEFINITIONS AND MODELS

*Elizabeth Schroeder*

Sex. Each reader will have her or his own response to that word: *Sex*. For some, an intimate act between two people will immediately come to mind. For many, that sex act will be penis–vagina sexual intercourse. Other readers may begin to muse about what *sex* is, knowing that former President Clinton's pronouncement that oral sex is *not* "sex" sparked an ongoing debate of which sexual behaviors do and do not qualify as sex. Still other readers will think of nonintercourse behaviors, and some will think of sex as the biological determination of a person as a man, woman, or intersex individual.

What, therefore, does *sexuality* mean? What do those six letters following the word *sex* do for the definition of the word? The answer is: Everything. Adding those six letters makes a three-letter word that, although rife with various meanings and connotations, is limited in scope explode with far greater meaning. *Sexuality* is an expansive term that pertains to far more than our biology or sexual behaviors, although those two elements are certainly integral parts. Dr. Mary Calderone, cofounder of the Sex (now Sexuality) Information and Education Council of the United States (SIECUS), said it best when she stated, "sex is what you do; sexuality is who you are."

For many sexuality educators, no definition could ring more true than what Dr. Calderone summarized in her simple phrase. At the same time, however, disagreement remains over what is or should be included in sexuality education. In a sexually charged society such as the United States, which one might expect to be progressive about sexual issues, government-supported sexuality education has focused and continues to focus primarily on disease and pregnancy prevention. Currently supported sexuality education programs place emphasis on talking young people out of being sexually active without explaining what *sexually active* even means. The "just say no" approach—as with the message once promulgated to youth about drugs—does not work and simply tries to frighten young people out of being sexual with another person because they could end up with a sexually transmitted infection (STI), particularly HIV. Programs teach girls negotiation and refusal skills because "boys will be boys"—leaving girls responsible for maintaining the moral boundaries around sexual behaviors in male–female relationships. Programs tend to ignore nonheterosexual and non–gender-congruent individuals (those who are lesbian, gay, bisexual, and/or transgender), mention them in passing, or discuss them exclusively within the context of HIV and AIDS. Sexuality experts maintain that all of these emphases are short-sighted and ineffective, and they reduce sexuality to a small, untamed beast that lives inside of everyone and that only needs to be suppressed until one's wedding night when it is deemed acceptable to release it.

Instead, many sexuality educators—including myself and the coeditor of this set of books—encourage people to see *sexuality* as a much broader term that covers a wider array of topics, as shown in Figure 1.1. This model shows a much more holistic view of sexuality, one that should be the roadmap for sexuality education programming and interventions.

There are several aspects of the model of which one should take note. First, it is imperative to consider the vast range of topics addressed in the circles identified in Dr. Dailey's model. Although the majority of sexuality education programs throughout the United States (and in many places around the world) have safely remained within the circle of "Sexual Health and Reproduction," being restricted to that circle leaves out many important issues that real people—and especially young people—deal with. For example, it is clear that attempting to address the reasons why a young person engages in sexual behaviors at an early age may be related to his or body image, which is part of the "Sensuality" circle, a wider circle than "Sexual Health and Reproduction" as shown in the figure. A girl with a poor body image may think that she will feel better about herself by being intimate with another person, regardless of the reality. Or, looking at another circle in the figure—the Intimacy circle—a boy might do something sexual at an early age because of his developmentally related sense of risk-taking; consistent with the fact that adolescents see themselves as impervious to the potentially negative consequences of their actions, including sexual activities. Or, expanding even broader to the "Sexualization" circle, a young person might imitate unsafe or too-early sexual behaviors they have seen in the media, or they may not even have had a choice about whether to become sexually active because they were sexually assaulted, harassed, or abused in some way. Clearly, teaching sexuality exclusively within the "Sexual

**Figure 1.1**
**A Model of Holistic Sexuality**

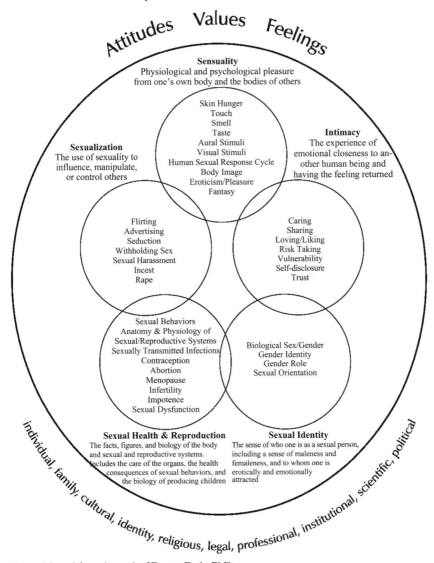

*Source*: Adapted from the work of Dennis Daile, PhD.

Health and Reproduction" circle is limiting and does a disservice to learners of all ages.

## LIFELONG LEARNING: UNDERSTANDING AGE AND WHAT IS DEVELOPMENTALLY APPROPRIATE

When I tell parents of younger children that I am a sexuality educator, I am often met with a response to the effect of, "Well, my child is only 7—I'm so glad I don't have to deal with that yet." Imagine the looks I receive when I reply, "Well . . . actually, it's a really good idea to start now." My response reflects the knowledge that I and other sexuality educators have—that sexuality starts from birth and that curiosity and questions about sexuality are normal parts of growing up.

Parents fear sexuality partly because they and other adults remain fixated on the "sex" part of sexuality, which implies the sex act, and they forget those extra six letters, "uality"—which encompasses all the other important aspects that are reflected in the Five Circles model. If adults do not discuss anything related to sexuality with young people until adolescence, those young people have already learned volumes from their peers and the media. Sadly, much of what they learn will be inaccurate, a lot will be confusing, and none will be provided by a trained professional. Books and resources such as those listed at the end of this volume can help parents, other adults, and professionals in health and other fields provide age-appropriate information to people of all ages.

When it comes to formal school-based learning about sexuality, many of us who have taught at the college level have found it tragic that higher education is often the last opportunity for people to learn about sexuality in a formal setting. Yet, if sexuality is an integral component of our lives from birth to death, why do we stop learning about it in our early 20s? How can we possibly be sexually healthy at age 50 if we have not learned anything new about sexuality in 30 years?

Age, however, is not the only factor. Any school- or community-based professional working today is likely to see a growing number of students with learning or emotional challenges or disabilities. What this means for sexuality education is that a 10th-grade student who has the developmental level of a 4th-grade student should not be placed in the same sexuality education class as her or his 10th-grade contemporaries. It is vital that age not be the sole factor in determining what is appropriate for an adolescent or adult to learn about sexuality.

## NON–SCHOOL-BASED SEXUALITY EDUCATION

School is the natural place for sexuality education—yet, once a person has stopped going to school, at whatever level that may be, there are vastly fewer opportunities to learn about sexuality in any formal way. This is where different types of and venues for sexuality education come in. Not all sexuality education takes place in a formal classroom setting. Learning about sexuality—providing accurate information to adults—can happen through a variety of settings or media. For example, sexuality education can be provided in one-on-one interventions by medical doctors and clinicians, counselors, and therapists. In fact, sexuality-related complaints are among the most common issues that bring adult couples into therapy or counseling, including differences in sex drive, boredom in the bedroom, pain, performance concerns, difficulty reaching orgasm, or a desire by one partner to try something nontraditional that is not desired by the other.

Sexuality education is also provided through the media. In the United States, and throughout the world, especially where countries have access to U.S.-created television, film, and other media, people are bombarded by graphic sexual messages and images. Many complain that programming, including "reality TV" shows, does more to reinforce stereotypes, perpetuate myths, and create controversy than educate. Thankfully, efforts have been made, and continue to be made, to use media in a more positive way—to educate via films, soap operas, radio shows, and other venues. Some of these efforts are presented in this book series, particularly in volume four. They include the use of video games to teach about sexuality, Web-based sexuality education, and much more.

## CONCLUSION: WHO ARE SEXUALITY EDUCATORS?

The term *sexuality educator* is as broad a phrase as the word *sexuality* itself. There are those of us who have been trained specifically as sexuality educators, for whom this is our exclusive work. Others are teachers of other topic areas—such as health or science—within whose bailiwick teaching sexuality may fall according to the school curriculum. Some of us are trained as counselors, therapists, social workers, or youth-serving professionals who may provide information and education about sexuality either directly (e.g., by answering questions) or indirectly (e.g., by modeling how to maintain appropriate interpersonal boundaries). Some are media professionals who help educators in more traditional settings reach the public with their important work. And some are young people and adults who serve as peer educators, learning and sharing their learning with their same-age teens, friends, and classmates.

Sexuality education can be provided in many ways, using a range of pedagogies, methods, techniques, and resources. Regardless of the manner in which we teach people about sexuality, being a sexuality educator is an enormous responsibility, one that must be taken with seriousness for what we teach and a sense of joy for the hopeful outcome of helping people to feel good about themselves and their relationships throughout their entire lives.

Chapter Two

# A CRISIS OF IDENTITY IN SEXUALITY EDUCATION IN AMERICA: HOW DID WE GET HERE AND WHERE ARE WE GOING?

*Eva S. Goldfarb*

Over the first hundred-plus years of organized sexuality education in the United States, there have been two distinct, somewhat incompatible, competing philosophies about its goals and purposes. One philosophy envisions what was then referred to as *sex education* as a means to affect the behaviors and morals of society. This approach was first articulated and advanced by social reformers who focused on sexual behaviors and advocated for education as a means to reduce out-of-wedlock sex and pregnancies, as well as venereal disease, masturbation, prostitution, and any nonprocreative sexual behaviors. The second philosophy took a broader view of sexuality as a life-long human force—and as a source of pleasure—that needed to be understood and appreciated for better mental, physical, social, and spiritual health. The discrepancy in world views represented by these two visions was, and continues to be, reflected even in the language used to describe the field. The social reform movement, seeing this as largely an effort to control behaviors, tended to use the term *sex education*, while increasingly, those with a broader view tended to (and still do) use the term *sexuality education*. While many people today use these two terms interchangeably, they really represent two different schools of thought that have evolved over much of the twentieth century in the United States.

These two competing views shifted in and out of favor from the late nineteenth century up until the 1970s, when political and social forces would converge to join them together under the term *comprehensive sexuality education* (CSE). What has resulted since that time is an identity crisis within the field that has exposed the difficult reconciliation of opposing world views about the role of sexuality in people's lives as well as how to educate people about it. From the vantage point of 2008, the past three decades have seen a struggle over several issues central to the identity of the field of sexuality education itself. These issues are:

1. What are the appropriate goals and objectives for sexuality education?
2. Into what discipline(s) does sexuality education best fit? Or is it a discipline unto itself?
3. Who should teach sexuality education?
4. What role should sexuality education play in American society? What role should it play in the education of young people?
5. What is/should be the future direction of the sexuality education field?

## EARLY SHAPING FORCES

There is little doubt that sex education as envisioned by its early pioneers was a way to preserve the rapidly vanishing morality of the nineteenth century in the face of a society experiencing dynamic changes. The growth of urban development brought the break up of the traditional family, in which children tended to grow up and stay close to home. As young men and women went off to seek employment in the cities, they found a life that provided increased anonymity and the lure of prostitution. In short order, however, new implications for sexual relationships as a result of medical advances with treating venereal disease, the push for women's suffrage, and, in particular, the work of activist Margaret Sanger in the fight for the dissemination of birth control information to the public supported a new philosophy of sex for pleasure.

Although there were scattered attempts to teach sex education in the nineteenth century, through Universities, the YMCA and YWCA, and organizations such as the American Purity Alliance ("Some High Points in the History of Sex Education in the United States," 1938), the organized movement for sex education in the United States largely began at the start of the twentieth century (Bigelow, 1935). Dr. Prince Morrow, a physician, is largely considered to be the originator of the behavior-focused social reformer sex education movement in this country. His efforts to combat venereal disease began in the nineteenth century, and by the early 1900s, he was calling for the implementation of educational programs in the public schools to deal with the problem. In 1905, Morrow formed the American Society of Sanity and Moral Prophylaxis. Composed of medical professionals, this group's major concern was the eradication of venereal disease through medical treatment and education. In their own words, the organization aimed to:

protect the community against the spread of venereal disease by enlightening adults as to their dangers, inspiring the youth of both sexes to lead pure lives and by minimizing the appeal of the prostitute and the opportunity of the quack doctor. (The American Society of Sanitary and Moral Prophylaxis, 1910, p. 4)

The fact that the earliest sex education efforts were focused on venereal disease prevention can be understood by a confluence of factors present at the time. There were major breakthroughs in the understanding of venereal disease that came during the end of the nineteenth and beginning of the twentieth centuries. The identification of the gonorrhea organism in 1879 and the syphilis organism in 1905, the development of the Wasserman test (an antibody test for Syphilis) in 1906, and the discovery of a treatment of syphilis in 1910 brought increased interest in combating venereal disease. The control of venereal disease was also being given a lot of attention by European scientists. Over a number of years around the turn of the twentieth century, there were a series of international conferences for "Combating the Venereal Peril" held in Brussels, Belgium, which were attended by Morrow and 14 other American physicians (Cook, 1972). These events, together with a growth of interest in "moral education" and the rise in international interest around the regulation of prostitution, gave these reformers the perfect platform from which to make their case for education that would eradicate the vices that led to venereal disease.

The most characteristic aspect of the ensuing decade was the proliferation of organizations dedicated to sex education. In 1910, some of the more prominent among these groups merged to form the American Federation for Sex Hygiene (Cook, 1972). Believing that education was the most effective means of preventing venereal disease, this group carried out public campaigns for sex education aimed at adults and young people alike.

In 1914, the American Federation for Sex Hygiene joined forces with another important organization called the American Vigilance Association whose main concerns were to fight commercialized vice (prostitution) and to provide moral education. The emergence of this new group, the American Social Hygiene Association, was significant in that the original purpose of sex education, the prevention of venereal disease, was broadened to include other forms of "social vice" (Kassoy, 1931). The social reform model was thus cemented and would come to characterize programs aimed at behavior change and moral guidance.

## Philosophies of Sex Education

Though these growing numbers of organizations can be credited with first making the subject of sex education a salient public issue, early philosophies of sex education seemed to reflect divergent viewpoints about the role of sexuality in life. It was largely during this period, through philosophical discussions and debates waged in medical journals and the popular press, that sex education began to develop a unique identity. Priorities were being set, old assumptions were beginning, albeit slowly, to be challenged, and a recognition that sex education was a necessary discipline unto itself began to emerge. Early in the new century, however, while much of the country's thinking was toward the future, the sexual morality of the sex education pioneers remained, for the most part, rooted in the Victorian nineteenth century.

For some sex education advocates, the purpose of sex education was to develop strong moral character in young people by emphasizing high ideals. The moral approach had many proponents during this period; Dr. Morrow (1904) wrote that "all moral teachings which inculcate self-control, personal purity, reverence for women, and respect for the dignity and sacredness of marriage are conducive to the subject in view" (p. 359).

This philosophy, based on an old nineteenth-century morality, demanded the repression of all sexual activities except for procreation. Sexuality educator Bryan Strong (1972) writes that the morality of:

> repressed sexuality was believed to provide the force for creating values; chastity and sexual restraint were directly related to the middle-class constellation of values that included work, industry, good habits, piety, and noble ideals. Indeed, without sexual repression it was believed impossible for such values to exist in an ideal character. (p. 130)

Not surprisingly, scientific thinking at the time coincided with and supported this view, including, for example, the semen theory of bodily fluids. This theory held that semen, being a vital fluid necessary for a man's health, must be kept within the male body and that failure to do so would result in ill health (Klein, 1982). The semen theory of bodily fluids suggested not only the desirability but the necessity of chastity before and moderation and restraint even after marriage (Strong, 1972).

This attitude, Strong argues, was consistent with the attempt to de-eroticize sexuality by changing it into a means for achieving socially proscribed ends rather than its own instinctual end of pleasure:

> Despite their insistence that sex was pure, the reformers believed that it was pure only insofar as its circumstances and objects were pure. If men and women made love for the pleasure of the act, whether in or out of marriage, then sex was impure; if, on the other hand, they made love in order to conceive, then sex was pure, for its ends were pure. If men made love with loose women or prostitutes, then sex was vulgar; if they made love with their wives, who were presumably pure, then sex was noble. The underlying theme of these ideas concerning purity was that sex was pure only if it were not passionate, for if sex were for procreation, then pleasure was only an accident accompanying the act. If men made love with their wives it was assumed that the purpose was procreation. (p. 142)

Other philosophies, however, existed as well. One was expressed by those who believed specific facts (mainly about the cause and effects of venereal disease) should be the main goal of instruction. Much of the sex education that has been provided to young people in public schools and elsewhere in the last part of the twentieth century and into the twenty-first century has continued to espouse this philosophy despite calls of its inadequacy by many experts in the field. In the early 1900s, this group was mostly made up of physicians and social workers (Cook, 1972), an interesting alliance that brought together the physical and social aims of early sex education. A leading author of early sex education matters, Winfield Hall, emphasized the hygienic aspect in an article he wrote in 1908.

> It is the inherent right of every adolescent child to know enough about his sexual equipment so that he will be able not only to guard against disease, but to keep the sexual apparatus and other parts of the body which depend more or less upon it, and through the sympathetic nervous system indissolubly connected with it, in a state of vigorous good health. (p. 131)

Still, much of the hygienic approach at the turn of the century was intended not to encourage positive sexuality but to maintain a morality of sexual repression, though the approach was somewhat different from that of the moralist advocates. Though the sex reformers abandoned the old belief that masturbation led to insanity or death, they would not accept self-stimulation as a legitimate mode of sexual expression. In fact, one aim of the hygienic teachings was to emphasize the danger of masturbation. If one could instill a proper attitude toward masturbation in children and adolescents, it was believed, one could curtail immorality because masturbation was thought to be "predisposing to sexuality" (Strong, 1972, p. 144). Maurice Bigelow, a social hygienist and early sex educator who published the first major work on sex education in 1916, expressed this in his writing:

> The habit should never be described to children except as unnecessary handling of the sex organs. It is dangerous to suggest to children, as certain books do, that there is any pleasurable sensation resulting from manual manipulation of the organs. (pp. 142–143)

## ROOTS OF COMPREHENSIVE SEXUALITY EDUCATION

There were other trends in the sex education movement at the turn of the twentieth century that represented the early expression of a philosophy that would characterize the goals of the sexuality education movement of the 1960s and 1970s. The men and women in this early period who became advocates of sex education believed its ultimate goal to be a realization of the positive, constructive, and pervading force of sex in the life of every human. Thus, they laid the groundwork for the articulation of the CSE model that would come from sexuality education advocates in the 1960s. This view encouraged (as it did in the 1960s and 1970s) sex education programs that would give individuals "a realistic idea of the sexual focus as a prime motivator in human life" (Cook, 1972, p. 61). Without emphasizing either the pathological or the moral aspects of sex, this approach advocated paying equal attention to all aspects. Important sex education leaders supported this approach. One of the leaders of the early sex education movement, Thomas Galloway (1913), wrote in an address to the National Education Association (NEA):

> In advocating sex instruction thru [sic] the home and school and other available social agencies, we are not meaning primarily that the young shall get such knowledge of the pathological conditions and the dangers as powerful agencies of restraint. Nor do we mean merely that they shall understand those laws of inheritance which may enable them to mix judgment with the process of falling in love, to mate well, and to contribute sound and healthy offspring to society. We mean, rather, that they shall have such clean and reliable knowledge and training in all the constructive and inspiring facts of sex that they shall properly sense its mental and spiritual contributions to full and normal life. (p. 642)

This latter view, encouraging a more positive role of sexuality in life, continued to gain increasing favor among many leaders in the developing field of what would later be envisioned as CSE. For the time, however, the hygienic and moral aspects continued to be the dominant influences on the content and methodology of sex education.

## Early Shaping of Contemporary Issues

There is evidence that early sex education reformers recognized and struggled with many of the problems that continue to challenge sexuality educators today. One of the big debates to characterize the early sex education movement was over the proper implementation of sex education. Should education about sexuality be done as a separate subject, as some argued, or should it be integrated into other already established areas such as biology, physiology, health, and physical education? The majority of thought at the time was that sex education needed to be integrated into these other fields of study. The reasoning behind the sentiment, apparent in this statement from a 1913 Bulletin of the Bureau of Education, is familiar to the arguments many sexuality education advocates make in the same case today:

> The subject of sex hygiene must be taught as one intimately and obviously related to other subjects in the curriculum . . . To detach the subject of sex and teach it to

young children as an unrelated course not only is illogical and unscientific but it gives undue prominence in the childish mind. (U.S. Bureau of Education, p. 37)

Other questions that still draw debate among today's sexuality educators were being grappled with by the early sex education reformers. One of these concerns was regarding the appropriate age for a child to begin receiving education about sex. The prevailing sentiment of the time was that during the stage of puberty or shortly thereafter was the best time for a person to receive such education (Cleaves, 1906; Morrow, 1904; U.S. Bureau of Education, 1913). The only education related to sexuality being offered in some elementary grades was in the form of reproduction in plants and some lower animals, with the connection to human beings left to the children to make suppositions on their own (Cook, 1972). This approach too, has not changed much in almost one hundred years.

Another important issue concerning the focus of sex education involved the differing needs of males and females and whether or not there should be gender-separated classes. Among the authorities writing at the time, it was believed that because boys manifested interest in sex earlier and had greater sex drives than girls, they needed an earlier education on sexual matters than did girls. The latter were thought to be more reticent about such matters and not in need of instruction until they were at the age where marriage and child-bearing became important concerns (Cook, 1972; Valentine, 1906). The most common procedure was to segregate the genders for sex instruction after the students reached puberty. In an address to the American Academy of Medicine, Professor C. F. Hodge (1910) offered support to this idea:

A good deal of expert testimony from the side of teachers who have been studying the problem indicates the wisdom of dealing with boys and girls separately in these lessons, mainly because the instruction needs to be radically different. (p. 307)

Not everyone agreed with this sentiment, however. Charles Henderson, a sociologist and member of the National Society for the Scientific Study of Education, noted the few opinions that favored mixed gender classes:

Other teachers . . . favor frank instruction in mixed classes in biology and hygiene and claim that it is done by many teachers without embarrassment or injury. They reason that if young people are separated for such instruction it is surrounded with an air of mystery and evil, as if there were something debasing per se in the facts of sex, and that this very mystery debases the tone of thought and feeling on the subject. (Henderson, 1909, pp. 32–33)

There is evidence, then, that there was not unanimous agreement on the issue of class segregation. Apparently, even during this early, experimental period in the history of sex education, there were people who saw segregation as a cue to the students that something special and different was involved in sex education for boys versus girls.

The debate over who should teach about sexuality also raged. There were those who argued, as it is argued today, that sex education belonged exclusively in the home and was the responsibility of the parents, and others countered that parents were either not able or not willing to educate their children fully in these matters so that much of the burden of education on this very important topic properly fell onto the public school. Early proponents also argued over the proper role of the public school, the church, and the medical field in providing sex education.

Strength was added to the arguments of those who opposed sex education in the public schools by the fact that teachers were not at all prepared, emotionally or intellectually, to deal with such subjects. Furthermore, teacher preparation became a major obstacle to the early development of the sex education movement. Morrow's response to this dilemma was that sex instruction should be given by a physician because no one would question his authority in matters of hygiene (Morrow, 1904). Many others echoed his sentiment, and, in fact, lectures in hygiene given by physicians brought into the schools specially for this purpose were extremely common.

There were many people at the time who did not agree with Morrow's solution. These sex education advocates felt that a visiting physician was too detached from the students to understand individual needs and would likely place too much emphasis on the pathological aspects while giving too little attention to the esthetic aspects of human sexuality (Cook, 1972). Understanding the need to prepare teachers for sex instruction, Henderson (1909) observed:

> The teachings of science in regard to the sex function are always in accordance with the physical interests of the individual. Who shall teach the teachers is largely a pedagogic problem. There is no doubt an urgent need for organization of a course of special training for teachers for this work. In my opinion no better solution of the problem could be found than the establishment in schools of pedagogy of a special course of instruction in the difficult art of teaching a delicate subject. (p. 35)

Many other educators made pleas for the establishment of formal instruction in sex education for preparing teachers, and as a result, a few schools began to offer courses that would help teachers to meet these requirements. Even so, the lack of qualified teachers was critical in this early period, and the special guest lecturers, including physicians and social hygienists, continued to be the primary means of sex instruction in many schools for several decades after World War I (Cook, 1972).

Though the original intent of the physicians and educators who made up the early sex education reform movement was to preserve an old morality of sexuality through repression of sexual ideas and activities, the field continued to evolve through the early decades of the twentieth century. Fast-paced changes in academic, medical, political, and social arenas were forcing those concerned with sex education to grow and adapt to the new needs of the country's citizens. As the field of sex education became more structured and organized, the philosophical, methodological, and political issues that would come to characterize it up through the beginning of the twenty-first century began to be articulated, debated, and further refined.

## 1930s–1950s

### Background

The stressful and chaotic years of the depression and World War II had a huge impact on sex education. During the uncertainty of the 1930s, traditionally relied upon safeguards were no longer dependable. Marriages were in decline, juvenile delinquency was growing, prostitution was stronger than ever, and the incidence of venereal disease was on the rise. Within this context, Cook (1972) writes, "there was a general rebellion against, or at least disillusionment with, legislated morality" (p. 117). There was a growing sense that the old educational methods that stressed fear of disease and sexual repression were not effective in dealing with these social problems.

### Education

As an important social institution, education came under particularly heavy scrutiny as people looked with some desperation for causes and solutions to the problems brought about by the society's turmoil during the era of the depression and World War II. Longstanding conflicts over basic educational philosophies became intensified. Many blamed the "progressive" educational philosophy, which was popular during this time for many of society's problems (Cook, 1972).

### Increased Support for Sex Education

An important shift of emphasis that resulted from the vocal disputes was a growing belief that education played an important role in the reconstruction of American society and that schools should emphasize a child-and-society approach. While earlier progressive programs had been based on the interests of students, new concepts were being developed that increasingly focused on the needs of students (Cook, 1972). Sex education was increasingly seen by educational professionals as being important in meeting some of the vital needs of young Americans, and the period of the late 1930s through the 1940s saw increasingly wide and vocal support for sex education from those in the education community.

In 1938, the Educational Policies Commission of the NEA published a report titled *The Purposes of Education in American Democracy,* which proposed four major objectives for education. Two of those were self-realization and human relationships. Because sex education was seen as meeting important needs relative to these objectives, sex education advocates saw the report as further support for their subject (Cook, 1972).

## The Emergence of "Sexuality" Education

With a new understanding of sexuality, the role of the schools in sex education underwent philosophical and methodological change. Beginning in the 1940s, with the support of the American Association of School Administrators and the U.S. Public Health Service, sexuality education began to experience changes in its goals and its scope. Rather than advocating repression of sexual thought and behavior, the new role became contributing "to the long-term sexual adjustment of individuals" (Penland, 1981, p. 307). It was at this time that sex education began to take a positive, life-enhancing approach rather than a negative, repressive approach to sexuality as the definition and importance of the concept of sexuality became progressively broader and more encompassing. Although it would continue to be referred to as sex education for a time to come, this time period marked a shift in support for what was evolving into *sexuality* education.

It was also during this period that sex education advocates began to realize the importance of emphasizing not only facts but values as well. It can be argued that values were always the guiding force behind sex education. At this time, however, they became overtly recognized and expressed. Within this context, the sex educator's new role was not only to impart facts but also to help guide behavior and the personal development of students.

The new trends in psychology, emphasizing the socialization process, encouraged the notion that sex education should be a continuous process from birth through adulthood. The National Congress of Parents and Teachers reflected this new sentiment in its calls for sex education to be instituted in the public school systems of the United States, beginning at the preschool level and continuing throughout public school and into education for adults (Ross, 1944). The philosophy that sexuality is a pervasive force within a person from birth to death was articulated before the end of World War II.

A program developed in 1941 for high school students in Toms River, New Jersey, provided evidence of the rapidly evolving concept of sex education. Within the broad framework of "family life education," sex education was given a central focus. As Elizabeth Force, the architect of this program, wrote:

We saw sex as a thread running through all of life and therefore essential for our consideration. Physical aspects of sex, we agreed could not be isolated from the emotional, social and spiritual life of an individual. We did not devote special blocks of time to this but took up issues related to sex as they naturally arose. (1962, p. 15)

Along with a growing preference for the term *family life education*, which seemed to shift emphasis toward more inclusive and positive aspects of sexuality, other basic changes reflected evolving goals for sexuality education. The biggest change was the removal of venereal disease education from the curriculum to be included, instead, within the topic of communicable diseases in science and health classes. This meant that sexuality education became more and more focused on the healthy aspects of sexuality rather than on the pathological. Though this represented a radical change in one way, the underriding rationale for the change was partly based on a fear of being seen as advocating sex outside of marriage (Klein, 1982). For similar reasons, specific information about birth control, sexual techniques, and sexual perversions continued to be seen as being inappropriate for inclusion in a sex education curriculum. Nevertheless, the more inclusive view of sex education that was evolving made the physician lecture method seem less appropriate. It also supported the concept, first articulated decades earlier, of the integration of sex education with the regular curriculum.

The move to a broader family life perspective represented a shift away from a primary focus on the genitals and toward more social aspects of sexuality. This evolution led to greater support for the integration of males and females for instruction, at least at the high school level. Because social relationships occurred between the sexes, advocates argued, most interpersonal problems and issues could best be discussed and understood in mixed classes (Cook, 1972).

The 1950s was a period of relative calm with regards to sex education, and support for it continued to grow as increasing numbers of schools adopted family life education into their programs. The superficially quiet 1950s, however, was a period in which continuing trends within the field laid the groundwork for the major shifts that would come in the 1960s.

## The Sexuality Education Revolution

Characteristics of sexuality education programs in the 1960s and 1970s that distinguished them from earlier programs were: broadness in scope dealing with subject matter; increased emphasis on individual attitudes and values around sexuality instead of sole emphasis on factual information; a focus on individual decision making rather than on compliance with absolute norms and moralities; and a well-designed comprehensive approach rather than a crisis approach, which focused on disease and pregnancy prevention almost exclusively. Part of this new plan included an expanded role for the school in providing sex education.

The major shift in emphasis included a broadening of the definition of sexuality to include the physical, mental, emotional, social, economic, and psychological aspects of human relations. Beginning in the late 1960s, program objectives began to reflect the theme of sexuality as a natural part of the total personality of the individual. Having come a long way from the early sex education movement, which focused on avoidance, control, and suppression of sexual understanding, the new sexuality education took on a broad perspective studying the role of sexuality in human life.

Amidst technical and scientific advances, which brought, among other things, new and effective ways of controlling fertility, people seemed to be becoming more in control of their lives and their environments. In turn, they also seemed to be faced with new moral and ethical questions previously unknown.

By the mid-1960s, many students and educational leaders were beginning to argue that education had ignored the needs, desires, and interests of individual students in favor of some vision of "national good" that had been fueled by anxiety sparked by Sputnik and the cold war. By the end of the 1960s, there was a return to more individual-centered education, and educational objectives began to be more individually and subjectively based. Students began to demand relevancy, self-determination, student involvement in classroom decision making, process-centered experiences, and a gender humanizing of the curriculum (Somerville, 1971).

Most of the ideas and concepts being espoused within the sex education movement in the 1960s were extensions of previously articulated philosophies. What set apart this decade in the history of sex education in this country, however, was the tremendous upsurge in the number and variety of groups supporting these ideas, as well as the proliferation of new programs. In the 1960s, long argued-for concepts that formed what would become known as comprehensive sexuality education were finally to come to fruition. The term *sexuality education* reflected this broader, life-long view of sexuality.

With growing support for sexuality education, many programs began to spring up. Unfortunately, most of these new programs were implemented without any real organization or clear goals. The formation in 1964 of the Sex Information and Education Council of the United States (SIECUS; later the organization would change the term "Sex" to "Sexuality") was a key development in the growing movement toward a unification and articulation of shared goals and philosophies in the field. SIECUS espoused a philosophy that sexuality should be seen as a healthy entity; it emphasized openness of approach to and study of sexuality and the importance of scientific research designed to lead to greater understanding (Fulton, 1965).

One of the founders of SIECUS, Lester Kirkendall, published a study guide on sex education that reflected the philosophy of the organization. In it, he marked a clear separation from some of the older philosophies and methods of sex education as he set out what were to become the guiding priorities and ideologies for the field in the following decades:

> The purpose of sex education is not primarily to control and suppress sex expression, as in the past, but to indicate the immense possibilities for human fulfillment that human sexuality offers. Sex education must attempt to give the individual sufficient understanding to incorporate sex most fruitfully and most responsibly into his present and future life. (Kirkendall, 1965, p. 14)

The writings of Kirkendall, as well as cofounder and pioneer sexuality educator and physician Mary Calderone, and others, would lead the way in the development, organization, and articulation of the goals, methods, and philosophy of what would become known formally as comprehensive sexuality education (CSE). It represented a clear departure from the social reform model of controlling sexual behaviors and moral development and decisively moved sexuality education into the realm of the health field. The emergence of SIECUS was an enormous step for sexuality education. While there had been other organizations since the turn of the twentieth century that had supported education about sexuality, it was always as part of a broader philosophical framework. However, SIECUS represented the first organized effort directed solely at sexuality education.

Increasingly, sexuality education advocates successfully made the case that public school was an appropriate place for education of this sort where, it was believed, a student would have the opportunity to learn about sexuality as naturally and openly as with other subjects:

> The important thing in sex education is to deal with human sexuality openly and fully in a classroom climate that makes the student feel safe and free to express his feelings of wonder, pride, and concern about his sexuality. (Schiller, 1968, p. 19)

Cook (1972) wrote that, in the 1960s, schools were beginning to develop more CSE programs beginning usually at the 5th grade level:

> By making sex education a natural part of the education process, educational leaders stated that sexuality could be more easily related to life as a natural part of the total personality. It was, in fact, this positive approach to sex which was most characteristic of the 1960s and which separated the sex education of this period from earlier times. (p. 244)

One of the main issues that characterized discussions among sex education professionals was over the role of values in courses on sexuality. As emphasis moved away from providing solely information and toward the broader discussion of sexuality in its biological, sociological, and psychological aspects, it became clearer that the discussion of values was important and necessary.

Some groups opposed to sex education argued that they did not want schoolteachers imposing their personal values on the children. The initial response from school educators was to aim for values-free sex education in which teachers only provided facts but did not engage in any discussions of values. By the 1970s, however, opposition within the field grew in response to this approach. Education, including sex education, it was argued, never had been, and never should be, values free. The growing sentiment was that by trying to deny the existence of values in education, sexuality educators set themselves up to fail. Sol Gordon, an important leader in the newly evolving sexuality education movement, wrote:

> Education cannot be conducted in a value-free context. In social studies, for example, the teacher doesn't say, "All forms of government are equally good. Choose one." The teacher explains that democracy is what American founders thought was best. Democracy, in their understanding, offers the maximum benefits to the most people and protects them from exploitation. The notion of democracy, then, is value-laden. (1988, p. 1)

Many leaders in the field argued that the only way to ensure effective sex education was by using a facts and values approach (Calderone, in Safran, 1968; Ferm, 1971; Hoyman, 1974; Kirkendall, 1970). Hoyman identified seven functions that fall within the school's role in sex education. Of those, two directly addressed the emphasis of values:

> To help youth evaluate conflicting sexual standards and value systems and to think things through, in relation to our guiding ethical principles and core values and laws in American democracy . . . To help young people make sound and responsible value judgments and decisions and choices; and to develop a normative ethical code that justifies their life styles and goals. (p. 67)

The argument by those who opposed value-laden education, however, was not without merit. One of the issues that continued to plague the field of sexuality education was the lack of qualified, educated teachers. Part of this dilemma lay in the fact that the question of which discipline(s) were in the best position to address this topic was never fully resolved, therefore, few disciplines took up the charge within higher education to develop courses of study for future sexuality educators. The question was: "Was human sexuality best taught from the perspective of sociology, psychology, medicine, health, physical education, or home economics?" The ongoing lack of formal education and training continued to deepen the crisis of identity for the field and represented the area of least advancement since the earliest years of the sex education movement. If there was no formal discipline, then basically anyone could develop and teach sex education. The sixties saw a rise in self-designated family life and sexuality educators (Somerville, 1971). These educators, many of whom were not formally trained, often did "show an inability to examine value systems objectively" (p. 25).

Rapidly changing cultural, technological, economic, and social forces of the 1960s enabled Calderone, Kirkendall, and others to gain support for their vision of CSE. Although their ideas were not entirely new, the social context of the 1960s was. While behaviors may not have changed much, popular culture, including the mass media, reflected a more open attitude toward sexual matters and celebrated a new freedom of sexual expression. The moment in time for CSE had arrived.

Comprehensive sexuality education fit in nicely with trends in education and psychology and with a growing distrust of authority and moralistic preaching, as played out in the growing feminist and black liberation and antiwar movements toward the end of the decade. The new kind of sexuality education espoused by SIECUS and its supporters represented a deliberate philosophical shift away from the overriding goals of the early sex education movement. Yet, while some of the specific goals had changed, in many ways it still maintained the broader goals of the social reform model—the idea that sexuality education could have a major impact on the social mores, values, and behaviors of society (Moran, 2000).

This broad and ambitious vision would have a major impact on the direction that the field would move in the later part of the twentieth and into the next century. Another shift in focus brought about by the sexuality education reformers of the sixties was the idea that a better understanding of sexuality in all its dimensions would lead to improved "sexual health." This placement of education about sexuality firmly into the arena of health (albeit being informed by many other disciplines), unwittingly or not, paved the way for the transition back to a pregnancy and disease prevention model that was to come in later decades.

## A CLASH OF COMPETING PHILOSOPHIES AND GOALS

In the 1970s, the government and social scientists began to pay increasing attention to what they perceived as a growing crisis in "out-of-wedlock" teenage pregnancies. Although the CSE model unveiled in the 1960s had focused primarily on the positive aspects of sexuality rather than on the crisis and disease-prevention approach of previous decades, it seemed like a natural fit for sexuality education to take on this issue of out-of-wedlock pregnancies because it already advocated helping young people to have access to and information about contraceptive services. As Moran (2000) writes, some CSE supporters, including Mary Calderone, were concerned that this new emphasis on trying to solve crises and bring about specific behavior change would undermine their goals of focusing on more positive sexuality. Nonetheless, most sexuality education advocates rallied around this cause and saw an opportunity to build even greater inroads and support for sexuality education in schools. In retrospect, it represented a shift back from a decades-long trend away from single-focused, behavior-changing goals that would have a long-lasting impact on the direction of the field and how it came to be perceived for decades to come.

In 1979, the U.S. Department of Health, Education, and Welfare and the Centers for Disease Control and Prevention (CDC) commissioned a comprehensive examination of sex education programs in the United States from Mathtech (Kirby, Alter, & Scales, 1979). Part of the study's purpose was to identify important features and outcomes of sex education programs. Based on a comprehensive review of studies on sex education, discussions with various professionals, and meetings with sex education experts and adolescents enrolled in sex education classes, the authors of the study compiled a list of what the most important aspects of sexuality education should include. Program features were identified within categories that included content, teacher, classroom, and program characteristics. Program outcomes were identified within categories that included changes in areas of knowledge, understanding of self, values, self-esteem, interaction skills, and fear of sex-related activities.

The authors of the study envisioned a causal relationship in which the identified features of a sex education program would lead to certain outcomes of the program, which in turn would lead to what the study identified as the two most important goals of sexuality education (Kirby et al., 1979). These goals, which were given equal weight, were:

1. The facilitation of a more positive and fulfilling sexuality, and
2. A reduction in unplanned pregnancies.

The articulation of these two goals in the Mathtech study represented the ongoing struggle between two very different philosophies about the role and purpose of sexuality education in this country as well as the once-again increasingly visible role sexuality education was playing in pregnancy and, later, in disease prevention.

Are the goals of behavior change (related to pregnancy and STI prevention) and facilitation of positive and fulfilling sexuality compatible? The marriage of these two goals over the ensuing decades would bring together advocates and experts from different arenas and disciplines, and, at times, at cross-purposes with one another, under the redefined umbrella of CSE.

## Conservative Backlash

Beginning in the late 1970s, cultural conservatives unhappy with rising abortion rates and what they saw as a growing liberalism related to sexuality in general (e.g., the rise of women's and gay rights) began, once again, to become very vocal in their opposition to sexuality education, which, they argued, despite all of the scientific evidence to the contrary, was increasing sexual activity among adolescents. These opposition groups became increasingly confident of their position in the wake of President Ronald Reagan's election in 1980 and their growing influence within the federal government. The following year, Congress passed what would be the first of the abstinence-only-until-marriage programs that would come to dominate the federal government's approach to funding for sexuality education.

The Adolescent Family Life Act (AFLA) was designed to prevent teen pregnancy by promoting chastity and self-discipline and denied funding to most programs that provided abortions or abortion counseling, or that provided information about contraception as a method of pregnancy prevention (Kempner, 2001). The conservative backlash of the 1980s included other attempts by Congress to cut funding to many sexuality education programs that strayed from an abstinence-only-until-marriage (AOUM) message. This represented a clear return to the social reform ideas at the turn of the twentieth century with its focus on repression of nonprocreative, nonmarital sexual behaviors and its clear moral reform message.

Within this context, which put CSE advocates very much on the defensive, was the emergence of the HIV/AIDS crisis. With many sexuality education advocates feeling pressure to justify themselves and their programs, this new and barely understood epidemic presented what seemed like a perfect opportunity to demonstrate the importance of sex education. As Moran (2000) noted:

> Recognizing the growing importance of sex education, many politicians and public health officials readily turned to the schools for a solution. As a majority of the 1987 [congressional Select Committee on Children, Youth, and Families] argued, "Until a vaccine or cure is found and becomes available, education is the only tool we have to prevent the spread of this deadly disease." (p. 207)

As it became clearer that HIV/AIDS was not, in fact, a "gay disease" and that many of the people infected with HIV were originally infected as adolescents, pressure grew to broaden the provision of explicit education about safer sex to a majority of the nation's adolescents. Despite two Republican administrations that cut funding for HIV/AIDS programs, the CDC, a less political arm of the federal government, began to provide hundreds of millions of dollars to HIV/AIDS prevention education, and increasingly, states began to mandate HIV/AIDS education.

The impact of this new focus resulted in a proliferation of sex education programs throughout the country in schools and community-based settings. In one sense, then, government and public support for sex education had grown. The programming that grew out of this mandate and that was required in almost every state, however, focused on HIV/AIDS prevention. The result, probably unforeseen by many sexuality education advocates, was that in many cases, HIV/AIDS education replaced what had been more comprehensive programs that had focused on the broader goal of positive and fulfilling sexuality. Programs that had included discussions of gender and gender roles, sexual orientation, healthy relationships, and even decision making around contraception and abortion were replaced with discussions of HIV/AIDS built very specifically on a disease-prevention model. This represented a clear break from decades before in which sexuality education had been steadily moving away from the pregnancy–disease prevention model. Advocates of CSE, such as Calderone, Kirkendall, and others after them, had argued that pregnancy and sexually transmitted infection (STI) prevention were not appropriate or even possible goals to guide the development of, or evaluate the effectiveness of, CSE programs.

This dramatic shift put the field of sexuality education into an impossible bind. On the one hand, programs were growing in every part of the country and, in some cases, with approval for more explicit sexual discussions than ever before. On the other hand, this mandate now required specific demonstrated results; sexuality education was to reduce HIV/AIDS and, by extension, other STIs and unintended pregnancies. With pregnancy and HIV reduction in the public spotlight, it would only be a matter of time before the unresolved issues that had characterized the field of sex education for decades—the lack of a unified philosophy and agreement on appropriate goals for the field, teacher preparation, the standing of sexuality education as its own discipline, with standards and identified bodies of knowledge, understanding, and expertise— would impede its progress and make it difficult for supporters to make the case to the public for the need for CSE.

In 1997, the National Campaign to Prevent Teen Pregnancy released a report by sexuality education researcher Douglas Kirby titled, *No Easy Answers: Research Findings on Programs to Reduce Teen Pregnancy*. Among Kirby's findings was that programs that were most successful at reducing pregnancy were programs that focused narrowly on the reduction of pregnancy rather than on a wider range of topic areas. In other words, CSE, which took a broader approach to sexuality in all of its many aspects, was not the most effective way to reduce unintended pregnancies. This news came as a blow to many staunch supporters of CSE. They had put all their eggs in a basket that was never really meant to hold them, and now, they were once again on the defensive. In addition, all throughout the 1990s, despite the increase in funding for HIV/AIDS education, the chorus of conservative opponents had been rising steadily. In the face of some of the highest unintended pregnancy and STI rates in the industrialized world (Darroch, Singh, & Frost, 2001; Feijoo, 2001), conservatives continued their charge against what they saw as a root cause: sexuality education that recognized and acknowledged that unmarried adolescents were having sex.

## Comprehensive Sexuality Education Redefined

The conservative movement, very organized in its aims, began to compare sexual abstinence programs (which promote abstinence-only-until-marriage or AOUM) to what they defined as comprehensive sexuality education (CSE). In their definition, any program that included the discussion of contraception options and condoms represented CSE. These programs, they argued, not only gave permission and even encouraged young people to have sex, but they also did nothing to reduce pregnancies or STIs. The ability of these opposition groups to frame the language and the debate had a major impact on the field of sexuality education. Due to the lack of a unified approach to sexuality education, and the split focus on positive sexual health on the one hand and pregnancy and disease reduction on the other—among different factions all identifying as sexuality education supporters—the field was unable to provide a clear, unambiguous message to counter the charges from conservative opponents. Although sexuality education supporters throughout the twentieth century had moved steadily away from the social reform movements that sought to discourage unmarried sexual behavior, they found themselves right back in the middle of a debate many did not want to have ("What is the best way to reduce pregnancies and STIs?") and that they could not possibly win. (Unlike the social reform model, CSE was never intended primarily as a disease and pregnancy prevention effort.) Additionally, they were fighting it the debate on terms that were never theirs to begin with because conservative opponents successfully reframed CSE as any program that discussed abstinence, contraception, and safer sex. More and more, sexuality education advocates found themselves forced to address sexual abstinence as part of any discussion of sexuality education and to defend education about contraception as important in helping to reduce pregnancies and STIs. As sociologist Janice Irvine observed about the end of the twentieth century:

A decided conservative victory was that "comprehensive" sex education atrophied, coming to increasingly resemble abstinence-only programs. The term no longer implied the integrated, K12 course of instruction SIECUS had recommended. "Comprehensive" had become a code for programs that stress abstinence but also teach about contraception. (Irvine, 2002, p. 188)

Several social and political forces had converged upon a field that was struggling internally over its identity and goals. In some ways, "the field," despite the strong influence of organizations such as SIECUS, was not (and may never have been) a cohesive discipline with a shared vision. Within this context, organized opposition groups were able to exert as much influence on the shaping of sexuality education, especially in the public's eye, as were any of the leading sexuality education advocates and leaders.

The last decade of the twentieth century and first decade of the twenty-first saw steady and dramatic increases in federal funding for AOUM programs. By 2008, the federal government had spent over $1.5 billion on programs that had the reduction of sex outside of the confines of marriage as their primary focus. The goals of many of these programs are much more rooted in enforcing a particular religious morality than in promoting public health outcomes. Nevertheless, this is what represents much of what is called sex education in the early twenty-first century.

Given the huge amount of resources given to AOUM programs and the lack of funding for other types of sexuality education, supporters of CSE have engaged in a debate about whether AOUM programs or CSE programs that teach abstinence as well as other information are better at pregnancy and STI prevention. This is a debate that is not likely to be resolved in the arena of public opinion because there is no agreement from the many sides about definitions, evaluation, or even what "success" looks like.

## The Current Crisis

The crisis for sexuality education is that the field is as un-unified as it has ever been. Without a clear identity, role and purpose, and coordinated goals, sexuality education will not be able to have as substantial an impact on the sexual health of young people and adults as it might. The questions that were debated in 1908 continue to dominate the field in 2008, the most predominant of which is: What is (or should be) our ultimate goal? While the health education field as a whole moved away from a disease-prevention model to one of health promotion, sexuality education has not followed suit.

Regardless of which direction sexuality education eventually takes, it is important to differentiate between programs with primarily behavior-change goals and those with primarily broader sexual literacy and sexual health goals.

Both are defensible depending on current and emerging social, political, and community needs. They are not, however, interchangeable. The very narrow focus that has been found necessary for successful behavior change programs is not sufficient for the comprehensive, life-long, positive sexual health model, which values broad and interdisciplinary consideration of issues. Perhaps the convenient partnering of these two philosophically different worldviews has lost its value. Social reform and behavior change advocates, more aligned with the term *sex education*, serve a very important role. Advocates of CSE serve an equally important but different role. The two philosophies are not at odds with one another in their aims for sexually healthier individuals and a healthier society, but nor are they cut from the same cloth. It is important for advocates of both approaches to work together but with clearer differentiation of their goals. Then, possibly, some of the unresolved issues that have continued to plague sex and sexuality education—the need for well-prepared, trained educators; the appropriate role of sexuality education in American society and in young people's lives; the goals of sexuality education—can be more clearly defined and resolved. While pregnancy and disease prevention efforts are critical (and are part of, but only one part of, CSE), they should not define the field of sexuality education, nor be the criteria by which we assess the effectiveness of all sexuality education.

Comprehensive sexuality education as first envisioned over a century ago, and clearly articulated by sexuality education reformers such as those involved in SIECUS in the 1960s, has its own very important role to play in the social and sexual health of people's lives.

## REFERENCES

The American Society of Sanitary and Moral Prophylaxis. (1910, January 7). *Journal of Social Diseases, 1,* pp. 4–7.

Bigelow, M. (1916). Sex education: A series of lectures concerning knowledge of sex in its relation to human life. New York: MacMillian.

Bigelow, M. (1935, January). The past and future of the educational program of the American Social Hygiene Association. *Journal of Social Hygiene, XXI,* pp. 10–15.

Cleaves, M. (1906, February). Education for young working women. *Charities, 15,* pp. 721–724.

Cook, James R. (1972). *The evolution of sex education in the public schools of the United States, 1900–1970.* Unpublished doctoral dissertation, Southern Illinois University, University Microfilms International, Ann Arbor, Michigan.

Darroch, J., Singh, S., & Frost, J. (2001, November/December). Differences in teenage pregnancy rates among five developed countries: The roles of sexual activity and contraceptive use. *Family Planning Perspectives, 33*(6), pp. 244–250.

Educational Policies Commission. (1938). *The purposes of education in American democracy.* Washington, DC: The National Education Association.

Feijoo, A. (2001). Adolescent sexual health in Europe and the United States: Why the difference? *Advocates For Youth.* Retrieved May 14, 2008, from http://www.advocatesforyouth.org/publications/factsheet/fsest.pdf.

Ferm, W. (1971). *Responsible sexuality now.* New York: The Seabury Press.

Force, E. A. (1962). *Teaching family life education.* Edited by P. Vahanian. New York: Teachers College Press.

Fulton, W. (1965). Why is there an Information and Education Council of the United States? Why a new, separate organization? *The Journal of School Health, 35,* 232–233.

Galloway, T. W. (1913). Sex instruction. Journal of Proceedings and Addresses of the National Education Association of the United States, 51, pp. 640–647.

Gordon, S. (1988). The case for a moral sex education: A response to extremists. Fayetteville, NY: Ed-U Press.

Hall, W. S. (1908). The teaching of social hygiene and the bearing of such teaching on the moral training of the child. *Religious Education, III* (October), 129–132.

Henderson, C. R. (1909). Education with reference to sex: Eighth yearbook of the National Society for the Scientific Study of Education. Bloomington, IL: Public School Publishing Company.

Hodge, C. F. (1910). Instruction in social hygiene in the public schools. *Social Science and Mathematics, XI,* 305–314.

Hoyman, H. S. (1974). Sex education and our values. *The Journal of School Health, 44*(2), 62–69.

Irvine, J. (2002). Talk about sex: The battles over sex education in the United States. Berkeley: University of California Press.

Kassoy, I. (1931). A history of the work of the American Social Hygiene Association in Sex Education, 1876–1930. Unpublished Master's thesis, College of the City of New York.

Kempner, M. (2001). Toward a sexually healthy America Abstinence-only-until-marriage programs that try to keep our youth "scared chaste." New York: Sexuality Information and Education Council of the United States [SIECUS], p. 69.

Kirby, D. (1997, March). *No easy answers: Research findings on programs to reduce teen pregnancy.* Washington, DC: National Campaign to Prevent Teen Pregnancy, pp. vi, 19.

Kirby, D., Alter, J., & Scales, P. (1979). *An analysis of US sex education programs and evaluation methods. Volumes I–VI.* Atlanta: Centers for Disease Control and Prevention and Mathtech, Inc.

Kirkendall, L. (1965). Sex education. *SIECUS Study Guide* (No. 1). New York: SIECUS.

Kirkendall, L. (1970). How shall counselors deal with moral values? In J. P. Semmens & K. Krants (Eds.), *The adolescent experience* (pp. 349–371). New York: The Macmillan Co.

Klein, D. (1982). *Exemplary sex education programs: An analysis of perceptions in significant populations.* Unpublished doctoral dissertation, Southern Illinois University at Carbondale.

Moran, J. (2000). Teaching sex: The shaping of adolescence in the 20th century. Cambridge, MA: Harvard University Press.

Morrow, P. A. (1904). *Social diseases and marriage.* New York: Lea Brothers and Company.

Penland, L. (1981). Sex education in 1900, 1940, and 1980: A historical sketch. *The Journal of School Health, 51*(4), pp. 305–309.

Ross, B. N. (1944, May 3–7). Social hygiene. Proceedings of the National Congress of Parents and Teachers, XLVIII, Chicago, 339–340.

Safran, C. (1968, March 3). Parents' questions about sex education in the classroom. *Family Weekly.*

Schiller, P. (1968). Sex education that makes sense. *National Education Association Journal,* 57(2), 19.

Some high points in the history of sex education in the United States. (1938). *Journal of Social Hygiene, XXIV* (December).

Somerville, R. (1971). Family life and sex education in the turbulent sixties. *The Journal of Marriage and the Family, 33*(1), pp. 11–32.

Strong, B. (1972). Ideas of the early sex education movement in America, 1890–1920. *History of Education Quarterly, 12,* 130.

U.S. Bureau of Education. (1913). Sex hygiene" by Fletcher Dresslar. Bulletin No. 18. Washington, DC: Government Printing Office.

Valentine, F. C. (1906). Education in sexual subjects. Transactions of the American Society of Sanitary and Moral Prophylaxis, I, pp. 96–97.

Part II

# UNDERSTANDING OUR HISTORY

Chapter Three

# SCHOOL-BASED SEXUALITY EDUCATION: A CENTURY OF SEXUAL AND SOCIAL CONTROL

*John P. Elia*

That there are some most strenuously opposed to instruction in sex hygiene can be truthfully granted, but the consensus of opinion from educators, sociologists, physicians, and nurses is that the time is ripe for instruction to be given in matters of sex. But there is almost universal agreement that the giver of instruction must do it carefully, veiling to a certain extent sex emphasis, giving it without self-consciousness, helping untrained minds to see facts in their right position and proportion; helping not only the mind to see, but the character to act aright and develop in strength and purity.

Elizabeth Cocke (1912, pp. 382–383)

[E]ducation was a persistent and quiet route to reform. Prostitution and venereal disease might not disappear in the current generation, but the rising generation, educated in the proper spirit about sex, might avoid these dangers to a greater degree, and might in turn teach stronger morality to their own children.

Jeffrey Moran (2000, p. 38)

Sexuality education has been a part of American schooling for about a century.[1] Since its inception, school-based sexuality education has caused quite a stir. Not only have people argued about whether or not such a subject merits being taught in school, but also much heated discussion has ensued about the nature of what sexual topics ought to be taught. What is remarkable, as we will see a little later in this chapter, is that both attitudes about sexuality education as well as the curricular content have remained remarkably constant for nearly a century.[2] This chapter traces the history of school-based sexuality education from its earliest days in the early twentieth century to the early twenty-first century. Before turning to the initial sexuality education efforts, this chapter provides a brief historical overview of the attitudes about sexuality in the United States that set the stage for such an educational enterprise. Next, the chapter turns to the precise context in which sexuality education was introduced in the schools, that is, the social hygiene movement. Then, the chapter explores major themes in school-based sexuality education from its debut in 1913 through the first decade of the twenty-first century.

## A BRIEF HISTORICAL OVERVIEW: ATTITUDES ABOUT SEXUALITY IN THE UNITED STATES

Gaining a thorough understanding of the history of school-based sexuality education in the United States requires a general background on the history of sexual attitudes and values. Throughout much of the nineteenth century, Victorian sexual morality reigned supreme. It was not necessarily that everyone subscribed to the kind of sexual prudery that was inherent in Victorianism, but such propriety was at least the "public face" of daily life in the sexual sphere. Sexual activity in the marital bedroom for purposes of procreation was the only truly acceptable form of sexual activity. This firmly held belief had its roots for the most part in the Western world as a result of Judeo-Christian sexual morality. Marital reproductive sexuality was highly valued while other forms of sexual activities—of the nonprocreative sort—were condemned and severely frowned upon. What is interesting to note is that these sexually restrictive edicts were deeply embedded in the institutional discourses of not only religion but also in medicine, the law, and, as we will see later in this chapter, in education.

Regarding the power of the discourses in these institutional contexts, historians of sexuality John D'Emilio and Estelle Freedman (1988) observe, "In the decades after the Civil War . . . a new spirit of 'scientific charity' replaced the benevolence of earlier reforms, and doctors began to supplant clergymen as male authorities over sexual matters . . . The medical profession became the second major group to mobilize sexual reform movements in America" (p. 145). Sexual behaviors outside of marriage, which were *de facto* considered sinful, became medicalized, making them medical disorders as well. To add to the religion-based and biomedical discourses about sexuality was the legal discourse of the late nineteenth century. An exemplar of the legal aspects was Anthony Comstock, who was a strong proponent of anti-obscenity. In fact, in 1873, the Comstock Act was passed making the mailing of obscene materials (e.g., birth control information, indecent writing and advertisements, and paraphernalia for abortions) through the U.S. postal service illegal (D'Emilio & Freedman, 1988). Comstock could not have had such an impact alone. He had the support of wealthy businessmen who were connected to the YMCA and the initial support of the Women's Christian Temperance Union (WCTU) (D'Emilio & Freedman, 1988). The strong impact of Comstock can be seen in the battles that ensued between Margaret Sanger, the feminist and staunch supporter of contraception, and him. In addition to Comstock's antiobscenity crusade, the Mann Act was passed in 1910, which prohibited bringing women across state lines for "prurient purposes" in an effort to prevent sex trafficking (Moran, 2000). Essentially, it was antiprostitution legislation (Imber, 1982). In any event, there was a strong wave of sexual conservatism that could be felt across the country.

A number of scholars have noted that toward the end of the nineteenth and early twentieth centuries the robust traditional family was being "threatened" on a number of fronts. Sociologist Kristen Luker (2006) observes that there was a decline in marriages, and smaller family sizes were becoming common. She also notes, "If later and fewer marriages were not bad enough, the divorce rate skyrocketed in the first years of the new century . . . The ratio of divorces to marriages went up by a third between 1880 and 1900 and almost doubled between 1910 and 1920" (p. 47). This created deep concern by those individuals who were invested in the perpetuation of marriage and family life as they knew it. Second, besides the marriage issue, there was growing unease about "sexual vice, prostitution, and venereal disease in the first two decades of the twentieth century [and] they [urban reformers] began to suspect that these carnal errors were a direct result of the public's massive sexual ignorance" (Moran, 1996, p. 481). This, in large part, gave rise to the social hygiene movement, which had as its chief organization the American Social Hygiene Association (ASHA).

While Prince Morrow, a physician, was primarily responsible for spearheading this movement, he was not the only individual concerned with such matters. Along the lines of Anthony Comstock's abhorrence of moral decay, there were organized groups in existence in nineteenth-century America that worked diligently to uphold moral standards. In fact, there were "a number of 'moral education societies' [that collectively became the] American Purity Alliance, which then combined with the National Vigilance Committee in 1912" (Moran, 2000, p. 31). Initially, members of these moral purity groups were generally mistrustful of the burgeoning social hygiene movement. However, by roughly the end of the first decade of the twentieth century the purity reformers joined forces with the social hygienicists.[3] This demonstrates the medical establishment's ability to communicate about expected and proper morality in combination with the prevention and treatment of diseases. It almost goes without saying that teasing apart moral and medical issues—especially in relation to sexuality—was difficult if not impossible during that time. In the end, there were individuals from many walks of life who participated in the social hygiene movement, including physicians, teachers, social reformers, and philanthropists (Imber, 1982).

## THE SOCIAL HYGIENE MOVEMENT

Many social hygienists believed that an effective way to achieve their goal of combating wayward sexuality—that would lead to venereal disease or extramarital sexual activities—was through public school sexuality education (Imber, 1982). It was believed that both publicity and educational efforts would be effective in dampening carnal desires (Moran, 2000). The details of the social hygiene movement shed light on the impact it had on initiating a broad-based sexuality education effort in the public schools.

The social hygiene movement, although seemingly progressive in that it brought sexuality into the public light and in doing so shattered the "conspiracy of silence" on sexual matters, was extraordinarily wedded to traditional values. Prince Morrow (1846–1913), a dermatologist in New York, was one of the first and certainly one of the most prominent individuals to sound the alarm about sexual dangers to public health (Bullough, 1994; D'Emilio & Freedman, 1988). Morrow focused much of his career on the prevention and management of venereal disease, and he viewed prostitution as the major source of venereal disease (Bullough, 1994; Brandt, 1987; D'Emilio & Freedman, 1988). As the panic about the destructive forces of venereal disease on the American family gained momentum, the effort to launch a public campaign became more urgent. But the legacy of Comstock's fanatical stance raised its ugly head, and Morrow's efforts to put his concerns about venereal disease out to the public were met with opposition. The press refused to print a word about such matters (Brandt, 1987). The dissemination of materials was a long, arduous process.

The press was not the only entity reluctant to make available to the public materials on sexually transmitted diseases. Public opinion similarly disdained any discussion of sexual disease. For example, the editor of the *Ladies' Home Journal* published several articles on venereal disease in 1906, which resulted in the loss of approximately 75,000 subscriptions (Bok, 1920; Brandt, 1987; Bullough, 1994; Morrow, 1906). While a few progressive social welfare publications, namely, the *Survey* and *Charities and Commons,* published pieces on venereal disease, newspapers continued to refuse to publish such information (Brandt, 1987). The campaign to silence such matters was completely realized when Margaret Sanger published her pamphlet on "What Every Girl Should Know" in 1920. After her words of wisdom were distributed, the U.S. Post Office confiscated several copies because literature on gonorrhea and syphilis was considered obscene, based on the Comstock Act.

Pleas for public discussion about sexuality were met with tremendous opposition and, at the least, considerable apprehension. Who wanted sexuality education? It was quite clear that individuals such as Prince Morrow, who in 1905 founded the American Society for Sanitary and Moral Prophylaxis, advocated public sexuality education in the schools to "prevent the spread of diseases which have their origin in the social evil" (Brandt, 1987, p. 24). Even a cursory examination of most of the major proponents of sexuality education reveals that these individuals treated sexuality as dangerous and disease-producing. Sexuality education aimed to: (1) eradicate venereal disease; (2) teach youngsters the virtues of good old-fashioned Victorian morality; and (3) destroy the "conspiracy of silence."

Like all of the other issues in the social hygiene movement, opinion was divided about whether school-based sexuality education ought to exist. We have already discussed why the proponents of such an educational campaign felt so strongly: essentially, to curb the spread of venereal disease, instill traditional morality, and promote and safeguard marriage and the traditional family. Several people, however, deeply questioned the efficacy and appropriateness of sexuality education, even condemning it as a form of propaganda that would actually promote licentious activity and "impure" thoughts (Brandt, 1987; Carter, 2001). Even so-called sexuality education experts displayed much apprehension about the subject. A prominent academic, Max J. Exner "cautioned that undue attention to the 'sordid aspects of the sex question' would undoubtedly have a deleterious impact on impressionable adolescents" (Brandt, 1987, p. 27).

Yet another example of this kind of educational asceticism is characterized by some educators in the late nineteenth century. Professor Earl Barnes of Stanford University recalls that, when asked whether educators should answer students' questions about sexuality, "some advised answering all questions simply and directly; others would on no account shock the child with the fact that he was once carried under his mother's heart; but would instead tell him that he came from God, or that he must wait for information till older" (Barnes, 1892, p. 201). It is obvious from the context of this quote that the fear and apprehension concerning the place of sexual information in schooling was staggering. The fear about the impact of such information and how students would use it paralyzed many an educator. Also, other social pressures (namely, Comstockery) encouraged silence about such matters.

Many theoreticians and practitioners were deeply conflicted about the merits and pitfalls of school-based sexuality education. On one hand, sexuality educators in the early twentieth century aspired to eliminate tawdry and immoral thoughts and curiosities. On the other hand, it was a bit disconcerting to think that teaching about various aspects of sexuality could incite thoughts that might have precisely the very outcome that educators wanted to avoid (Tyack & Hansot, 1992). For this reason, Dr. Ferdinand C. Valentine maintained that sexuality education was dangerous. The famous early sex educator Maurice Bigelow (1872–1955), who taught sex hygiene at Columbia University Teachers College, echoed similar sentiments. He contended that day dreaming about masturbation was more harmful than actually doing it because one could be preoccupied about such thoughts constantly (Brandt, 1987). The eminent developmental psychologist G. Stanley Hall was equally tentative about this matter. He expressed a need to protect against the dangers that could arise from sexuality, but he suggested that this be done without the slightest allusion to sex (Hall, 1914). It was truly a paradoxical situation!

Charles W. Eliot, Harvard University's President Emeritus and president of the newly formed American Social Hygiene Association in 1913, voiced similar concerns about the great need for sexuality education in schools. Like Hall, Eliot suggested sexuality education "be high-minded, and free from suggestions which might invite youth to experiment in sexual vice" (Eliot, 1914, p. 2). Among other things, Eliot reported that the American Social Hygiene Association's major goal was the eventual eradication of venereal disease. To accomplish this goal, sexual abstinence was strongly recommended along with other lifestyle modifications to avoid venereal disease and "sexual perversions." Some of these lifestyle regimens included bodily exercises; eating in moderation; and abstinence from drugs, alcohol, tobacco, and hot spices and other drugs that might impair self-control (Eliot, 1914). Self-control was vitally important because it was a crucial element for sexual abstinence. Sexuality education, according to Eliot, ought to take place gradually and under certain conditions. In elementary schools, he suggested pupils receive instruction in elements of biology, and in secondary schools, social hygienic measures. Eliot strongly recommended that pupils be segregated according to their sex: boys with boys and girls with girls. This explains why sexuality instruction and health education became the responsibility of physical education teachers because these classes were among the few times in the daily school schedule when sex segregation occurred. It seems that mere convenience, and not expertise, was the reason why physical education teachers taught social hygiene, including the sexuality segment of that curriculum. Additionally, it was thought that physical exercise during a physical education class would help to dissipate sexual energy, which undoubtedly was viewed as beneficial at that time.

Not all educational interventions took place in the public schools. Various medical societies, the Young Men's Christian Association (YMCA) and the Young Women's Christian Association (YWCA), benefit societies, boys' and girls' organizations, health and life insurance companies, and a number of other organizations joined in the effort to eliminate venereal disease and promote "morality" (Eliot, 1914). An educational campaign of this magnitude was propelled and sustained primarily because many people thought that if something was not done to curtail the spread of venereal disease, the entire civilization would be annihilated.

The function of sexuality education was to desexualize society, excepting only the marriage bed (Tyack & Hansot, 1992). Teaching about sexual matters was motivated more by an effort to uphold the traditional morality of the day, rather than exploring how such activity could be intrinsically pleasurable and fulfilling (Strong, 1972). The way to do this was to convince the populace of the dangers of contracting venereal disease and to urge them to accept that the height of civility was to repress carnal energies and avoid autoerotic activity. During this time it was thought that masturbation could potentially cause medical problems. The campaign about these evils can be traced back to the mid-eighteenth century. Scare tactics about venereal disease and masturbation were often employed to teach children and the general population about the deleterious effects of inappropriate sexual activity. Preventing disease and inculcating morality into the minds of the young were priorities.

## Gender Roles and the Social Hygiene Movement of the Early Twentieth Century

Gender stereotypes were promoted by teaching sexual hygiene. The double standard for men and women was stark. For girls, there was an extremely high regard for innocence, which unequivocally meant ignorance; the more "innocent" she was as a potential mother, the better (Brandt, 1987). Many feminists of the time insisted that they should protect themselves from the double standard of morality, but some thought that girls from genteel backgrounds ought to be spared the details about venereal disease and other sexual matters. It is interesting to note that some argued that if girls were subjected to this kind of instruction, it might disrupt their thoughts about getting married. Some girls became frightened of dancing, of drinking out of water fountains, and of boys because of the terror of contracting venereal disease (Gould, 1916). This approach to education created hysteria and made it difficult to view sexuality in a positive light.

Another factor that reinforced gender roles for school girls was the introduction of home economics classes at the turn of the twentieth century. There were concerns about urbanization, industrialization, rapid immigration, and the marked increase of working women. Furthermore, the traditional family was eroding. Divorce and high rates of infant mortality were blamed on women, and to make them more "responsible" homemakers, schools across the country institutionalized home economics classes. Ironically, several women spearheaded this educational reform, forming coalitions and formal committees (Tyack & Hansot, 1992). This is more evidence that, either wittingly or unwittingly, the education of girls was along very traditional gender lines. This "making better domestic engineers" through home economics classes was splendidly compatible with the kind of messages girls supposedly received in their sexuality education classes: Be virtuous, get married, and have children. Boys took woodworking, while girls took home economics and also learned millinery and sewing—and it was a big deal if girls chose or insisted on taking woodworking in this era. While Tyack and Hansot assert that it would be erroneous to attribute a conscious and deliberate attempt to "change or give constancy" to gender policies in curriculum, it is extraordinarily difficult to believe that the shoring up of gender stereotypes was not intentional on the part of curriculum reformers and others.

Boys were taught to repress their sexuality, while girls were taught to be wary and careful of boys (Brandt, 1987). Also, boys were warned about the perniciousness of visiting prostitutes (Sanger, 1927). Given the double standard, it makes sense that boys had to be warned about premarital sex. After all, boys had more access to some girls, which encouraged boys to collect experiences while their brides-to-be waited passively (Gay, 1984). This created the Madonna/whore dichotomy, which severely stigmatized young women who engaged in premarital sexual activities. But boys often had no more knowledge about sexuality than their virgin wives (Gay, 1984). This must have created tension in boys, given that educational reformers insisted on boys practicing sexual abstinence. Boys were taught that if they remained sexually continent their sperm would reabsorb into their bodies, thereby keeping them pure and supplying them with additional energy to invest in "virtuous" activities (Corcoleotes, 1973; Sanger, 1927).

The philosophical underpinnings of this educational campaign were equally austere and restrictive for boys and girls. One similarity is that unmarried members of both sexes were to abstain from sexual activity (Imber, 1980). As fear about venereal disease reached its zenith, the double standard of males having license to "sow their wild oats" before marital commitment became a thing of the past.

Sexual instruction for boys and girls was often approached from the standpoint of biology, with a particular focus on reproductive anatomy and physiology. Russell Babcock's (1936) article "A Seventh Grade Course in Sex Education" provides an excellent illustration of how matters of sexuality were broached with youth. He pointed out that students first learned about the reproductive process of plants and gradually moved into mammalian reproductive physiology ("the birds and bees"), finally ending up with a discussion of human reproduction. Following this, a terribly serious discussion about the dangers of venereal disease and prostitution took place.

In sum, sexuality education both in and out of public schools at the turn of the twentieth century had very specific aims. Due to moral panic and the threat of sexually transmitted diseases (STDs; known as "venereal diseases" [VD] at the time), sexual instruction tried to shore up waning emotional, social, and physical hygiene. An ever-quickening fear was that the destruction of the traditional family was near. Obscene materials loomed large, birthrates steadily declined since 1800, venereal disease interrupted and permeated marriages, industrialization and urbanization threatened the "old-fashioned" stable family unit, and, of course, vociferous feminists and suffragists, best exemplified by Margaret Sanger, deeply questioned the whole idea of women becoming baby factories. They urged women to take control of their own fertility and not mindlessly have many children.

## TRIUMPH OF THE SOCIAL HYGIENE MOVEMENT

The social hygiene movement succeeded in working toward stemming the tide of prostitution as well as educating youth and adults about proper sexual behavior. This success, in part, was due to a few organizations joining ranks as well as a plethora of lay people involving themselves in this social and education reform. Michael Imber (1982) notes the impact of the ASHA: "In a relatively short time, ASHA, a small group with no official standing within education, succeeded in making sex education an important issue of debate within communities, schools, and professional education organizations. The key to this success seems to have been the Association's enlisting of support from high status individuals whose interest made sex education important" (p. 359). Originally, in 1906, the American Purity Alliance and the National Vigilance Committee worked conjointly to eradicate prostitution. Together they were able to secure the Mann Act, in addition to numerous statewide antiprostitution laws (Imber, 1982). It did not take long for the antivice and social hygiene groups to join forces because the social hygiene groups genuinely supported the antivice groups, and both memberships realized that there would be more efficiency and strength in numbers (Imber, 1982). Perhaps the most important reason for consolidating their efforts is that they viewed "sex education as potentially their most effective weapon" (Imber, 1982, p. 345). And, indeed, these groups carried on protecting the American public from sexual debauchery and family disintegration.

There were, however, tensions and ironies in these social reform movements. After all, the beginning of the twentieth century marked the progressive era in U.S. history. D'Emilio and Freedman (1988) note that "Historians have debated the meaning of Progressivism at great length ... As a number of writers have pointed out the Progressive movement embodied sharply conflicting impulses—social order as well as social justice, efficiency along with uplift, faith in the power of education as well as determination to coerce the recalcitrant" (p. 203). While social hygiene advocates often identified as progressive reformers, their views on sexuality were reminiscent of nineteenth-century middle-class, conservative values (Strong, 1972). Even so, the social hygiene movement was fraught with controversy and opposition.

Some authors have written about the social hygiene movement as if it were monolithic, uncomplicated, and unchallenged movement in the early twentieth century. As mentioned earlier, although it succeeded in pushing school-based sexuality education, it had ongoing tensions and challenges both from within the movement and from the outside. From within, the challenges ranged from great apprehensiveness that sexuality education would awaken the sexual curiosity and carnal desires of youngsters to those who had conflicting points of view about the ways in which sexuality education ought to be carried out. Regarding the opposition that emanated from outside social hygiene circles there were those who questioned the effectiveness or practicality of sexuality education (Imber, 1982). There were those outside of the movement who believed that teaching sexuality education would take the focus and energy away from other subjects in schools, and finally there were those traditionalists who were opposed to offering sexuality education because they believed that this would interfere with the parental role in handling such delicate matters and disrupt the privileges of home life. Traditionalists also vehemently opposed the idea "that religion, the family, and the community needed to be replaced as institutions of social order. Instead, many opponents broadened their criticism of sexuality education to condemn the general tendency of state institutions to encroach on traditional prerogatives of the family and community" (Moran, 2000, p. 64). In addition, there were yet other detractors from the radical camp who believed that sexuality education was being taught incorrectly. As just one example, Margaret Sanger certainly went against the status quo even to the extent of being arrested for her work on contraception and her publications. In the end, however, with all of the turbulence surrounding sexuality education, the social hygiene movement put school-based sexuality education on the proverbial map as a public issue. For instance, historian Jeffrey Moran notes that "in 1907 Dr. Helen Putnam had investigated schools in some twenty cities and uncovered little evidence of sex education in any form" (2000, p. 36). However, by 1920 and 1927, two surveys of high schools were sponsored by the U.S. Public Health Service that revealed that 40 percent of high schools claimed to offer some type of sexuality education in 1920, and by 1927, this statistic rose to 45 percent (Moran, 2000). Historian of education Michael Imber (1982) notes that the ASHA "campaign became increasingly sophisticated and diligent until depression era financial problems imposed severe limitations on its activities. However, it never fully succeeded in overcoming its opposition, much of what continues to this day" (p. 341).

Yet another factor that led to the prominence of the Social Hygiene Movement was World War I. During the nineteenth century and early in the twentieth century, before WWI, people were generally of the opinion that youth ought to "remain in the dark" about sexual matters. Additionally, the U.S. government paid little if any attention to the activities of the ASHA (Imber, 1984). However, wartime brought about a different stance on sexuality education. When it was discovered that venereal disease was a threat to U.S. servicemen, federal money was granted to ASHA to educate military personnel about prevention of venereal disease. Imber avers that "venereal disease was the second greatest cause of absence from duty throughout the war, far ahead of battle wounds and injuries [and VD was only second to the world-wide influenza pandemic of 1918]" (p. 50). At last, there was an educational campaign to combat venereal disease in the military, and ASHA played a prominent role in this enterprise, producing pamphlets, educational films, and other curricular materials. Ultimately, in July 1918, the Chamberlain-Kahn Act was passed, which funded antivenereal disease activities for the civilian population (Brandt, 1987; Imber, 1984; Moran, 2000). Certainly as a result of the attention venereal disease received during WWI, sex education efforts in schools during the 1920s were more common than in the prewar era (Imber, 1984).

## 1920s

The 1920s witnessed a bit of a shift from the previous years. As early as 1916 there was a move away from "emergency" sex education classes (which constituted a special class in sex education, or a series of lectures offered by "sex specialists" [Imber, 1982] on specific sexual topics) to a more integrated curriculum in which sexuality education was to be taught throughout the curriculum. Social hygienists Benjamin Gruenberg (1922) and Maurice Bigelow (1916) were proponents of such integration, which meant that sexuality education materials would be included in biological science, social studies, health and physical education, English, home economics, and so on (Kirkendall, 1981). In general, the 1920s was a more sexually permissive era and less uptight than the two previous decades (Moran, 2000). However, the focus continued to be on living a sexually wholesome lifestyle, stopping prostitution, and curbing the spread of venereal disease. Sexuality education efforts for the most part followed along these lines. To illustrate an example of such education, David Campos (2002) writes about a prominent social worker, Florence Richards, who gave an address to the National Conference of Social Work in 1923. She said "In social studies, for instance, youth could learn about the biographies of great men and women, the menace of venereal diseases, gonorrhea as a depopulating factor, and syphilis as a source of insanity and degeneration" (p. 68). Although with a softer tone than Richards, Max Exner wrote an article in 1929 titled "Progress in Sex Education" in which he commented on how the spirit and practice of sexuality education shifted from being shame-based in earlier years to being more focused on the wholesome aspects of sexuality. While he states that sexuality education should be integrated into the general curriculum and that sexuality education ought to be progressive, he also claims that in the process of their sexuality education youth ought to have a "wholesome" approach to sexuality and how they should exemplify respectable and ideal sexual conduct. Although perhaps sexuality educators and social hygienists might have had a looser reign on sexual matters, the relics of the Victorian past were part of the approach to sexuality education in the 1920s.

School-based sexuality education continued to have a presence in the 1920s. There were a number of studies and reports on sexuality education produced during this decade.[4] Also signaling that sexuality education was deeply a part of the educational system is the fact that many of the normal schools of education (teacher training schools) included a treatment of sexual topics as a part of teacher education (Campos, 2002; Moran, 2000). In addition, the integrated sexuality education curriculum had gained momentum since 1920 (Moran, 2000). As the 1920s drew to a close with the Great Depression on the horizon, the U.S. Public Health Service withdrew financial support for sexuality education (Moran, 2000).

## 1930s

The Great Depression greatly hampered the sexuality education effort. While there were a few integrated sexuality education programs left after the funding dried up, most school-based sexuality education efforts languished. The programs that remained were more liberal and inclusive than earlier sexuality education approaches in terms of covering more in the curriculum than reproductive biology and the facts about venereal disease. The historical literature suggests that the 1930s witnessed more extracurricular sexuality education and encouragement for parental involvement as far as sexuality education was concerned. For example, in the *Journal of Social Hygiene* in December 1938, Maurice Bigelow wrote that the field of sex education had evolved and grown over the past decades and that "health experts recognized that sex education was critical at home, school, and church. Libraries now carried books and pamphlets on sex education, and youth learned about more than venereal diseases in sex education" (Campos, 2002, p. 77). Perhaps due to the paucity of funding for integrated sexuality education in schools, this educational enterprise branched out to include—some might say became diluted by—community-based educational efforts (e.g., YMCA), the distribution of pamphlets, and so forth. Although the 1930s was a decade in which sexuality education had become about much more than the study of venereal diseases, the cloud of venereal disease as a pressing topic loomed large. This had been the case ever since the end of World War I when soldiers brought VD home to their wives. Hence, sexuality education was not able to fully put VD in the background because there was money flowing from the federal government in 1938 to fund the Venereal Disease Control Act, which was initiated and backed by the Surgeon General, Dr. Thomas Parran (Moran, 2000). Ultimately, public health officials "urged their state legislature to pass laws mandating venereal disease education for high school students, and elsewhere state boards of health sent out traveling lecturers to all the schools" (p. 115). Just as there was some hope that sexuality education would be broadened well beyond the biomedical model, circumstances would have it that many school-based sexuality education efforts would be reduced to "venereal education." In addition, Jeffrey Moran astutely observes:

> Although leaders in sex education tried to accentuate the "positive" aspects of sexuality, especially marital sexuality, actual teachers in the classroom proved unwilling to accept adolescent sexual impulses as romantic or even validly sexual. Rather, they echoed the parents in their community in treating premarital sexual activity as a medical problem removed from the emotional realm but still somehow susceptible to moral condemnation. (p. 117)

Sexuality educationalists of the 1930s began showing some promise of being more comprehensive in their approach, but they fell far short of their optimal sex education. It is interesting to note, however, in the late 1930s there were college and university courses offered on marriage and the family, including the course that Alfred Kinsey, a famous American sexologist, offered at Indiana University (Gathorne-Hardy, 1998; Pomeroy, 1972). The 1940s were about to dawn with yet a new era for sexuality education.

## 1940s

The 1940s was an interesting time for sexuality education. There was not only renewed interest in trying to realize the broad sexuality education plans of the 1930s, but there was also much going on regarding the field of sexuality in general. For instance, "In 1940, the U.S. Public Health Service strongly advocated for sexuality education in the schools, labeling it an urgent need" (Pardini, 2002). Sexuality education responded to this call and continued to grow throughout the 1940s. During the 1940s there was a marked focus on personal development, marriage, parenthood, and the family (Moran, 2000).

One factor that impacted sexuality education was the advent of penicillin during World War II. This meant that the threat of syphilis and gonorrhea was quickly diminishing. Given that much of the sexuality education effort since the early days of the social hygiene movement was to eradicate venereal disease—particularly during the World War I era—this influenced the direction of sexuality education. However, even though the cure for venereal disease was a reality, the old social hygienists clung to the idea that the behavior that got them in trouble with VD was a moral issue and that the disease was a by-product of improper sexual behavior. Nonetheless, the focus of education efforts had very much to do with marriage and family issues and other matters squarely in the domestic realm.

Prior to WWII, there were a fair number of marriage and family life courses offered at colleges and universities. Following along similar lines, some high school teachers taught comparable lessons—to the university classes—and expanded the curriculum and attempted to "reach boys as well as girls through units offered in biology and social studies, or through stand alone courses in family life" (Moran, 2000, p. 128). There was a strong emphasis on family life education with particular attention paid to educating young men and women about child rearing. While sexuality educators' admonitions against sexually transmitted diseases—gonorrhea and syphilis—were beginning to fade, they nonetheless continued their stern moral tone similar to those sexuality educators from earlier times (Moran, 2000). Meanwhile, during the WWII era, there was brewing what would become a significant contribution to sexology by a zoology professor at Indiana University.

Dr. Alfred Charles Kinsey of Indiana University departed from his life's work of studying gall wasps and began engaging in sex research in the late 1930s and 1940s. This research culminated with his first book—sometimes known as the Kinsey Report—*Sexual Behavior in the Human Male* in 1948 (Kinsey, Pomeroy, & Martin) and his companion volume, *Sexual Behavior in the Human Female*, published in 1953 (Kinsey, Pomeroy, Martin, & Gebhard). His findings were revolutionary, and he demystified sexuality for many Americans. In fact, his books sold extraordinarily well (in spite of being written in dense statistical prose), which in many ways can be seen as a form of sex education, or at the very least dissemination of sexuality information, and on topics that were certainly not easily broached in polite company.

All told, "even though there were some advances in the 1940s toward a more progressive sexuality education, restrictive messages were still an important component of the curriculum. Masturbation, petting, and necking were discouraged because their practice might cause difficulties in subsequent sexual relationships" (Yarber, 1994, p. 5). Additionally, there was concern that if these behaviors got started they would lead to other more intense sexual activities. The focus of sexuality education was undeniably on family life along fairly conservative lines.

## 1950s

The 1950s experienced an even stronger focus on family life education as the American School Health Association began a prominent and widespread program in family life education. At this time sexuality education was refashioning itself as family life education. According to Moran (2000), all of this focus on marriage and family created higher standards for families. He puts it best when he avers, "The movement for family life education was the high point of the American educational system's attempt to train adolescents to conform to middle-class family life standards" (p. 155). In many ways, the family life education movement cast a shadow over sexuality education as it had been accomplished during earlier years. Furthermore, many family life educators stayed mostly silent about sexual matters. They mostly taught basic skills regarding daily family living, such as "balancing a check book, applying for a job, learning to date, planning a wedding, finding a hobby . . . jewelry and furniture shopping" (Moran, 2000, p. 150). There was unrelenting attention paid to various and sundry aspects of family life from a practical standpoint.

While sexuality education was overshadowed by family life education, it was neither entirely forgotten nor defunct. The American Medical Association in collaboration with the National Education Association produced five pamphlets focusing on sexuality of young adults that enjoyed widespread national usage (Haffner & di Mauro, 1991; Yarber, 1994). The publication of Kinsey's volume on female sexuality in 1953 and the debut of Hugh Hefner's *Playboy* magazine in that same year were the harbingers of a more sexually liberal decade ahead in the 1960s.

## 1960s

During the 1960s, sexual standards were changing, and there was a "youth revolution" afoot. Times had changed. The once conservative researcher of family and sexuality education, Lestor Kirkendall, who in the 1940s and 1950s condemned premarital sexuality, was opening up to the possibility of its merits during the 1960s. Along the same lines, Mary S. Calderone, who was the medical director of Planned Parenthood of America and who was prosexuality as long as it "buffered marriage" (Moran, 2000), was beginning to rethink her position on sexual matters. What was evolving was a breakthrough in sexuality education. In 1964, Dr. Mary Calderone cofounded the Sex Information and Education Council of the United States (SIECUS),[5] a clearinghouse of information about sexuality. It focused—as it does to this day—on frank, non-judgmental information and educational materials about sexual matters. Soon after its founding, SIECUS published "study guides; sex education, masturbation, and homosexuality were the topics of the first guides" (Yarber, 1994). Kirkendall joined Calderone in her effort to depathologize sexuality and look to its potential as an integral positive part of the human experience. Calderone (1969) advocated for breadth in sex education as she states, "I believe that sex education is education in the broadest sense about this aspect of our lives. It should not focus exclusively on coitus and reproduction but should consider all aspects, and they are many, of sexuality" (p. 106). In terms of her positive approach to sexual matters, she claims, "If our culture has portrayed human sexuality to our young people in all of these negative or over-emphasized ways, and also as a *problem,* something to be controlled, it is not our social responsibility to balance these aspects with the positive and creative aspects of the sexuality with which man was endowed?" (Calderone, 1969, p. 108). Clearly, Calderone advocated for a balanced approach to sexuality education, and she was a staunch believer in reconceptualizing this educational endeavor.

What Calderone and other supporters urged was not universally accepted. In fact, there was a backlash to sexuality education's revival as a more progressive and "sex positive" enterprise. Specifically, such organizations as the "John Birch Society, Parents Opposed to Sex and Sensitivity Education (POSSE), and Mothers Organized for Moral Stability (MOMS) emerged. Their impact was far-reaching, contributing to numerous state legislatures abolishing or restricting sexuality education, and several local communities experiencing fierce battles over the implementation of sexuality education" (Yarber, 1994). The 1960s were, indeed, turbulent times. On the one side, this decade witnessed the advent of "The Pill" in 1960 and the Hippie Movement and counterculture activities of the late 1960s. On the other side, there was the formation of conservative anti–sexuality education organizations, as mentioned previously. While there were those interested in pushing forward with a more updated and socially responsive sexuality education, others were desperately mobilizing to keep it shackled as a dangerous topic in need of staying contained in the old, Victorian biomedical model.

## 1970s

Sexuality education sustained continued criticism and attack by a number of conservative groups such as the "Christian Crusade, the John Birch Society MOTOREDE (Movement to Restore Decency) and a host of other organizations—MOMS (Mothers Organized for Moral Stability), PAUSE (Parents Against Unconstitutional Sex Education), POSSE (Parents Opposed to Sex and Sensitivity Education), POSE (Parents Opposed to Sex Education)" (Campos, 2002, p. 91). These are only some of the groups that vociferously opposed sexuality education during the 1960s and 1970s. As the names of these groups indicate, many of them were parent focused. At first glance it might appear that the majority of parents were against school-based sexuality education. However, historically—at least in the last half of the twentieth century—parents have generally supported sexuality education. Judith Levine (2002) points out, "The majority of American adults champion sexuality education at school: the very first Gallop Poll, in 1943, found 68 percent of parents favoring it, and even the heaviest right-wing fire in the 1980s and 1990s didn't manage to blast away the base of that support, which consistently bested 80 percent" (pp. 108–109). While many parents wanted a form of sexuality education that stressed abstinence, they were also realistic in terms of wanting a variety of sexual topics covered.

Besides the issues directly pertaining to sexuality education in the 1970s, there were a few major issues that revealed deeply held beliefs and attitudes about sexuality: One was the landmark Supreme Court case *Roe v. Wade* regarding abortion rights, and the other issue involved the possible expulsion of gay and lesbian school teachers in California. While these were not the only sexuality-based issues of significance at that time, they do represent momentous issues that were pivotal in the history of sexuality in the United States and ultimately influenced the politics of, and discourses about, sexuality education as we will see later in this chapter. Let's now turn to *Roe v. Wade*.

In 1973, *Roe v. Wade* was one of the most controversial U.S. Supreme Court cases in U.S. history. The Court handed down a decision, based on privacy, declaring laws prohibiting abortions to be unconstitutional. This "legalized a woman's right to terminate her pregnancy before the fetus has reached the age of viability . . . defined as the fetus's ability to survive independently of the woman's body—an ability that develops by the sixth or seventh month of a pregnancy" (Crooks & Baur, 2008, p. 306). This created a firestorm of criticism at the time and ultimately galvanized antisexuality education groups to influence how sexuality education would be taught in schools across the country. Let's turn from abortion rights at the national level to the proposed Brigg's Initiative at the state level in California during the late 1970s.

Although not directly related to sexuality education, California in the late 1970s witnessed a threat to gay and lesbian and teachers. In 1978, California State Senator John Briggs put forth an initiative (Proposition 6) known as the "Briggs Initiative." Essentially, it proposed to rid California of gay and lesbian teachers. It was bitterly contested and was ultimately defeated by California voters. Again, while this was not about sexuality education per se, it illustrated the anxiety about, and prejudice toward, teachers who were sexual *others* (those other than heterosexual teachers). It fits in with the conservatism of the various groups that opposed sexuality education based on moral grounds.

Turning to a different theme that emerged in the 1970s, William Yarber (1994) notes that "a newer goal for sexuality education emerged: the promotion of sexual health. In 1975 the World Health Organization (WHO) defined sexual health as 'the integration of the physical, emotional, intellectual, and social aspects of sexual being in ways that are positively enriching and enhance personality, communication, and love . . . every person has a right to receive sexual information and to consider accepting sexual relationships for pleasure as well as procreation'" (pp. 6–7). In many ways, this was antithetical to the views of those who belonged to the anti–sexuality education groups, espousing beliefs ranging from the idea that sexuality education was patently immoral and indecent to the thought that it was a communist plot (Campos, 2002). During the 1970s and 1980s there were many deft political moves made by conservative groups—which came to be known as the "New Right"—that impacted sexuality education (McKay, 1998; Weeks, 1986). Clearly, there were divergent views about sexuality education during the 1970s, and these were mostly continued in the 1980s.

## 1980s

Perhaps one of the most influential policies that set the tone and direction for sexuality education in the United States during the 1980s was the Adolescent Family Life Act (AFLA) of 1982.[6] The AFLA reflected a conservative, restrictive sexual ideology and was the genesis of the federally supported abstinence-only-until-marriage sexuality education (McKay, 1998). It focused primarily on prevention of teenage pregnancy and favored adoption over abortion. The conservative abstinence-only sexuality education programs *Teen Aid* and *Sex Respect* were spawned as a result of AFLA. This restrictive view was fueled, in part, by two issues: abortion and the AIDS epidemic starting in the early 1980s (Irvine, 2002).

As discussed earlier, *Roe v. Wade* created much controversy and outrage on the part of those who constituted the New Right and the Religious Right—sexual conservatives. The AIDS epidemic created an intense interest in school-based sexuality education and ended up being a polarizing issue. On the one hand, conservatives used AIDS as an occasion to buttress their arguments about the merits of the "Just Say No" campaign. On the other hand, those who believed in a more comprehensive, permissive sexuality education used AIDS to leverage teaching about sexuality from a broader perspective including lessons about safer sex. In the mid-1980s, Surgeon General C. Everett Koop articulated the seriousness of AIDS and made it quite clear that school-based sexuality education not only ought to happen "at the lowest possible grade" (Irvine, 2002, p. 89), but also it should teach about gay/lesbian relationships and heterosexual relationships alike (Yarber, 1994). Nevertheless, the battles fought by individuals and groups over sex education ensued.

One individual who fought bitterly to keep sexuality education out of schools was Phyllis Schlafly, a nationally recognized leader of the Far Right and author of *Child Abuse in the Classroom* (1985). This book consists of a series of testimonials for the U.S. Department of Education about how children have been victimized in the classroom. Regarding sexuality education, Schlafly includes a number of testimonials about how children are exposed to issues such as birth control, bisexuality, homosexuality, masturbation, teen sexuality, and other forms of sexuality. According to Schlafly and her contributors, by virtue of children's exposure to such information, they have been abused! In the foreword of her book, Schlafly boldly and unabashedly asserts that "classroom courses have confused schoolchildren about life, about standards of behavior, about moral choices, about religious loyalties, and about relationships with parents and peers" (p. 11). She goes on to explain how the various testimonials reflect "how schools have alienated children from their parents, from traditional morality such as the Ten Commandments, and from our American heritage" (p. 12). She also charges that children have been neither learning to read, write, add, subtract, nor learning about the basics of history, geography, and civics and that children in school learn "to be 'sexually active,' take illegal drugs, repudiate their parents, and rationalize immoral and anti-social conduct when it 'feels' good in a particular 'situation'" (p. 12). Albeit Schlafly was not the only individual to express such vitriolic views about school-based sexuality education, she exemplified and even embodied those who vigorously opposed such educational efforts.

Throughout the 1980s, various groups (e.g., the American Family Association, Focus on the Family, the Eagle Forum, Moral Majority, etc.) and individuals "mounted major campaigns to discredit comprehensive sexuality education and to promote their 'just say no' approach" (Yarber, 1994). The debates about the aims and objectives of school-based sexuality education remained deeply contested and unsettled. Not much would change in the 1990s.

## 1990s

The debates about what ought to be covered in sexuality education in the schools in the 1990s were similar to those of the 1980s. The hope, among some, of making substantial progress in terms of being able to offer a less restrictive and much more permissive, comprehensive sexuality education in schools during the 1990s was dashed with the passage of the welfare reform legislation of 1996, which earmarked $50 million annually for abstinence-only-until-marriage sexuality education (Elia, 2000). Those communities and schools who accepted the funding were—and are currently—mandated to teach the abstinence-only approach, including teaching that:

> there are social, psychological, and health advantages of abstaining from sexual activity until married; the only way to prevent out-of-wedlock pregnancy and STDs is by sexual abstinence; monogamy within the context of marriage is the socially expected standard for sexual conduct; sexual expression outside of marriage will probably have detrimental mental and physical effects; and having a child out-of-wedlock often has deleterious effects on the child. (Elia, 2000, p. 341; originally taken from Daley, 1997)

This federal legislation had a significant impact on school and community-based sexuality education across the nation. When the abstinence-only funding first became available, it was widely accepted, which clearly indicates that the majority of school-based sexuality education was taught from an abstinence-only approach.

Another indicator of the conservative stronghold and censorship in the United States regarding sexual issues in the mid-1990s was the firing of Surgeon General Joycelyn Elders of the Clinton administration for mentioning that children might learn about masturbation. According to Judith Levine (2002), "this remark, according to one congressman, was part of a social movement that was 'killing the moral fiber of America' and just one symptom of a decline also manifested in reckless driving, an indecisive military policy dubbed 'mission creep,' and homosexuals in the Boy Scouts" (p. 185). While people of all walks of life were quite shocked by the draconian nature of why Dr. Elders was fired, this occurrence was a chilling reminder of both how "sex negative" we are as a society and the sheer power of sexual conservatives who continue to be alarmed and called to action about the supposed moral decay associated with various aspects of sexuality. To be sure, this incident reverberated through sexuality education circles, not to mention that it was the subject of both extensive and extended media coverage.

## 2000 TO THE PRESENT

Abstinence-only school-based sexuality education continues to be one of the leading issues regarding school-based sexuality education. However, there is a shift occurring in which a number of states have slowly begun to reject the abstinence-only funding. In fact, as of this writing approximately 20 states have not accepted such funding. This clearly indicates disapproval—or apprehensiveness, at the very least—about the nature of the abstinence-only curriculum. The most pressing concern is that abstinence-only efforts do not offer medically accurate information, are not scientifically based, and do not adequately reflect the lives of youth. According to journalist, Rob Stein (2007), "The reasons given for passing up the federal money vary from state to state. Some governors publicly repudiated the programs. Others quickly let their applications lapse or blamed tight budgets that made it impossible to meet the requirement to provide matching state funds. Still others are asking for more flexibility" (p. A-3). Without a doubt, there is a major shift afoot since the federal money was first made available over a decade ago.

## CONCLUSION

School-based sexuality education in the United States has had quite a journey since its inception in the early twentieth century. As we have learned, it began as an effort to curb the spread of venereal disease and inculcate Victorian sexual morality and propriety into the minds of the young. At the same time, however, there was a lot of consternation about whether or not broaching such a topic with youngsters would stir their sexual curiosities and carnal desires. There was much debate about what constituted appropriate pedagogical approaches to sexual instruction. In mainstream sexuality education the focus has been mostly on reproductive sexuality within the confines of marriage and the traditional family. During the early days of the social hygiene movement, venereal disease was a real public health issue. There is much documentation to support this (see Allan Brandt's [1987] *No Magic Bullet*, for instance). However, it is very likely that the venereal disease scare was leveraged as a tool of social and sexual control to promote (and even insist on) marriage and the family during the times—late nineteenth and early twentieth centuries—when marriages were failing or being postponed.

Over the approximately one hundred years since school-based sexuality education's debut, there have been battles about what ought to constitute sexuality education, or if it is even appropriate to offer school-based sexuality education. Much of the reactivity about moral and social decay, sexual impropriety, and disease has been, for the most part, the result of moral panics. Social and sexual control has been a theme throughout the history of sexuality education in the United States. In the end, what is most remarkable is that although the cast of characters and the names of movements and curricula are different, the deep concern over proper sexual behavior and the prominence of marriage and the family along with reproductive sexuality have been the foci of school-based sexuality education for the past century. Not much has changed. We can fully anticipate that given the controversial nature of sexuality and the place it has in society and, more specifically, in the curriculum, it will always be an area of deep controversy.

## HISTORICAL TIMELINE OF EVENTS RELATED TO SEXUALITY EDUCATION

| | |
|---|---|
| **1873** | *Comstock Act:* Federal law prohibits the mailing of obscene materials including, but not limited to, information about contraception and sexuality education.[7] |
| **1904** | G. Stanley Hall publishes his two-volume work *Adolescence.* |
| | Prince Morrow starts campaign to combat venereal disease and sexual immorality. |
| **1905** | Prince Morrow founds the *American Society for Sanitary and Moral Prophylaxis* to prevent spread of venereal disease. |
| **1907** | Helen Putnam's research on the prevalence of school-based sexuality education reveals that little, if any, exists. |
| **1910** | Mann Act passes making the trafficking of women across state lines for immoral purposes illegal. |
| **1913** | Founding of the American Social Hygiene Association (ASHA). |
| | First school-based sexuality education in Chicago schools. |
| **1914** | Beginning of World War I. |
| **1916** | "Emergency Sex Education" (having sex specialists visit schools to give lessons on particular sexual topics) becomes less popular. |
| **1916/1917** | Margaret Sanger opens first birth control clinic in the United States. |

| | |
|---|---|
| 1918 | Chamberlain-Kahn Act passes, which earmarks federal funding for social hygiene efforts to stem the tide of venereal disease in the civilian population. |
| 1920 | Margaret Sanger publishes *What Every Girl Should Know*. |
| | Public Health Service Survey results claim that 40 percent of high schools offer some form of sexuality education. |
| 1927 | Public Health Service Survey results claim that 45 percent of high schools offer some form of sexuality education. |
| 1929 | Great Depression results in the U.S. Public Health Service withdrawing financial support for sexuality education. |
| 1938 | Venereal Disease Control Act is initiated and backed by U.S. Surgeon General Thomas Paran. |
| 1939 | Beginning of World War II. |
| 1948 | *Sexual Behavior in the Human Male* is published by Alfred Kinsey and others. |
| 1953 | *Sexual Behavior in the Human Female* is published by Alfred Kinsey and others. |
| | Hugh Hefner publishes first issue of *Playboy*, which serves as an informal form of "sexuality education." |
| 1964 | Mary Calderone cofounds the Sex Information and Education Council of the United States (SIECUS). |
| 1973 | U.S. Supreme Court decision *Roe v. Wade* is passed, giving women the right to terminate pregnancies (legalizing abortions). |
| 1978 | Briggs Initiative (Proposition 6) in California, proposing to purge gay and lesbian school teachers from California's schools, is defeated. |
| 1982 | Adolescent Family Life Act (AFLA) earmarks federal funds to teach abstinence-only sexuality education. |
| 1984/1985 | Phyllis Schlafly publishes *Child Abuse in the Classroom*, which purports that the mere teaching of sexual matters in schools constitutes child abuse. |
| 1996 | Welfare Reform Bill (Social Security Act, Title V) provides federal funding for abstinence-only (A-H) sexuality education. |

## NOTES

1. Until recently the term *sex education* was used. In recent years, the term *sexuality education* has been used to reflect the varied and multifaceted aspects of sexuality.

2. It is important to note here that the actual school-based sexuality education curricula (what was actually taught in schools) remains elusive. The historical scholarship on this topic consists of primarily intellectual histories of social and educational reform and the discourses used to galvanize such reform efforts. Much of what is referred to in this chapter follows along similar lines. There needs to be more historical scholarship that chronicles and analyzes what was actually taught as opposed to the history of sexuality education reform efforts.

3. For a detailed historical account of why and how the moral purity groups joined the larger social hygiene movement headed by Prince Morrow, see Moran (2000, pp. 31–32).

4. For a comprehensive account of various studies and reports on sexuality education in the United States during the 1920s, consult Campos (2002). Specifically, see chapter 3 titled "A Historical Perspective of Sex Education in the Twentieth Century," pages 64–71, which deals specifically with the 1920s.

5. Originally, SIECUS was an acronym that stood for Sex Information and Education Council of the United States. Recently, it changed its name to Sexuality Information and Education Council of the United States (with the emphasis on "sexuality" rather than "sex" to suggest the broader and more encompassing category of sexuality).

6. For a complete description and detailed analysis of the Adolescent Family Life Act (AFLA), see, for example, Irvine (2002, pp. 88–106).

7. This historical timeline is not intended to be comprehensive or exhaustive. There are other historical events that could have been included, but I decided to highlight the events mentioned in this chapter. Moran (2000) was especially helpful as I constructed this historical timeline.

## REFERENCES

Babcock, R. B. (1936, May). A seventh grade course in sex education. *Progressive Education, 13,* 374–382.

Barnes, E. (1892, February). Feelings and ideas of sex in children. *Pedagogical Seminary, 2,* 199–203.

Bigelow, M. (1916). *Sex education.* New York: Macmillan.

Bok, E. (1920). *The Americanization of Edward Bok.* New York: Charles Scribner's Sons.

Brandt, A. M. (1987). No magic bullet: A social history of venereal disease in the United States since 1880. New York: Oxford University Press.

Bullough, V. L. (1994). Science in the bedroom: A history of sex research. New York: Basic Books.

Calderone, M. S. (1969). Sex and social responsibility. In G. P. Powers & W. Baskin (Eds.), *Sex education: Issues and directives* (pp. 99–112). New York: Philosophical Library.

Campos, D. (2002). *Sex, youth, and sex education: A reference handbook.* Santa Barbara, CA: ABC-CLIO Press.

Carter, J. B. (2001). Birds, bees, and venereal disease: Toward an intellectual history of sex education. *Journal of the History of Sexuality, 10*(2), 213–249.

Cocke, E. (1912). Sex hygiene. *The American Journal of Nursing, 12*(5), 382–387.

Corcoleotes, G. (1973). American attitudes on sexual hygiene and ethics, 1877–1914: A study of the ideology in the works of John Harvey Kellogg, periodical literature, and manuals of advice. Unpublished master's thesis, San Francisco State University.

Crooks, R. & Baur, K. (2008). *Our sexuality* (10th ed.). Belmont, CA: Thomson/ Wadsworth.

Daley, D. (1997). Exclusive purpose: Abstinence-only proponents create federal entitlement in welfare reform. *SIECUS Report, 25*(4), 3–8.

D'Emilio, J., & Freedman, E. B. (1988). *Intimate matters: A history of sexuality in America.* San Francisco: Harper and Row.

Elia, J. P. (2000). The necessity of comprehensive sexuality education in the schools. *The Educational Forum, 64*(4), 340–347.

Eliot, C. W. (1914). President's address of the annual meeting of the American social hygiene association. *Social Hygiene, 2,* pp. 1–5.

Exner, M. J. (1929). Progress in sex education. *Journal of Social Hygiene, 15*(2), 80–85.

Gathorne-Hardy, J. (1998). *Kinsey: Sex the measure of all things.* Bloomington, IN: Indiana University Press.

Gay, P. (1984). The bourgeois experience. Victoria to Freud: Education of the senses. New York: Oxford University Press.

Gould, M. C. (1916, April). The psychological influence upon the adolescent girl of the knowledge of prostitution and venereal disease. *Social Hygiene, 2,* 195.

Gruenberg, B. (1922). High schools and sex education. Washington, D.C.: U.S. Government Printing Office, Revised edition, 1939.

Haffner, D., & di Mauro, D. (1991). *Winning the battle: Developing support for sexuality and HIV/AIDS education.* New York: Sex Information Education Council of the United States.

Hall, G. S. (1914). Education and the social hygiene movement. First Annual Report: 1913–1914 of the American Social Hygiene Association, 73–79.

Imber, M. (1980). Analysis of a curriculum reform movement: The American social hygiene association's campaign for sex education, 1900–1930. Unpublished doctoral dissertation, Stanford University.

Imber, M. (1982). Toward a theory of curriculum reform: An analysis of the first campaign for sex education. *Curriculum Inquiry, 12*(4), 339–362.

Imber, M. (1984). The First World War, sex education, and the American social hygiene association's campaign against venereal disease. *Journal of Educational Administration and History, 16*(1), 47–56.

Irvine, J. (2002). Talk about sex: The battles over sex education in the United States. Berkeley: University of California Press.

Kinsey, A. C., Pomeroy, W. B., & Martin, C. E. (1948). *Sexual behavior in the human male.* Philadelphia: W. B. Saunders Company.

Kinsey, A. C., Pomeroy, W. B., Martin, C. E., & Gebhard, P. H. (1953). *Sexual behavior in the human female.* Philadelphia: W. B. Saunders Company.

Kirkendall, L. A. (1981). Sex education in the United States: A historical perspective. In L. Brown (Ed.), *Sex education in the eighties: The challenge of healthy sexual evolution* (pp. 1–18). New York & London: Plenum Press.

Levine, J. (2002). *Harmful to minors: The perils of protecting children from sex.* Minneapolis: University of Minnesota Press.

Luker, K. (2006). When sex goes to school: Warring views on sex and sex education since the sixties. New York: WW Norton.

McKay, A. (1998). Sexual ideology and schooling: Towards democratic sexuality education. Albany: State University of New York Press.

Moran, J. P. (1996). "Modernism gone mad": Sex education comes to Chicago, 1913. *The Journal of American History, 83*(2), 481–513.

Moran, J. P. (2000). *Teaching sex: The shaping of adolescence in the 20th century.* Cambridge, MA: Harvard University Press.

Morrow, P. A. (1906, June 14). Sanitary and moral prophylaxis. *Boston Medical and Surgical Journal, 154,* 676.

Pardini, P. (2002). The history of sexuality education. *Rethinking Schools Online.* Retrieved December 4, 2006, from http://www.rethinkingschools.org/sex/sexhisto.shtml

Pomeroy, W. B. (1972). Dr. Kinsey and the institute for sex research. New York: Harper & Row.

Sanger, M. (1920). *What every girl should know.* Springfield, IL: United Sales Co.

Sanger, M. (1927, Original publication date). *What every boy and girl should know.* New York: Maxwell Reprint Company.

Schlafly, P. (Ed.). (1985). *Child abuse in the classroom* (2nd ed.). Alton: Pere Marquette Press.

Stein, R. (2007, December 16). States spurning abstinence funds: At least 14 tell federal government they'd rather teach comprehensive sex education. *San Francisco Chronicle*, A-3.

Strong, B. (1972). Ideas of the early sex education in America, 1890–1920. *History of Education Quarterly, 12*(2), 129–161.

Tyack, D., & Hansot, E. (1992). Learning together: A history of coeducation in American public schools. New York: Russell Sage Foundation.

Weeks, J. (1986). *Sexuality.* New York: Tavistock Publications.

Yarber, W. L. (1994). Past, present and future perspectives on sexuality education. In J. Drolet & K. Clark (Eds.), *The sexuality education challenge: Promoting healthy sexuality in young people* (pp. 3–28). Santa Cruz, CA: ETR Associates.

Chapter Four

# FAMILY LIFE AND SEX EDUCATION IN THE TURBULENT SIXTIES

*Rose M. Somerville*

The 1960s began on an expansive note. The sixth White House Conference on Children and Youth (1960) recommended that:

> the school curriculum include education for family life, including sex education [and] family life courses, including preparation for marriage and parenthood, be instituted as an integral and major part of public education from elementary school through high school.

This positive indication of nationwide interest in and theoretical support of family life and sex education found no consistent reflection, however, in the actual local situations. Nor did the conference offer specific plans for action in the future on federal, state, or local levels.

Despite some notable accomplishments to be detailed, efforts to expand and enrich community and school programs had consistently met obstacles of various kinds. These obstacles were to loom even larger in the clouded atmosphere of the late 1960s. Among such obstacles were the following: (1) difficulty in defining the goals of family life and sex education programs; (2) competition among the disciplines for major responsibility in formulating and implementing programs; (3) low academic status of functional courses; (4) dependence upon volunteer efforts in gaining citizen support and coordinating contributions from laymen and professionals; (5) fear and uncertainty in facing changes; (6) reluctance to modify existing schedules and traditional classroom procedures; (7) lack of professionalization, related to inadequate teacher preparation opportunities and lack of any established standards for family life and sex educators; and (8) limited male participation on teaching and student levels.

The list could continue. The fact that some of the difficulties are contradictory, as in the competition among disciplines and the low academic status of the programs, or mutually reinforcing, merely compounds the problem.

In this perspective, the emphasis on sex education that was to come with dramatic force in the mid-decade can be seen as a kind of surgical intervention with a somewhat unprepared patient. The professionals in the field (teachers, counselors, administrators) played the role of involved kinfolk and became increasingly polarized over the issue. Some maintained that the sick man of family life and sex education was beginning to grow stronger in the early 60s and needed only time and attention in a quiet atmosphere. Others considered the dormancy akin to death and defended more extreme measures on a now-or-never basis. As in all crises, those affected can learn from the inevitable stocktaking, the assessment of strengths remaining, and mistakes to be avoided. The 1970s can build on a foundation of experience, particularly in facing the forces of organized opposition that exposed the vital issues in the field.

## THE ISSUE OF DEFINITION

The difficulty of defining family life and sex education that marked the earlier decades of the twentieth century continued into the 60s. Some professionals were impatient with this; others saw definitions as essential both in forcing goal clarification and in providing one of the essentials in surveying and evaluating the field.

The lack of precise information as to how much family life and sex education existed or now exists in the United States has frustrated efforts to pinpoint trends or to describe broad historical changes. Contradictory assertions mark the field: "The sex education boom came at about the time of World War I" (Kerckhoff, 1964, p. 883); "Unquestionably, there was little sex education in the schools in the 1920s, 1930s, and even in the 1940s" (Kirkendall & Libby, 1969, p. 8).

On the local scene, community organizations and schools found it difficult to determine how much family life education, if any, they were offering at a given time. "A survey of the offerings of organizations with educational programs relating to family life had been attempted, but the central sponsoring committee was not satisfied with the results and wanted the study repeated," one report recalls (Brown, 1953, p. 37). Much depended on the definition, and consensus on the definition was lacking.

At the college level, confusion was somewhat lessened, but even here there was some question as to whether only functional courses were to be counted as family life education or also those courses considered institutional because they stressed history and family organization. (Some of these latter had been in existence for more than a decade before Ernest Groves pioneered in the 20s in offering Marriage Preparation in Boston University and then at the University of North Carolina.)

There was also some question as to whether child development or marriage counseling courses were to be considered under the family life education rubric. (In secondary schools child development units were a considerable part of family life education.) The two major college-level surveys, by Bowman in the 40s and Landis in the 50s, differed in their definitions, the former excluding child development and institutional family courses (1949, p. 415), the latter broadening the definition and accepting each college's interpretation of "courses in marriage and the family" (1959, p. 21).

The teacher's view of whether family life education was being offered was not always reliable, especially when no operative definition was offered. In the elementary schools of a county project described by Brown (1953, pp. 49–50), an effort at precision was made by having a form on which the teacher could record details of one lesson considered to be family life education. When the forty-five lessons were sorted they were found to fall into three categories: those definitely related to family life, some that could have been but were not, and some that definitely were not. It is evident that any nationwide survey based on teacher report without definition or detail would have yielded exaggerated returns.

Nor was the administrator's view of whether family life education was being offered always trustworthy. A survey in 1965 of Minnesota schools found principals reporting courses or units which in sixteen instances proved illusory; the teachers contacted said they were not teaching them (Martinson, 1966, p. 197). Similarly a survey of Indiana public high schools in the late 50s had found principals naming teachers as family life educators, "but fully one-third of the present returns (around seven hundred or 71 percent) from these teachers indicate that they do *not* teach family life" (Dager & Harper, 1959, p. 387).

The issue of definition, particularly in delimiting the goals of family life education, relates also to the competition among disciplines that was to mark the 30s, 40s, and 50s and grow even more tension-filled in the 60s.

At the college level, the majority of courses had been initiated in the two decades prior to the 60s, most typically within sociology departments. The instructor was not inclined to think of himself as a family life educator for several reasons. First, the given course (Marriage and Family, Preparation for Marriage, or Courtship and Marriage, the most common titles) was only part of his teaching load; second, the term *family life educator* tended to be preempted by home economics departments, which had lesser academic status on most campuses; and third, the courses taught had some functional and some institutional dimensions, and there was a tendency to associate family life education only with the former. These three considerations continue to operate today.

If sociology departments had a commanding position in the 40s and 50s, they began to lose some ground to home economics and health education departments in the 60s. Health education began to rise on the crest of the sex education wave of the late 60s. The Board of Directors of the American Association for Health, Physical Education, and Recreation in March 1966 passed a resolution urging that sex education be offered in the schools as part of health education. While the home economics definition of their responsibility has long included education in child care and family relationships as integral parts of a functional program, it is precisely in these areas that weakness has persisted. At the end of the 1960s, the response to a questionnaire survey representing about ten percent of the nation's colleges and universities found "the most popular courses in the home economics field were those associated with food and nutrition. Courses in clothing and textiles ranked second as a major field of study for both four-year and two-year institutions" (DeNichols, 1970, pp. 24–25). Child development and family relations ranked third. While an occasional breakthrough occurred, as at The Pennsylvania State University and the University of Connecticut, college departments largely staffed with clothing-and-textiles and foods-and-nutrition teachers gave sparingly of their resources for expansion in child development and family relations.

Some of this has historical roots. In 1917, the federal government declared homemaking a basic vocation for women (an event worthy of note by feminist historians, coming as it did on the eve of suffrage and the increasing involvement of women in gainful employment), and Congressional funds were voted to teach homemaking throughout the country. With state aid grants, vocational education expanded. If it is recalled that at that time there were no child guidance or research centers, no nursery schools, no public programs in parent education (Frank, 1962, pp. 208–209), it will not be surprising that "for many years . . . work in this educational area tended to focus narrowly on the teaching of specific skills, particularly cooking and sewing" (Brown, 1953, p. 3). This emphasis has persisted despite a series of landmark critiques clearly revealing the inadequacies of home economics programs. In what is termed "one of the important historical documents of homemaking education" (Brown, 1953, p. 12), Dean Stoddard of the University of Iowa found the program concentrating on "technical and traditional offerings for girls" and "relatively deficient in child growth and development, adolescent and pre-marriage guidance, sex education, personality development and adjustment, marriage and family counseling, husband and wife relationships, mental health, economic and social impacts upon the home."

Whatever improvements have been made in the home economics curriculum to increase attention to the behavioral sciences, progress tends to be uneven. In some of the professional journals there seems to be a continued uncritical acceptance of old content under new labels. Thus, as recently as the May/June 1970 issue of *What's New in Home Economics* (Currie, 1970), an article titled "Elementary School Program Prepares Children for Family Role" makes it evident that cooking and sewing are the mainstay of the program reported, and role definitions are broadened only to allow boys into these activities. Recent pronouncements by some home economists seem to recognize the need for reordering priorities but still do not put the study of family and child development at the head of the list (McConnell, 1970, p. F-89). Others, however, continue to reveal an insistence on the traditional skills ("Skills Found Lacking," 1968, p. 12). Moreover, some journals for home economists were as late as 1970 still including materials for units on self-understanding and personality that would not pass scientific scrutiny ("Follow the Signs," 1970, pp. 34, 36, 38). The unevenness finds reflection in out-of-school activities arranged for young girls. While the YWCA through questionnaires and reading lists directs attention to broadened conceptions of women's roles (Southard, personal communication, November 18, 1970; 1971), the elaborate self-evaluation study of Camp Fire Girls in 1964–1967 continues to define program activities to stress the "mother-role," with emphasis on "sewing for home" (McCune & Jones, 1967).

At the secondary school level, social studies has played a very minor role in family life and sex education. In most schools history and geography are taught without any account of the history of the family or the ecological component in family functioning. It is ordinarily not until college that the student can find these bases for broader understanding in anthropology and sociology of the family. Some improvement can be anticipated in the 70s as a result of efforts by the American Sociological Association in the late 60s to improve social studies in the secondary schools. The year-long high school sociology course, Inquiries in Sociology, which had its national trials in the spring of 1969, found especially positive student reaction to the sections on socialization and social change. New materials for teachers and students will be issued in the 70s (ASA, 1970). These developments may reduce the variation among states in the 50s and 60s so far as social science involvement in family life and sex education is concerned. State surveys of secondary schools have indicated that in Indiana, sociology had offered nine percent and government, economics, history, and problems five percent of the schools' 973 units in family life education (Dager & Harper, 1959, p. 386). In the state of Washington, social science departments had only 3 semester courses and 15 units in contrast to 67 and 137 for home economics and 25 and 107 for health education (Baker,

1969, p. 229), while in Minnesota, social studies had offered 74 units to 94 by home economics and 23 by health (Martinson, 1966, p. 199).

## PROGRAMS, COURSES, AND UNITS

At the start of the 60s there were few family life programs in school systems or in communities in the sense of an integrated complex of experiences. A survey of Indiana high schools reported in 1959 there were only 108 courses but 973 units within other courses (Dager & Harper, 1959, p. 386). A survey of Minnesota high schools had found 23 semester courses in 1959 and 93 units, whereas in 1965, there were 20 and 117, respectively (Martinson, 1966, p. 197). In Washington, a survey of the state in 1969 found 104 semester courses and 301 units (Baker, 1969, p. 229).

At the college level, a course in marriage and the family might be offered in the sociology department and a similar one in home economics, but with little or no cooperation between them. Also, both psychology and home economics might be offering a course in child development. Few institutions were offering enough courses to constitute a family relations major. At the graduate level, a bare dozen institutions were preparing men and women for leadership in family life education: Florida State, Michigan State, Pennsylvania State, Utah State, Ohio State, Merrill-Palmer, Cornell University, Purdue, and Universities of Hawaii, Oregon, Minnesota, and Connecticut. The distinguished interdisciplinary program at Teachers College of Columbia University, which had staffed many of these graduate programs throughout the country, was in the process of being phased out soon after the demise of its charismatic leader Ernest G. Osborne, in whose name an annual teaching award in family life education was established in the mid-1960s by the National Council on Family Relations.

Generally, sociology departments had too few courses on the family to encourage masters and doctoral degrees in family sociology to an equal extent with, for example, urban sociology. However, the trend was upward, and during the 60s there were clues to considerable growth. While only occasional articles on family sociology continued to appear in *The American Sociological Review*, the official journal of the American Sociological Association, the *Journal of Marriage and the Family* published by the National Council on Family Relations, expanded markedly in the second half of the decade. Its pages became so replete with research studies on the family that a separate journal was established, *The Family Coordinator*, in which family life education, formerly covered in the "Teacher Exchange for High Schools and Colleges," a section of the *Journal of Marriage and the Family*, could receive extended coverage. (The new journal was a successor to *The Family Life Coordinator*, which had been published since the early 50s by an educational foundation.) The American Sociological Association started a "Family Section" in the 60s, as a result of which its annual meetings, especially in the latter part of the decade, featured more papers on marriage and the family than ever before.

While there was some expansion in home economics departments at both graduate and undergraduate levels in the 60s, few of the women who went into the secondary school systems were well prepared to teach the occasional unit on the family assigned them. The several state surveys made in this decade, as well as local studies, emphasize the lack of teacher education in family life either in home economics or in health education. In Minnesota, three of eleven teachers assigned to teach semester courses had no prior family life education, and twenty-seven out of forty-nine were unprepared to teach the unit in family life assigned them (Martinson, 1966, p. 200). In the state of Washington, "more than 70 percent of the teachers evaluated their academic preparation to teach family life and sex education as inadequate" (Baker & Darcy, 1970, p. 231).

Because so few high schools offered courses in child development and family relationships, colleges were not preparing teachers in this area in great number. Hence, there were few people available to teach courses when parents and community agencies sought curriculum expansion. Harassed administrators generally sought a solution through in-service education, selecting a few teachers from an assortment of disciplines. The very shallow educational experience tended to ensure a separation of family life from sex education. In none of the states did certification machinery either encourage curriculum expansion at the teacher preparation level or recognize and reward the expanded efforts of a few institutions that took the initiative. Students in the human development program at Pennsylvania State University, for example, who come from departments of psychology and sociology and wish to teach family life and sex education in the secondary schools of that state, are not eligible for certification which is limited to home economics education and requires courses they have not had, in textiles and similar subjects. In all states, the sociology major who went to teach in high school was certified in social studies and, like the home economist, had to teach an array of courses in which family relationships were allowed to play only a small part, if any. Despite workshops to upgrade the competencies of high school family life teachers, problems persist of limited behavioral sciences backgrounds as much of the undergraduate program had included cooking and sewing to permit students to be certified as home economists.

## THE FEMALE CLASSROOM

For many home economists the level of understanding is limited by the almost exclusively female environment. Careful inquiry usually reveals that only a minority of classes in secondary school or college that are called home economics attract male students and even in these classes the boys are severely outnumbered. A survey of Minnesota high schools showed the situation was worse in full semester courses (456 girls and 68 boys) than in units of courses (1,556 girls and 673 boys; Martinson, 1966, pp. 200–201). In some states the sex imbalance increased after Sputnik when new definitions of "essential subject matter" and "frills" shook the American educational world. In California, for example, a study in 1956 had found 44 percent of family life courses given in social studies classrooms, which were coeducational; replication of this study in 1964 found little offered in social studies owing to the Casey bill (Landis, 1965). The public image is that of a female-centered discipline. Those addressing teachers of home economics tend to assume their students are girls (Calderone, 1963).

It is increasingly recognized that even if an intellectual understanding of male and female role changes can be achieved in the predominantly or wholly female classroom, it is questionable whether emotional and social preparation for the teaching role can be. It is a curious development that the movement for women's studies sponsored in the late 60s, while critical of traditional home economics classes as limiting female aspirations both in vocational and domestic roles, lays stress on some campuses on the desirability of all-female classes. The unfinished struggle for coeducation thus finds new opponents in the very groups of avant-garde women who, in a previous century, were its firmest adherents.

On the colleague level, as well as in teacher preparation, home economics teachers tend to live in a one-sex world. Indeed, the effort in the 60s to attract men has raised issues of sexism. Women who prepared for the family field at interdisciplinary graduate facilities are often not acceptable to sociology departments, which question the EdD degree, or there are not enough family courses to warrant hiring a specialist in the area. Now the emphasis on recruiting males in Home Economics departments creates, ironically, problems of unemployment in a field marked by a shortage of doctoral degrees. The value of creating a coeducational world for students by attracting boys to classrooms with male teachers and for teachers by balancing the sexes in the department obviously conflicts with the value of judging teachers on competencies. The dilemma of the 60s is likely to continue into the next decade.

Because of the predominance of women in secondary school teaching of family life, as well as the use of teaching materials that, in the years up into the early 60s, gave scant coverage to the sexual dimension of various topics, an image had developed of conventionality or indeed of prudery in relation to home economics teachers. Biology teachers were often unprepared and reluctant to teach about human reproduction, and their textbooks often omitted this subject. Health educators were similarly unprepared for the most part, although less reluctant, to tackle the emotional and social dimensions of venereal disease, masturbation, and illegitimacy. In serving as consultant to a number of school systems on the east and west coasts in the 60s, the writer found principals and superintendents somehow more reluctant to consider social studies and home economics teachers for new programs than teachers in the other disciplines.

It should be evident that the difficulty with teacher readiness and teacher images originated in colleges in which the teachers were undergraduates, colleges that offered few courses in the family field. Such preparation for life and for teaching could have had profound effects on teacher and citizen performance. It would have ensured that every teacher in elementary and secondary schools, regardless of subject matter, would have been prepared to use the "teachable moment" and focus on the relevance of the given phenomenon to personal and family living. With teachers alerted by their own undergraduate and graduate education to the biological, sociological, psychological, and historical dimensions of family functioning, they would be ready and able to use this knowledge in their classrooms. The specialist might still serve a purpose as a coordinator of the many school and community experiences that would be offered, and certification might still be necessary for such specialists, or at least the establishment of standards. Undoubtedly, this would require wholesale revision of present undergraduate programs and educational philosophy. This may occur in the 70s if student demands of the 60s for relevancy, self-determination, student involvement in classroom decision making, process-centered experiences, and a general humanizing of the curriculum grow more persistent.

However, this is only one side of the coin. The other is community readiness, involving adult education and its specialized branch, parent education. The latter has been largely mother education. It was in the 20s and 30s that parent education began to spread beyond the few "relatively well-educated and unusually sophisticated urban families" with whom it had begun (Frank, 1962, p. 225). It must be said, however, that it never reached the proportions that would ensure an informed citizenry in the area of family life education. The turn of the century had seen the beginnings of child care literature that contributed to "faith in the power of new knowledge to guide the rearing of children" (Frank, 1962, p. 209). This literature was to grow dramatically in each decade, but reliance upon traditional beliefs and customary practices was to continue to be as dominant a strain in the American household in the 60s as the scientific approach.

Opportunities for parents to sift through their own feelings about themselves, their children, and society are present in only a small quantity. When controversial issues involving family life and sex education are raised in any community, this very uncertain background of knowledge and value clarification becomes a quicksand in which reason stands a strong chance of floundering. It is a likely hypothesis that the citizen who has been in a family life education program, as a student in school and later as an adult, is less apt to panic than the one who finds sudden challenge to views accepted on faith through succeeding generations. There is need for research to discover whether communities in which parent education programs have been carried on for many years under the federal government's Department of Agriculture, with a Cooperative Extension Service based in land-grant colleges (MacArthur, 1967), did indeed weather the national organized opposition of 1968 and 1969 more successfully than those without this educational opportunity. Brown reported in 1964, concerning Extension Service, that "Interest in the study of child development, human relations, and family living has grown so rapidly over the last 25 years that 33 states now employ 41 specialists in these subject matter areas" (p. 831). Nongovernment programs of adult education, including the Child Study Association, the General Federation of Women's Clubs (Home Life Department), the National Congress of Parents and Teachers, and the Association for Family Living, may also wish to study themselves or be studied to determine how effective their past efforts have been in preparing parents and other adults to meet the exaggerated criticisms that made the last years of the decade so crisis-filled.

There is considerable room for disagreement to be sure, on the answers to the complex questions facing family life education today. The uncertainty exists in the public at large, among the experts to a lesser degree perhaps, and inevitably affects the way a school system interprets its responsibility. Most administrators have, for the past few decades, been more influenced by the opposition, real and anticipated, in their communities than by the demands of those seeking curriculum expansion in family life and sex education.

## COMMUNITIES AND SCHOOLS

Much work had been done to bring communities and schools together for joint solving of problems in the family life area. In some communities a number of promising programs were allowed to die out. On the other hand, some older programs lived on and, for their very endurance rather than for any growth demonstrated, were deemed "successful." Irony reached a high point when in the controversy of the late 60s a number of these older programs were cited as models for more advanced communities to follow.

It was difficult to ascertain in the 60s just how much was left of the work that had been carried on for community and school family life education in the three previous decades with federal agency and private support. Two particularly notable efforts had been made, the first beginning in the 30s and the second in the 50s. These have been selected because of their broad coverage. In addition, it should be noted, individual states were engaged in pioneering work. Oregon, in particular, forged ahead under the leadership of educators associated with the University of Oregon, aided by the half-million dollars left for the establishment of the E. C. Brown Trust. Films and courses were developed and publications issued, all with emphasis on "sex education as part of family life education," which were to be helpful in other parts of the country (Avery, Brody, & Lee, 1969, pp. 17–26). In 1933, the Home Economics Education Service, along with the Bureau of Vocational Education in which it functioned, was transferred to the United States Office of Education. These were the years of the Great Depression, and a sense of urgency concerning families, which were faltering with the economy, pervaded national agencies. The Works Progress Administration (WPA), under Harry Hopkins, had authorized federal funds for nursery schools and parent education programs. The Home Economics Education Service decided to work with one community in each of four different states that shared a belief in family life education, that is, a view that "an educational program which aids in making family life function more effectively is of primary importance to society and that every person as a member of a home should have an opportunity for an expanding educational experience dealing with this phase of his life, from early childhood into adulthood and parenthood" (Brown, 1953, p. 16). A county in Utah, another in Tennessee, a city in Ohio, and another in Kansas began to participate in the project. The details of organizational efforts will not be of concern here, although they bear reading for the contrasts presented with some of the relatively hurried efforts at community organization for family life and sex education in the 60s.

What is of more significance was: (a) the failure to achieve official status for family life education in government bodies locally, and (b) the tendency for activities to cluster where there was paid leadership to ensure their continuance. Thus, in the Utah county, the central sponsoring committee for the community family life education program sought to become a subcommittee of the county planning board but was unsuccessful. This may not be unrelated to the fact that in 1950 the program came to an end. The improvements in the high school did continue, however. The county in Tennessee focused mainly on health education, with nutrition and tuberculosis central concerns, along with setting up family recreation centers. Evaluations tended to be consistently overenthusiastic. For example, the judgment that "cooperative, creative problem-solving has become a community habit in the county" as a result of these efforts finds little substantiation in reports that an adult education program was lacking, "Negroes have not yet really been included" (Brown, 1953, p. 89), and efforts to establish a nursery school were unavailing.

The question of how family- life- education-minded a community remains after years of guided effort has implications for policy formation today. The study of communities in which parent education organizations and agencies have long labored should include examination of the degree to which the communities in the project under consideration were able to withstand the organized attacks on family life and sex education in the late 60s.

The account of the Ohio city project reveals the vulnerability of partial programs to exigencies of the moment. "So often progress made in one year or one semester is lost the next because of schedule changes or the resignation of a teacher" (Brown, 1953, p. 121). When few teachers are prepared, replacement becomes difficult or at least a good excuse for reluctant administrators to terminate a program. Nursery schools are important adjuncts to high school courses in child development. The two WPA nursery schools in the Ohio city were discontinued, however, even before the war was over because "there were no longer enough eligible children in the neighborhood to keep it going" (Brown, 1953, p. 117). The community had evidently not been sufficiently educated to the values of nursery schools to resist definitions of eligibility that ensured their demise. Back of administrative failure often lies the assumption, sometimes correct, of community indifference to family life and sex education.

The city in Kansas was able to build on a parent education program already under way when federal encouragement of family life education began in the late 30s. However, as in any program where Home Economics provides leadership, there is a tendency for lessons in food, clothing, and home decoration to figure more prominently than parent–child relationships. As in the other three communities of the project, cooperation was sought amongst the many agencies on the scene, from the YMCA's to service clubs, PTA's, and Junior League, which could further the program. An innovation in the city of Kansas was the showing at successive meetings of a series of films prepared by the Commission of Human Relations of the Progressive Education Association. How arid was the soil in which family life education considered as human relations education was being planted is revealed by the commentary on the film program: "In some ways the results of this experiment were disquieting. Children and grown-ups frequently responded in terms of old stereotypes and prejudices" (Brown, 1953, p. 170). While some progress had undoubtedly been made by the 60s, the negative experiences of the earlier decades may also be seen as clues to the depth of cleavages that were to emerge in the late 60s.

The second and larger of the two nationally organized efforts to expand community and school family life education began in 1953 and continued until 1962. It was under the auspices of a private agency, the American Social Health Association (ASHA), which was aided by private foundation funds amounting to almost three-fourths of a million dollars. ASHA considers its nine-year demonstration in family life education to be "the most comprehensive such program in the history of the movement" (ASHA, 1966, p. 14). Five regional projects involved 23 states and the District of Columbia. Unlike the earlier project, the ASHA plan did not start with assumptions of the superiority of one discipline over another in the family life education responsibility. Perhaps more important than its consequent ability to gain greater cooperation among various disciplines was the ASHA awareness of the focality of teacher preparation and its attempts to involve teacher education institutions in the regional projects.

The ASHA projects concentrated on the *education* in family life education. There was recognition, to be sure, that food, clothing, and shelter were essentials in family functioning and that family life education could facilitate and accompany the development of community efforts to solve these problems as well as those of recreation and health care.

ASHA defined family life education as "a body of knowledge and an active process as well—includes what we know, feel, and do as family members. In other words, family life education deals primarily with the behavior of people not merely as individuals but as members of a family and of other groups" (ASHA, 1966, p. 10). It saw as the primary aim of such education "to provide the knowledge and develop the attitudes which will raise the standards of home life and enable people of all ages to live more constructively" (ASHA, 1966, p. 10). Churches, professional health and welfare agencies, youth agencies, and civic groups were viewed as capable of forming their own programs in family life education as well as lending support to program development in the schools (ASHA, 1966, p. 11).

The nine-year projects were an intensification of efforts that had characterized ASHA soon after its founding in 1914. In the 40s, its educational program had included lectures, conferences, and teacher workshops in response to requests from community organizations and school systems. Much of the work was carried out by the affiliates in the various states and localities.

While the nine-year projects sought to build programs in communities with a high degree of readiness, ASHA proceeded on the assumption that "readiness can be created," that a concentrated and sustained effort to encourage leadership among teachers and administrators would have as its consequence increased community appreciation for the role that family life education could play in schools, and outside, to provide children, youth, and the older generations with the perspectives and interpersonal skills that allow more effective personal and family functioning.

The ASHA projects secured the cooperation of key bodies, such as the National Education Association (NEA), the American Association of Colleges for Teacher Education (AACTE), and the National Congress of Parents and Teachers. Project staff members served as consultants to local schools and agencies. Thus, the decade preceding the 60s saw unprecedented activity in the Midwest (Minnesota, Iowa, North and South Dakota), the Central Atlantic (Delaware, Maryland, North Carolina, Virginia, West Virginia, and the District of Columbia), New England (Massachusetts, Connecticut, Maine,

Vermont, New Hampshire, and Rhode Island), the Middle States (Colorado, Kansas, Nebraska, and Missouri), and the Rocky Mountain States (Utah, New Mexico, Arizona, and Nevada).

The reports of the ASHA projects, which extended into the 60s, are replete with details of concrete accomplishments. In each region materials of high quality were prepared for publication. These served as models in many parts of the country in the 60s. In the Midwest project, a curriculum guide for teacher education institutions, followed by another for teachers in elementary and secondary schools, received distribution in a majority of the states. Workshops begun at teachers colleges became annual events. Television series and library commissions broadened community awareness. In the Central Atlantic project, resource guides were compiled, containing ideas and methods still useful today, and in-service workshops involved thousands of teachers. In New England, public school systems in a number of cities and counties introduced courses and units, and various teachers colleges increased their offerings. Similarly, in the other projects there was an expansion of curriculum and teacher workshops, the development of exhibit material (shown at the 1960 White House Conference on Children and Youth as well as at various state conferences), the use of radio and television.

In the Middle States project, a questionnaire survey of the status of family life education in teacher preparation institutions in the four-state area revealed that of the 71 colleges responding (almost three-fourths of those queried), 87 percent offered special courses in family life education, and 84 percent gave some attention to it in other courses. Undoubtedly, the expansion in college courses encouraged by ASHA accounts in part for the quantitative growth reported by Landis (1959).

It should be noted that these projects, which extended well into the decade under review here, pioneering and dedicated as they were, rarely affected a majority of schools or communities in the various states. Even where a state board of education approved family life courses and drew up guidelines for teaching the courses, little was done for years afterward (Brantley, 1966).

## A SPECIAL DECADE

Each part of the decade, the early 60s, the middle 60s, and the late 60s, saw different forces at play, with different consequences for family life and sex education. Almost every issue raised in the latter part of the 60s had already received some consideration in the earlier years. What was to become evident was that there had been little resolution of differences. These issues were as follows:

    a. sexual behaviors, especially premarital intercourse
    b. sex education apart from family life education

c. privacy
d. home and school roles in family life education
e. teacher preparedness
f. child readiness, especially in K–4
g. moral codes and attitudes toward masturbation, homosexuality, etc.
h. interdisciplinary cooperation
i. value differences between teachers and parents, parents and children, states and communities
j. legislation mandating or prohibiting programs
k. audiovisual materials

If the issues were common to several decades, the social matrix in which they occurred varied greatly. The 60s represent a very special decade in American history so far as the sexualization of society is concerned. In the mass media, the use of sex in advertising reached new levels of exposure. New publications appeared, such as *Playboy,* easily available in the supermarket and displayed on newsstands. Films were increasingly imported from countries with less traditional attitudes or produced in this country under relaxed interpretations of the codes. National magazines devoted covers and pages to "Sex in the United States: Mores and Morality" (*Time,* 1964) and "The Morals Revolution on the U.S. Campus" (*Newsweek,* 1964). While viewing with alarm, particularly in adult contemplation of youth's manners or morals is not new, the sheer quantity of attention given sex in periodicals and books was undoubtedly unique. Television and the radio reflected and encouraged a new freedom of discussion by bringing into the home talks about and depictions of childbirth, abortion, VD, and illegitimacy.

All these nonacademic forces had an impact on parents, teachers, and students alike. Private schools as well as public ones felt these pressures. In 1964, the National Association of Independent Schools, an organization with 750 member schools, held a much publicized conference to discuss what curriculum changes would be appropriate in the face of the new pressures. Particularly in New York, where the sexual component was at that time almost wholly omitted from instruction, private schools perceived themselves as having the needed flexibility to innovate changes without excessive delay and to serve as models for public school programs (Southard, 1967). Schools tended to lag behind more informal socializing agencies in open discussion, however. Textbooks in the early 60s tended to reflect the fears of adults, not necessarily of those who wrote them, but of the administrators who approved them for purchase and the publishers who continued to *assume,* as they had in prior decades, that open discussion of sexual issues would decrease sales in traditional markets.

On the professional scene, changes were becoming more evident. Professional journals and books as well as national conferences began to discuss the findings of sex research to an even greater degree than when the Kinsey findings first appeared a decade or more earlier. It is noteworthy that, in most of these publications, schools were not regarded as contributing significantly to the sexual scene. The special edition of the *Journal of Social Issues* (April, 1966) devoted to "The Sexual Renaissance in America" contains barely more than a sentence and a footnote on sex education (Reiss, 1966, p. 133).

In the 50s and into the early 60s, curriculum guides for home economists, even those with newer emphasis on concept development and readiness to use the contributions of psychology and sociology, rarely included sex in topics where it would have seemed unavoidable (Pieretti, 1963, p. 128). The ASHA, long experienced with sex education programs, had sought to incorporate the sexual dimension into the nine-year projects. Their optimistic assessment of the outcome may overstate the realities. "Although sex education aspects of family life education were viewed with some misgivings by school leaders at first, the content relating to sex soon became a natural part of the whole. Through workshops, administrators and teachers became more competent and confident in handling sex education as part of the family life programs" (ASHA, 1966, p. 16). Because so many family life educators tended to avoid the sexual dimension, the titling of courses and programs began to change in the 60s to remind teacher and student alike of the interconnection of family life and sex education (Morgan, 1966; Somerville, 1967).

The recommendation in 1948 of the National Conference on Education of Teachers that sex education be part of the curriculum for all teachers had not been implemented. Several studies show sex among the areas receiving least attention in teaching at the secondary level (Martinson, 1966, p. 202). Moreover, the discomfort with which even biologists, doctors, and nurses face when discussing sexual matters suggests the inadequacy either of the total college and professional curricula or of the system of required and elective subjects, which makes it likely that most college graduates have not encountered any frank discussion in their classes (Coombs, 1968).

Partly as a result of the reluctance of family life educators to handle the sexual component, there sprang up a movement for sex education as a separate subject. Warnings against this had been offered in each decade. One early figure in the field had declared, "In my opinion it is a mistake to confine sex teaching to a single course such as health or personal hygiene, since its ramifications in human behavior are so broad" (Beck, 1955). Later, Reiss (1966) was to declare, "In light of the goals of sex education, it may well be better to build broad social science course materials in all grade levels . . . rather than just adding an isolated sex education course at the junior high school level" (p. 134).

A demand in the 60s to start "putting the sex back into sex education" indicated the path that had been taken by the separate sex education programs in the previous decades (Strriven, 1968, p. 485). Many agreed with the judgment that "Sex education so far has usually been a half-hearted venture into the physiology of reproduction with some vague remarks about dating behavior" (Strriven, 1968, p. 486). The American Association of School Administrators (AASA) in its Sixteenth Yearbook had declared:

> The fairly common practice of inviting a physician to speak to boys or girls may be seriously inadequate. Few physicians (except psychiatrists) by training or practice have studied the essential problems of sex. They have been taught the names, functions, and physical disorders of various sex organs, but that is a minor contribution to the great problems of affection, courtship, and marriage in modern society. Most of the conflicts that keep youth awake in troubled nights are psychological and social problems . . . persons well trained in psychology and sociology will be able to help much more than any but the very exceptional physicians. (1938)

The separate course in sex education offered in some school systems was usually offered under health education or physical education auspices. Few teachers in these fields were prepared to offer sex information, let alone sex education. The shortcomings lay in the education they had received as undergraduates, in the hypocrisy of community leaders who tended to demand of schools and teachers preachments of behavior they were not themselves willing to live by, and in the poor scheduling and in-service practices of the schools. To be sure, some of this was to change in the later 60s when health educators and others began to come to serious grips with the challenge to upgrade their offerings ("Growth Patterns," 1967).

## NEW ORGANIZATIONS

It was against this background of the sexualization of American society on the one hand, and the inadequate attention given in schools, churches, and social agencies to the sexual aspects of man and society, that a new organization was announced in 1965 after months of preparation. The Sex Information and Education Council of the United States (SIECUS) created a stir from its beginning, both among professionals and in the public at large.

After five years of SIECUS there are still marked differences among professionals in calculating the outcomes. Most would agree perhaps that until it was attacked in 1968 and 1969, it was "the single most important force in the realm of sex education today" (Powers & Baskin, 1969, p. 13). Space will not permit a detailed examination here of various SIECUS activities. Mention of these can be found in the SIECUS Newsletter, which, together with eleven brief study guides and a handbook, comprises almost the totality of SIECUS publications. The spoken word rather than the written, whether in speeches, panels, or consultancies, has been most used.

Discussion here will be limited to the ways in which the founding of SIECUS brought to the surface uncertainties and confusions in the whole field of family life and sex education as well as new opportunities.

SIECUS defined itself as a health organization and its goal, "To establish man's sexuality as a health entity." To some professionals this seemed to give a clearer mandate to health education than to other disciplines despite SIECUS's mention of "a broad interdisciplinary approach" in publications and speeches. The unsettled issue of which disciplines should take primary responsibility came to the fore again.

Related to this was the issue of separate sex education or including the sexual component within the study of individual and family development. SIECUS seemed to speak both of a "sharp and direct" focus on human sexuality and of bringing about "within the framework of family life education" constructive dialogue between youth and adults (SIECUS, 1965). Kirkendall (1970) reports that "in the first informal meetings at which the formation of SIECUS was discussed, the question arose as to whether the incorporation of such an organization would retard or advance the cause of sex education. Some believed it meant pulling 'sex out of context' and spotlighting sex in an undesirable way." He himself had long been inclined to question the appropriateness of a family life context for all sex education. "How does one teach about sexuality among the permanently unmarried in a 'family life context'?"

Thus, the establishment and functioning of SIECUS reminded professionals of the unsatisfactory state of terminology in the field. "Family life education" is a name no one is too comfortable with. Some think the individual and society are more certain pivots and prefer *human relations education* or *human development education,* with sexuality and family relations only aspects of the larger area of study. However, some prefer to use *family life education* as the umbrella term, maintaining that the individual always carries with him the impact of his family of origin, and therefore, even if he does not enter into a family of procreation, his sexual and other relational behaviors can be viewed in the family life framework. However psychologically sound this argument may be, there is an equally astute consideration to counter it, that "because the word 'family' suggests dependency and restraint at a time when they are striving to sever the psychological umbilical cord with their family group," adolescents will react more favorably to the study of Human *Relations* than Family *Living* (Lindquist, 1968, p. 59). Sex education has connotations of emphasis on the physiological, and *Sexuality* Education has been suggested in its place. A compromise term, *family life and sex education,* came to be frequently used in the 60s despite misgivings that "and" suggests divisibility of subject matter.

SIECUS also reminded professionals of their divided state on the issue of special courses versus integration of family life and sex education into all parts of the curriculum. The thrust of the E. C. Brown Trust and its leaders,

Avery and Johannis, had been in the direction of integration, and this was to be echoed by Barr (Avery et al., 1969; Barr, 1967). The impact of SIECUS, however, had been in the direction of the separate course or unit on sex, not that this was advocated in any of its publications, but because the public, and educational institutions responding to that public, interpreted it this way and because some departments saw this as a path to speedy enlargement of student enrollments. "SIECUS barnstorming conveys a sense of urgency which coincides with nationwide concern over the sexual morality of the rising generation," one volume comments (Powers & Baskin, 1969, p. 14). Those who listened to the speeches by SIECUS representatives, particularly those on television and radio, did not always read the publications, which warned against haste and the need for thorough community study before program formulation. If the mailbags of existing organizations such as NCFR and ASHA had been heavy in the early 60s as communities and schools demanded help in getting teaching materials for family life and sex education, they were swamped, as was SIECUS, in the mid-1960s when TV appearances of Mary Calderone made sex education a household topic (Jewson, 1967; Somerville, 1967). "One New York school system which recently received nationwide publicity for its program of sex education was inundated with over 3,000 requests for its curriculum guide" (Burleson, 1967, p. 9). The fact that the guide was of questionable quality in the view of some professionals did not stem the flow. Criticisms were not welcomed or taken seriously. There was general awareness that qualified teachers were in short supply, but the issue was not raised in all its seriousness until almost the eve of the reaction of 1968 and 1969 (Malfetti & Rubin, 1967). The National Council on Family Relations, aware of the influx of self-designated family life and sex educators into the field in the mid-1960s, appointed a number of commissions and committees to look into the establishment of teaching criteria. The writer chaired the Committee on Educational Standards and Certification for Family Life Educators in 1968 and 1969, which formulated a set of Criteria accepted by NCFR at its Washington meeting. These criteria seek to ensure that whatever departments are involved in offering courses and units, the teachers will have multifaceted professional preparation (Somerville, 1970).

The establishment in 1968, with the aid of the Commonwealth Fund, of the Center for the Study of Sex Education in Medicine, under the leadership of Dr. Harold Lief, Director of the Division of Family Study in the University of Pennsylvania, is an example of the attempt to establish standards within a given profession. It marked the culmination of more than five years of effort to get medical schools to broaden their curriculum to include education about sexuality. The NCFR, AAMC, SIECUS, and other organizations cooperated with medical leaders, and by 1968 there were 35 medical schools in contrast to three in 1964 with expanded curriculum (Lock, 1964; Mathias, 1966).

## THE ISSUE OF TIME

The new programs tended to underestimate even more than the older ones the amount of time needed not only to prepare the teacher but how much time he would need to explore the subject with his classes. Even the often-cited programs, at Anaheim, Evanston (Furlong, 1967), San Diego, Flint (Somerville, 1966), and Winnetka (Marland, 1961), gave at most five weeks and in some instances only days in any given year. Often expediency is at work and brings on a tendency to accept what seems possible over what is more defensible but difficult to obtain. For the most part, however, there seems to be a genuine misconception concerning the nature of the task among parents, administrators, and teachers. Thus, an educator offers the view that in the second year of high school "the program need not be lengthy. One class period for imparting information and another for discussion should be sufficient." Perhaps it is not unexpected that he hastens to add, "The teacher is on safe ground if he sticks to the broadly accepted sexual standards" (Wake, 1966).

In teacher education, the 60s brought the establishment of a few graduate and undergraduate programs offering broad preservice preparation. The main reliance, however, was on the brief workshop. It is likely that haste in teacher education in the 60s was encouraged by precedents in health education of introducing brief VD and drug units as well as other "crisis" material into ongoing programs (Kaplan, 1967).

The 60s did not contribute to the resolution of an old dispute in teacher education: whether the workshop should be regarded as a refresher for the experienced professional rather than as the main way of preparing family life and sex educators. The long-established tradition of workshops has to some extent both mitigated the difficulties caused by lack of preservice teacher education opportunities and increased those difficulties by seeming to offer an adequate solution. In the 60s, the number of workshops, especially in the summer months, seemed to increase, with listings appearing in the *NCFR Newsletter*, the *Journal of Home Economics*, the *SIECUS Newsletter*, and other publications. Most of these workshops, having been "developed entirely independently of SIECUS" (SIECUS, 1970, p. 3), were not subject to the vicissitudes of that organization when it became the main target of organized opposition in the late 60s. They can be expected in the 70s to be affected by new criteria adopted by NCFR and by several state departments of education, as, for example, the Pennsylvania Department of Education's Recommended Standards for Sex Education Teachers (Somerville, 1970). SIECUS called a small working conference in 1970 with a view to developing "a unified curriculum for training teachers." Dissertations in the graduate schools are likely to help focus attention on this issue of teacher preparation in the next decade (Shimmel & Carrera, 1970).

It should be noted that there are differences among workshops not only in quality of teaching personnel but in time. Some run only for a week of two, some six weeks (Luckey, 1968, p. 90). Some have as their students mainly professionals with graduate degrees in related disciplines, while some have people for whom the course work is almost entirely new. Workshop outcomes will obviously vary, depending not only on time allotted but on quality of faculty and of students. Time is stressed in this discussion because it has received least attention. Its importance is suggested by the experience of a teacher workshop in Winston-Salem that, with a brilliant roster of resource persons available to them in a "medical school town," nonetheless found the 33 hours inadequate for needed discussion and reflection.

Class size became an increasing problem in the 60s. So few courses are offered in the colleges that are helpful in the preparation of future family life and sex educators that when a class is scheduled, enrollments are apt to rise spectacularly. When there is an entire program rather than a single course, a large class with an inspiring teacher may serve an introductory function, with detailed discussion to be found in other classes. There is the danger, unless criteria are carefully observed, that the student and the administrator may evaluate this large-class experience for more than it actually offers. The 70s will undoubtedly see the enrollment battle still being fought out. Underlying the issues of time and class size is the assumption of the importance of discussion: the dialog-centered classroom. While this has strong professional support, it is by no means unanimous.

## OTHER UNSETTLED ISSUES

While SIECUS was the main organizational target of the highly publicized attack on sex education in 1968 and 1969, family life education came under criticism, too. The most obvious reason was the misuse of the latter designation by those who devised programs that omitted the family and social contexts in which sexual behavior occurs. Whatever resistance family life education had met in the earlier decades was mild in comparison with national nervousness over sex education. Newspapers, magazines, radio, and TV devoted an unusual amount of time and space to the attacks. Only occasionally was a fair picture presented by inviting both sides to comment or summarizing the issues on a pro and con basis. Often the pictures that accompanied stories, as in *Life* and *Look*, "spoke more than a thousand words" in revealing the nature of the opposition and are testimony for the need for adult education. In the furor of the late 60s, many family life programs were curtailed along with sex education. It may be painful for some life educators to realize that several of the questions concerning sex education can logically be raised about family life education, especially when the latter meets its responsibility of handling the sexual component. These questions, which were raised in an atmosphere of hostility in the 60s, will need to be answered if the 70s are to proceed on a basis of greater agreement.

## Home, School, and Church

The roles of these three socializing agencies have not been clearly demarcated for many years, particularly where children and youth are concerned. It is a rare textbook or syllabus that does not take an apologetic tone to some degree, either stating or implying that if parents were only better equipped with knowledge and fortitude there would be no need for formal programs in family life and sex education.

All agree that some learnings take place in the home concerning family and sex, if only by the models offered and the emotions developed and suppressed there (Calderone, 1965; Force, 1970). However, an analogy may distinguish this from more formal learnings. Parents are not regarded as historians because they discuss a recent world event at the dinner table or reveal by their body tension their disagreement with a TV commentary. Similarly, parents can plant the seeds for an appreciation of art or literature, but these disciplines exist, and the school offers knowledge and skills the home cannot be expected to supply. It is only in relatively simple societies that the family can fulfill the total educational function.

One of the complaints against family life and sex education most frequently heard in the latter part of the 60s, but certainly not unknown before then, was that family life and sex education usurps the parental prerogative. Some would hold, however, that even the best educated parent cannot handle this responsibility alone for lack of time, knowledge, and teaching skills and, perhaps above all, for lack of the essential component in such education: a group of peers for interaction. Some would hold that the incest taboo and inbuilt role conflict necessitate that others than the parents take on the formal educational task (Mace, 1963). This does not mean that family life and sex education for parents and other adults is not valuable. Indeed, it may be, along with teacher education, a prerequisite for the successful functioning of school programs for youth. It may also be essential if the informal learnings in the home are to make a positive contribution (Calderone, 1965; Kirkendall, 1970).

It is probably the issue of values, however, that dominates the feeling behind the "parental prerogative" argument. This is not lightly dismissed or quickly settled. As Christensen succinctly puts it: "Values are the mental and emotional sets which aid persons in judging the relative worth or importance of things, ideas, or events . . . In decision-making theory, values, simply stated, are the criteria one used for choosing among alternatives" (1964, p. 969). It is claimed that "Probably most leaders in the field today agree that family life education should not consist of foisting one set of values, the teacher's, in place of another set, the pupil's" (Kerckhoff, 1964, p. 898). It would be difficult to make this statement about teachers rather than leaders. With inadequate teacher preparation, it is not unexpected that teachers often show an inability to examine value systems objectively.

One contributing factor may be the ubiquitous use of "wholesome" and "healthy" when attitudes are mentioned in curriculum guides and professional writings. It is not easy to find consensus on such value-laden concepts. According to Rutledge and others (1961) after a three-day effort, "As we discuss the sexual area of life it becomes increasingly clear that vast chasms exist not only between what is taught and practiced, but between professional viewpoints of what is health or unhealth, healing or destructive." Awareness of difference and of diversity is characteristic of the writings of leaders in the field. As Luckey (1967) puts it, "Most social scientists agree that it would be difficult if not impossible to define the norm of sexual behavior in contemporary American society," and "Just as there is no unified political opinion in this country, nor single religious belief. there is no one ethic." In recognition of this, religious leaders in an Interfaith Statement on Sex Education issued in June 1968 to supplement an affirmation in 1966 urge that "Sex education in the schools must proceed constructively, with understanding, tolerance, and acceptance of differences." Chilman (1969) suggests that "Values about sex which are different from those to which the student has been exposed at home or in his neighborhood can be presented as another way of looking at the subject, not as *the* way, or a *better* way."

Thus, when parents insist that the teacher present all sides of a question rather than propagandize for one view, they are on firm educational ground. However, there is a tendency for parents and other adults (including some teachers) to accept traditional propagandizing and to become critical of the classroom only when material not supportive of their particular value position gets presented. Sometimes this is only inferable, but in the late 60s, many of the more extreme opponents, such as LaHaye (n.d.), frankly condemned those who preferred "education over indoctrination." Moreover, any attempt to get beneath the majority assent to sex education reported in polls, such as the Gallup poll of 1967, is likely to find parents either demanding that the teacher believe in chastity or teach it as an absolute if a course in their school is to be required. Even in the sample from a suburban town with higher economic and educational levels than in the country at large, almost three out of five parents thought the teacher should teach that chastity before marriage is best in order for the sex education program to be required (Libby, 1970). A journalist's account of the situation in Anaheim in 1969 reveals in personal interviews some of the more extreme processes of the organized opposition on the value issue (Breasted, 1970).

In the late 60s, the long-smoldering hostility toward secular education because of its emphasis on science spread to family life and sex education. One point of entry was the contrast between the traditional Judeo-Christian position held by many Christian evangelical as well as orthodox Jewish groups that sex outside of marriage is wrong, and the view of situational ethics supported by many other religious bodies, which holds the moral implications of an act to be different at different times, places, and circumstances (Duvall, 1965). While the issue of sex, premarital and extramarital, became an important weapon in the arsenal aimed at family life and sex education in the late 60s, actually it was, together with masturbation, abortion, homosexuality, illegitimacy, and other related topics, only part of the total argument. The dispute can be seen to center on church–state relationships, the use of science rather than revelation in teaching about the family and sex, and the kind of society sought by conflicting political groups.

With the best of motives but with inadequate appreciation for the complexities and the irreversibilities, many parents wanted the schools to act as a brake on the runaway train of change. Few parents were willing to recognize that they in their own youth and in present marital relationships did not live up to the preachments they were asking family life and sex educators to enunciate in the classroom. In the 60s, the Kinsey reports were often cited as though they described the youth of today instead of their parents and grandparents (Somerville, 1968).

It is a principle of religious freedom in the United States that people may indeed live by the dictates of their churches. Many family life and sex education workshops and meetings have been made available within the framework of church educational programs (National Council of Churches, Synagogue Council of America, & United States Catholic Conference, 1968). Many church leaders have sought to keep up with the research findings in the family field by membership in NCFR and by attendance at its annual meetings. Special conferences have also taken place in the 60s, such as a week-long set of meetings called by the Canadian Council of Churches and the National Council of Churches of Christ in the USA in 1961, where more than 500 Protestant clergymen met with sociologists and psychologists (Duvall & Duvall, 1961).

Just as the teaching of evolutionary theory in schools has been opposed and still is in some jurisdictions (California State Department of Education, 1969, p. 64), there is fear that the scientific approach in family life and sex education will reduce religious faith. The split among churches on this issue became dramatically evident in the late 60s when the more extreme attacks on family life and sex education programs were tied in with political movements, some of which sought to violate the constitutional guaranties of separation of church and state and to prevent the application of pluralistic principles.

Despite the hue and cry in the late 60s (Ulman, 1969; "Why the furor," 1969; Zazzaro, 1969), most of the family life and sex education programs in this decade as in previous decades had been supportive of conventional sex-value systems and only faintly reflective of the franker level of discussion that characterized the arts and the mass media. A national magazine had concluded that "most sex education tries to perpetuate by sweet reasonableness, the same morality that was once enforceable by social or religious canon and parental fiat" ("Sex in the U.S.," 1964). Of the Anaheim program, brought to a close in 1969 with the election of a new school board, it was said: "Though the moralizing is camouflaged, the course relies heavily on case histories which point up the dread consequences of unwanted pregnancies and the danger of contracting venereal diseases" (Powers & Baskin, 1969, p. 22).

## The Young Child

The fears of some parents and teachers that family life and sex education will be "the wrong kind," came to a head in the late 60s on the issue of such education for the very young. This was not immediately discernible. As late as 1967, even a responsible journalist could declare: "In the early grades, sex education, far from being controversial, strikes most people as rather cute" (Goodman, 1967, p. 65). But, by 1969, another widely distributed journal was reporting that "The issue is sex education for little children," and "the recent shift of sex education to the elementary grades has stoked anger, fear, and mistrust" ("Facing the 'Facts of Life,'" 1969).

Kindergarten and elementary schools as logical starting places for family life education, however informal and flexible the actual teaching, had been endorsed and to some extent used in the decades preceding the 60s. Good teacher education in early childhood programs had stressed the teachable moment, the desirability of allaying fears and satisfying curiosity, and helping young children develop acceptance of themselves, their friends, and their families. Some teachers used "organized conversations," puppets, and reading aloud as means for allowing feelings to be expressed and knowledge to be acquired. The 40s and 50s were marked, perhaps, by a tendency to overemphasize happiness in family relationships, to take a somewhat narrow view of "proper" family structure and functioning, and to make short work of sex questions. One guide declared in the 40s: "Questions about sex, if there are any . . . should be answered simply and not elaborated upon" (Stevenson, 1946, p. 51). In the 60s, more specific sex education programs were directed at the primary grades (Medical World News, 1965; Minnesota State Department of Education, 1970; "Sex Education in the Elementary Schools," 1967).

During the conflict of the late 60s, both sides tended to blame the other for making an issue of sex education for young children. Moreover, many parents were not able to reconcile themselves to having children able to discuss sex with relative ease, since their own educational experiences rarely had given them the same competency. The moral issue was raised, too. The various assurances given that sexual promiscuity was more rooted in a poor self-image and ignorance of consequences and that early sexual play among children was common in any case were not accepted by large numbers of anxious parents.

At the adolescent level, similar parental fears but with different curriculum implications intruded into the educational picture of the 60s. Many sought extended sex education as a kind of vaccination against premarital intercourse, abortion, unplanned pregnancy, and venereal disease. The arguments for sex education expansion offered by many community councils of parents, educators, and representative citizens bore little relation in some instances to the more cautious view of the seasoned family life educator expressed in the literature: "While specific social and personal problems dramatize our lack of knowledge, insights and competence, family life education does not focus primarily on promiscuity, delinquency, illegitimacy, incorrigibility, and the like. Its focus is on how individuals as parts and products of family life may become physically healthy, emotionally secure, understanding, disciplined, responsible, tolerant human beings, with the capacities to support themselves and to care about other human beings" (ASHA, 1966, p. 11).

There was widespread anticipation among many professionals of mental health benefits from both reduction of guilt as a basis for decision making and the support that school family life and sex education programs could offer youth in coping with negative consequences of unwise decisions. However, it became evident in 1968 and 1969 that many parents, in addition to the organized opposition, were not reconciled to guilt reduction, regarding guilt as insurance against evil behavior and as deserved punishment for departures from traditional codes.

In addition to these value gaps that split the population in a number of different segments, there was uneasiness in the communities as it became evident that some parental fears concerning programs and teacher qualifications had a realistic basis. There is little agreement among educators as yet concerning the sequential family life and sex education experiences that should be offered at any stage of the individual life cycle. Careful evaluation of differing programs might suggest the variables involved, but little has yet been done in comparison of programs. As Chilman (1969) puts it, "No research has been done on how information about sex is best imparted, what its content should be, or what the effects of sex education are" (p. 65). Most family life and sex education programs have not been open to outside observation and evaluation, and as a result, there has been almost complete dependence on self-report of those involved in the given program. Moreover, with the diversity of course goals, time, quality of faculty, school atmosphere, etc., the measurement of a single program or a group will not permit easy generalization.

A case in point is the issue of separation of the sexes in the classroom. Some hold that the communication barriers between men and women are widespread, and there is a need for more rather than fewer opportunities in which boys and girls search together for definitions of roles and clarification of expectations. Community demand for segregated classes sometimes derives from standards of modesty that do not fit well into the out-of-school experiences of young people. Again, there would seem to be a need for the community to permit various kinds of programs to be tried and for the professionals to test their hypotheses and at the least to recognize them as such rather than as proven truths.

## Who Shall Teach?

While parental fears about teacher competency have been complicated by issues of values, there has undoubtedly been justifiable concern about level of knowledge in the family life and sex education classes. The issue became particularly acute in the late 60s when it became evident that the rush into sex education of the mid-60s had proceeded without adequate attention to teacher preparation. Manley (1969) sees "the curriculum for prospective teachers of health" as "generally inadequate," with no attempt to deal with sex "as a teaching area in which a future teacher would have to be proficient" (pp. 54, 55). Malfetti and Rubin (1967), serving as consultants to a survey undertaken by the Information Center on Population Problems, declared, "There is a shortage of persons equipped to teach even the most rudimentary facts of human reproduction." Few teacher education institutions were found in the 1967 survey to be preparing sex educators in any definition of the term (Information Center on Population Problems, 1967). A survey of school districts involving almost a million students in 1961–1963 showed that in the majority of such districts physical education teachers tended to be "also the health education instructors" (Slipcevich, 1964, p. 27). Colleges were urged to revise their curricula (Johnson, 1967).

The National Council on Family Relations has taken the position that those who teach in family life and sex education programs need to have certain academic and field experiences along with opportunities for self-awareness and supervised practice. The establishment of criteria avoids the fruitless struggle among disciplines for hegemony in the field (Somerville, 1970). However, there may still be some disagreement in colleges and universities as to which disciplines should be involved in offering the core experiences. In one institution it may be the psychology department, in another home economics, in still others health education or sociology or a combination of these. While certification of teachers has come increasingly under criticism in some fields, it has not been tried in family life and sex education and may be one of the mechanisms whereby the many disciplines involved can be encouraged to meet nationally recognized standards. Clark Vincent (1967) points out that we require certification for language teachers and none for teaching family life and sex education, "although marriage and human sexuality are far more complex subjects than any foreign language" (p. 51). The issue of who shall teach will undoubtedly persist well into the 70s. In addition to NCFR criteria, several state departments of education have formulated their own standards. Doctoral dissertations will undoubtedly be increasingly devoted to the issue. It is not difficult to foresee a problem in reconciling the various sets of criteria and possible confusion for college administrators and public alike.

## The Issue of Privacy

Still unsettled in the aftermath of the turbulent final years of the decade is the issue of privacy. Parents are understandably concerned about revelations children may make in family life and sex education classes involving their own family life. Just as the doctor or social worker is the recipient of much personal data and is expected to maintain high standards of confidentiality, so, too, the family life and sex educator with better preparation will be less liable to violate professional standards. At the same time, parents will have to recognize that schools are not to be blamed for the negative view their children may have of marriage and family life. In a study of thousands of 8th through 12th graders, Duvall (1965) found "less than half of these students wanting their marriages to be like their parents'." In the industrial areas, only four percent of the boys wanted to reproduce their parents' patterns in their own plans for marriage" (p. 97). It is important for the classroom to permit that kind of airing of discontent that permits inconsistent and unrealistic expectations of marriage and family life to come to light and to encourage students to examine causes of behaviors and alternative solutions to problems. Moreover, many teachers have learned to develop classroom safeguards that allow the problem, and not the child or his family, to become a discussion focus. On the other hand, parent education may help reduce excessive concern with privacy as parents learn to reevaluate their own attitudes and personal behaviors. The 1960s offered little improvement in teacher skills and parent tolerance, and the privacy issue loomed even larger by the end of the decade (Kerckhoff et al., 1970). Crude legislative intrusions did little to solve a delicate problem. Thus, Senate Bill 669, approved by Governor Reagan, July 31, 1968, changed the California Education Code by requiring written notification to parents and written permission from parents before any pupil in K–12 classes can be given a "test, questionnaire, survey, or examination containing any questions about the pupil's personal beliefs or practices in sex, family life, morality, and religion" or any questions about his parents' beliefs and practices in these areas.

## FAMILY LIFE AND SEX EDUCATION OVERSEAS

The ferment that marked the American scene in the 60s had its counterparts abroad, although no country had anything similar to the organized opposition to family life and sex education that developed in the United States at the end of the decade. The Groves Conference on Marriage and the Family, meetings of the International Planned Parenthood Federation, and meetings of NCFR, ASHA, and SIECUS all brought attention from 1965 to 1970 to the development of new programs in many parts of the world. Some took paths not widely trod in the USA, as in the reliance upon volunteers, while others watched the American scene closely and used materials and personnel from here. Only brief mention can be made of a few of the highlights.

Canada, the site of the NCFR annual meeting in 1965, had at that time no university offering any course specifically to prepare the teacher of family life or sex education. Some of the local schools had been offering boys and girls separately a brief unit on reproduction within the health or science course or in special evening lectures by doctors or nurses. Some schools called this family life education as "a less disturbing name" than sex education (Guest, 1966). Also, in many schools aspects of family life and sex education had been included within a variety of subjects: Personal Development, Psychology, Sociology, and Home Economics (Alberta Province) as well as in Biology (Saskatchewan and Ontario). It was only after some twenty years of this pattern (Canadian Education Association, 1964) throughout Canada that in the mid-60s an effort was made in Winnipeg to create an interprofessional committee in which representatives from the clergy, the YWCA, health educators, the Child Guidance Clinic, and the Home and School Associations would meet on a regular basis for a year or two to work out the kind of program they would like their community to offer (Canadian Education Association, 1964). The founding of the Vanier Institute of the Family in Canada in 1965 resulted in a number of activities. Family Life Education is one of its concerns, and it has sponsored a survey that was begun in 1967, and is currently still under way, to discover and classify all programs now offered in churches, schools, social agencies, and other institutions in Canada. Preliminary returns indicate that 1,529 schools among those responding have reported involvement with family life education, while almost twice that number, 2,946, reported no involvement. In universities and colleges, 163 of 308 responded, and of these, 136 were involved and 27 were not (Vanier Institute, 1969a, pp. 25–27). There would seem to be some basis for the announcement in 1970 that "Family life programs are springing up all over" (Vanier Institute of the Family, 1970). Both reflective of this expansion and a spur to it was the National Consultation on Family Life Education sponsored in 1969 at Baniff by the Vanier

Institute (1969b), which brought government and organization representatives together from the various provinces to make recommendations concerning family life education. One college in Canada has begun to publish *The Family Life Educator,* a newsletter reporting new courses, books, and teaching concerns. With all this activity, there is, however, a degree of reliance upon teacher educators from the United States as staff for Canadian workshops, which suggests a lag in development yet to be overcome.

In Great Britain, family life and sex education is at an early stage quantitatively, even more so inside the schools than outside, where youth clubs and adult organizations have had various brief series offered them. Health education personnel predominate in the school program of a city such as Leeds (Paget, 1965, p. 58), serving as peripatetic teachers in the familiar San Diego pattern, while in Gloucester teachers in the school are given brief training for this responsibility (Paget, 1965, p. 54). The use of volunteers, carefully selected by the National Marriage Guidance Council (NMGC) and given some preparation, became widespread when the counselor movement spread to the family life and sex education field in the 60s. "The education work of the NMGC has grown steadily during the last twelve years," it was reported in 1968, "and today our counsellors, who are all volunteers, are also running discussion groups in schools, colleges, youth clubs and other institutions, in many different parts of Great Britain" (Sanctuary, 1968). In mid-decade only the University of Edinburgh among 23 responding to a researcher's request for information had a university program in family life education. The lack of parent education programs was also seen as a retarding influence.

In Australia in the 60s, a pattern developed similar to Britain's in which there is mainly as yet reliance upon Marriage Guidance Organizations to "offer lecture courses or discussion programmes in marriage and family living to help young people prepare for marriage" (Attorney-General, 1966). The organizations approved by the Attorney-General as marriage guidance organizations in the first half of the 60s include welfare agencies and religious institutions as well as regional branches of the NMGC.

In New Zealand, where the Justice Department decided early in the decade to enter the field of marriage counseling in order to safeguard standards and, as in Britain, have the national government offer financial aid in selection and preparation of personnel, the work was extended by mid-decade to family life and sex education in secondary schools. As in Britain, lay people were accepted for training as counselors and family life educators. Unlike professionals, their accreditation has to be newly established in each community in which they work. While there had been nothing in the law to stop the introduction of family life courses in primary or secondary schools, the lack of prepared teachers had been a factor in delay. By using the men and women volunteers selected and trained by the MGC, schools could test parent response and, if this were negative, withdraw them more easily as the courses would not be a firm part of school curriculum and teacher assignment (Clements, 1970).

The International Planned Parenthood Federation (1970), interested in having population programs in formal educational systems in order to help develop "rational knowledge of sex and reproduction, together with an understanding of the responsibilities involved in interpersonal relationships," brought representatives of fourteen countries together in late 1969 to identify common aims in Responsible Parenthood and Sex Education (REPASE) and to arrive at standards concerning content and teacher selection. Recognition of the need for an informed body of parents and of a receptive public generally led to the conclusion that early efforts in family life and sex education would place reliance upon volunteers and concentrate on innovative programs to establish what can be done.

In Chile, preparation for family life education to be introduced into the school system included visits to the United States and Europe to ascertain what kinds of programs and teacher education were found effective. The team included a psychologist and a sociologist. Their tour in this country was financed by the United States government (Social Health News, 1969). The demand for such education had been voiced by teenagers in 1967 when a public session on Youth and Sex had been opened to them in Santiago by an international conference ("Students Turn Out for Sex," 1967).

In the African nations where family patterns are changing rapidly and traditional sources of sex education are less available to the urbanized population, the usefulness of new programs is recognized. Many obstacles exist, including the need to develop a behavioral sciences base; the desirability of including secular groups in an area dominated by religious pressure, especially because the traditional emphasis is often inappropriate; and the lack of published material pertinent to the local conditions.

Sweden and Denmark attracted the attention of American magazines in the 60s to an extent that makes fact and fiction difficult to separate in the realm of family life and sex education. This served to confuse the public, many of whom thought Sweden, for example, had had a model program and that its inadequacies foredoomed American attempts (Moskin, 1966). The professional was aware through the corrective of authoritative books such as Linner's (1967) or reports at conferences such as Wickbom's (1967) that the Scandinavian experience was not offered as a model but modestly recognized its own problem in teacher preparation and parental consensus. Swedish sex education, begun in the 40s and made compulsory in the 50s, was integrated into the national curriculum for all school-age children from first grade on in 1962. "Sex education is given chiefly in the biological lessons but according to recommendations from the National Board of Education it is touched upon also in . . . other subjects in which questions of sex may arise naturally," the headmaster of Katrineholm Secondary School, near Stockholm, reported recently. In the final year of compulsory schooling, the ninth grade when boys or girls are 15 and 16, the amount of time in the school curriculum is increased, and for students who continue in school, the teachers' handbook on sex instruction issued by the Royal Board of Education includes additional topics to be covered. Television and radio add to school coverage. However, not all teachers feel adequately prepared, and there is some tendency to avoid the responsibility.

In France, schools are not permitted to include sex education in the curriculum. Evening courses are arranged for parents. There has been little study as yet of the kind and extent of children's learnings through the parents, or indeed of the parents' own learnings.

In the countries of Eastern Europe, a lack of family life and sex education programs has persisted; the repeated demands for curriculum expansion in this direction may be supported by recently increased research on the family and the publication in educational journals of proposed new courses (Somerville, 1965; Zverev, 1968).

## SUMMARY

For four decades, family life and sex education has struggled against an array of disciplinary, conceptual, and public relations obstacles to achieve a secure place in community and school programs. Many governmental and private agencies have contributed funds, personnel, and imaginative effort. In the 60s, the sudden burgeoning of specialized programs in sex education, although unsupported by a commensurate reckoning of teacher preparedness, brought strong public reaction, at first favorable and often overeager but, in the final years of the decade, questioning and, among some groups, harshly critical. In some instances, proponents of such programs were vulnerable on the grounds of ill-defined goals or questionable premises. In others, political malice grossly exaggerated shortcomings. The situation threatened to polarize family life educators. The irrationality and the political machinations of fundamentalist and antidemocratic minorities alienated most professionals, however, and both individuals and organizations were stirred to dissociate themselves from the extreme attacks. Position statements were issued by various organizations stating their belief in the validity of family life and sex education.. The challenge for family life educators to recognize more fully the sexual dimensions of their subject matter, and for sex educators to recognize more fully the psychosocial dimensions, has brought a measure of theoretical unity to the whole field. However, many issues have not been settled. Evaluation studies, experimental programs, agreement on teacher preparation criteria, and expansion of teacher education and parent education may have to be high on the priority lists of the 70s if progress is to be made. While undoubtedly more education of the public will be necessary to offset the confusion sown by the organized opposition, a recent survey shows that this confusion, although serious, has not stopped many communities from undertaking or continuing the study of ways of developing programs (Force, 1970). There seems to be little retreat among some of the religious groups. A survey by the United States Catholic Conference Family Life Division found one-third of the dioceses offering or preparing to offer programs (Bolton, 1969), and it is expected that increasing numbers of the 12,000 Catholic schools, with their five million elementary and secondary school students, will follow suit (McHugh, 1968). The variety of the Catholic programs reveal awareness of community differences and cooperation with secular school systems in workshops for teachers and adaptations of teaching guides (McHugh, 1969).

Undetermined yet is the amount of governmental aid that can be expected in the 70s. Here and there, mention is made of federal funds that have underwritten new programs, such as that at New York University. There is a general impression that the change of political administration curtailed some financial support on the federal level. The Children's Bureau had announced in the 60s that improving family life education was one of its current emphases, and it was cooperating toward this goal with several other federal agencies through a Subcommittee on Parent and Family Life Education of the Interdepartmental Committee on Children and Youth. The establishment of the Office of Child Development in 1970 within the Department of Health, Education, and Welfare may have positive effects on the Federal Government's recognition of the need for studying and expanding family life and sex education programs. Major reliance will undoubtedly continue to be on private foundations, university grants, and the donation of time and effort by leaders in the field.

Legislatively, the field of family life and sex education continues to be wide open. According to one survey, as late as June 1969, "most states had no law either authorizing or prohibiting the teaching of sex or birth control education in their schools" (Rodick, p. 157). However, this can change abruptly, and the California experience has shown that restrictions on material to be used in the classroom, as in the Schmitz bill, can in only a few months so threaten teacher effectiveness that new legislation must be proposed, such as the Rodda bill, to lessen the negative consequences. Governors' Councils continued to function in the 60s (Somerville, 1969).

The flood of materials that poured over the educational scene in the mid-1960s will need careful evaluation to ensure that only the best are adopted for classroom use. Wholesale condemnation based on connection with SIECUS is irrational. California has outlawed not only the few publications offered by that organization but even the books and films recommended by them. Many of these were high-grade materials reviewed and recommended in various professional journals. Similarly, reevaluation will have to be made in the 70s of materials rejected earlier. The TV series "A Time of Your Life," including its most controversial segment, "A New Life," is currently finding additional uses in teacher and parent education. Even for schools, a national magazine reports that "In California, Hawaii, and New York, the opposition has tended to lose its bite as the programs are actually aired" (Jobin, 1970). Generally, the fate of a local program in the menacing atmosphere of the late 60s should not prejudge the materials issued in connection with it or the books written by those temporarily removed from positions of influence (Cook, 1969; Schulz & Williams, 1968).

The turbulence of the 60s shook up the family life and sex education field and left in its wake the need to take stock and to rebuild along new lines offering greater shelter against unexpected or unreasonable furies.

## NOTE

Previously published by the *Journal of Marriage and the Family*, Vol. 33 No. 1, Decade Review, Part 2 (Feb. 1971), pp. 11–35. Published by National Council on Family Relations.

## REFERENCES

American Association of School Administrators (AASA). (1938). Sixteenth Yearbook. Author.

American Social Health Association (ASHA). (1966). *Family life education—A cause for action.* Author.

American Sociological Association. (1970). *SRSS Newsletter* (Spring).

Attorney-General's Department, Canberra, Australia. (1966). Organizations approved by the Attorney-General as marriage guidance organizations under the provisions of the Matrimonial Causes Act 1959–1966.

Avery, C. E., Brody, D. S., & Lee, M. E. (1969). *Sex education: Concepts and challenges.* Eugene, OR: E. C. Brown Center for Family Studies.

Ayres, W. H., & McCurdy, M. (n.d.). Time of your life: Family life and health education for intermediate grades. *Preliminary Teachers Guide,* Programs 10–15, KQED Instructional Television Service.

Baker, L. (1969). The rising furor over sex education. *The Family Coordinator* (July).

Baker, L., & Darcy, J. B. (1970). Survey of family life and sex education programs in Washington secondary schools. *The Family Coordinator* (July).

Barr, D. (1967). Sex, love, and modern education. *Columbia College Today* (Fall), 35–39.

Beck, L. (1955). The Bulletin of the National Association of Secondary School Principles (December), 16.

Bolton, B. (1969). Bishops open drive for sex education. *Daily Californian* (September 26).

Bowman, H. (1949). Marriage education in the colleges. *Journal of Social Hygiene.*

Brantley, L. (1966). How far should schools go in family life education. *Winston-Salem Journal.*

Breasted, M. (1970). *Oh! sex education?* New York: Praeger.

Brown, M. (1953). *With focus on family living.* Washington, DC: U.S. Government Printing Office.

Brown, M. (1964). Organizational programs to strengthen the family. In H. Christensen (Ed.), *Handbook of marriage and the family.* Chicago: Rand-McNally.

Burleson, D. L. (1967). Sex education: What are the issues? *Scholastic Teacher* (April 21).

Calderone, M. (1963). Sexual energy—constructive or destructive. *Western Journal of Surgery, Obstetrics and Gynecology* (November–December).

Calderone, M. (1965). Sex and social responsibility. *Journal of Home Economics* (September).

California State Department of Education. (1969). Guidelines for moral instruction in California schools. Report accepted by State Board of Education (May 9).

Canadian Education Association. (1964). The present status of sex education in Canadian schools. Canadian Education Association (September).

Carrera, M. A. (1970). Guidelines for the preparation of high school teachers of sex education. Chapter IV. Mimeographed.

Chilman, C. S. (1969). Some social and psychological aspects of sex education. In C. Broderick & J. Bernard (Eds.), *The individual, sex and society.* Baltimore: Johns Hopkins Press.

Christensen, H. (1964). The intrusion of values. In H. Christensen (Ed.), *Handbook of marriage and the family.* Chicago: Rand McNally.

Christensen, H. (1969). The impact of culture and values. In C. Broderick & J. Bernard (Eds.), *The individual, sex, and society.* Baltimore: Johns Hopkins Press.

Clements, L. C. (1970). Criteria for selection of sex educators: A New Zealand experience. Paper prepared for SIECUS Conference.

Cook, P. W. (1969). Family life and sex education program in the Anaheim Union High School District. Mimeographed.

Coombs, R. (1968). Sex education for physicians: Is it adequate? *The Family Coordinator* (October).

Currie, B. (1970). Elementary school program prepares child for family role. *What's New in Home Economics* (May–June).

Dager, E. Z., & Harper, G. (1959). Family life education in Indiana public schools: a preliminary report. *Marriage and Family Living* (November).

DeNichols, W. (1970). A marketing specialist looks at Home Economics. *Focus* (May).

Duvall, E. M. (1965). How effective are marriage courses. *Journal of Marriage and the Family* (May).

Duvall, E. M., & Duvall, S. M. (1961). *Sex ways—In fact and faith.* New York: Association Press.

Follow the signs. (1970). *What's new in home economics* (November–December).

Force, E. (1970). Family life education survey report: Western region, February 15–March 3, 1970. *American Social Health Association.* Mimeographed.

Frank, L. (1962). The beginnings of child development and family life education in the twentieth century. *Merrill-Palmer Quarterly* (October).

Furlong, W. B. (1967). It's a long way from the birds and bees. *The New York Times Magazine* (June 11).

Goodman, W. (1967). The new sex education. *Redbook* (September).

Guest, H. H. (1966). Interim report of the Interprofessional Study Committee on family life education to the Winnipeg School Board, May 3. Mimeographed.

Growth patterns and sex education: A suggested program, kindergarten through grade twelve. (1967). *Journal of School Health* (May).

Information Center on Population Problems. (1967). News release.

International Planned Parenthood Federation, Working Group. (1970). *Proceedings of the 1970 International Planned Parenthood Federation, London.* Mimeographed.

Jewson, R. H. (1967). Family life education as viewed from the NCFR mailbag.

Jobin, J. (1970). The sex battle takes on a new meaning. *TV Guide* (May 2).

Johnson, W. R. (1967). The sexual revolution and the colleges: A challenge to higher education. *The Journal of the American College Health Association* (May).

Kaplan, M. (1967). Schools extend V.D. instruction. *New York Times* (May 19).

Kerckhoff, R. (1964). Family life education in America. In Harold Christensen (Ed.), *Handbook of Marriage and the Family.* Chicago: Rand-McNally.

Kerckhoff, R., et al. (1970). Community experiences with the 1969 attack on sex education. *The Family Coordinator* (January).

Kirkendall, L. A. (1970). *Kirkendall on sex education: A collection of readings.* Eugene, OR: E. C. Brown Center for Family Studies.

Kirkendall, L., & Libby, R. (1969). Sex and interpersonal relationships. In C. Broderick & J. Bernard (Eds.), *The Individual, Sex, and Society.* Baltimore: Johns Hopkins Press.

LaHaye, T. F. (n.d.). *A Christian view of radical sex education.* San Diego: Scott Memorial Baptist Church.

Landis, J. T. (1959). The teaching of marriage and family courses in colleges. *Marriage and Family Living.*

Landis, J. T. (1965). *Family life education in California.* Paper presented at the Miami Meeting of NCFR, Miami, FL.

Libby, R. W. (1970). Parental attitudes toward high school sex education programs. *The Family Coordinator* (July).

Facing the "facts of life." *Life* (September 19).

Lindquist, R. (1968). Teach sex education as the fourth "R." *What's New in Home Economics* (February).

Linner, B. (1967). *Society and sex in Sweden.* New York: Pantheon.

Lock, F. R. (1964). The challenge of change. *Obstetrics and Gynecology* (September).

Luckey, E. B. (1967). Helping children grow up sexually: How? When? By whom? *Children* (July–August).

Luckey, E. B. (1968). Sex education and in-service training program. *The Family Coordinator* (April).

MacArthur, A. (1967). Family life education through extension programs. *Journal of Marriage and the Family* (August).

Mace, D. (1963). *Should parents undertake sex education at all?* Paper presented at the Groves Conference on Marriage and the Family, Baltimore, MD.

Malfetti, J., & Rubin, A. (1967). Sex education: Who is teaching the teachers? *Teachers College Record* (December).

Manley, H. (1969). Starting a program of sex education. In C. Broderick & J. Bernard (Eds.), *The Individual, Sex, and Society.* Baltimore: Johns Hopkins Press.

Marland, S. P., Jr. (1961). Placing sex education in the curriculum. *Phi Delta Kappan*, 43(December), 132–134.

Martinson, F. M. (1966). Sexual knowledge, values and behavior patterns: With especial reference to Minnesota youth. St. Peter, MN: Gustavus Adolphus College.

Mathias, J. L. (1966). What doctors don't know about sex. *Medical Economics* (December 12).

McConnell, E. (1970). The history of home economics education. *Forecast for Home Economics* (Part 1, September; Part 2, October).

McCune, S. D., & Jones, B. (1967). Camp fire girls final report, Potomac Area Council, December 1967. Washington, DC. Mimeographed.

McHugh, J. T. (1968). Sex education in the Catholic schools: An overview of Diocesan programs. *Catholic School Journal* (March).

McHugh, J. T. (Ed.). (1969). *Sex education: A guide for teachers.* Washington, DC: Family Life Division, United States Catholic Conference.

Medical World News. (1965). Biologist suggests sex talks to toddlers. *Medical World News* (December 3).

Minnesota State Department of Education. (1970). Guidelines for family life and sex education, grades K–12. *Curriculum Bulletin* (32).

The Morals Revolution on the United States Campus. *Newsweek* (April 16).

Morgan, M. (1966). Family life and sex education in the schools. *Social Health News* (June).

Moskin, J. R. (1966). Sweden's new battle over sex. *Look* (November 15).

National Council of Churches, Synagogue Council of America, & United States Catholic Conference. (1968). Interfaith statement on sex education. (June 8).

Paget, N. (1965). Education for family living in the United Kingdom. Buffalo, NY: De-Grey.

Pieretti, G. (1963). A guide for teaching personal and family relationships. *Home Economics Education* (November).

Powers, G. P., & Baskin, W. (1969). *Sex education: Issues and directives.* New York: Philosophical Library.

Reiss, I. (Ed.). (1966). The sexual renaissance of America. *Journal of Social Issues* (April).

Rutledge, A. L., et al. (1961). Sex ethics, sex acts, and human need: a dialogue. *Pastoral Psychology* (October–November).

Sanctuary, G. (1968 *Family life education in Britain.* Paper presented at the Groves Conference on Marriage and the Family, Boston, MA.

Schulz, E. D., & Williams, S. R. (1968). *Family life and sex education: Curriculum and instruction.* New York: Harcourt, Brace and World.

Sex education in the elementary schools. (1967). *Scholastic Teacher* (April 21).

The Sex Information and Education Council of the United States (SIECUS). (1965). SIECUS Newsletter.

The Sex Information and Education Council of the United States (SIECUS). (1970). SIECUS Newsletter.

Sex in the U.S.: Mores and morality. (1964). *Time* (January 24).

Shimmel, G. M., & Carrera, M. A. (1970). Guidelines for teacher preparation programs. *SIECUS Newsletter* (April).

Skills found lacking. (1968). *What's New in Home Economics* (April–May).

Slipcevich, E. (1964). School health education study: Summary report of a nationwide study of health instruction in the public schools, 1961–1963. Washington, DC.

Social Health News (1969). *Social Health News.*

Somerville, R. M. (1965). The family in Yugoslavia. *Journal of Marriage and the Family* (August).

Somerville, R. M. (1966). New materials for study of the family: Study of sexual aspects of family relationships. *Journal of Marriage and the Family* (August).

Somerville, R. M. (1967). The relationship between family life and sex education. *Journal of Marriage and the Family* (May).

Somerville, R. M. (1968, March 1). *The sexual revolution?* Keynote address at the Symposium on Sex and Family Life Education, University of California, Irvine.

Somerville, R. M. (1969). Governors' councils and family life programs. *The Family Coordinator* (January).

Somerville, R. M. (1970). Family life and sex education: Proposed criteria for teacher education. *The Family Coordinator* (April).

Southard, H. (1967). The revolution in sex education: What schools can do. *Teaching and Learning*.

Southard, H. (1971). Readers' guide. *YWCA Magazine* (January).

Stevenson, E. (1946). Home and family life education in elementary schools. New York: John Wiley.

Striven, M. (1968). Putting the sex back into sex education. *Phi Delta Kappan* (May).

Students turn out for sex. (1967). *Planned Parenthood News* (May).

Ulman, N. (1969). A delicate subject: Sex education courses are suddenly assailed by many parent groups. *The Wall Street Journal* (April 11).

Vanier Institute of the Family. (1969a). Annual Report for year ended December 31, 1969. Mimeographed.

Vanier Institute of the Family. (1969b, September 7–10). A kaleidoscope report of a National Consultation on Family Life Education, Baniff, Alberta. Mimeographed.

Vanier Institute of the Family. (1970). *Transition*.

Vincent, C. (1967). The pregnant single college girl. *The Journal of the American College Health Association* (May).

Wake, F. R. (1966). Are parents the best sex educators? *PTA Magazine* (November).

White House Conference on Children and Youth. (1960). *Recommendations: Composite report of forum findings*. Washington, DC: U.S. Government Printing Office.

Why the furor over sex education. (1969, August 4). *U.S. News and World Report*.

# Chapter Five

# SEXUALITY EDUCATION IN THE ONGOING SEXUAL REVOLUTION OF THE 1970s

*Konstance McCaffree and Jean Levitan*

When reflecting on the history of sexuality education during the 1970s, it is critical to examine the cultural context in which those educational efforts took place. Consequently, before discussing the various programs and curricula that were offered during that time, we will highlight the significant political and cultural events that informed the perspectives of the decade. Both authors will also share their personal experiences, both as students and educators.

The 1970s were remarkable for sexual openness and growth, yet the decade was clearly influenced by the 1960s. Though it is common to use the phrase "sexual revolution" for the late sixties and early seventies, scholars disagree about whether there was indeed a sexual revolution (Leo, 1983). As in other time periods during the twentieth century, researchers conducted studies on sexuality with the traditional focus on: marriage and divorce rates, number of children, reported rates of premarital sex, reported rates of homosexual sex, and attitudes toward selected sexual matters. What distinguished this decade, however, was the impression that sexual behavior and attitudes were changing rapidly.

Clearly, the 1960s laid the foundation for political action and change centered on civil rights in the broadest sense of the term. The Reverend Dr. Martin Luther King, Jr.'s leadership brought attention to discrimination based on race, with President Lyndon Johnson signing the Civil Rights Act in 1964, which protected basic human rights based on race and sex.

The publication of *The Feminine Mystique* (Friedan, 1963) led women to examine their roles in life. That book's author, Betty Friedan, was influential in the formation of the National Organization of Women, an organization arguing for equal treatment based on sex. In 1969, the Stonewall Uprising took place, where gay and transgender individuals in a bar in Greenwich Village, New York, fought back against police harassment. That event was considered to be the start of the gay rights movement. Overlapping it all was the antiwar movement, with growing student activism committed to ending the Vietnam War.

For much of the 1960s, contraception was illegal and so was abortion. People were encouraged to marry and have children. Though there was evidence that women were sexually active before marriage, no one really knew because asking unmarried women about their sexual practices was not acceptable (Luker, 2007). Getting pregnant outside of marriage was shameful, and the woman was the one who was blamed, rather than sharing that blame with her male partner. If the pregnancy did not lead to a quick marriage, women, especially white women, were sent away to keep the pregnancy hidden; the mothers were counseled to place their babies for adoption (Fessler, 2006). By the 1970s, more women were keeping their babies, yet when an unwed mother kept her baby, she risked being fired from her job and refused services (such as diaper delivery) once it was discovered that she was unmarried. A related bias was that a man could be refused condoms if a pharmacist knew he was unmarried (Solinger, 1992).

By 1975, the world just described had ended. Contraception was legal for everyone regardless of marital status, including teenagers and adults. Condoms, contraceptive jellies, and foams were openly available for sale in stores and regularly advertised in women's magazines. The decade of the 1970s began with public discourse on issues of what was right and fair in the treatment of people based on race, sex, and sexual orientation. The decade ended with whispers of a terrible infection showing up among gay men in New York City and San Francisco, an infection that would have an impact on sexuality that no one could have imagined.

## THE POLITICAL CLIMATE OF THE 1970s

At the beginning of the 1970s, Richard Nixon was serving as President of the United States. In May of that year, four students were killed at Kent State University in Ohio during a protest against the Vietnam War. People in the country had been watching news reports about deaths in Vietnam on television, an experience unlike the reporting of earlier wars; media exposure helped Americans better understand the horrors of war. Hearing about four individuals shot by the National Guard on a college campus, however, shocked the nation, especially college students. The events at Kent State led to many colleges and universities being shut down by student protests, often pitting students against police.

During the 1960s, people witnessed the assassinations of their leaders—President John F. Kennedy, Reverend Martin Luther King, Jr., and Senator Robert Kennedy. The 1970s brought the resignation of Richard Nixon (1974) for fear of impeachment due to criminal activity, the subsequent inauguration of Gerald Ford, and the election of Jimmy Carter in 1976. Americans were able to watch the Watergate Hearings on television, where the Senate interrogated Nixon's staff and exposed the unethical practices that led to his resignation. The decade ended with a folksy president name "Jimmy" who seemed to embody honesty and a down-home style, coupled with close ties to born-again Christian religious beliefs. Surprisingly, Carter crossed traditional boundaries when he gave an interview to *Playboy* magazine (November, 1976) admitting: "I've looked on a lot of women with lust. I've committed adultery in my heart many times" (Scheer, 1976). Earlier presidents may have had affairs, but no president had ever agreed to an interview with what was considered a "soft porn" magazine. Carter also distinguished himself by advocating for sexuality education.

In between Nixon and Carter was the presidency of Gerald Ford. What was particularly interesting about that presidency was the role model set by his wife, Betty. During his years in the White House, Betty confronted two serious health problems and spoke openly and publicly about both. She was struggling with an alcohol and drug problem, and she was diagnosed with breast cancer. To many, she brought embarrassing health issues out of the closet and into the public domain. Many women went for mammograms for the first time and felt somewhat better able to talk about the experience of a breast cancer diagnosis. Today, the Betty Ford Clinic for drug rehabilitation is well known, with that First Lady having helped to remove the stigma of treatment.

Throughout the decade there was continued activism around civil rights. Women's groups were involved in a national campaign to add an "equal rights" amendment to the U.S. Constitution. The language of the Equal Rights Amendment (ERA) was to read: "Equality of Rights under the law shall not be denied or abridged by the United States or any state on account of sex." The ERA had been introduced in Congress starting in 1923 and was passed in 1972, but despite national efforts at the state levels, it was never ratified by the requisite number of states by the deadline of 1982; consequently, it never became part of the Constitution (Rothenberg, 2001, p. 493).

During the decade, Phyllis Schlafly became a national leader in the fight against the ERA. Her anti-ERA group later became the Eagle Forum

(Diamond, 1995), a well-funded conservative group whose agenda included efforts to preserve traditional marriage, with women home to raise the children, and limiting sexuality education in the public schools. Her conservative base never seemed to question the hypocrisy of a working attorney and mother of several children, traveling across the United States, lecturing on the dangers of having women become independent and treated equally under the law. Schlafly later joined forces with those opposing gay rights, another threat to the nuclear family; years later, her own son was "outed" in an attempt to puncture her antigay efforts.

As various single-issue groups—such as, abortion rights, gay rights, and ERA—argued the civil rights agenda, what came to be known as "the religious right" became better organized. Anita Bryant, a popular female vocalist, previous Miss Oklahoma, and runner-up in the Miss America contest, became a national figure in her crusade against gay rights. In 1977, she successfully campaigned for the repeal of a Dade County, Florida, ordinance that prohibited discrimination based on sexual orientation. Her antigay views stemmed from her strong conservative religious background, and she argued that Christianity viewed homosexuality as a sin. Because homosexuals couldn't have their own children, she argued, they would be likely to "recruit" other people's children. She began the organization Save Our Children, which grew nationally, expanding its efforts to block gay civil rights measures. Bryant also worked as a spokesperson for the Florida Citrus Commission, promoting orange juice as part of a healthy breakfast. One victory for gay rights groups was their successful threat to boycott orange juice; Bryant's contract was not renewed.

By the end of the decade, Reverend Jerry Falwell was becoming known as the leader of The Moral Majority, a fundamentalist Christian group opposed to sex education in the schools, gay rights, abortion, and pornography. The group was committed to developing a voting block to secure their agenda, which also included putting prayer back into public schools (Right Web, 2008). Falwell referenced the Bible and God, advancing the "pro-family" and "pro-life" positions. The nuclear family was to be protected, as was the life of the "unborn child." There was no desire to separate church and state issues, and "secular" became another "dirty word." Above all, Falwell helped to hijack the concept of morality, pointing an accusing finger at those who argued for gender equality, freedom of speech, and sexual civil rights.

## THE MEDIA'S INFLUENCE ON THE SEXUAL CLIMATE

During the 1970s, people relied upon newspapers, magazines, radio, and television to learn about the world. There were three major networks—ABC,

NBC, and CBS—with local stations bringing television options to perhaps a total of seven channels. *Time* and *Newsweek* were popular magazines, summarizing the critical events of the week. At various times during the decade, attention was given to sexuality issues. With the publication of *People* magazine in 1974, the lives of entertainers, sports figures, politicians, and others of public interest came under increasing scrutiny. Issues of sexuality moved into more mainstream publications over the course of the decade, with various issues getting prominent attention. Dr. David Reuben's *Everything You Always Wanted to Know About Sex—But Were Afraid to Ask* had been published in 1969, facilitating more open discussions about sexuality in public. In 1972, Woody Allen's film of the same name, loosely based on Reuben's book, used comedy as he framed out the answers to selected questions about sexuality. The August 24, 1970, issue of *Newsweek* featured Reuben on the cover with "More than you want to know about sex." The public was treated to a naked Burt Reynolds as the centerfold in *Cosmopolitan* magazine in April of 1972, a very radical move for that time. In March 1977, *Time* magazine featured Marabel Morgan's book *Total Joy* and the headline "Fighting the Housewife Blues." Morgan had earlier distinguished herself as an author of *The Total Woman*, advising women on how to satisfy their husband's sexual needs and keep him happy.

Clearly, greater public access to sexuality information was a hallmark of the 1970s. The irony was that while mainstream media addressed sexuality issues more openly, there was a simultaneous growth of and organization by those opposed to the essence of sexual openness and tolerance. Feminists were telling women to find their own voices at the same time that Marabel Morgan, a married woman publicly identified with born-again Christianity, was advising women to be sexy and focus on their husbands. Phyllis Schlafly was traveling the United States advising women to stay home with their children. People were talking about sexuality and making allegiances with others like themselves. And the media was there to report it all.

## PORTRAYALS OF SEXUALITY IN THE MEDIA

During the 1970s, books that honestly explored issues around sexuality became more visible in mainstream bookstores. Alex Comfort published *The Joy of Sex* (1972), which, along with two later volumes, aided heterosexual couples in their pursuit of mutual pleasure. The Boston Women's Health Book Collective wrote *Our Bodies, Ourselves* (1973), which encouraged women to understand their bodies, take charge of their health, and share their stories to help others. Lonnie Barbach wrote *For Yourself* (1975), a guide to help women learn to orgasm. Shere Hite became a very public figure with the publication of *The Hite Report: A Nationwide Study of Female Sexuality* (1976); that book provided women with both "data" and personal descriptions about sexuality. In 1977, *The Joy of Gay Sex* (Silverstein & White) became available in mainstream bookstores. What was revolutionary for the times was the accessibility of sexuality-related books and the increasing comfort with which they were publicly discussed.

Television during the 1970s both contributed to and reflected what was seen as a sexual revolution. Among the variety of shows designed for entertainment came a host of images and messages reflecting new attitudes toward sexuality. Norman Lear was able to infuse challenges to bigotry in his successful sitcom *All in the Family;* over the years that show addressed issues of gender roles, coming out as gay, rape, and sexual swinging. *Maude,* a spin-off program, devoted two episodes to the topic of rape. *Charlie's Angels* was a show about three female investigators who solved problems while setting new standards for sex appeal. *Three's Company* not only showed a single man living with two single women but also had a middle-aged woman character complain about her husband's sexual performance. Afternoon television offered numerous soap operas where the complicated sexual lives of the characters were openly portrayed for viewers. *Saturday Night Live* was first produced in 1975, taking comedy to a new level, albeit beginning at 11:30 P.M. (Kingwood College Library, 2008). Sexual issues were well-represented, although the use of proper terminology in programming would have to wait.

Even though there has been public concern about suggestive sexual material on television since the early 1960s (Steiner, 1963), extensive objective examinations of sexual content on television only began in the late 1970s. Inference made from the existing research supports the premise that television does contribute to the sexuality education of America's youth. In 1977, television awareness training sponsored by the United Methodist Church and other church groups instituted workshops in communities around the United States to assist participants in developing critical viewing skills through awareness and knowledge (Rubinstein, 1981). These same skills were later utilized by educators in schools to help students evaluate what they were viewing.

The movies of the 1970s pushed the proverbial envelope for how sexuality would be portrayed on the screen. *A Clockwork Orange* (1971) graphically depicted the violence of rape and a behavior modification treatment for the crime. *Chinatown* (1974) had Faye Dunaway's character confess that her sister was also her daughter, having been impregnated by her father. In *Last Tango in Paris* (1973), Marlon Brando engages in anal intercourse on the floor with his young lover. In *Coming Home* (1978), Jon Voigt portrayed a partially paralyzed Vietnam veteran who explained to his girlfriend that he enjoyed oral sex and got aroused by keeping on the lights during lovemaking. *Deep Throat* (1972) and *Behind the Green Door* (1972) were both "porn flicks," yet they became popular and mainstream and were distributed nationally. Marilyn Chambers, a model for Proctor and Gamble, caused a scandal when she became the star of *Behind the Green Door,* and it led to the company's recall of all Ivory Snow products with her image. For many, *Annie Hall* (1977) became a reference point for the struggles and humor inherent in opposing sexual complaints.

Live theater also addressed sexuality in bold new ways. One example was *Let My People Come* (1974), which opened in Greenwich Village, New York. The actors simulated a range of explicit sexual behaviors, including orgies, male and female homosexuality, and oral sex. The music was both funny and serious, with the overall atmosphere of the show upbeat and fun (Ward, 2002). Plays from the late 1960s, such as *Hair* and *Oh! Calcutta!* had prepared audiences for nudity on stage; *Oh! Calcutta!* was revived on Broadway in 1976 and ran for 13 years. *Let My People Come,* however, simulated behavior in a way never before shown on the stage.

Overall, the sexual culture of the 1970s made human sexuality something to be talked about, witnessed, and appreciated increasingly in a public arena.

## SEXUALITY CONCERNS OF THE 1970s

The women's movement had a significant impact on the way sexual issues were addressed during this period of time. Traditional gender roles were questioned, with growing respect for more egalitarian relationships between men and women. Women were supported as they fought to change the way rape was handled by police, hospitals, and courts. There was a growth in rape crisis centers and better practices established to deal with victims of assault.

The fight for reproductive rights led to better access to birth control. In 1965, the Supreme Court ruled in *Griswold v. Connecticut* that married couples had the right to use contraception. That decision was followed in 1972 with *Eisenstadt v. Baird,* guaranteeing those same rights to single individuals. The 1973 *Roe v. Wade* decision ensured that women could have medically safe first trimester abortions in all states in the United States; the availability of, and regulations relative to, second trimester procedures were to be determined at the state level. Planned Parenthood centers across the United States were able to provide care in clinics, some only offering birth control services, with others providing abortion services as well.

Toward the end of the 1970s, there was growing public concern about the high rates of teen pregnancy, with descriptions being made of an "epidemic." Careful analysis of the statistics on teen pregnancy would show that the pregnancy rate had remained constant despite increased reporting of sexual activity. A Senate inquiry in 1978, however, focused on the rates of out-of-wedlock births among teens and the disproportionate birth rates for African American teens compared to white teens (Moran, 2000, pp. 200–201). Joseph Califano, Jr., the Secretary of Health, Education, and Welfare, testified before a Senate Committee that teenage parenthood was associated with poverty, health problems for the mother and child, poor education, poor job prospects, and welfare dependency. In response, Congress passed the Adolescent Health Services and Prevention and Care Act of 1978, which, although consistently underfunded, became one source for the funding of family life and sex education services (Moran, 2000, p. 201).

As in earlier decades, the negative outcomes of sexual activity—unintended pregnancy and venereal diseases—would have the attention of public health officials. While gonorrhea and syphilis remained the two infections commonly addressed, a new viral infection began to get attention—herpes simplex II. By the end of the decade, articles appeared talking about the viral infection one would have "for life."

The gay rights movement also impacted policies and practices of the decade. In 1973, the American Psychiatric Association removed "homosexuality" from the list of mental illnesses cited in the *Diagnostic and Statistical Manual II.* Increasingly, gay and lesbian rights activists were working publicly to ensure greater civil rights. The first Gay Pride Parade took place in New York City in June 1970, commemorating the one-year anniversary of the Stonewall riots, and led to an annual tradition that takes place across the United States.

## THE STATE OF PUBLIC SCHOOL EDUCATION

As stated at the outset, the political climate and culture provide a context in which public schools educate youth. While the 1970s could be viewed as progressive, the decades prior were not. During the 1950s and 1960s, more and more secondary schools had adopted some elements of sexuality education. Public school sexuality education in the mid-sixties had seemed fragmented and incomprehensive (Irvine, 2002). In a few large school districts there were ambitious programs, yet there was no systematic program development. Evanston's (Illinois) family life education program was an interdisciplinary course integrated into the overall curriculum starting in kindergarten. In Anaheim, California, the family life education program proposed to teach high school students not only about anatomy and physiology but also about pregnancy, parenting, and topics such as masturbation, homosexuality, and abortion (Irvine, 2002). The impetus for more comprehensive sexuality education in the early 1970s came in response to perceived changes in teenage sexual behavior. Parents, school administrators, and teachers became concerned and supported courses in sexuality education. In some cases, the content was incorporated into health and other disciplines that included marriage, family, and personal development.

The openness and freedom of the youth culture of the 1960s laid the foundation for the growth and development of sex education in the 1970s. While youth were exploring the use of hallucinogens, making love not war, and protesting establishment rules, sexuality educators of the decade wrote books attempting to keep the lid on the sexual revolution. Adult concerns were reflected in some of the books, with authors condemning premarital sex and homosexuality and discouraging masturbation. In *Modern Sex Education*, girls were warned about their behavior on a date, which might lead to premarital sex, pregnancy, and abortion. The authors describe "that homosexuals are made, not born" (Julian & Jackson, 1967, p. 55), implying that homosexuality could be changed if the culture changed. School administrators were still somewhat wary of introducing sexuality education into the school curriculum. There was a strong belief that teaching children more about sex and contraception would encourage them to engage in sex at a younger age. There was an even stronger belief, however, that information was an important antidote to the exploding sexuality of the sixties. In author McCaffree's own school district, the school board and administration gave permission to offer a comprehensive course in human sexuality for high school seniors as long as there was parental permission for the course.

In many ways, the decade of the 1970s was a honeymoon for sexuality educators. When communities became frightened by the arrival of drugs, they decided that schools needed to do something to combat the issue. Concern for the welfare of youth led to the establishment of courses that dealt with drugs, alcohol, and sex education. The inclusion of sexuality education was supported by the medical community, which saw an increased prevalence of venereal diseases (VD), today referred to as sexually transmitted infections (STIs). It was not unusual in the 1970s for schools to invite doctors to speak to students about disease and the growing problem of unwanted pregnancy. "In Connecticut, Governor Tom Meskill brought attention to VD and labeled it more of a concern and more prevalent than measles, mumps, chicken pox and diphtheria combined—and therefore a public health problem" (R. Selverstone, personal communication, April 28, 2008).

Some communities were very open to "liberal," creative, and experimental programs in all aspects of the curriculum (i.e., open classrooms where entire schools were built without walls and a large group of students of varying skill levels would be in a single, large classroom with several teachers overseeing them). School administrators supported courses for high school youth that might include any topic in sexuality, including abortion, pornography, and so forth. Some would require permission slips from parents; others invited parents to visit the class or come to special lessons on topics the children were learning.

The Sex (now Sexuality) Information and Education Council of the United States (SIECUS) had been arguing for sexuality education programs that were value-neutral, information rich, and nondirective in approach because "By the end of the 1970s, sexual liberalism was at its high tide, and it lifted SIECUS and its comprehensive program in value-neutral sex education along with it" (Moran, 2000, p. 202). In 1974, SIECUS updated their "Statement of Beliefs" about sexuality. They now endorsed the rights of people to live according to who they are regardless of their sexual orientation and the distribution of contraceptives to children without parental consent. Materials from Planned Parenthood manuals provided positive messages that described sex as being good when one was ready for it, able to act responsibly, and wanting to engage in it (Donovan, 1994).

When Congress passed the Adolescent Health Services and Prevention Care Act in 1978, grant monies were made available to public and private agencies that would offer pregnancy testing and provide family planning services, health services, and sexuality education. As mentioned, the 1970s were a creative, sex-positive period of time.

## SUPPORT FOR SEXUALITY EDUCATION

Both Planned Parenthood and SIECUS have a long history in championing sexuality education. In 1966, the National Education Association (NEA) had created its first resolution endorsing "sex" education. "From its inception, SIECUS campaigned for realistic sexuality education for individuals of all ages and for the necessary preparation of educators in schools, churches, and other institutions to achieve that goal" (Calderwood, 1981, p. 192). In 1970, federal Title X funding of reproductive health programs began. During this year, meetings between Planned Parenthood and SIECUS were held, and it was decided that SIECUS would promote sexuality education, while Planned Parenthood would promote educational materials in its clinic work. Teenagers would be getting the same message in the schools as they were getting once they arrived at the Planned Parenthood clinic. With the passing of the

National Family Planning Service and Population Research Act in 1970, the federal government greatly expanded the sexuality education offered by family planning centers (Scales, 1981a). Dr. Harold Lief, president of SIECUS in 1970 and a longtime member of the Planned Parenthood National Medical Committee, suggested the two groups find ways to work behind the scenes together (Lief, 1978). Thus, the Planned Parenthood Medical Committee formally recommended that the organization incorporate sexuality education in all of its programs.

For years, Dr. Mary Calderone, a medical doctor and director of SIECUS, had attempted to persuade the American Medical Association (AMA) to support a resolution "that the physician's role in handing out information about sexual matters and in population control should be primary" (Donovan, 1994, p. 5). The resolution was passed in 1964, but it took more than a decade for the leadership of the AMA to actually consider it.

Starting in 1965, Title III of the Elementary and Secondary Education Act was used for funding teacher-training programs in human sexuality. The federal government greatly expanded the sexuality education offered by family planning centers when it passed the National Family Planning Service and Population Research Act in 1970 (Kirkendall, 1981).

## TRAINING SUPPORT

SIECUS received Title X funding to develop a training manual, and Planned Parenthood developed its first training program for in-clinic sexuality educators. From that effort, the Sexual Attitude Reassessment, commonly referred to today as SAR, was born. While not referred to as SAR at the time, the training program began with a mini-marathon of explicit visuals designed, as it explicitly said in the grant, "to desensitize the participants and to get them to accept a variety of sexual behaviors" (Donovan, 1994, p. 8). Such desensitization was considered basic in the training sessions and was replicated in training programs sponsored in medical schools and other higher education institutions across the country. SARs were intended to help participants learn that it is all right to be sexual, to know all there is to know about human sexuality, to banish sexual myths and replace them with facts, and to identify ways to help participants, patients, and special populations have a better sex life (National Sex Forum, 1975).

## PARENT SUPPORT

Parents and parenting also received support during this time. The National Institutes of Mental Health (NIMH) had given a grant to the Institute for Family Research and Education, located at Syracuse University. In this three-year project, groups of parents were taught how to better communicate with their children about sexuality. Most of the federal government's support during the '70s involved "Education for Parenthood" programs designed for youth (Kirkendall, 1981, p. 13). Youth-serving groups, such as the Boy Scouts, Girls' Clubs, 4-H, and others, received funding from the Office of Education, NIMH, and the Administration for Children, Youth, and Families to develop programs designed to educate young people on the responsibilities of parenthood, with the hope of discouraging early childbearing (Kirkendall, 1981, p. 14). Unfortunately, evaluations done in 1977 concluded that only about 10 percent of all the educational sessions had any content dealing with human sexuality (Scales, 1981b, p. 14).

## SERVICES FOR ADOLESCENTS

Throughout the 1970s, federal support of programs developed by SIECUS and Planned Parenthood increased. In 1978, the Carter Administration reauthorized the federal Title X Program and explicitly included an authorization to provide services for teenagers. This was the first federal initiative to deal with teenage pregnancy, but other federal initiatives supportive of sexuality education had emerged in the early 1970s. In 1971 the U.S. Commission on Population Growth recommended that adolescents be provided sexuality education that would include contraceptive information (Kirkendall, 1981, p. 12).

Additionally, because there was an attempt to build a marriage between school sexuality education and Planned Parenthood clinics, some of the first school-based clinics were created (Donovan, 1994). School-based clinics are health clinics located on school campuses that provide students with a variety of primary health care services, such as physical examinations, treatment of illness and minor injuries, personal counseling, and reproductive health services. Though not all clinics distributed contraceptives, the first clinic to prescribe and dispense contraceptives did so in 1973. There has been continued discourse about the effectiveness and the effect on encouraging sexual involvement by youth, yet the numbers of these centers has increased, and by the 1990s, there were more than 178 school-based health clinics (Kirby, 1992). As of 2000, there were more than 1,100 operating in the United States (Brodeurk, 2000).

## OPPOSITION TO SEX EDUCATION

The unsettled political climate of the 1960s supported both sexual liberalism and the uniting of the right-wing movement. In the 1960s, the

John Birch Society, an ultraconservative organization, pushed schools to eliminate sex education programs in the classroom. Their claims that classes were immoral or a communist plot to poison the minds of American children rallied other organizations to join the battle cry. Opposition to sex education seemed to catalyze action by conservative groups and signaled a growing political visibility of the right wing. The attacks seemed to foster the alliance between various fear-based groups. Single-issue groups of this time helped launch the more consolidated movement of the "new Right" (Irvine, 2002, p. 41).

Some feared that learning about sexuality would be harmful to children and adolescents. Strong opposition came in particular from the Catholic Church and Christian Scientists (Kirkendall, 1981). Some argued that the materials produced to meet the needs of education—books, pamphlets, slides, and films—were unsuitable for children, especially films that were regarded by some as pornographic. There was also opposition to sexuality education that focused on venereal diseases and the fact that sexuality education was not integrated with other subjects.

For his doctoral dissertation, Deryck Calderwood (1970) communicated with all 50 states to review the statewide policies on sex education in the schools. Responses ranged from states that had requirements for an approved curriculum or curriculum guidelines, to philosophical statements approving sex education, to those with no policies or rules. Only one, Nebraska, prohibited sex education courses and programs and forbade any SIECUS materials from being distributed.

## TEACHER PREPARATION

In the early 1970s, a coach or physical education teacher primarily taught sexuality education classes. Few of these teachers, however, were trained to teach sexuality education. Classes were often segregated by sex, with boys learning about physiology and masturbation and girls about menstruation. As the decade progressed, Planned Parenthood educators were invited into schools to provide educational services, usually free, on birth control (J. Helmich, personal communication, May 22, 2008). Though there was little formal training, now that birth control was legal in every state and premarital pregnancy was a societal concern, Planned Parenthood was eager to expand their services beyond that of family planning and gynecological services for women to include school-based sexuality education.

The selection of teachers to become sexuality educators in the public schools was a major concern for parents. Teachers often needed to be assigned to teach sexuality education because there were no certifying requirements for the teaching of sexuality education. Each state had different requirements for certifying teachers. Being an effective sexuality education teacher was not deemed something just anyone could do. There should be, it was posited, an emphasis on good facilitation skills, understanding of group process, content knowledge, and self-understanding (Tatum, 1981, p. 143).

Workshops and programs began to be offered to help professionals learn more about the sexual issues involved in youth culture. In the Northwest in 1971, a group of 12 met together quarterly and created the Association for Sexuality Education and Training (AASET). By 1976, 30 or 40 educators attended these meetings. This core group became involved in teaching a very popular course called "Sex Ed for Teachers" through Central Washington University, an extensive training program supported by Title X funding.

Some schools and communities were willing to invest resources into the education of their youth on health issues. Even in the wake of budget cuts elsewhere, schools encouraged double staffing of classes. It was considered important to have both a male and female teacher in each sexuality education class (R. Selverstone, personal communication, April 28, 2008). Schools also hired specialists to help the teachers develop programs. Psychologist Sol Gordon, a veteran author and educator, was hired to help train teachers. Peggy Brick, another well-known sexuality education pioneer, developed two new courses in psychology and sociology in Dwight Morrow High School, Bergen County, New Jersey. "During the final week of school, the kids came to the auditorium for 'Sex Week', which involved films and Sol answering the kids' questions . . . all with great humor" (personal communication, April 16, 2008). Eventually, Brick developed a 10-week "Human Sexual Behavior Unit" for the last few weeks of the high school year.

The 1970s saw progress toward professional education. The National Council on Family Relations published criteria for teacher education in sexuality. The American Association of Sexuality Educators, Counselors and Therapists (AASECT) developed criteria for teacher certification and conducted seminars around the country to train educators. By 1977, 81 percent of medical schools offered instruction in human sexuality (Lloyd & Steinberger, 1977). Many seminaries and schools of social work included course work in sexuality as well.

## SEXUALITY EDUCATION AND RELIGIOUS SUPPORT

As far back as 1968, an Interfaith Statement favoring sex education was jointly disseminated by the National Council of Churches, the Synagogue Council of America, and the U.S. Catholic Conference. Other support was found in protestant denominations such as the Lutheran Church of America, United Methodist Church, United Presbyterian Church, and the Southern Baptist Convention (Selverstone, 1985, p. 146). By the end of 1970, one-third of U.S. Catholic dioceses had sexuality education (Donovan, 1994).

In 1970, the Unitarian Universalist Association published a sexuality education course, About Your Sexuality (AYS), that was first used in Unitarian Universalist congregations for youth ages 12–14. It was made available to other organizations and revised several times during the 1970s and early 1980s. Originally developed by New York University human sexuality professor Deryck Calderwood, the course materials were unique for sexuality education courses of the time. The program incorporated visuals that depicted human sexuality in what was considered a graphic and realistic manner. Filmstrips showed images of real heterosexual and homosexual encounters. There was no attempt to hide the genitals or the acts of penetration. Other media used in the curriculum included audiotapes of interviews with transgender, heterosexual, and homosexual men and women discussing their sexuality.

Though it was considered controversial at the time and was replaced in 2000 by *Our Whole Lives* (*OWL*), a series of sexuality education curricula that cover grades K–12, the AYS curriculum was utilized for sexuality education in the Unitarian Universalist education programs for almost 25 years. It was considered to be an example of a complete sexuality education program (Levine, 2002). Then, as today, the curriculum was used in secular settings as well as religious ones. A specialized training was provided for the teachers to help them utilize the curriculum to its most effective end.

## CURRICULAR CONTENT

Educators strived to broaden the understanding of sex education with a focus that went beyond reproductive anatomy. They began to use the term *sexuality* education, which emphasized not just the physical but also the social, emotional, psychological, and spiritual aspects of being human (Scales, 1989, p. 173). Curriculum guides contained exercises that teachers could use to help students increase their self esteem. A popular manual used by teachers of school students was *Education for Sexuality, Concepts and Programs for Teaching* by Burt and Brower Meeks (1975). It included both content and lessons on love, biology, human sexual response, pregnancy, childbirth and lactation, contraception, abortion, venereal diseases, intelligent choice of a sexual lifestyle, masturbation, and homosexuality. For elementary children there were lessons on families, including animal families, growing organisms from seeds or eggs, friendship, heredity, where babies come from, and discovering oneself.

Another resource, one that emphasized the use of group process and interaction to more effectively teach, was *Group Strategies in Understanding Human Sexuality: Getting in Touch* (Kaplan, Brower Meeks, & Segal, 1978). The individual lessons focus on getting in touch with knowledge, attitudes, and values on many topics, such as abortion, adoption, body image, dating, fantasy, homosexuality, love, relationships, sexual variance, and virginity.

While the purely biological approach toward sexuality education remained during the 1960s and 1970s, the role of the school in helping young people make responsible decisions in dealing with sexual issues began to take hold. There was growing support for the belief that dealing with sexual issues objectively could contribute to students' sexual morality and character development (Klein, 1983). Values clarification became a popular topic and process for learning as sex education continued to evolve. *Values in Sexuality* by Eleanor Morrison and Mila Underhill Price (1974) assisted teachers in developing activities to engage students in examining their values. The belief was that values clarification increased self-awareness and catalyzed individual thought and critical assessment that would assist in guiding their behavior.

Programs were also developed during the '70s for different populations. Carrera and Juliana (1977) developed a human sexuality program in a residential treatment center for boys. Books and films were developed for those working with special populations. *Sex Education and Counseling of Special Groups: The Mentally and Physically Handicapped, Ill and Elderly* (Johnson, 1975), and *Ripple in Time* (Sutton, 1974) are the foundation for resources utilized today.

## OTHER RESOURCES

Teachers and parents were looking for resources for both learning and teaching about sexuality. Accurate information on a wide variety of sexuality topics was not easily accessible, though there were many popular books written during this time. Textbooks were also limited. The texts may have been more direct and included more language than in previous years, with a focus on dating and appropriate gender roles of males and females, yet there was little connection to the sexual revolution that had invaded the culture. College-level texts by James McCary (1973) or Katchadourian and Lunde (1972), both University professors who wrote the texts for use in their own classes, were sometimes used as resource information for secondary teachers.

Comprehensive textbook choices continued to be developed for college populations, yet texts for public school-aged students were limited.

Pamphlets focusing on what young people should know about sex were developed and provided to college students in various communities. SIECUS published a series of study guides that were used by some for accurate information. Topics such as homosexuality, masturbation, and teenage pregnancy (prevention and treatment) were included as well as those on morals and values. *Sex, Science, and Values* (Christensen, 1976), *Masturbation* (Johnson, 1968), and *Homosexuality* (Rubin, 1965) were among the fourteen guides. Children's books such as *Where Did I Come From?* (1973) and *What's Happening to Me?* (1975) by Peter Mayle were very popular in the later '70s. Both books relied on cute cartoons yet described puberty changes, sexual intercourse, variations in the timing of puberty, and so forth in an honest and accurate manner. One colleague recalls visiting the doctor's office as a child, and seeing *Where Did I Come From?* He says, "I was intrigued, picked it up and it was like something inside me went 'BOING!' I started looking through it and began to read the print and drink in the pictures, only to have the nurse call me and my mom in to the doctor's office. I quickly put the book down and went in to see the doctor. I do remember feeling embarrassed, but constantly telling my mom I was feeling sick so I could go back to the doctor's office!" (B. Satterly, personal communication, April 17, 2008).

In some schools, menstruation was discussed with sixth- and seventh-grade girls using a Walt Disney film *The Story of Menstruation*. In others, materials provided by Tampax were distributed to girls on a mother–daughter night run by the school nurse. This one evening with the school nurse remained the definition of sex education in the elementary school for decades to come.

Toward the end of the decade, two very popular films on puberty were produced. The first, *Am I Normal?*, was released in 1979 and had real teen actors discussing their concerns and angst about bodily changes. The second, *Dear Diary*, was released in 1981 and again used real teen girls to portray the issues. They were so popular among teachers, and students seemed to be engaged in the storyline, that they continued to be used into the 1990s. Students could see both movies and learn about the emotional and physical development of both males and females. The teacher *could* present the film as the education in the class without having to discuss it.

In contrast to the aforementioned resources that are still used, the book *Show Me*, created as a picture book for children and published in 1975, is now illegal in the United States because of the use of explicit photographs of naked children. In the 1970s the book could be purchased at any major bookstore. It was created in Germany, translated to English, and was used as a guide for parents to discuss various sex topics with their child. In the early 1970s, adults were worried and hotly debated whether or not to provide students with information about abortion and contraception. Within a few years, others were utilizing explicit pictures to educate their children.

## EVALUATION OF PROGRAMS

In the late 1970s, the U.S. Centers for Disease Control and Prevention initiated a research effort to learn more about and potentially improve sexuality education. A national study was funded for the Mathtech research organization to examine the barriers to sexuality education. The experiences of 23 communities throughout the United States were studied. The researchers found that the barriers to sexuality education included: (a) administrators' fear of opposition, more than opposition itself, and (b) supporters' inadequate political skills. These two findings helped explain the struggles that schools were facing in their attempt to develop and support their sexuality education programs (Scales, 1984).

## SEX EDUCATION FOR UNDERGRADUATES

There is no way to know even today how many colleges present instruction in sexuality because it may be integrated into a number of subjects. During the 1970s, colleges offered independent classes within psychology, sociology, biology, and health departments. In 1970, a pilot study of 35 institutions conducted by SIECUS found that 83 percent offered "some type of course" for academic credit that dealt with "some aspect of sexuality" (Katchadourian, 1981, p. 173). Textbooks were often created by the professors teaching the class and were then utilized for the training of teachers implementing sexuality education in the secondary schools. Though it increased the number of books available on sexuality and provided education for young adults, it was problematic in that material appropriate for younger adolescents, and adults working with adolescents, was often more developmentally advanced for these youth.

## GRADUATE PROGRAMS IN HUMAN SEXUALITY

In 1968, the New York University degree-granting graduate program in human sexuality was initiated (Kirkendall, 1981, p. 13). Two major universities in the east established programs for training graduate students in sexuality: New York University (NYU) and the University of Pennsylvania created their education programs using the explicit video model (SAR). NYU created summer abroad programs where students were immersed in culture outside of the United States and encouraged to explore their values and behaviors outside of their cultural understanding. In addition, the Institute for the Advanced Study of Human Sexuality in California trained educators and therapists in San Francisco. The Kinsey Institute, long a part of Indiana University in Bloomington, began to establish week-long programs. It was now possible for people to secure professional training in the area of human sexuality.

Deryck Calderwood (1981) developed a model that utilized both films and experiential exercises to assist educators in increasing their attitudes, knowledge, and skills, which had become universally promulgated largely through the influence of SIECUS (p. 192). He described the basic components in professional education for human sexuality as SURE: "S" is Self-evaluation, "U" is the Unlearning, "R" is Relearning, and "E" is for Exercise, which is the making use of the training in creating change (pp. 194–198). The SURE model was a form of the SAR using other experiential activities, which sometimes included visuals but more often did not.

## REFLECTIONS OF TWO EDUCATORS WHO EXPERIENCED THE 1970s

The 1970s were an exciting time to be a graduate student in sexuality. Both authors attended New York University, earning doctorates in health education with a specialization in human sexuality, marriage, and family life education. The program coordinator was Deryck Calderwood, PhD, who also designed curricula, developed educational materials, and served on the Board of Directors for SIECUS. Students had the opportunity to study in New York City as well as abroad, with summer programs run in Sweden, Denmark, Kenya, Japan, and Thailand. The authors share their reflections as a way to highlight the differing ways professional preparation was applied in educational settings.

*Konnie McCaffree* was a public school teacher beginning in the mid-sixties. She has worked with elementary, middle school, and senior high youth. As an athletic coach, she learned about the many issues with which young people struggle. Her work specific to sexuality education began in 1970, and she was privileged to have an administration that supported her efforts to develop a truly comprehensive program for secondary students. She utilized this experience to develop the sexuality education program for the graduate school training of professionals at University of Pennsylvania and Widener University. In addition to being a professor, she is an educational training consultant. She has led research projects that measure the outcomes of educational interventions, developed curricula for HIV/AIDS education, worked with international communities on the provision of sexuality education, and trained sexuality educators.

The following is Konnie's personal narrative:

Teaching in the '70s was fun. I loved having a career, living on my own, and working with youth. They seemed more eager in my memory than the youth of today.

I moved to a new community in Pennsylvania in the early seventies and interviewed for a job teaching health and physical education. I remember being asked in the interview questions that I doubt could be asked of a future employee today: "How long before you will quit teaching to have children?" "Why don't you want children?" "How can you be a teacher and not want to have your own children?" It was even more challenging because the course they wanted me to teach that no other teacher wanted was "Marriage and Family Life." Questions followed on how I would be able to teach if I did not have a family.

Once hired, I was given a warning. My department chair explained that I was not to use any materials by a radical group called SIECUS. He explained that a group called the John Birch Society opposed them and that he didn't want any trouble from parents. Of course I knew nothing of either and went right out to find out what SIECUS was. Years later, I spent 10 years as a SIECUS Board member.

Today, I still have some of the SIECUS pamphlets on teaching sexuality topics. On the front cover of the "Masturbation Study Guide" it clearly states, "This study guide is intended primarily for professional people in positions of responsibility for programs for children and youth and/or counseling programs for parents and teachers, nurses, physicians, clergymen, and other professionals." The SIECUS purpose was: "To establish man's sexuality as a health entity; to identify the special characteristics that distinguish it from, yet relate it to, human reproduction; to dignify it by openness of approach, study, and scientific research designed to lead toward its understanding and its freedom from exploitation; to give leadership to professionals and to society, to the end that human beings may be aided toward responsible use of the sexual faculty and toward assimilation of sex into their individual life patterns as a creative and re-creative force" (Johnson, 1968, p. 2). I wasn't sure what that all meant, but somehow it seemed to connect to me.

I actually didn't know much about teaching that subject, but they hired me anyway. I learned quickly that students really wanted to talk about topics other than marriage, and using the anonymous question technique, I gathered many ideas for what they wanted to learn about. At a nearby university there was a class on "Teaching about Family and Relationships" that I thought might help. Little did I know that that class focused on what we would now term *sexuality*. It stimulated my interest to enter graduate school at New York University where there was a doctoral program in sexuality education.

The graduate program included night courses in New York City and summers abroad studying in Sweden and other cultures of the world. My sexological worldview expanded, and my teaching was never the same. The study abroad program at NYU was a reflection of the times. Students, ranging in age from 20 to 60, were eager to explore their own sexual and emotional boundaries. There was exploration through nude saunas, massage, and open discussion of feelings. The experience literally changed my life. I had always been an independent thinker, but the interaction with my peers outside of my own culture allowed me to learn how others thought, lived their lives, and expressed their sexuality. Interestingly, it taught me that I could maintain my core values and still accept others' whose views and actions may be different from my own.

In my first high school class, males and females were separated. I recognized the need for a different type of class for the youth that included conversations with the each other on these issues. The school district allowed teachers to submit proposals for new classes, so I created a co-ed human sexuality elective to be offered to seniors that included talking about such topics as sexual orientation, sexual assault, abortion, pornography, and prostitution, to name a few. As an elective, it would also include a parental permission component. The administrators and school board approved the proposal, fully believing as was stated to me several times that "no parents would give permission for the course." The course not only filled, but after the first year other sections were added.

Though it was not part of the course proposal to the board, I held a companion class for parents that met three to four times throughout the school year. The parents who attended were eager to learn more about sexuality and continued to be supportive. (It was not until the late '80s and '90s that a few parents only came to meetings so they could complain about topics the children were talking about. These parents would not give permission for the class, but their children were hearing the information and discussions from their peers who did take the class.)

It was exciting to develop a class that utilized what I was learning in graduate school. I brought to the group a variety of guest speakers, all who had grown up in our community and were representative of people the students would know. Guests represented included people who were rape survivors, pregnant while in high school, gay, lesbian, and transgender, all sharing their stories.

The class met in a classroom where the desks were removed, and we sat in a group circle. There was no lecture or presentation of facts other than what was integrated during the group process. Students could talk about any issue, and we met in small groups as well as large groups. There were projects where students researched topics of interest, including visits to community agencies or through inventories. I was able to meet with students daily, which included a minimum of 80 50-minute class meetings. We utilized videos and filmstrips that were more sexually explicit than anything that could be used today.

I also created a different format for the health classes taught to tenth graders. Students in these classes were separated by gender part of the year so that girls could work together on topics of their interest. Boys spent time with a male teacher discussing topics that we thought they would be more embarrassed to discuss honestly with girls present. For the majority of the school year, however, classes were co-ed. These classes also had projects for assignments. One of their favorites was to visit a pharmacy and study the many products available for sexual and reproductive health. They were often surprised to find that some pharmacists kept the condoms hidden.

They also practiced being parents. Instead of focusing on how hard it is to take care of a baby, they were to choose the children's books they would use to teach their child about sex and sexuality. Their remarks indicated that they were not as comfortable with a child knowing about sexuality, especially on how babies were conceived.

When the '70s began, I had been teaching biology and physical education for several years. I also had contact with many adolescents as a counselor and coach. I experienced several situations where knowledge of sexuality was needed, and I had none. I had grown up in a small town in the Midwest, gone to Catholic school, and other than a limited amount of socializing (where kissing was the most I ever did), I was naïve about sexuality. My college preparation for teaching included health, biology, and adolescent psychology courses that had no mention of the words *sex* or *sexuality*, not even in the study of human reproduction.

Before *Roe v. Wade* in 1973, I had two students who asked me for help with a pregnancy, both wanting abortions. I had no idea how to help them, and thankfully, their parents were supportive and helpful. I had several students who were labeled lesbians (no gay or transgender youth indicated such). No one spoke of homosexuality openly; it was innuendo and connected to two female physical education teachers who shared a house together and students somehow "knew" they were lesbians. I have no idea if they were lesbians because no one ever said anything. I also experienced what I now know as sexual harassment from another male teacher in my school. I ended up quitting at the end of the school year because another teacher, married with small children, was always watching me through the window of my classroom. I thought I must be doing something to attract his attention, and I had no realization that my discomfort was something I could discuss with others and had the right to stop.

*Jean Levitan* began her professional career as a counselor in a privately run abortion clinic. In 1973, she began teaching at the college level, where she continues today offering undergraduate courses in human sexuality, reproductive rights, and women's health. Her graduate training during the 1970s prepared her for educational and professional training opportunities. She has helped educate public school teachers, administrators, and mental health professionals on sexuality issues. During the mid-1980s, she worked to evaluate the mandated Family Life/Sex Education program for the New York City public schools.

The following is Jean's personal narrative:

At the beginning of the 1970s, I was a sophomore in college, attending Case Western Reserve University in Cleveland, Ohio. I was living in an all-female dorm, where for the first time keys were distributed and curfew rules abolished. At the end of that year, the University agreed to establish co-ed dormitories as a future living option. My close friends and I moved with great excitement into co-ed dorms for the remainder of our two years in college.

The climate on campus was always an exciting one for me. I was learning in a much more diverse environment than that of high school, asked to question my thoughts and beliefs. Dr. Benjamin Spock was a professor at the medical school, and his anti–Vietnam War activism and leadership undoubtedly were responsible for bringing the antiwar activist Jerry Rubin, who advised "not to trust anyone over 30," and actress Jane

Fonda, who had befriended the North Vietnamese, onto campus. Cleveland was less than 100 miles from Kent State, making the National Guard shootings (1970) on that campus all the more real.

By my senior year in college, I knew that I wanted to pursue graduate work in the sexuality field. During my sophomore year, I had a brief sexuality class within my gym requirement. I loved my "Marriage and Family" class within the sociology department. I had completed an internship at Planned Parenthood in their teen clinic and volunteered giving piano lessons at the Booth Memorial Home for unwed mothers. Both those experiences opened my eyes to the reproductive needs of teens. The home for unwed mothers, in particular, exposed me to girls close to my age who were pregnant and left there by disappearing boyfriends and family who would not, or could not, take in them and their babies.

I completed an independent study in sociology my senior year, using Masters and Johnson's *Human Sexual Inadequacy* (1970) as a text. On a weekly basis, I discussed sexuality issues with a Dr. Condon; I always worried that I would call him *Dr. Condom*. Through a friend of my parents, I became aware that New York University was offering a Master of Arts in Health Education with a specialization in Human Sexuality, Marriage, and Family Life Education. I applied and was accepted.

I graduated from Case Western Reserve in May 1972 and immediately began my master's program in June. I was able to begin my program with an internship at an abortion clinic in New York City. I worked at Parkmed, at that time the only clinic in Manhattan to offer general anesthesia for the procedure. I was there for six months before the U.S. Supreme Court issued its decision in *Roe v. Wade*, making first trimester abortions available in every state in the United States. Parkmed was averaging 400 abortions per week, with patients coming to them from all over the United States. They expected the patient load to drop as more states established their own facilities. I was not there to witness the changes in the clinic population, though, as I moved on to full-time work.

My first full-time position was as an instructor in the Department of Health and Recreation at Kean University in New Jersey. Along with other health courses, I regularly taught the undergraduate course in human sexuality. There were a couple of textbooks from which to choose, and I was one of three faculty members who offered this very popular elective class. I had total freedom of speech in the classroom and never had to worry about parental or community reactions to what I was teaching. In order to be eligible for tenure, however, I had to obtain a PhD; what made the most sense to me was to continue at NYU.

Along with teaching full time and going to graduate school, I also made myself available for speaking engagements and consulting work. I remember my first consulting job with a public school system on Long Island; the year was 1974. I was invited to discuss curriculum development for their family life program. The curriculum guidelines were sent to me along with instructions that I was not to include any material on homosexuality, abortion, and "human" sexuality. I think I've blocked out the details of that one visit; I felt totally unprepared to help with such ridiculous restrictions, having just completed classes that taught excellent ways to create programs. I had been exposed to the curricular work of Schultz and Williams (1968) and was naively assuming I could adapt their developmentally appropriate curriculum for this Long Island community. Instead, I spent a few hours with frustrated teachers who had to make do with lessons on anatomy and traditional families.

My graduate work during the 1970s had a profound effect on my thinking. I was living in Greenwich Village, an extremely diverse community with seemingly high standards for mutual respect and tolerance. My graduate program required tremendous amounts of self-analysis and values clarification. I studied in Sweden and Denmark during the summer of 1975 and was exposed to two countries with long histories of tolerance and respect for sexual diversity. Above all, I learned the power of openness and trust that could be built between students to enhance learning.

Throughout the seventies, I continued to regularly teach undergraduate sexuality classes. I also developed a course in women's health, which coincided with the growth of the women's movement. I cherished my copy of the book *Our Bodies, Ourselves* and ended the relationship with my gynecologist when in response to an informed question I was told, "you read too much." I also remember sitting at a NYC women's center and deciding that this "odd and lengthy" questionnaire I was offered wasn't worth the trouble to answer. Little did I know that the responses would be turned into *The Hite Report,* that qualitative research effort where women told their stories. And to learn that so many women were faking orgasm to please a male partner! That became newsworthy. Lonnie Barbach's *For Yourself* (1975) spoke honestly to women, and her words to women to be responsible for their own sexual response were incredibly powerful. She, along with other feminist leaders, was helping women find their voices. I was working to develop mine.

Toward the end of the 1970s, I moved to William Paterson University, where I continued to teach undergraduate sexuality classes along with women's health. The number of textbooks from which to choose was growing. There were visual materials that were prefaced as "explicit," useful for stimulating discussion among students. The growth of the gay rights movement enabled speakers to "come out" to students and help them appreciate the similarities of life, rather than continue making assumptions about assumed differences. Greenwich Village remained my home, and I continued to be formed by the openness of the decade.

## THEN AND NOW

Looking back over our long careers in the field, some things have changed and many things have not. Students still hunger for sexuality information and opportunities to talk about the issues. Today, the information is more readily available, with Internet access taken for granted. Ironically, the opportunity to talk about the issues in schools has become more limited with the unfortunate restrictions imposed by the abstinence-until-marriage programs at the public school level. At the university level, some of the materials first developed in the 1970s are still being used—such as explicit films on sexual response. What has not changed is the freedom to talk about sexuality. What is surprising, however, is that despite the increased availability of information, college students today sometimes seem less informed than their counterparts from decades past.

The fight for comprehensive sexuality education in the schools continues, and it continues to amaze so many in the profession that we still have to fight for what should be an obvious right—the right to factual, bias-free information.

## REFERENCES

Barbach, L. (1975). For yourself: The fulfillment of female sexuality. New York: Signet Publishing.

Boston Women's Health Book Collective. (1973). *Our bodies, ourselves.* Boston: New England Free Press.

Brodeurk, P. (2000). School-based health clinics. *Robert Wood Johnson Foundation Anthology.* Retrieved June 8, 2008, from http://www.rwjf.org/files/publications/books/2000/chapter_01.html

Burt, J., & Brower Meeks, L. (1975). *Education for sexuality, concepts and programs for teaching.* Philadelphia, PA: W. B. Saunders.

Calderwood, D. (1970). Adolescent appraisals and opinions concerning their sex education in selected institutions. Unpublished doctoral dissertation, Oregon State University.

Calderwood, D. (1981). Educating the educators. In L. Brown (Ed.), *Sex education in the eighties: The challenge of healthy sexual evolution.* New York: Plenum Press.

Carrera, M., & Juliana, J. (1977). A human sexuality program in a residential treatment center. *Child Care Quarterly, 6*(3), 224–228.

Christensen, H. (1976). Sex, science, and values. SIECUS Study Guide No. 9. New York: SIECUS.

Comfort, A. (1972). *The joy of sex.* New York: Simon and Schuster.

Diamond, S. (1995). Roads to dominion: Right wing movements and political power in the United States. New York: Guilford Press.

Donovan, C. (1994). Lecture, Human Life International National Sex Education Conference in St. Louis, MO. Retrieved March 25, 2008, from http://www.vidahumana.org/english/family/sexed-history.htm

Fessler, A. (2006). *The girls who went away.* New York: Penguin Books.

Friedan, B. (1963). *The feminine mystique.* New York: W.W. Norton & Company.

Hite, S. ( 1976). *The Hite report: A nationwide study of female sexuality.* New York: Macmillan Publishing Company, Inc.

Irvine, J. (2002). Talk about sex. The battles over sex education in the United States. Berkeley, CA: University of California Press.

Johnson, W. (1968). *Masturbation. SIECUS Study Guide No. 3.* New York: SIECUS.

Johnson, W. (1975). Sex education and counseling of special groups: The mentally and physically handicapped, ill and elderly. Springfield, IL: Charles C. Thomas.

Julian, C., & Jackson, E. (1967). *Modern sex education.* New York: Holt, Rinehart and Winston, Inc.

Kaplan, R., Brower Meeks, L., & Segal, J. S. (1978). *Group strategies in understanding human sexuality: Getting in touch.* Dubuque, IA: Wm. C. Brown Company.

Katchadourian, H. (1981). Sex education in college. In L. Brown (Ed.), *Sex education in the zighties: The challenge of healthy sexual evolution.* New York: Plenum Press.

Katchadourian, H. & Lunde, D. (1972). *Fundamentals of human sexuality.* New York: Holt, Rinehart and Winston.

Kingwood College Library. (2008). American cultural history: 1970–1979. Retrieved May 23, 2008 from http://kclibrary.nhmccd.edu/decade70.html

Kirby, D. (1992). School-based programs to reduce sexual risk-taking behaviors. *Journal of School Health, 62*(7), 280–286.

Kirkendall, L. (1981). Sex education in the United States: A historical perspective. In L. Brown (Ed.), *Sex education in the eighties: The challenge of healthy sexual evolution.* New York: Plenum Press.

Klein, D. (1983). Sex education: A historical perspective. Retrieved March 25, 2008, from http://eric.ed.gov/ERICWebPortal/custom/portlets/recordDetails/det

Leif, H. (1978). Sex education in medicine. In N. Rosenzweig & F. Pearsall (Eds.), *Sex education for the health professional.* New York: Grune and Stratton, Inc.

Leo, J. (1983). The revolution is over. *Time.* Retrieved March 25, 2008, from http://www.time.com/time/printout/0,8816,1714248,00.html

Levine, J. (2002). *Harmful to minors.* Minneapolis: University of Minnesota Press.

Lloyd, J., & Steinberger, E. (1977). Training in reproductive biology and human sexuality in American medical schools. *Journal of Medical Education, 32,* 74–76.

Luker, K. (2007). *When sex goes to school.* New York. W.W. Norton & Company, Inc.

Masters, W. & Johnson, V. (1970). *Human sexual inadequacy.* Boston: Little, Brown, & Company.

Mayle, P. (1973). *Where did I come from?* Secaucus, NJ: Lyle Stuart.

Mayle, P. (1975). *What's happening to me?* Secaucus, NJ: Lyle Stuart.

McCary, J. (1973). *Human sexuality.* New York: D. Van Nordstrom.

Moran, J. P. (2000). Teaching sex: The shaping of adolescence in the 20th century. Cambridge, MA: Harvard University Press.

Morrison, E., & Price, M. (1974). *Values in sexuality: A new approach to sex education.* New York: Hart Publishing Company, Inc.

National Sex Forum. (1975). SAR: Sexuality Attitudes Restructuring: A training program for couples. San Francisco: National Sex Forum.

Right Web (2008). *Profile: The moral majority.* Retrieved on December 19, 2008 from http://rightweb,irc-online.org/gw/2803html

Rothenberg, P. (2001). How is happened: race and gender issues in U.S. law. In P. Rothenberg, (Ed.), *Race, class and gender in the United States* (5th ed.). New York: Worth Publishers.

Rubin, I. (1965). Homosexuality. SIECUS Study Guide No. 2. New York: SIECUS.

Rubinstein, E. (1981). Television as a sex educator. In L. Brown (Ed.), *Sex education in the eighties: The challenge of healthy sexual evolution.* New York: Plenum Press.

Scales, P. (1981a). Historical review of sex education efforts and barriers. In P. Scales (Ed.), *Facilitating community support for sex education. Centers for Disease Control final report.* Bethesda, MD: MATHTECH.

Scales, P. (1981b). Sex education and the prevention of teenage pregnancy: An overview of policies and programs in the United States. In T. Ooms (Ed.), *Teenage pregnancy in a family context: Implications for policy.* Philadelphia, PA: Temple University Press.

Scales, P. (1984). The front lines of sexuality education: A guide to building and maintaining community support. Santa Cruz, CA: Network Publications.

Scales, P. (1989). Overcoming future barriers to sexuality education. *Theory into practice, 28*(3), 172–176.

Scheer, R. (1976). The Playboy interview: Jimmy Carter. *Playboy, 23*(11), 63–86.

Schultz, E., & Williams, S. (1968). *Family life and sex education: Curriculum and instruction.* New York: Harcourt, Brace, and World, Inc.

Selverstone, R. (1985). Sex education and the adolescent: Perspectives from a sex educator. *Seminars in adolescent medicine, 1*(2), 145–151.

Silverstein, C., & White, E. (1977). *The joy of gay sex.* New York: Crown Publishers, Inc.

Solinger, R. (1992). Wake up little Susie: Single pregnancy and race in the pre-Roe v Wade era. New York: Routledge.

Steiner, G. A. (1963). *The people look at television.* New York: Knopf.

Sutton, L. (1974). *Ripple in time.* San Francisco: National Sex Forum.

Tatum, M. L. (1981). Sex education in the public schools. In L. Brown (Ed.), *Sex education in the eighties: The challenge of healthy sexual evolution.* New York: Plenum Press.

Ward, J. (2002, June). Come in my mouth: The story of the adult musicals of the '70's. Retrieved on May 23, 2008 from http://www.furious.com/Perfect/adultmusicals.html

Part III

# RESEARCH, RHETORIC, AND REACHING FOR CONSENSUS

Chapter Six

# DOES SEXUALITY EDUCATION "WORK"? AN OVERVIEW OF THE RESEARCH

*Leslie M. Kantor*

Sexuality education programs have been evaluated for more than two decades in order to understand whether they help people to learn important information, to have more positive attitudes about engaging in healthy behaviors, and to avoid unhealthy behaviors or engage in positive behaviors. Because sexuality education has often been controversial in the United States, research has also been critical in proving that programs do not lead to earlier or more frequent sexual behavior among participants. At this point, a significant body of well-designed, scientific studies have been published that definitively show that sexuality education programs with certain characteristics can have very positive impacts on adolescent sexual behavior and that fears that programs lead to more or earlier sexual involvement are unwarranted (Kirby, 2001, 2007, 2008). Increasingly, evaluations have been designed that are scientifically rigorous and allow researchers to have confidence that differences observed after participation in sexuality education are the result of those interventions and not due to other factors. Abstinence-only education, which has received increasing amounts of federal funding in the United States, has also been evaluated. Existing evaluations of abstinence-only education do not indicate that these programs help young people to postpone sexual behavior (Kirby, 2007, 2008). This chapter reviews the definition of *effectiveness,* the research on sexuality education programs and abstinence-only programs and their effectiveness, and the characteristics that are shared by programs that have been found to be effective.

## DEFINITION OF EFFECTIVENESS

When sexuality education is defined as "effective," that generally indicates that a program has helped young people to maintain or change their sexual behavior by either continuing to abstain from vaginal sexual intercourse or to use contraception and condoms when they do engage in sexual intercourse.

The reason effectiveness has been defined in this way is that other types of changes that may occur as a result of sexuality education programs, such as improvements in knowledge or shifts in attitudes and beliefs, are necessary but not sufficient for ensuring that healthy behaviors take place. People frequently know certain facts about health but still engage in behaviors that may put them at risk for poor health outcomes. For example, while the dangers of smoking are well-established and widely known, some people still smoke. Likewise, most people know that they should floss their teeth every day, reduce their intake of fatty foods, and never drive over the speed limit. Yet, even with that information, many people continue to engage in unhealthy behaviors despite their high level of knowledge. Therefore, in order to help people to change behaviors, health education programs must go beyond providing facts and help people to develop positive attitudes toward the behavior being encouraged, beliefs that they have the skills and abilities to implement the behavior in their lives (self-efficacy), and the actual skills they may need to begin and maintain healthy behaviors. In addition, while other sexual behaviors, such as oral sex or anal intercourse, also increase STI risk, many evaluations have not included questions about these behaviors because asking those questions is sometimes opposed by parents, administrators, or school districts that need to approve such surveys.

The broad public health impacts that sexuality education programs have generally sought are to reduce problems such as unintended pregnancy and sexually transmitted infections (STIs) because these outcomes have significant negative consequences both for the individuals involved and for society as a whole. While there has been improvement in reducing the number of teen pregnancies in the United States, over 750,000 pregnancies still occur annually among women aged 15 to 19 (Ventura, Abma, Mosher & Henshaw, 2006), and recent studies suggest that 25 percent of sexually active teens may contract a sexually transmitted infection (STI) every year (Forhan, 2008). Given these negative health outcomes, evaluations of programs seek to measure behavior changes, such as abstaining from intercourse or using contraception when engaging in intercourse, which are more proximal to reducing unintended pregnancy and STIs than knowledge and attitudes, which are somewhat further away from those desired outcomes. Figure 6.1 illustrates a basic diagram of the relationship between knowledge, attitudes, and skills and the behaviors needed to avoid unintended pregnancy and STIs. Certainly, numerous other

**Figure 6.1**
**Relationship between Knowledge, Attitudes, Skills, and Behaviors Needed to Prevent Pregnancy and STIs**

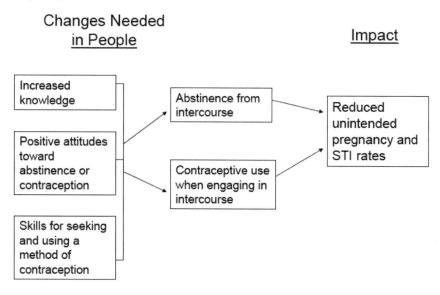

factors also influence health behaviors and are described in several theories of behavior change. That said, measuring actual changes in behavior is the best way to ascertain whether a program is actually effective.

There are certainly other important objectives that may be sought by high-quality sexuality education programs. The definition of *sexual health* is much broader than simply not getting pregnant accidentally or avoiding STIs. The U.S. Surgeon General's Call to Action on Sexual Health notes: "Sexual health is not limited to the absence of disease or dysfunction, nor is its importance confined to just the reproductive years. It includes the ability to understand and weigh the risks, responsibilities, outcomes and impacts of sexual actions and to practice abstinence when appropriate. It includes freedom from sexual abuse and discrimination and the ability of individuals to integrate their sexuality into their lives, derive pleasure from it, and to reproduce if they so choose" (Satcher, 2001, p. 1). As important as they are, concepts such as "integrating sexuality into their lives" and "deriving pleasure" are challenging to precisely define and measure, so existing evaluations of programs generally focus on examining shifts in knowledge, attitudes, and behaviors that result from sexuality education interventions.

Further work should be done to operationalize additional desirable sexuality education objectives and to broaden current definitions of effectiveness to include other aspects of sexual health.

## WAYS TO ASSESS EFFECTIVENESS

There are several methodologies for assessing the effectiveness of programs, though some are more scientifically robust than others. Within medicine, the gold standard for evaluating whether a treatment works is clinical trials utilizing random assignment that are "double blind." Such trials randomly assign people to either a group that receives the intervention, treatment, or medication being assessed or one that does not receive the intervention, treatment, or medication in a manner that ensures that the two groups match on key characteristics (such as age, gender, and health status). Further, even the clinicians who are administering the medication or treatment are "blind" to which group is getting the treatment and which is getting the placebo.

Measuring the effectiveness of a program cannot be done using the same methodology because participants will certainly know whether they are participating in a program that includes information on a given health topic, and similarly, instructors must know the content and purpose of the program. As a result, in these cases, other types of evaluation procedures are used. The most scientifically rigorous approach maintains many of the qualities of a clinical trial as described previously, by randomly assigning participants to either the program group or the no-program group. (In some cases, a program or intervention will be tested against the existing program or intervention rather than one group receiving nothing at all.) When random assignment is utilized, the evaluation design is referred to as "experimental" and is considered to be the most desirable type of research. Random assignment helps to ensure that the participants and the nonparticipants are truly comparable and are not different in some fundamental way that may affect the findings of the evaluation. There have been only a few sexuality education programs that have used this scientifically rigorous, experimental design. The main program that has been evaluated using random assignment is the Children's Aid Society-Carrera Program, which helped girls ages 13 to 15 to remain abstinent, to use both contraception and condoms when they did have sex, and to avoid pregnancy. The findings showed that girls in the program were 55 percent less likely to become pregnant than the girls in the control group (Kirby, 2007).

The use of random assignment can be difficult to structure in many school- and community-based settings. As a result, other types of evaluations are also utilized to determine whether programs work. The next best approach for evaluating the effectiveness of a program is to employ a quasi-experimental design. In these methodologies, random assignment may not be used, but other steps are taken to ensure that there is a comparison group that does not receive the program but is otherwise well-matched to the young people receiving the intervention. When evaluations are conducted appropriately, the one key difference between groups is the program being assessed, so that any differences observed after the program can be attributed to the program and not to other factors that would confound the results.

One way to judge whether the evaluation methodology used to ascertain effectiveness meets scientific criteria is to rely on studies that have been published in peer-reviewed, scientific journals. Studies in those publications have generally been sent to at least three outside experts that can comment on whether the way the evaluation was set up meets key criteria and whether the statistical analyses that have been performed are appropriate and accurately executed. Sexuality education programs have been rigorously evaluated for over two decades, and a great deal of research has been amassed. In addition, key "meta-evaluations" have been published that summarize all of the high-quality studies that have taken place on sexuality education (Kirby, 2001, 2007, 2008). Relying on peer reviewed journal articles and meta-analyses that assess the appropriateness and quality of evaluation methodology allows those interested in program effectiveness to trust that the methodology used to conduct research and the data analyses meet appropriate scientific criteria and that any conclusions drawn are sound.

## FINDINGS FROM KEY ANALYSES OF SEXUALITY EDUCATION

The most comprehensive review of the existing scientific literature on sexuality education programs examined evaluations of programs that had as their goal either reducing unintended teen pregnancy or reducing the likelihood of transmitting STIs, including HIV, and was published by the National Campaign to Prevent Unintended and Teen Pregnancy in 2007 (Kirby, 2007). The studies reviewed for the meta-analysis, *Emerging Answers,* were completed since 1990, were conducted in the United States or Canada, were run either with middle or high school students, included both baseline and follow up data, measured behavior change, included at least 100 people in both the program and comparison groups, and used either experimental or quasi-experimental design. The programs included in the analysis had to be curriculum- or group-based interventions rather than one-on-one interventions or media campaigns in a community. The studies also had to look at behavioral impacts such as initiating sexual behavior for the first time, frequency of sexual activity, number of sexual partners, use of condoms and contraception, and pregnancy or STIs.

In all, 56 studies were reviewed: 8 examined the effectiveness of abstinence-only programs, and 48 examined more comprehensive programs that included discussions about contraception and condoms (Kirby, 2007, 2008).

The results of the meta-analysis showed that, of the comprehensive programs, close to half delayed the initiation of sexual intercourse among participants, and none of the programs led to earlier initiation of intercourse among the participants. Forty-seven percent of the programs led to increased condom use among participants, and 44 percent increased contraceptive use. One program did decrease condom use. In addition, six programs reduced the frequency of sexual intercourse, and none increased the frequency. Eleven decreased the number of sexual partners overall (Kirby, 2007, 2008). All of these behavioral impacts would logically lead to reductions in the likelihood of pregnancy or STIs among the young people receiving the program. Programs that were effective in helping young people to maintain or adopt healthy behaviors included: Becoming a Responsible Teen, Cuidate! (Take Care of Yourself); The Latino Youth Health Promotion Program; Draw the Line, Respect the Line; Making Proud Choices: A Safer Sex Approach to STD, Teen Pregnancy, and HIV/AIDS Prevention; Reducing the Risk; Safer Choices: Preventing HIV, Other STD and Pregnancy; and SIHLE: Sistas, Informing, Healing, Living, Empowering.

Based on the research results and a comparison of those programs that have had positive behavioral effects compared to those that have not, researchers have concluded that there are 17 characteristics that are common to effective programs. In addition, when programs incorporate all 17 characteristics, they almost always have a positive effect on behavior, such as delaying the onset of intercourse or increasing the use of condoms and other forms of contraception when intercourse does take place. The characteristics can be grouped into three categories—factors related to how the curriculum was developed, the contents of the curriculum itself, and the process of implementing the curriculum (Kirby, 2007, p. 131). Table 6.1 lists the 17 characteristics common to effective programs.

Many of the programs that have been carefully evaluated and found to be effective are commercially available, and curricula and other program materials as well as training and technical assistance may be available for replicating these interventions in other school and community settings. It is worth noting that there are studies that show that when programs are not implemented with fidelity (e.g., replicated almost exactly the same way as how they were done when first evaluated), the same behavioral results are frequently not observed (Kirby, Laris, & Rolleri, 2006).

## STUDIES OF ABSTINENCE-ONLY PROGRAMS

Evaluations of abstinence-only programs require particular examination because the United States provides significant public funding for abstinence education that meets a particular definition (see Table 6.2 for the federal definition of abstinence education).

The first evaluations of abstinence-only programs often had methodological flaws that made any assessment of knowledge and attitudinal changes due to abstinence programs difficult to discern (Kirby, 1997, 2001). Further, many of these early evaluations did not seek data on the sexual behavior of youth participating in abstinence interventions. The evaluations that were scientific and met standard criteria for inclusion in peer-reviewed, scientific journals showed that abstinence-only programs did not help young people to delay the onset of sexual intercourse or to use methods of risk reduction such as condoms and other forms of contraception when they did have intercourse (Kirby, 1997, 2001).

There were eight studies of abstinence-only programs included in the *Emerging Answers* meta-analysis (Kirby, 2007). The most rigorous of the evaluations of abstinence-only programs completed to date showed that abstinence programs did not have an impact on the timing of first intercourse and did not reduce the number of sexual partners (Trenholm, Devaney, Forston, Quay, Wheeler & Clark, 2007). The study of four abstinence programs conducted by Mathematica Policy Research, Inc. examined *My Choice, My Future!* in Powhatan County, Virginia; *ReCapturing the Vision* in Miami, Florida; *Teens in Control* in Clarksdale, Mississippi; and *Families United to Prevent Teen Pregnancy* in Milwaukee, Wisconsin. The evaluation utilized an experimental design and analyzed data from 1,207 participants in one of the abstinence-only programs and 848 members of the control group. None of the individual programs had a statistically significant impact on sexual abstinence whether defined as always having been abstinent or as abstaining from sexual activity in the past 12 months. Youth in the programs also did not differ in the number of sexual partners from those in the control group. Youth in abstinence-only programs were no more likely to have unprotected sex than those that did not participate in abstinence-only programs. In both groups, slightly more than half of all young people remained abstinent, 29 percent reported always using a condom or another method of birth control, and 15 percent (program group) to 16 percent (control group) used a method only some of the time (Trenholm, Devaney, Forston, Quay, Wheeler, & Clark, 2007). Other abstinence programs examined in *Emerging Answers* also showed little or no behavioral impact.

## SUMMARY OF EXISTING RESEARCH ON SEXUALITY EDUCATION AND ABSTINENCE-ONLY PROGRAMS

A review of the available studies on sexuality education programs provides ample evidence that sexuality education programs that meet certain criteria are quite successful at helping young people to either postpone intercourse, use contraception and condoms when they do have intercourse, engage in sex less

**Table 6.1**
**Emerging Answers**

| The Process of Developing the Curriculum | The Contents of the Curriculum Itself | The Process of Implementing the Curriculum |
|---|---|---|
| | **Curriculum Goals and Objectives** | |
| 1. Involved multiple people with expertise in theory, research, and sex and STD/HIV education to develop the curriculum. | 6. Focused on clear health goals—the prevention of STD/HIV, pregnancy, or both. | 14. Secured at least minimal support from appropriate authorities, such as departments of health, school districts, or community organizations. |
| 2. Assessed relevant needs and assets of the target group. | 7. Focused narrowly on specific types of behavior leading to these health goals (e.g., abstaining from sex or using condoms or other contraceptives), gave clear messages about these types of behavior, and addressed situations that might lead to them and how to avoid them. | 15. Selected educators with desired characteristics (whenever possible), trained them, and provided monitoring, supervision, and support. |
| 3. Used a logic model approach that specified the health goals, the types of behavior affecting those goals, the risk and protective factors affecting those types of behavior, and activities to change those risk and protective factors. | | |
| 4. Designed activities consistent with community values and available resources (e.g., staff time, staff skills, facility space, and supplies). | 8. Addressed sexual psychosocial risk and protective factors that affect sexual behavior (e.g., knowledge, perceived risks, values, attitudes, perceived norms, and self-efficacy) and changed them. | 16. If needed, implemented activities to recruit and retain teens and overcome barriers to their involvement (e.g., publicized the program, offered food, or obtained consent). |
| 5. Pilot-tested the program. | | 17. Implemented virtually all activities with reasonable fidelity. |

**Activites and Teaching Methdologies**

9. Created a safe social environment for young people to participate.

10. Included multiple activities to change each of the targeted risk and protective factors.

11. Employed instructionally sound teaching methods that actively involved participants, that helped them personalize the information, and that were designed to change the targeted risk and protective factors.

12. Employed activities, instructional methods, and behavioral messages that were appropriate to the teens' culture, developmental age, and sexual experience.

13. Covered topics in a logical sequence.

*Source:* Kirby, 2007.

Table 6.2
**Federal Definition of Abstinence Education. Title V, Section 510 (b) (2) (A–H) of the Social Security Act (P.L. 104–193).**

**Under Section 510, abstinence education is defined as an educational or motivational program that:**

(A) has as its exclusive purpose, teaching the social, psychological, and health gains to be realized by abstaining from sexual activity;

(B) teaches abstinence from sexual activity outside marriage as the expected standard for all school age children;

(C) teaches that abstinence from sexual activity is the only certain way to avoid out-of-wedlock pregnancy, sexually transmitted diseases, and other associated health problems;

(D) teaches that a mutually faithful monogamous relationship in the context of marriage is the expected standard of human sexual activity;

(E) teaches that sexual activity outside of the context of marriage is likely to have harmful psychological and physical effects;

(F) teaches that bearing children out-of-wedlock is likely to have harmful consequences for the child, the child's parents, and society;

(G) teaches young people how to reject sexual advances and how alcohol and drug use increases vulnerability to sexual advances; and

(H) teaches the importance of attaining self-sufficiency before engaging in sexual activity.

frequently, or reduce the number of sexual partners. All of these types of behavior change lead directly to reductions in the likelihood of getting pregnant or acquiring or transmitting an STI. Much is known about the characteristics of effective programs. Interventions that lead successfully to behavior change last a sufficient amount of time for key information and skills to be taught, include a variety of teaching methods, are appropriate to the developmental stage and experience of the young people in the program, and are taught by teachers that are trained to provide sexuality education. Unfortunately, real-world constraints may hinder the ability of schools or community-based agencies to implement programs that have previously been found to be effective or align with the characteristics of effective approaches. For example, schools are under increasing pressure to ensure that students perform well on standardized tests and may feel unable to devote time to teaching substantive health curricula. In addition, sexuality education remains controversial in many communities and even evidence of effectiveness may not be enough to overcome the reluctance of school or program administrators to embark on interventions that may lead to opposition.

However, every effort should be made to provide young people with programs that are likely to have a meaningful impact on their sexual behavior in order to help them to avoid negative health outcomes and to enjoy the benefits of healthy decision making throughout their lives.

## REFERENCES

Forhan, S. (2008). Prevalence of sexually transmitted infections and bacterial vaginosis among female adolescents in the United States: Data from the National Health and Nutritional Examination Survey (NHANES) 2003–2004. Oral presentation at the 2008 National STD Prevention Conference, Chicago, Illinois.

Kirby, D. (1997). *No easy answers: Research findings on programs to reduce teen pregnancy.* Washington, DC: The National Campaign to Prevent Teen Pregnancy.

Kirby, D. (2001). *Emerging answers: Research findings on programs to reduce teen pregnancy.* Washington, DC: The National Campaign to Prevent Teen Pregnancy.

Kirby, D. (2007). Emerging answers 2007: Research findings on programs to reduce teen pregnancy and sexually transmitted diseases. Washington, DC: The National Campaign to Prevent Teen and Unintended Pregnancy.

Kirby, D. (2008). The impact of abstinence and comprehensive sex and STD/HIV education programs on adolescent sexual behavior. *Journal of Sexuality Research and Social Policy, 5*(2).

Kirby, D., Laris, B., & Rolleri, L. (2006). The characteristics of effective curriculum-based sex and HIV education programs for adolescents. Scotts Valley, CA: ETR Associates.

Satcher, D. (2001). *Call to action to promote sexual health and responsible sexual behavior.* Rockville, MD: Office of the Surgeon General, U.S. Department of Health and Human Services.

Title V, Section 510 (b) (2) (A–H) of the Social Security Act (P.L. 104–193).

Trenholm, C., Devaney, B., Forston, K, Quay, L., Wheeler, J., Clark, M. (2007). *The evaluation of abstinence education programs funded under Title V section 510: Final report.* Princeton, NJ: Mathematica Policy Research.

Ventura, J., Abma, J., Mosher, W., & Henshaw, S. (2006). *Recent trends in teenage pregnancy in the United States, 1990–2002.* Hyattsville, MD: National Center for Health Statistics.

# Chapter Seven

# FEDERAL INVOLVEMENT IN ABSTINENCE-ONLY EDUCATION: HAS THE BUCK BEEN PASSED TOO FAR?

*Michael Young*

Controversy concerning public school instruction about human reproduction and other topics related to sexuality is nothing new. Sociologist Janice Irvine (2002) noted that in the 1960s, even as our society became more open about sexuality issues, community debates about what, if any, sexual topics should be discussed in classroom settings intensified. In recent years, the controversy has been concerned with abstinence-only education vs. more comprehensive approaches to sexuality education. Many sexuality educators would agree with researcher Douglas Kirby (2001), who stated, "Postponing the initiation of sex or returning to abstinence should be an important goal of comprehensive pregnancy prevention initiatives" (p. 21).

If sexuality education professionals agree that encouraging abstinence is appropriate, then why the controversy? It may be because these same sexuality education professionals also agree that young people are entitled to information—accurate information—about sexuality, including methods to protect themselves against HIV and other sexually transmitted infections (STIs) and unwanted pregnancy for when they do begin engaging in sexual behaviors. Many proponents of abstinence-only education, however, are also strong supporters of the federal government's definition of abstinence education, which emphasizes the teaching of abstinence-only-until-marriage to the exclusion of accurate information about contraception. To qualify for federal abstinence funding, applicant organizations must agree to abide by this federal definition.

This chapter discusses the federal government's involvement in abstinence-only education and concerns expressed by many sexuality educators and public health professionals regarding this approach. This includes: (1) historical perspectives on federal involvement in abstinence-only education, (2) an analysis of the federal definition of abstinence-only education, and (3) a discussion of the federal funding of abstinence-only education curricula, which provide inaccurate information and have not demonstrated effectiveness in changing sexual behavior.

## HISTORICAL PERSPECTIVES ON FEDERAL INVOLVEMENT IN ABSTINENCE EDUCATION

Federal involvement in abstinence-only education began under President Ronald Reagan with the passage in 1981 of the Adolescent Family Life Act (AFLA), popularly known as the "Chastity Bill" (Benshoof, 1988). This act was the response of a conservative administration to a felt need to solve or prevent the "severe health, social, and economic consequences" that often result from "teen pregnancy and childbirth among unmarried adolescents" (Public Health Service Act, 1981, Sec. 2001). Language from the AFLA indicated its stated purpose was "to find effective means within the context of the family, of reaching adolescents before they become sexually active in order to maximize the guidance and support available to adolescents from parents and other family members and to promote self-discipline and other prudent approaches to the problem of adolescent sexual relations, including adolescent pregnancy" (Sec. 2001 (a), para. 11, sub. (C)(b)(1)).

The legislation authorized funding for demonstration grants (rather than service grants). The federal agency responsible for AFLA, the Office of Adolescent Pregnancy Programs (OAPP), currently indicates that grantees are "charged with demonstrating effective approaches that address the issues of abstinence education and/or issues related to pregnant and parenting adolescents and their families" (The Title XX Adolescent Family Life Program, undated, p. 1). The legislation directed these funded projects to "use such methods as will strengthen the capacity of families to deal with the sexual behavior, pregnancy or parenthood of adolescents and to make use of support systems such as other family members, friends, religious and charitable organizations and voluntary associations" (Public Health, 1981, Sec. 2003 (a)). Grant recipients were required to describe how they would involve such individuals and groups in the proposed project. The Act imposed limitations on the use of grant funds for family planning services and forbade granting funds to projects or programs that "advocated, promoted or encouraged" abortion (Public Health, 1981).

## The Kendrick Decision

This legislation was challenged in court by a group of federal taxpayers, members of the clergy, and a religious organization who were collectively represented by the American Civil Liberties Union (ACLU). In the original lawsuit, *Kendrick et al. v. Heckler*, the plaintiffs sought to have the AFLA declared unconstitutional on its face and as applied (J. Benshoof, personal communication, March 13, 1984). This case is important because it was this case and its settlement that led to additional federal involvement in abstinence education and the a–h definition of abstinence education (Title V, 1996). The concerns voiced by plaintiffs were twofold: (1) that the AFL Act (the legislation that provided for the federal funding of abstinence education programs) violated the U.S. Constitution's establishment of religion clause and (2) that many of the AFL projects were conducted by religious groups that provided inaccurate information and promoted their own religious beliefs. Thus, the plaintiffs alleged this had the effect of advancing religion and leading to the entanglement of church and state.

The Federal District Court agreed with the plaintiffs and found the AFL Act unconstitutional on its face and as applied. On appeal to the U.S. Supreme Court, however, the AFL Act was found to not violate the Constitution's establishment clause (*Bowen v. Kendrick* et al., 1990), which means that the Court found that the abstinence education legislation did not necessarily promote religion. In the decision the Court indicated that the promotion of abstinence did have a valid secular purpose; in other words, there are good reasons, separate and apart from religious reasons, to encourage young people to postpone sexual involvement.

One should note, however, that the AFL Act, while encouraging young people to postpone sexual involvement, did not include the a–h definition of abstinence education, nor did the legislation include a specific abstinence-until-marriage provision. The issue of whether the AFL Act was constitutional as applied was remanded (sent back) to the District Court. In the District Court's initial decision, many of the AFL grantees were characterized as "pervasively sectarian organizations." When the District Court's decision was appealed, the Supreme Court acknowledged that there was evidence of specific incidents of impermissible behavior by grantees. The Supreme Court also stated that the District Court had not indicated which grantee organizations were considered "pervasively sectarian," nor identified the criteria used for designating an organization pervasively sectarian, nor did the District Court design an appropriate remedy for the wrongful approval of grants (*Bowen v. Kendrick* et al., 1990). This basically meant that while the Supreme Court agreed with the plaintiffs that there were problems with the way in which OAPP awarded some of AFL grant funds and problems with the way in which some grantees used the funds that had been awarded, the Court also found that there were problems with the District Court's ruling. Thus, the Supreme Court remanded to the Federal District Court the issue of whether the act was constitutional as applied. This gave the District Court the opportunity to make revisions in its ruling, addressing the concerns expressed by the Supreme Court.

In 1993, before the District Court issued a new ruling, the plaintiffs and the government reached an out-of-court settlement. Under the terms of the settlement, the OAPP established a stringent review process for educational materials proposed for use in AFLA projects. Materials were to be reviewed for "medical accuracy" and "neutrality on religion" and could "neither encourage nor discourage abortion." Materials that did not pass the review had to be revised to meet OAPP standards or otherwise could not be used in OAPP-funded projects (*Kendrick et al. v. Sullivan*, 1993). The terms of settlement expired in January, 1998, but Patrick Sheeran, OAPP Director at that time (since retired), indicated his commitment to continue the review process (P. Sheeran, OAPP, personal communication, 1998). This settlement was not popular with many of the abstinence organizations that had been funded by OAPP or that had provided materials to grantees. This is because their materials, which had been widely used by OAPP grantees prior to the settlement, did not gain approval after the new review process was in place.

## THE FEDERAL DEFINITION OF ABSTINENCE EDUCATION

The OAPP review process did not prohibit organizations from revising their abstinence materials in order to meet the new rules and pass the review conducted by OAPP. In fact, such revisions were encouraged. However, it is a common statement in dealing with legal issues of a controversial nature that if one doesn't like the rules one option is to start a new ball game in which the rules are more to one's liking. In the case of abstinence-only education, the 1996 welfare reform legislation became that new ball game. The abstinence education provision of this legislation was inserted into the welfare reform legislation "during a process that is reserved for corrections and technical revisions" and became law without the benefit of public input or Congressional debate (Edwards, 1996, pp. 1–2).

This welfare reform version of abstinence education, developed by Robert Rector of the Heritage Foundation ("Abstinence Education," 2006), included a specific eight-point (provisions a–h) definition of abstinence education, as shown in Table 7.1.

The table shows that among other requirements, the a–h definition mandated that funded programs teach abstinence-only-until-marriage—setting marriage as "the expected standard of human sexual activity" (Office of State

Table 7.1
The Federal a–h Definition of Abstinence Education

Abstinence education means an educational or motivational program that:

(a) has as its exclusive purpose, teaching the social, psychological, and health gains to be realized by abstaining from sexual activity;

(b) teaches abstinence from sexual activity outside marriage as the expected standard for all school age children;

(c) teaches that abstinence from sexual activity is the only certain way to avoid out-of-wedlock pregnancy, sexually transmitted diseases, and other associated health problems;

(d) teaches that a mutually faithful monogamous relationship in the context of marriage is the expected standard of human sexual activity;

(e) teaches that sexual activity outside of marriage is likely to have harmful psychological and physical effects;

(f) teaches that bearing children out-of-wedlock is likely to have harmful consequences for the child, the child's parents, and society;

(g) teaches young people how to reject sexual advances and how alcohol and drug use increases vulnerability to sexual advances; and

(h) teaches the importance of attaining self-sufficiency before engaging in sexual activity. (Office of State and Community Health, 1997)

and Community Health, 1997, p. 10). The definition applied to OAPP as well as the new $50 million per year Title V program, which block-granted abstinence education funds to states. The definition has received a number of criticisms from sexuality educators and public health officials. These have generally focused on the restrictive nature of the definition, the imposition of a moral standard with which most of the American people do not agree, a lack of clarity regarding definitions of abstinence and sexuality activity (e.g., what specific activities do we want unmarried people to avoid? What about nonheterosexual individuals for whom legal marriage is not an option in most states?), and the promotion of inaccurate information (Young, 2004; Young & Goldfarb, 2000).

The guidance initially provided by the Maternal and Child Health Bureau (MCHB), the federal agency first given responsibility for administering the Title V program, indicated that programs did not have to meet all eight aspects of the definition but could not be inconsistent with any aspect of the definition. This allowed states and individual grantees more flexibility than would have been possible if they had been required to meet all eight aspects of the definition. States took different approaches in using the Title V funds. Some states funded media campaigns, while others provided grants to schools and community groups to conduct various types of abstinence education programs. Some programs used materials that did provide medically accurate information and were neutral on religion and abortion. Other programs did not.

This resulted in a hodge-podge of programs, many of which did not meet a strict interpretation of the a–h definition.

The OAPP also coped with the a–h standard by telling grantees that they could not be inconsistent with the definition. They could instruct students "to wait" or to "be abstinent." Grantees could not tell students to wait until they were "older" or more "mature." If the word "wait" or "abstinent" was followed by the word "until" then "until" must mean "until marriage" (L. Nestor, OAPP, personal communication, October 1998). Again, this type of flexibility circumvented strict compliance with all aspects of the a–h definition.

Self-appointed conservative watchdog groups insisted that both federal agencies and many states were violating Congressional intent, in that it was the intent of Congress that all programs funded under AFLA or Title V fully meet all eight aspects of the definition. For example, Julie Wright, executive director of a pro-abstinence organization, said it was the clear intent of Congress that programs incorporate all eight provisions of the definition and that her state (Minnesota) had not done that ("Safe Sex," 1997). House GOP leaders Bill Archer and Thomas J. Bliley, Jr. advised MCHB that it may not be following Congressional intent. They cited the fact that while three of the eight provisions of the definition specifically promoted marriage, a number of states had not even mentioned marriage in the plans they had submitted to secure federal abstinence education funding (Wetzstein, 1998). The argument was that simply running a program that was "not inconsistent" with the definition was not good enough. It must clearly meet all eight of the a–h provisions. It may seem a bit strange to some people for groups to argue Congressional intent about an issue that had not subject to Congressional debate but was only added in conference, however, that has not seemed to bother those who support a strict adherence to the a–h definition.

## SPRANS/CBAE Funding

Concerns by conservatives about programs not fully meeting all eight aspects of the definition, and concerns in some states that conservative groups did not receive Title V funds, led to several changes in the way these federal funds were administered. The first of these was the establishment of an additional federal abstinence education program, Special Programs of Regional and National Significance (SPRANS), which was also housed in the MCHB, along with the Title V program. This program gave community organizations the opportunity to apply directly to the federal government for abstinence education funding. These projects had to meet all aspects of the a–h definition. SPRANS funding was first available in fiscal year (FY) 2001. Applicants could ask for up to $800,000 per year, for three years ($2.4 million for a single project). In FY 2005, both the Title V Program and the SPRANS program were moved to the Administration for Children and Families. SPRANS became Community-Based Abstinence Education (CBAE). Funding limits were placed at $600,000 per year for five years ($3 million for a single project). To ensure that grantees used curricula that fully complied with the federal definition of abstinence education, a major part of the grant application process was for applicants to demonstrate that the materials they planned to use fully met all provisions of the a–h definition. Beginning with the 2006 CBAE Request for Proposals, applicants also have had to show how the materials met the "13 themes" embedded within the a–h definition. This also appears to be the brain-child of Robert Rector, author of the a–h definition ("Abstinence Education," 2006). The intent seems to be to require grantees to use only curricula that have the abstinence-only-until-marriage message as their clear focus.

## FEDERAL FUNDING OF ABSTINENCE EDUCATION CURRICULA: ACCURACY AND EFFECTIVENESS

### Accuracy

Concerns about federal involvement in abstinence education have been focused not only on the a–h definition, but also: (1) whether the programs provide accurate information, and (2) whether the programs funded have been effective in reducing/postponing sexual involvement or reducing risky sexual behavior. In December 2004, the U.S. House of Representatives released *The Content of Federally Funded Abstinence-Only Education Programs*, commonly known as the Waxman Report because it was commissioned by Congressman Henry Waxman (D-CA), an outspoken critic of federal involvement in abstinence-only education. The report examined the content of the abstinence education curricula most frequently used in projects funded under SPRANS and found that of the 13 most commonly used curricula, 11 contained "major errors and distortions of public health information" (p. 7), "false, misleading or distorted information about reproductive health" (p. i), and had "serious and pervasive problems" with the accuracy of the information provided (p. ii). The two curricula that did not contain major errors or distortions were "Sex Can Wait" (Core, Schutz, & Young, 2005; Core, Schutz, Young, & Young, 2005; Young & Young, 2005) and "Managing Pressures Before Marriage" (Howard, 2006a, Howard, 2006b, Howard, 2006c). These two curricula did meet the a–h definition. Because of the limitations imposed by the a–h definition, these curricula did not address issues that are discussed in some more comprehensive programs (e.g., neither program has lessons concerning contraceptive use or sexual orientation), but the information that is provided does not have major problems with accuracy. Scare tactics are not employed. Both curricula approach topics from a health behavior perspective, helping young people make sound decisions rather than imposing a religious, moralistic standard. "Sex Can Wait" and "Managing Pressures Before Marriage" were each used in 5 SPRANS-funded projects. The other 11 curricula were used in 69 projects. As of the writing of this chapter, the Administration for Children and Families is conducting their own review of "medical and scientific information" presented in abstinence education curricula used by their grantees (M. Watson, personal communication, June 6, 2008).

## Effectiveness

A number of sexuality educators, public health officials, and others have raised concerns about the effectiveness of abstinence-only programs. A review by Young and Penhollow (2006) found that at that time there existed 16 published evaluations of abstinence education programs/curricula in which the evaluation addressed the impact of the program on measures of sexual behavior. Five of these evaluations dealt with "Sex Can Wait." Four of the five evaluations of "Sex Can Wait" showed positive behavioral results. For example, a 1992 study of "Living Smart" (now the middle school component of "Sex Can Wait") found that students in health education classes who participated in the curriculum were less likely to report participation in sexual intercourse in the last month than students who took health education without "Living Smart" and students who did not participate in health education (Young, Core-Gebhart, & Marx, 1992). In another study concerned with "Sex Can Wait," Goldfarb and colleagues (1999) tested an intervention that included the upper elementary and middle school components of "Sex Can Wait" and activities from "Abstinence: Pick & Choose Activities" (Young & Young, 1996). They found that at post-test students from intervention schools were less likely to report participation in sexual intercourse ever and in the last month than students from control schools. Denny, Young, and Spear (1999) also studied the effects of "Sex Can Wait." They examined all three components of the curriculum series comparing intervention schools to control schools. No behavioral questions were asked of upper elementary students. At post-test, the behavioral trends (for both sexual intercourse ever and sexual intercourse in the last month) were in the desired direction (fewer students from the intervention schools reporting participation than students from comparison schools), but these trends were not statistically significant. Denny, Young, Rausch and Spear (2002) again examined the effects of all three elements of the "Sex Can Wait" series. This time there were significant differences at the high school level (but not at the upper elementary or middle school levels) between intervention and control students with regard to participation in both sexual intercourse ever and in the last month, with fewer intervention students reporting participation in intercourse. Finally, Denny and Young (2006) reported the results of an 18-month follow-up evaluation of the "Sex Can Wait" series. At follow-up, students who had experienced the curriculum at either the upper elementary or middle school levels were less likely than control students to report having sexual intercourse in the last month (both middle school and upper elementary) and sexual intercourse ever (middle school).

Since the Young and Penhollow (2006) review article, an additional evaluation article of an abstinence education curriculum, showing positive behavioral results has also been published (Weed, Ericksen, Lewis, Grant, & Wibberly, 2008). The researchers found that among students who reported at pretest that they had not had sexual intercourse, those who participated in the abstinence program were significantly less likely than students in the control group to report initiation of sexual intercourse by the 12-month follow-up.

It is important to note that only a small percentage of the abstinence education curricula that are currently in use have had evaluations published in peer reviewed journals. For example, of the 46 curricula listed, in the 2003 Abstinence Clearinghouse Directory of Abstinence Resources (http://www.abstinence.net/library), none have had evaluations that examined the effects of the curriculum on student sexual behavior outcomes published in peer-reviewed professional journals. Although an evaluation of "For Keeps" has been published (Borawski, Trapl, Lovegreen, Colabianchi, & Block, 2005), it is listed in the Directory under *program/training* and *speakers* rather than *curricula*. Of others that have claimed to have been evaluated, few of these evaluations have resulted in published articles, and of the evaluations that have been published, few have demonstrated positive results. Evaluations of abstinence education curricula not previously discussed here that have shown some positive behavioral results include: "Project Taking Charge" (Jorgensen, Potts, & Camp, 1993), "Stay Smart" (St. Pierre, Mark, Kaltreider, & Aiken, 1995), and "Making A Difference" (Jemmott, Jemmott, & Fong, 1998).

While positive results were reported for all four of these curricula, one cannot conclude from these evaluations that abstinence education curricula work. For example, authors of the "Project Taking Charge" evaluation noted that among students who reported they were virgins at pretest, the comparison group subjects were more likely than the intervention subjects to report initiation of sexual intercourse (Jorgensen, Potts, & Camp, 1993). In his review of program effects, however, Kirby (1997) apparently took issue with the way in which these researchers interpreted their results (counting a probability level of .051 as statistically significant, when less than .05 is the generally accepted standard) and reported the program had no effect. In the "Stay Smart" evaluation (St. Pierre, Mark, Kaltreider, & Aiken, 1995), the only behavioral difference was that at 27-month follow-up, among students who were nonvirgins at pre-test, there was an effect on the frequency and recentness of intercourse, and a combined measure of these two variables, for the "basic" program group—but not for the group that received the basic program, plus booster programs. One would expect that the basic program plus the booster program would produce improvements of at least the same degree as the basic program alone. This, however, did not happen.

The study that examined the "Making A Difference" curriculum did find that young people who participated in the program were less likely than those in the control group to report having sexual intercourse in the 3-month follow-up period (Jemmott, Jemmott, & Fong, 1998). At the 6- and 12-month follow-ups, however, these differences were gone. The curriculum encourages abstinence from risky behaviors but not necessarily from other types of sexual activity. Thus, while the researchers did utilize a rigorous evaluation design and did find positive, short-term behavioral change, the abstinence curriculum they studied does not appear to meet the a–h definition.

Borawski and coworkers (2005) found that sexually inexperienced students who participated in the "For Keeps" intervention were just as likely to initiate sexual intercourse by the 16- to 25-week post-test as sexually inexperienced students in the control group. Additionally, sexually experienced students receiving the intervention were no more likely to abstain from intercourse than control students. The positive findings were that among students who did report they had sexual intercourse at least once during the five-month follow-up period, students receiving the curriculum reported fewer episodes of sexual intercourse and fewer sexual partners than control students. Thus, while the program did demonstrate some public health benefit, it did not increase the number of young people who abstained from sexual intercourse. (See Young and Penhollow (2006) for more detailed comments on these evaluations and evaluations that did not have significant results.)

Several state evaluations of Title V abstinence education programs have also been conducted. These evaluations have shown little evidence that the programs have had an effect on reducing sexual behavior. Most of the evaluations used no control group (Hauser, 2004). Use of an appropriate control group is important because to make conclusions about the effects of an intervention, researchers really need to know what would have happened in the absence of the intervention. Thus, for the states that did not have a control group, the evaluations did not provide evidence the programs worked, but at the same time the evaluations provided relatively weak evidence that the programs did *not* work. None of these Title V evaluations have been published in peer-reviewed journals.

In 1998, Mathematica Policy Research, Inc., received funding to conduct a national evaluation of the state Title V programs. They initially selected 11 sites to participate in the evaluation. Their first report, dealing with the impact of these programs and released in 2005, presented a summary of findings from four selected school-based abstinence education programs (Maynard,

Trenholm, & Devaney, 2005). Behavior was not examined. In 2007, the Mathematica report dealing with the impact of the program on behavior was released. The findings indicated that the abstinence education interventions they examined had no effect on subsequent sexual behaviors (Trenholm, Devaney, Fortsan, Quay, Wheeler, & Clark, 2007).

The abstinence-only-until-marriage curricula that seem to be the most popular (e.g., "Choosing The Best," "WAIT Training," "Why kNOw," and "Me, My World, My Future") have had no evaluations published in peer-reviewed journals examining the impact of the program on sexual behavior. This is important, because while it is easy for people to say something "works," the scientific community looks to peer-reviewed publications as its standard of evidence. To increase the number of published evaluation articles that demonstrate the effectiveness of abstinence education programming, the Administration for Children and Families and OAPP have jointly sponsored two different National Abstinence Education Evaluation Conferences, the first in November 2005 and the second in March 2006. Additionally, guidelines for current CBAE grants require grantees to devote at least 15 percent of their budget to evaluation. Finally, most recent CBAE/Title V grantees conferences emphasized to grantees the importance of publishing project evaluations in scholarly journals (J. Donnelly, personal communication, January 31, 2008).

Because of concerns about the restrictive a–h definition of abstinence education, inaccurate information provided in many abstinence education curricula, and concerns that many curricula have not been shown effective in reducing participation in sexual behavior, a number of states have decided to opt out of the Title V abstinence education program. Washington (2008) reported Iowa was the 17th state to decline Title V funding. Other states to turn down the funding as of the writing of this chapter include: Ohio, Wisconsin, Connecticut, Rhode Island, Montana, New Jersey, California (Huffstutter, 2007), Maine, Virginia, Colorado (Stein, 2007), and Pennsylvania (Samuels, 2007).

## CONCLUSION

The federal government has spent a substantial amount of money—as of the writing of this chapter, more than $1.5 billion—on abstinence-only-until-marriage curricula and programs. Some of these funded projects have produced some evidence of positive results; most have not. Some programs do have a sound theoretical basis and provide fairly accurate information about reproductive anatomy and physiology, sexually transmitted diseases, sexual decision making and other related topics; most do not. Programs that receive federal abstinence education must operate under a restrictive definition of abstinence education, which limits access to important information that young people want and need. Encouraging young people to abstain from early sexual activity is not a bad thing. It is a legitimate goal of sexuality education. Most sexuality educators and public health professionals agree, however, that the current federal approach to abstinence education is not working and is not in the best interest of our young people. Many people opposed to the federal approach want the program abolished. Others, who support abstinence education, believe the program is working and should be continued and expanded. It should be clear to informed people that even if the program is continued, some changes need to be made if we are to provide our young people accurate information about sexuality, effectively encourage them to postpone too-early sexual involvement, and help them make positive decisions for their future.

## REFERENCES

Abstinence education grantees technical assistance conference call on A-H compliance with Mr. Robert Rector. (2006). Text of presentation, and questions and answers, May 17. Retrieved June 2, 2008, from, http://www.pal-tech.com/web/tacalls/05–17%20Transcript%20edited%2006–22–06.pdf

Benshoof, J. (1988). The Chastity Act: Government manipulation of abortion information and the first amendment. *Harvard Law Review, 101,* 1916–1937.

Borawski, E. A., Trapl, E. S., Lovegreen, L. D., Colabianchi, N., & Block, T. (2005). Effectiveness of abstinence only intervention in middle school teens, *American Journal of Health Behavior,* (5), pp. 423–434.

Bowen v. Kendrick et al. (1990). United States Supreme Court Reports, Lawyers Cooperative Publishing.

Core, P., Schutz, S., & Young, M. (2005) Sex can wait: An abstinence education program for middle school classrooms, Health Education Projects Office, University of Arkansas, Fayetteville.

Core, P., Schutz, S., Young, M., & Young, T. (2005) Sex can wait: An abstinence education program for high school classrooms, Health Education Projects Office, University of Arkansas, Fayetteville.

Denny, G., & Young, M. (2006). An evaluation of an abstinence-only sex education curriculum: An 18-month follow-up. *Journal of School Health, 76,* 414–422.

Denny, G., Young, M., Rausch, S., & Spear, C. (2002). An evaluation of an abstinence education curriculum series: Sex Can Wait. *American Journal of Health Behavior, 26,* 366–377.

Denny, G., Young, M., & Spear, C. (1999). An evaluation of the "Sex Can Wait" abstinence education curriculum series. *American Journal of Health Behavior, 23,* 134–143.

Edwards, M. (1996). Abstinence-only education. *SIECUS Report, 25*(4), pp. 1–2.

Goldfarb, E. S., Donnelly, J., Duncan, D., Young, M., Eadie, C., Castiglia, D. (1999) "Evaluation of an abstinence-based curriculum for early adolescents: First year changes in sex attitudes, knowledge and behavior," *North American Journal of Psychology, 1*(2), pp. 243–254.

Hauser, D. (2004). Five years of abstinence-only-until-marriage education: Assessing the impact. Washington, DC, Advocates for Youth. Retrieved June 6, 2008, from http://www.advocatesforyouth.org/publications/stateevaluations

Howard, M. (2006a). Managing pressures before marriage for preteens, Emory University Jane Fonda Center, Atlanta.

Howard, M. (2006b). Managing pressures before marriage for teens, Emory University Jane Fonda Center, Atlanta.

Howard, M. (2006c). Managing pressures before marriage for young teens, Emory University Jane Fonda Center, Atlanta.

Huffstutter, P. J. (2007, April 8). States are refusing Bush's abstinence-only sex ed. *The Los Angles Times.*

Irvine, J. M. (2002). Talk About Sex: The battle over sex education in the United States. Berkeley: University of California Press.

Jemmott, J. B., Jemmott, L. S., & Fong, G. T. (1998, May 20). Abstinence and safer sex HIV risk-reduction interventions for African American adolescents: A randomized controlled rial. *Journal of the American Medical Association, 279*(19), pp. 1529–1536.

Jorgensen S.R., Potts, V. & Camp B. (1993, October). Project taking charge: Six-month follow-up of a pregnancy prevention program for early adolescents. *Family Relations, 42*(4), pp. 401–406.

Kendrick et al. v. Sullivan. (1993). Settlement agreement, U.S. District Court for the District of Columbia, Civil Action No. 83–3175.

Kirby, D. (1997). *No easy answers: Research findings on programs to reduce teen pregnancy.* Washington, DC: The National Campaign to Prevent Teen Pregnancy.

Kirby, D. (2001). *Emerging answers: Research findings on programs to reduce teen pregnancy.* Washington, DC: National Campaign to Prevent Teen Pregnancy.

Maynard, R. A., Trenholm, C., Devaney, B., Johnson, A., Clark, M. A., Homrighausen, J., et al. (2005). *First-year impacts of four Title V, Section 510 abstinence education programs.* Washington, DC: U.S. Department of Health and Human Services, Mathematica Policy Research, Inc.

Office of State and Community Health, Maternal and Child Health Bureau, Department of Health and Human Services, Rockville, MD. (1997). Block Grant Application Guidance For the Abstinence Education Provisions of the 1996 Welfare Law, P.L. 104–193.

Public Health Service Act. (1981). Public law 97–35, Title XX, Adolescent Family Life Demonstration Projects.

Samuels, C. (2007). States turn down abstinence-only grants. *Education Weekly 26*(29): 5–12.

St. Pierre, T. L., Mark, M., Kaltreider, D. L., & Aikin, K. J. (1995, January). A 27-Month Evaluation of a Sexual Activity Prevention Program in Boys & Girls Clubs Across the Nation, *Family Relations, 44*(1), pp. 69–77.

Stein, R. (2007, December 16). Abstinence programs face rejection. *The Washington Post,* p. A03.

Title V, Section 510 (b)(2)(A-H) of the Social Security Act. (1996). Retrieved June 1, 2008, from http://www.ssa.gov/OP_Home/ssact/title05/0510.htm

The Title XX Adolescent Family Life Program. Retrieved June 1, 2008, from http://www. hhs.gov/opa/familylife/strategicplanning/whoisoapp_v2.pdf

Trenholm, C., Devaney, B., Fortsan, K., Quay, L., Wheeler, J., & Clark, M. (2007). *Impacts of four Title V section 510 abstinence education program.* Princeton, NJ: Mathematica Policy Research Inc.

U.S. House of Representatives, Committee on Government Reform, Minority Staff, Special Investigations Division. (2004). *The Content of Federally Funded Abstinence Education Programs, Prepared for Representative Henry Waxman.* Washington, DC.

Washington, L. (2008, February 29). Iowa refuses abstinence-only sex ed funding. *Iowa Independent.*

Weed, S., Ericksen, I. H., Lewis, A., Grant, G. E. & Wibberly, K. H. (2008). An abstinence program's impact on cognitive mediators and sexual initiation. *American Journal of Health Behavior, 32,* 60–73.

Wetzstein, C. (1998, February 9). Congressmen want states to use federal grant to urge abstinence—House Republicans on the use of grant intended for programs advocating marriage and other traditional social practices. *Insight on the News.*

Young, M. (2004). What's wrong with abstinence education? *American Journal of Health Studies, 19,* 148–156.

Young, M., Core-Gebhart, P., & Marx, D. (1992). Abstinence-oriented sexuality education: Initial field test results of the Living Smart curriculum. *Family Life Educator, 10,* 4–8.

Young, M., & Goldfarb, E. (2000). The problematic (a)-(h) in abstinence education. *Journal of Sex Education and Therapy, 25,* 156–160.

Young, M., & Penhollow, T. (2006). The impact of abstinence education: What does the research say? *American Journal of Health Education, 37,* 191–202.

Young, T., & Young, M. (1996). Pick & choose: Abstinence activities, ETR Associates, Santa Cruz.

Young, T., & Young. M. (2005). Sex can wait: An abstinence education program for upper elementary school classrooms, Health Education Projects Office, University of Arkansas, Fayetteville.

## Chapter Eight

# BITTER BATTLES: LESSONS FROM DECADES OF CONTROVERSY OVER SEXUALITY EDUCATION IN SCHOOLS

*Martha E. Kempner*

Though they may feel like the first person to ever deal with these issues, the educator whose classroom presentation about condoms sparks outrage in the community, the parent who suddenly learns that her child's sexuality education class is being led by a crisis pregnancy center, and the school board member who knows nothing about sexuality education yet finds himself trying to bridge the gap between a sharply divided community are all part of a decades-long tug-of-war.

What role schools should play in educating young people about sexuality has been debated since as early as the 1890s. This controversy plays out at all levels of politics and education with the federal government deciding what types of programs it should throw federal dollars behind, state governments imposing mandates, and local school boards choosing curricula.

This chapter looks at the historical controversy over sexuality education and how the modern Far Right, "pro-family movement" used it to gain power and brand its own type of sexuality education. It then tracks individual controversies in communities across the country to provide examples of how various issues from curriculum choices to what an individual teacher did or did not say in a classroom influence and are influenced by this national debate. And, finally, it provides some action steps that supporters of comprehensive sexuality education can take to seize the opportunities that are now emerging and to ensure that generations of young people to come will not be denied critical information just because sexuality education has been deemed controversial.

This chapter is designed to help the educator who is surprised by how controversial her annual condom demonstration has suddenly become, the mother who thought her son was learning about birth control but finds out he's simply being told that condoms don't work, and the school board member who never expected to become part of an age-old debate. By understanding how controversies in other communities have played out, these individuals can place their own situation in historical context, chart the best path forward, and avoid some of the mistakes others have made in the past.

## A CONTROVERSIAL HISTORY

The question of what role schools should play in sexuality education—indeed if they should play a role at all—has been debated for well over 100 years. In fact, the National Education Association (NEA) discussed the role of sexuality education in the school curriculum at its annual meeting in 1892. The NEA, like most professional health and education organizations, was supportive of sexuality education. In 1914, the NEA passed a resolution supporting specific training for teachers regarding sexuality education recommending "that institutions preparing teachers give attention to such subjects as would qualify for instruction in the general fields of morals as well as in the specific fields of sex hygiene" (Carrera, 1971, p. 99). The federal government further helped teachers in 1920 when it published the manual *Sex Education in High School* on how to teach about sexuality education in schools. School-based sexuality education also received support from other professional organizations such as the American School Health Association and the American Medical Association (Yarber, 1994).

From the beginning, however, there were those who opposed teaching sexuality education in schools. These individuals, often leaders or members of religious communities, suggested that schools were usurping parental authority, that they had no place in discussing what was primarily a moral and religious issue, and that such education would encroach on, and indeed permanently spoil, the natural innocence of children.

In the 1960s, a concerted effort to stop school-based sexuality education emerged (Yarber, 1994). A number of groups formed as organized and vocal opponents to school-based sexuality education programs. Some, like the John Birch Society and the Christian Crusade, were formed to take on a variety of social issues. The John Birch Society, for example, formed in 1958 to address what its leaders saw as growing threats to the U.S. Constitution, most notably communism (2008). Others, such as Parents Opposed to Sex and Sensitivity Education (POSSE), Mothers Organized for Moral Stability (MOMS), Sanity of Sex (S.O.S.), Parents Against Universal Sex Ed (PAUSE), and the Movement to Restore Decency (MOTREDE), were small groups of parents who organized specifically to protest the presence of sexuality education classes in school ("Sex in the Classroom," 1969; Yarber, 1994).

A *Time* magazine article published in June of 1969 highlighted controversies erupting over sexuality education across the country and explained that those who opposed teaching about sex in school raised a wide variety of arguments, "some plausible, some not." Among the more mainstream arguments was the concern that such courses would be "too specific, too early and too stimulating" ("Sex in the Classroom," 1969). According to this school of thought, exposure to sexual information too early left children obsessed with sex and threatened to turn them into perverted adults. Another common complaint from critics suggested that "schools are illicitly taking over an educative function that properly belongs in the home or with the churches" ("Sex in the Classroom," 1969).

Of course, many of the arguments used in the heated debated that sprung up around the country were less logical. As the *Time* article explained it, "At the lowest level, the attacks consist of nothing more than innuendoes that the teachers involved are degenerates eager to seduce youngsters into a life of blatant immorality" ("Sex in the Classroom"). Others were simply a reflection of the larger culture wars of the time. A widely released pamphlet, *Is the Little Red School House the Proper Place to Teach Raw Sex?*, published at the start of the 1968–1969 school year, warned parents, for example, that sexuality education was a gateway to communism. And the founder of the John Birch Society declared sexuality education "a 'filthy Communist plot,' akin to community fluoridation plans" ("Sex in the Classroom").

Battles over sexuality education never take place in a vacuum; they always reflect the larger political and social realities of their time. As Janice Irvine (2004) explains in *Talk about Sex*, "Passionate local debates tend to be read as though they are spontaneous, indigenous uprisings of outraged citizens. But they are not simply that. Rather they are profoundly shaped by national political rhetorics" (Irvine, 2004, p. 10).

In fact, Irvine explains that many of the modern Far Right groups used sexuality education as an issue that could both broaden their appeal and solidify their power. Groups such as Focus on the Family (and later its spin-off the Family Research Council), Eagle Forum, and Concerned Women for America organized around a whole host of social issues that they termed "pro-family." They opposed abortion, felt marriage was vital and cohabitation immoral, argued that homosexuality was a sin, and supported a return to "traditional" education. These groups, Irvine explained, used sex to demonize certain individuals, lifestyles, and values. "The right had found that drawing sexual boundaries and creating enemies through provocative sexual speech promised political rewards" (Irvine, 2004, p. 77). And they found that sexuality education was an issue that could draw in additional supporters.

However, instead of arguing that schools had no place teaching about sexuality, these new leaders of the Far Right positioned themselves as sexual experts in their own right and began to fight for their own policies and programs in schools (Irvine, 2004). Instead of using the original argument that the school house was no place to teach young people about sexuality, these groups acknowledged the importance of sexuality education but suggested there was only one proper teaching method. It was the school's responsibility, they said, to tell young people that sexual behavior outside of marriage was unacceptable.

This new tactic represented a change in the conservative movement but was also in many ways forced by the emerging AIDS epidemic, which raised the stakes on risky teen sexual behavior and unified many communities under the belief that sex education was imperative. In fact, in 1986, Surgeon General C. Everett Koop said, "There is now no doubt that we need sex education in schools" (Yarber, 1994, p. 7). Rather than argue with this new sentiment, organized opposition to sexuality education accepted it, indeed even sold it as their own idea, with one important caveat: the goal of sexuality education had to be to promote abstinence-only-until-marriage.

The Far Right very deliberately worked both from the top down and the ground up. They approached local school boards and national politicians with the same message: Sexual behavior among unmarried young people is dangerous, and we must stop it. They used the fear of AIDS and other problems such as teen pregnancy and rising rates of other STDs to gather support for the notion that teens simply shouldn't be having sex. They went as far as to suggest that abstinence was also the solution to the social ills they saw plaguing society, such as high divorce rates, poverty, and crime. They convinced parents and policymakers at all levels that what the country needed was a generation of abstinent teens and that their own brand of sexuality education—a brand that firmly told young people what they should and should not do—was how we would get it.

They created their own materials to support this brand of education. Throughout the 1980s and 90s, with ever-increasing financial support from the federal government, organizations around the country began offering easy-to-use, pre-packaged abstinence-only-until-marriage curricula. These curricula relied on messages of fear and shame to control young people's sexual behavior. They told students that premarital sex inevitably led to a whole host of consequences, from pregnancy and disease to loss of self-respect and a bad reputation. These fear-based curricula promoted heterosexual marriage as the only morally acceptable sexual relationship and included numerous biases based on gender, sexual orientation, and family type.

Hidden in these curricula was the conservative social agenda of the Far Right—an attempt to turn back the clocks on the social change of the 1960s and 1970s. Also hidden, sometimes in plain sight, were the blatant religious messages that drove the Far Right movement. In fact, early drafts of many fear-based curricula were written for parochial school audiences. The first draft of *Sex Respect*, for example, suggested that students take Jesus with them on a date as a way to avoid the temptations of sexual behavior. As the programs gained popularity with secular audiences these references were made more oblique. A late 1990s version of *Sex Respect*, for example, took out the word "religion" throughout the document and replaced it with "spirituality" (Kempner, 2001). Of course, religious ideology remains; the most recent edition gives students the following dating advice: "Set ending time for your date before you go out. Be home on time. Don't invite your date in. Lead yourselves not into temptation" (Mast, 2001, p. 102). While people rarely use the phrase "not into temptation" in daily conversation, it appears numerous times in the New Testament and is part of the Lord's Prayer.

Despite the underlying conservative values and religious messages, and in some places because of them, the Far Right was very successful in marketing this brand of sexuality education. They used moral and religious messages with their core supporters. For less religious parents, they tailored their message, preyed on fears of STDs and teen pregnancy, and then suggested the abstinence message was the only hope. After all, they argued, if schools teach kids about condoms isn't that tantamount to giving them a license to have sex? Even parents who did not believe in the underlying conservative social values (and there were many who simply did not realize these values were being passed on through abstinence-only-until-marriage programs) could be swayed to give this type of education a try.

When talking to politicians, the Far Right co-opted the public health messages that had always been used to support comprehensive sexuality education and argued, once again, that we needed to stop teen sexual behavior. They argued that at best "condom education" could provide risk-reduction for teens and suggested that complete risk-elimination that came with sexual abstinence was clearly superior when it came to fighting STDs and teen pregnancy, despite the fact that they had no evidence to back up these claims. However, they were hard to argue against. No politician wanted to be seen as in favor of promiscuous teens.

On the national level, by 2006, they had secured over $170 million each year for abstinence-only-until-marriage programs, money that allowed them to build a multimillion dollar industry worldwide. On the state level, they passed laws mandating an abstinence-only-until-marriage approach in schools. Perhaps, the true genius behind their strategy, however, was what they did on the local level.

## HISTORICAL CONTROVERSIES

The Far Right treated the grassroots movement as equally as important as their work on the national front. Large national organizations, such as Focus on the Family, encouraged supporters to get involved by approaching their own school board and demanding abstinence-only-until-marriage programs in their schools. In fact, in many cases, they encouraged their local supporters to run for the school board, an often neglected elected position, so they could make change from the inside.

Educators, school board members, and parents in communities across the country were unprepared to deal with this small but vocal minority of parents who approached the school board asking for any mention of contraception to be removed from the curriculum or for the district to replace the entire sexuality education program with a strict abstinence-only-until-marriage curriculum. Communities across the country were faced with what seemed like "spontaneous, indigenous uprisings of outraged citizens," (Irvine, 2004, p. 10) but what was in fact, a concerted nationwide effort to restrict what young people learn about sexuality in schools.

This section takes a look at a number of controversies that occurred in communities across the country between 1990 and 2008. It looks at efforts to institute abstinence-only-until-marriage programs as well as the counter efforts of supporters of comprehensive sexuality education to keep these programs out of schools. It looks at the early debates surrounding elementary education and discusses why this may become an issue once again. It also looks at controversies around the amount of information given to young people and those topics that are most likely to cause debate. Individually, the controversies show us how communities handle decisions over sexuality education in different ways. Together, these controversies paint a picture of where sexuality education has been and how advocates for more comprehensive approaches can ensure that it begins to move in the right direction.

## Instituting Abstinence-Only-Until-Marriage Programs

Though the abstinence-only-until-marriage movement may have had its largest successes in the halls of Congress, in many ways it began in town halls and high school auditoriums. The majority of early controversies tracked by advocates of comprehensive sexuality education such as the Sexuality Information and Education Council of the United States (SIECUS) involved a small number of parents, often armed with materials from a national Far Right organization, approaching the school board with a request for a specific abstinence-only-until-marriage program. In some communities, this meant a request to replace an existing, medically accurate, more comprehensive curriculum with an abstinence-only-until-marriage program, a more moralistic approach to teaching. In others it represented the first time a community would provide any sexuality education.

In 1993, the Vista, California School Board voted to replace "Values and Choices," a comprehensive sexuality education curriculum, with the fear-based, abstinence-only-until-marriage curriculum "Sex Respect," a program originally written for parochial schools that continues to rely on catchy, simplistic slogans, such as "Pet Your Dog, Not Your Date," as inspirations to students to wait to engage in high-risk sexual behaviors. They also voted to limit classroom discussions. Teachers were only allowed to discuss masturbation and homosexuality with students at the invitation of their parents and could only discuss contraception with 11th and 12th graders—and only in the context of marriage. A similar decision was made in Hendersonville, North Carolina, when the school board voted to replace the local curriculum, which covered a number of topics including contraception, with "Teen Aid," also a fear-based abstinence-only-until-marriage program. The board did allow teachers to use additional lessons from the old curriculum but said that contraception could only be taught within the context of a marriage relationship (Kempner, 2003, p. 33).

In 1999, Taunton, Massachusetts, became divided on how to approach sexuality education with its students. The Health Curriculum Advisory Board approved revisions to the curriculum that would change the focus of health classes from pregnancy and disease prevention to abstinence-only-until-marriage. At a heated community forum, a physician from the National Consortium of State Physician's Resource Councils, then a national opponent of comprehensive sexuality education with ties to Focus on the Family, told parents: "HIV is an adult fear not a child fear. When you teach it to ninth graders, you are impinging on their latency period" (Price, 1999). This harkens back to the argument used in the debates of the 1960s that suggested that teaching young people about sex too early causes psychological damage. The community voted on a compromise curriculum that would put a priority on teaching abstinence while also clearly communicating the risks associated with sexual activity and the use of contraceptives (Kempner, 2003, p. 33).

The school board in Waterbury, Connecticut, was approached in 2002, not by a parent, but by one of its own members, who recommended replacing instruction on birth control with discussions about the physical, social, and emotional damage that can result from teen sexual behaviors. "I feel like I've got dirt on my hands if I tell [teenagers] to use a condom and you'll be safe. That's a lie. That's a flat-out lie" (Associated Press, 2003). Other school board members, however, supported a more comprehensive approach. The school board decided not to make the change (Batchelder, 2003, p. 5).

In recent years, we have seen far fewer of these classic controversies play out at the local level. While fewer communities struggling with requests for abstinence-only-until-marriage programs may seem like a positive development, it may, in fact, be just the opposite. As the federal investment in abstinence-only-until-marriage programs increased over the years, many communities adopted them more willingly, both because they were often completely funded and because the federal dollars were perceived as the government's stamp of approval for this type of program. In addition, many communities, fearing a controversy similar to those that had occurred in neighboring towns, saw abstinence-only programs as the path of least resistance. After all, supporters of this restrictive approach were always more likely to complain than their peers who wanted comprehensive programs.

## Rejecting Abstinence-Only-Until-Marriage Programs

The good news is that there have always been communities dubious of the abstinence-only-until-marriage approach. In 1998, Idaho Springs, Colorado, rejected "WAIT (Why Am I Tempted) Training," a popular fear-based abstinence-only-until-marriage curriculum. At a school board meeting, a teacher demonstrated an exercise from the program in which a goldfish is removed from its bowl and left gasping for air on the table until a student steps forward to help it. The exercise is meant to show that just as fish belong in water, sex belongs in marriage (Kempner, 2003, p. 34). This exercise has been removed from subsequent editions of "WAIT Training."

The even better news is that, as the years go by, more and more communities question the wisdom of providing abstinence-only-until-marriage programs, criticize the programs that are being used, and demand that school districts do better. At a January 2005 meeting, parents in DeKalb County, Georgia—many of whom were scientists, physicians, and researchers from nearby Emory University and the Centers for Disease Control and Prevention—challenged the use of the fear-based curriculum produced by Choosing the Best, Inc. in Shamrock Middle School. The parents felt it was biased, based on religion, and inaccurate and pointed out that the program had never been vetted by the school board. A month later, the superintendent asked all middle schools to stop using the program despite the fact that it was free to the district (Ciardullo, 2005, p. 16).

Other communities have also turned down or discontinued programs even though they come with federal dollars attached to them. In 2007, both Charlottesville and Albermarle County, Virginia, resisted pressure to adopt a fully funded abstinence-only-until-marriage program sponsored by a local crisis pregnancy center despite the fact that five neighboring districts allow Pregnancy Centers of Central Virginia's "Worth Your Wait" program into their schools. Pregnancy Centers of Central Virginia is, like many recipients of federal funding, a crisis pregnancy center (CPC). CPCs typically advertise medical services and then use antiabortion propaganda, misinformation, and fear and shame tactics to dissuade women facing unintended pregnancy from accessing abortion services. As a result of the abundance of funding, CPCs have branched out and begun providing abstinence-only-until-marriage programs (Ciardullo, 2008, p. 4).

The programs provided by CPCs are often the most blatantly ideological and religious, and in recent years, a number of communities have rejected them. In 2003, a parent in Mt. Diablo, California, worked tirelessly to get "Crybabies" removed from her son's middle school. She felt the program was biased, inaccurate, and did not include sufficient information on how to prevent pregnancy or STDs. She explained that she became concerned when she saw a homework assignment in which her son had listed "killing a child" as a "disadvantage of abortion" (Batchelder, 2003, p. 8).

Parents in Montgomery County, Maryland, also objected to their district's outsourcing of sexuality education to a local CPC. The Montgomery County Public Schools (MCPS) were in the midst of a separate and protracted battle over additions to their middle and high school curriculum, but the district was quick and decisive in its response to complaints about the Rockville Crisis Pregnancy Center.

Its program is based on the belief that "pregnancy is not the root problem, but a symptom of a lifestyle that is outside of God's will" (Fisher, 2007). In one abstinence-only-until-marriage lesson, the CPC, which had been invited into some MCPS high schools for nine years, uses a shared piece of chewing gum to represent the dangers of STDs. District officials assured parents that the group would not be invited back (Ciardullo, 2008, p. 3).

As mentioned earlier, these controversies do not take place in a vacuum but inform and are informed by larger political and social issues. The recent shift in community attitudes toward abstinence-only-until-marriage programs and funding reflects what has been happening nationwide. First, a number of research studies have been released in the last year showing that abstinence-only-until-marriage programs have no impact on young people's sexual behavior. As a result, at least 17 states have chosen not to participate in the federal government's Title V abstinence-only-until-marriage funding stream. Moreover, the media, in particular newspapers and magazines, have begun to look skeptically upon abstinence-only-until-marriage programs, and many local newspapers have used their editorial pages to call for an end to these programs. It is likely that as more research is released and additional negative press is generated, even more communities will choose not to provide this kind of programming.

## Elementary Education

As mentioned earlier in this chapter, some of the initial arguments against sexuality education focused on the innocence of children and how sexuality education would invariably and irrevocably rob children of this state. Though these arguments were not limited to children in elementary school, they were certainly used to try to rid younger grades of sexuality education.

Proposed updates and revisions to the elementary school curriculum in Westfield, New Jersey, for example, were rejected in 1994 because community members feared that teaching fourth graders about HIV/AIDS would open the door for explicit discussions. In 1995, Schenectady, New York, decided to wait until fifth grade to teach lessons on reproduction and puberty that had been previously taught in the third and fourth grade. The next year, Sheboygan, Wyoming, voted to eliminate its K–3 sexuality education program against the advice of the Human Growth and Development Advisory Committee. The Board wanted proof that this type of education would prevent unplanned pregnancy and STDs later in life.

In 2002, the school board in Rochester, Michigan, eliminated reproductive health and HIV/AIDS instruction from Kindergarten through third grade and added "modesty" and "respect" as key concepts. In addition, it removed family planning and STD benchmarks (learning objectives) from the sixth-grade curriculum and added abstinence (Kempner, 2003, p. 37).

In recent years, however, far fewer controversies have revolved around elementary school education. It is hard to say why this has occurred, but it seems that as opponents of comprehensive sexuality education focused less on removing courses from school and more on changing the emphasis to abstinence-only-until-marriage they spent most of their time working in middle schools and high schools. Still, it is important for advocates to remain aware of objections to teaching younger students as such protests are still frequently part of debates over banning topics and materials. Moreover, as the popularity of abstinence-only-until-marriage programs wanes and communities become more resolved to providing older students with accurate information, the Far Right may once again shift its focus to elementary-aged students.

## Too Much Information

Regardless of the age of the students, parents and administrators often feel that some classroom conversations and curricula go too far. Unlike controversies over curricula that take place in advance of a teacher setting foot in a classroom, these controversies often erupt as a "she said what?" reaction to a class that has already been taught or a question that has been asked and answered.

In Odessa, Texas, parents became upset in 1998 because the new fifth-grade sexuality curriculum included definitions of vulva, clitoris, testis, penis, erection, orgasm, and ejaculation. Although the parents felt it was "sexually explicit," no changes were made.

Oral sex was the problematic topic in Belton, Missouri, where a teacher was placed on involuntary leave in 1997 after she answered a question that a student had placed in an anonymous question box. Parents felt she should have simply avoided the topic. An anonymous question box was also at the heart of a controversy in Beech Grove, Indiana, where parents felt misled when a question paved the way for classroom discussion on masturbation during the 1997–98 school year. And, parents in Bryant, Arkansas, were upset when questions about oral sex and genitalia were answered by a former health teacher during a presentation in 1998. The school board apologized and agreed to better screening for speakers.

The role of the school board in vetting speakers and controlling classroom conversations varies widely. In some schools it is standard practice for all presentations to be preapproved by the board or a school administrator, while in others, classroom teachers have more freedom in what they say and who they bring in to speak.

Some states and communities, however, have restricted how teachers can answer questions. In 1994, the school board in Merrimack, New Hampshire, voted to eliminate the anonymous question box after parents complained about students asking inappropriate questions. In 1997, teachers in Franklin County, North Carolina, were specifically told that if students ask questions about birth control they can only be told about the failure rates of contraception and referred to their parents or guardians for more information. And in 2000, lawmakers in Utah attempted to legislate how teachers answer questions. They passed a bill stating that when teachers are asked questions that "skirt the state approved curriculum," such as questions about homosexuality, they must pull students aside to answer the question or refer students to a school counselor. The author of the legislation felt that if you allow teachers to answer every question, "the class would be driving the curriculum" (Kempner, 2003, p. 39). The effects of such laws and regulations have not been formally documented; however, it seems probable that under such restrictive policies teachers are more likely to censor themselves because it is simply safer to say less.

Some communities, however, have recognized how important it is for teachers to be trusted sources of information. In 2003, the school board in Leander, Texas, voted to allow teachers, beginning in eighth grade, to discuss oral and anal sex with students when teaching about STDs and to use the specific phrases "oral sex" and "anal sex." The changes were first proposed by teachers who became frustrated with their inability to address these topics despite what they perceived as students' ignorance (Batchelder, 2003, p. 9).

In 2006, the school board in the Portland suburb of North Clackamas, Oregon, decided on a similar provision during a curriculum update. In addition to approving abstinence plus HIV- and teen pregnancy–prevention curricula for middle schools and high schools, the board also gave teachers the go-ahead to answer questions from students on a list of sensitive topics including homosexuality, abortion, pornography, and some sexual acts.

While two-thirds of the board voted in favor of the updates, some members were extremely vocal in their opposition. "The curriculum normalized behavior that I believe is inappropriate, immoral, and abnormal, particularly for students in middle school," argued one member, though he refused to specify the behaviors to which he was referring (Ciardullo, 2008, p. 13).

Despite such vocal opposition, it is clear that school boards are becoming more willing to allow teachers the flexibility they need to fully inform and educate their students.

## Lightning Rods

As these debates show, not all discussions have equal potential to stir controversy. Topics such as oral sex, anal sex, and masturbation are among those considered controversial, but over the years, there are two topics that have caused the most trouble for communities across the country: condoms and homosexuality.

Though research has shown over and over again that teaching young people about condoms does not increase their likelihood of becoming sexually active but does increase the chances they will use condoms when they do, the myth of condoms as "a license for sex" persists and communities continue to struggle with this debate. For this reason, opponents of comprehensive sexuality education often term it *condom education* and suggest that such courses encourage sexual behavior by sanctioning condom use. Many community controversies have erupted when teachers have honest discussions about the benefits of condoms with their students. In 1997, the school board in Hemet, California, denied a request to include contraceptive information in the ninth-grade curriculum. In 1999, the school board in Freemont, California, voted to cut a condom demonstration from a play that had been performed in the district for 14 years. And, in 2002, a teacher in Collier, Florida, was fired after he had students in his class demonstrate how to put a condom on a banana (Kempner, 2003, p. 40).

There are signs that debates over condom discussion are waning, however, condom demonstrations remain a controversial issue that many school boards simply choose to avoid. For example, New York City recently adopted a comprehensive sexuality education curriculum. Advocates and educators worked hard to find the appropriate curriculum and were disappointed when the school system decided not to include the curriculum's condom demonstration. An administrator explained that while he agreed this was an important part of the program, the school system had lost a chancellor in an early-1990s controversy that centered, in part, around condom demonstrations and distribution and that officials were not willing to open up that issue again.

Currently, no sexuality-related discussions are as heated as those about sexual orientation, which remains the single most controversial topic in sexuality education. Controversies around including information about homosexuality in class, student clubs, and even gay teachers have been common since SIECUS began our tracking. While many other topics seem to be becoming less controversial as the years go on, sexual orientation remains divisive.

In 1995, school administrators in Solon, Iowa, cancelled a presentation about sexual orientation when members of the community, including the director of the American Family Association in Iowa, voiced opposition. The cancellation came despite the fact that the presentation had been conducted the previous year with positive results; some students who attended were moved to send letters apologizing for having harassed a gay couple who lived across the street. In 1997, teachers in Franklin County, North Carolina, were told that if students asked about HIV/AIDS they were to explain that it is a "virus transmitted primarily by contaminated needles and by a homosexual act that is illegal in North Carolina" (Kempner, 2003, p. 40).

That same year, the school board in Clayton, Georgia, chose videos about AIDS and teen pregnancy with the understanding that they could not "represent homosexuality as an acceptable lifestyle." This idea of condoning or "promoting" homosexuality is at the center of many debates. In 1995, the school board in Merrimack, New Hampshire, passed "Prohibition of Alternative Lifestyle Instruction," a highly restrictive policy that prevented teachers from providing any instruction to support "homosexuality as a positive lifestyle." The policy went far beyond sexuality education. For example, it forced a teacher to stop showing a film about Walt Whitman because it mentioned that the poet was gay. Community outrage over this decision resulted in the election of a new school board that rescinded the policy and replaced it with language saying the school would have "no program or activity which is intended to promote sexual activity or any sexual orientation." A similar situation occurred the following year in Elizabethtown, Pennsylvania, when the school board adopted a "pro-family resolution" stating that the "traditional family is under relentless attack by those who want to redefine family to include homosexual and lesbian couples and to indoctrinate children to pro-homosexual propaganda against their parents' wishes" (Kempner, 2003, p. 40). The school board modified the policy after hearing objections from hundreds of community members.

One of the more recent examples involved a video shown to students in Evesham Township, New Jersey, during the 2006–2007 school year. *That's a Family,* shown to third graders in an effort to encourage tolerance, portrays families with step-parents, adopted children, mixed-race parents, and bilingual parents. It was, however, the inclusion of families with same-sex parents that caused a furor among some residents in the school district.

The controversy broke in January 2007 after some parents, angry that their children had seen the video, complained to school administrators. In response, administrators held a forum for parents to voice their concerns. Local media outlets covered the event, which was sometimes less than civil. One parent screamed that homosexuality was a "horrible concept" and as such had no place in the Golden Rule—doing unto others as one would do unto oneself. Another called the depiction of same-sex families in the video "absolutely appalling." And, a third claimed that the school district did not have the right to show something that she felt was morally wrong.

District officials initially defended the video as an important tool in teaching tolerance of diversity. The curriculum director said, "The video makes no judgment about lifestyles . . . the video is to teach respect for the diversity of all children." Another parent agreed with the school board, saying, "You have to acknowledge that these different kinds of families exist" (Quinones, 2007).

The argument over the video continued through the summer until the school board voted 7–1 in September 2007 to stop using it. The board reasoned that the video had simply created too much controversy within the community. One board member said, "I look out here and see a community tearing itself apart. It's obvious that this video is a lightning rod" ("School District Bans Diversity," 2007).

An even more protracted battle over teaching about sexual orientation spanned at least three school years in Montgomery County, Maryland. The Montgomery County School Board originally approved a curriculum update for middle and high school health classes in November 2004. The program included a video in tenth-grade health classes that showed students how to put on a condom and a pilot program for selected schools to discuss homosexuality in the eighth- and tenth-grade Family Life Curriculum.

A small group of parents and community members disagreed with the changes and formed an organization called Citizens for Responsible Curriculum (CRC). The group campaigned against the curriculum and brought in representatives from national conservative organizations, such as Concerned Women for America and Family Research Council, to speak against it.

When the district pushed ahead with its plan to pilot the program despite the opposition, CRC and its new allies, Virginia-based Parents and Friends of Ex-Gays and Gays (PFOX) and the Liberty Council, brought a federal lawsuit against the school system. The lawsuit claimed that allowing discussions about homosexuality to take place in the schools and distributing resource materials that included information on gay-positive churches and religious groups gave preference to religions that are tolerant of homosexuality and ignored those churches that teach that homosexuality is wrong. In addition, the lawsuit claimed the school board has an "irrational phobia of the ex-gay community" (Ciardullo, 2008, p. 5).

The case was eventually settled when the school board voted to scrap the controversial curriculum and begin building a second curriculum from the ground up. Though the lessons on condoms and sexual orientation ultimately made it into the second revision of the curriculum, many parents felt that the new tightly scripted lessons were neither comprehensive nor youth-friendly. Students in the pilot program were similarly unimpressed. "Our teacher ... she read straight from the manual . . . It was very strict. Like, you couldn't ask questions," one 14-year-old explained to a reporter at the *Washington Post* (de Vise, 2007).

Still, opposition groups worked desperately throughout the summer of 2007 to postpone implementation of the curriculum. First, they appealed to the Maryland State School Board asking it to step in and halt the lessons. When the state school board refused to get involved, the groups filed an administrative appeal in circuit court in hopes of overturning its ruling. A circuit court judge ended the delay tactics in October 2007 when he ruled that the lessons could be implemented. Nonetheless, opponents vowed to continue their crusade against the program (Ciardullo, 2008, p. 5).

Again, the fact that these battles are so frequent and so heated may say less about sexuality education and more about society as a whole. It is not a coincidence that these battles have become more incendiary as the issue of same-sex marriage became the subject of front page news, lawsuits, and ballot initiatives. In fact, many people who watched the Evesham controversy unfold felt that those who spoke out against the video were so vehement in their opposition, at least in part, because they were disappointed by a state court and legislative decision that ultimately allowed same-sex civil unions in New Jersey. At the same time, it is also becoming clear that these debates are in many ways the last hold that vocal conservative minorities have over communities.

## THE FUTURE OF SEXUALITY EDUCATION

There is no question that opponents of sexuality education have been remarkably successful in the past decade when it comes to promoting their brand of "sexuality education." Not only have they built a multimillion dollar industry with federal funds, but they have also used the issue of sexuality education, and their call for abstinence-only-until-marriage, to shore up members and support. For many years, opponents really called the shots in communities across the country. They were the vocal ones, the organized ones, the ones who got themselves elected to the school board, and as a result, they were often the ones who won. Even in communities where sexuality education never erupted into a controversy, there was a growing sense that it was better to play it safe and talk about less.

But their stronghold on this issue may be changing. As we watched the Far Right's brand of sexuality education rise throughout the last two decades, we seem to be watching it fall now. Research confirms that these programs are not helping young people delay sexual behavior. Despite two decades of programs, there are no published studies in the professional literature that show that abstinence-only programs will result in young people delaying sexual intercourse. In fact, a federally funded evaluation of Title V abstinence-only-until-marriage programs, released in April 2007, found these programs to be ineffective. The study, conducted by Mathematica Policy Research, Inc., on behalf of the U.S. Department of Health and Human Services, found no evidence that abstinence-only-until-marriage programs increased rates of sexual abstinence among participants. Students in the abstinence-only-until-marriage programs had a similar age of first sex and similar numbers of sexual partners as their peers who were not in the programs (Trenholm, Devaney, Fortson, Quay, Wheeler, & Clark, 2007). In addition, a "meta-study" published in the *British Medical Journal* examined the results of 13 evaluations of abstinence-only programs, which together included almost 16,000 students. The study found that abstinence-only-until-marriage programs were ineffective in changing any of the behaviors that were examined, including the rate of vaginal sex, number of sexual partners, and condom use. The rates of pregnancy and sexually transmitted diseases (STDs) among participants in abstinence-only-until-marriage programs were unaffected. As a result of this meta-study, the researchers concluded that recent declines in the U.S. rate of teen pregnancy were most likely the result of improved use of contraception rather than a decrease in sexual activity (Underhill, Montgomery, & Operario, 2007).

Concern is growing among parents, educators, and politicians as new statistics show that the teen birth rate is on the rise for the first time in over a decade and that the rates of STIs among young people, especially young women, is alarmingly high. A recent study by the Centers for Disease Control and Prevention found that one in four adolescent girls had an STI (Forhan, 2008). Between 2005 and 2006, the teen birth rate rose by 3 percent; this was the first increase in a decade (Ventura, 2007). Moreover, countless public opinion surveys show that broad-based support exists for teaching young people about sexuality and even about those topics—abortion, sexual orientation, and contraception, to name a few—with a history of controversy behind them.

So, now is a perfect time for advocates of comprehensive sexuality education to become more involved and make changes. Whether it is denying a request to restrict sexuality education, ridding a school of an abstinence-only-until-marriage program, or instituting a comprehensive curriculum where none previously existed, advocates can take advantage of the turning tides and improve the state of sexuality education in their community. A few simple ideas and rules can help prevent controversy or, at the very least, move it along quickly.

## Know the Facts

Anyone who wishes to advocate for sexuality education must start by becoming fully informed about what is being taught in the schools, who makes decisions, and the issue as a whole.

While debates over sexuality education often make it seem like an either/ or issue—communities are either providing comprehensive sexuality education *or* strict abstinence-only-until-marriage programming—more often than not the real program in a school falls somewhere in-between. Perhaps it is an abstinence-only-until-marriage curriculum that the teacher supplements with lessons on contraception or a comprehensive sexuality education from which lessons on condoms and sexual orientation have been removed.

Advocates for comprehensive sexuality education must find out exactly what is being taught in their schools. They can do this by reading through the curriculum (which most schools make available to parents) and talking to those individuals most involved in its implementation, such as the district's health coordinator and the classroom teachers responsible for the subject matter. In addition to finding out what is taught, advocates should use these discussions to try and discern how these individuals feel about sexuality education and whether they think the current program is adequate. Their opinions can be very valuable when making a plea for a change.

Knowing what young people are and are not learning can help advocates for comprehensive sexuality education point to the need for improved programs. Other local information can also help, especially statistics on teen sexual behavior, STDs, and pregnancy. Many communities are spurred into action when they realize the health issues that their teens are dealing with. For example, a number of years ago, advocates in Hartford, Connecticut, were able to move the community toward a comprehensive approach to contraception education when they made it broadly known that in one year more teen girls gave birth than graduated from high school. Similarly, in October of 2006, in St. Lucie County, Florida, school officials, health professionals, and community members came together as the Executive Roundtable to explore the possibility of revising the county's sexuality education and HIV/AIDS–prevention programs in public schools after learning that, among other things, St. Lucie County has the highest incidence of HIV/ AIDS among African Americans in any Florida county (Ciardullo, 2008, p. 11).

Local controversies, however, always take place in the broader context of the national debate over sexuality education. As such, advocates also need to know the current research and the arguments that opponents are using. The same arguments have been and will be used for years, and knowing these arguments in advance can help advocates keep their cool and respond quickly. (SIECUS's *Community Action Kit,* www.communityactionkit.org, can help advocates with this homework by taking them step-by-step through the arguments opponents use against comprehensive sexuality education and the information they need to counter these arguments.)

## Know the School Board

Advocates not only need information about local education and statistics, but they also need to become knowledgeable about local politics. Most local debates over sexuality education cannot be resolved without the input of the school board because this body sets curricula direction for schools. Not only is it important for advocates to understand how their school board operates, it is important to know the opinions of each of its members. Historically, school board members vary widely in their knowledge of and commitment to sexuality education. Some, especially in communities that have experienced controversies in the past, may have used this very issue to get elected, while others may have given this issue nary a thought before joining the board. Understanding where each board member is coming from, through personal conversations, can be very enlightening. When there is no debate over sexuality education (or other often-contested issues such as the budget), school board meetings are notoriously underattended; so it is easier for any individual attendee to approach the board members, ask questions, and gather information. Frequent attendance at meetings can help advocates know and become known by members of the board.

Moreover, school boards often create advisory committees to help guide curricula decisions. Some states actually mandate that each district has such a committee. These committees, made up of parents, educators, clergy, students, and communities members appointed by the school board, often have a significant say in how the school board will ultimately vote. Advocates for sexuality education can make a real difference by becoming part of these committees.

For example, in 2007, the AIDS/Safe and Drug-Free Schools Advisory Committee in Crawfordsville, Indiana, which is composed of local doctors and nurses, public health personnel, school staff, parents, community members, and students, suggested that the school expand its eighth-grade sexuality education to include a two-day lesson on contraception. The school had been using "Creating Positive Relationships (CPR)," an abstinence-only program produced by an organization of the same name that received a grant from the Indiana Department of Health through the federal Title V abstinence-only-until-marriage funding stream. The pastor of a local Baptist church asked the board to stick with the abstinence-only-until-marriage curriculum, saying that he's worried more comprehensive lessons will follow. The school nurse, however, said that although teachers are happy with the CPR program, "it was kind of weak on teaching about HIV, disease prevention and pregnancy prevention." She believes the new lesson will better inform the nearly half of the student body that is already sexually active. The board adopted the committee's recommendation by a 3–2 vote in May 2007 (Ciardullo, 2008, p. 10).

Stories like this show that these organized groups of citizens can, in fact, make a large difference in what young people are learning.

## Work the Press

Another important way for advocates to get their message out is to develop a relationship with local press. The press, primarily local newspapers, has the ability to set the tone of a controversy. Local education reporters seize on controversy related to sexuality education for the same reason advertisers use women in bikinis to sell toothpaste: sex sells. Moreover, because controversy sells in the media, an article that simply states a school board has reached an amicable decision about sexuality education will not be as interesting as one in which two sides of a seemingly intractable debate each declare themselves to be right. Advocates for comprehensive sexuality education need to watch the media carefully and try as best as possible to shape press coverage. This can be especially difficult—sometimes the best thing you can have is good press, and sometimes no news is good news. (The SIECUS *Community Action Kit*, www.communityactionkit.org, provides more specific advice on how to work with the press.)

For example, by allowing the press to cover it, school administrators in Evesham turned what should have been a small meeting of those parents whose children had seen, or were going to see, the controversial video on diverse families into a national media event. The press coverage culminated in Fox News Channel's talk show host Bill O'Reilly declaring that he, in fact, knew what was best for the students of this community he'd never visited. This type of media circus can sometimes be avoided if advocates and school administrators work together to control press coverage.

Parents in Loudon County, Virginia, did just that and used the media to their advantage when they wanted to ensure that abstinence-only-until-marriage speaker Keith Deltano was never again invited to their schools. Deltano, who describes himself as an "educational comedian," was invited to speak by the principal despite the fact that parents objected to his inaccurate, fear-based performance. By contacting the press and using professional public relations techniques, such as a press release, parents were able to call attention to this issue. In fact, a story ran in the *Washington Post* under the headline "The Abstinence Shtick, Minus Jesus" (Ciardullo, 2008, p. 4).

Each situation is different, and advocates must decide if and when to involve the press in the controversy with the understanding that those on the other side may do so at anytime. The most important thing, however, is that advocates are prepared to bring a story to the media's attention, or to correct misinformation that appears in the media, by contacting reporters or issuing press releases.

## Parents Are the Most Important

The most important group of people in any community debate is very simply those parents whose children are impacted by the outcome of that debate. The best spokespeople for either side of an issue—whether they are speaking to the school board or the press—are parents who have a passionate opinion about what they want for their children. The Far Right certainly knows this. Advocates for comprehensive sexuality education, therefore, must organize and galvanize parents supportive of their views.

It is also helpful to know what parents in the community are thinking before an issue about sexuality education is brought up. Administrators and parent groups often conduct polls. Some are formal, while others are simply a survey of parents leaving the grocery story. Either way, finding out what parents want can help advocates make change and avoid controversy.

For example, district officials in Howell, Michigan, charged with reviewing the sexuality education curriculum utilized local polling to engage parents on the issue. In April 2006, more than 600 parents responded to the Web-based poll, which relied on standard language developed by the Michigan Department of Education. When asked, most parents wanted schools to talk about condoms as a method of disease prevention, birth control, and even sexual orientation. With these reassuring numbers in hand, the sexuality education advisory board proposed new changes to the seventh grade curriculum (Ciardullo, 2008, p. 15).

It is important to remember, however, that not all parents in a district have, or should have, equal say in each decision. The most important voices are always those parents whose children are currently in a program or likely to be in the program soon. Many of the parents complaining about the family diversity video that was at issue in Evesham, New Jersey, had older children who had not seen the video and were not scheduled to do so. And, a recent debate over a peer education program in Gloucester, New Jersey, made media headlines despite the fact that those parents who were complaining did not have children in the program, and the parents who did were very pleased with it. The program required parental permission before students could participate and as such, parents of students not in the program had no grounds for complaint. School administrators and school boards should consider limiting participation in public forums and debates to those parents who have children in the program being discussed.

Perhaps the single most important lesson we can take from the Far Right's success is the benefit of organizing even a very small group of parents. Advocates for comprehensive sexuality education can start by organizing groups of parents with students at each grade level. Together these parents can argue for sexuality education throughout the school years, and if there is ever a question of a program at a specific grade level, advocates can call on those parents in particular.

## Include Students as Advocates

Students are in a unique position to know both what their peers need from sexuality education and what they are and are not getting. Over the years, many students have voiced their concerns about the inadequate education they were receiving, and in many communities they played an integral role in making change. For example, a group of students at Franklin High School in Macon County, North Carolina, assessed the results of the Youth Risk Behavior Surveillance System—a survey of a wide variety of behaviors conducted biennially by the Centers for Disease Control and Prevention (CDC)—and decided that sexual activity was the most troubling issue among their peers. The students pointed to the sizeable number of girls in their high school who were pregnant and determined that while illicit drug use (including alcohol) is routinely addressed in schools, sexual activity remains taboo and shrouded in myths and misinformation.

The students, with help from the North Carolina Department of Public Instruction, the Macon County Health Department, SIECUS, and others, developed a new peer-education program titled "Sexy Abs—Sense Enough to Expand Your Awareness About Sex." "Sexy Abs" was designed to be a "peer talk program," which would be presented to area middle-school students by trained high-school students.

The students presented an outline of the program to the school board in April 2007 and board members were supportive. Though he had initially also been supportive, the superintendent rejected the program without any board input saying, "there would be no kids teaching kids about sex" (Seay, 2007).

Still, the students were successful in making the school board aware of the need for more sexuality education. One school board member "expressed disappointment" when she learned that the issue would not go forward. "I think they would have done a fine job," she said. "We need to have people stand up and say this is something that is needed" (Seay, 2007). Another board member also felt let down: "We got an email with the rough draft . . . with a few changes, I would have no problem with it" (Seay, 2007). Many other members of the board also felt that the topic was prematurely pulled from discussion (Ciardullo, 2008, p. 18).

Advocates for comprehensive sexuality education should remember that students are most impacted by decisions about sexuality education. Parents, school board members, administrators, and educators should solicit young people's opinions in designing programs as well as ask them to weigh in on ideological debates. Moreover, advocates in the middle of any kind of controversy should consider using students—either current high-school students or recent graduates from the school—as spokespeople who can provide decision makers and the media with a front-line view of what is being taught and why it is important or how it can be improved.

## Outside Groups

There are groups on the national, state, and local level dedicated to promoting either sexuality education or abstinence-only-until-marriage programs. SIECUS is, of course, one of those groups, as are the groups such as PFOX and the Family Research Council mobilized against teaching about sexual orientation in Montgomery County. These groups certainly have a role in local sexuality education debates. As experts on their position and professionals who have been through it before, these groups understand the issues well and can help advocates prepare arguments and get their message out.

At the same time, as outsiders who do not live in the community or send their children to the schools, these groups should never be considered the most important voice in a debate. It is far more important that administrators and school board members listen to the voices of the parents whose children will be directly impacted by their decisions. SIECUS is very cognizant of our role in debates. We are happy to serve as advisors and cheerleaders, and when asked we are happy to speak at forums or engage reporters. However, we whole-heartedly believe that ours is not the most important opinion in a community debate, and we don't feel it is appropriate for us to be the only or even the loudest voice. Moreover, we have learned that it is often best for us to work with advocates behind the scenes, as our reputation precedes us and in some communities our involvement does more harm than good.

Advocates need to weigh the benefits of having outside organizations involved with the risks, and any good advocacy organization can help them do just that.

## IT IS OUR TURN

The old adage, "the squeaky wheel gets the grease," may be the simple statement that gave rise to the abstinence-only-until-marriage movement. The Far Right was organized, it was unified, and it was loud.

Today, however, the momentum has shifted. Advocates for comprehensive sexuality education are in a perfect position to approach school boards and defend or improve programs. The research is in, states have spoken by rejecting abstinence-only-until-marriage funds, and even the media, especially print media, has begun to treat abstinence-only-until-marriage programs as a failed concept. Advocates should not waste this important opportunity.

No one is saying this is going to be easy. Even with a new administration, the federal government's funding for abstinence-only-until-marriage programs will not dry up overnight. It will take effort at all levels. Advocates for comprehensive sexuality education at the national level will need to continue to call for an end of funding for abstinence-only-until-marriage programs and ask Congress to shift some of those monies to more comprehensive programs. On the state level, advocates will need to ask their lawmaker to stop participation in the federal abstinence-only-until-marriage program (if they haven't already done so) and to remove all mention of abstinence-only-until-marriage programs from state law. And on the local level, advocates need to spend time educating school board members to make sure they are on the right track and won't be easily knocked off by controversy.

There is work to be done for sure, but there is an opportunity here that cannot be wasted. The Far Right's success shows the importance of organizing on the local level, approaching the school board, and making a demand. Now, it is our turn.

## REFERENCES

Associated Press. (2003, June 27). Push on to teach abstinence, rather than birth control." *The Advocate* (CT).

Batchelder, M. (2003). Trends 2002–2003: A tug-of-war between abstinence-only and comprehensive sexuality education. *SIECUS Report, 31*(6), 5–16.

Carrera, M. (1971). Preparation of a sex educator: A historical overview. *The Family Coordinator, 20*(2), 99–108.

Ciardullo, M. (2005). Advocates on both sides are as passionate as ever: SIECUS controversy report 2004–2005 school year. *SIECUS Report, 33*(4), 4–19.

Ciardullo, M. (2008). Controversy report 2006–07 school year: Pendulum begins to swing back: Communities and schools moving towards more practical approaches to sexuality education. New York: The Sexuality Information and Education Council of the United States.

de Vise, D. (2007 March). Montgomery starts sex-ed pilot program. *The Washington Post.* Retrieved March 7, 2007, from www.washingtonpost.com/wp-dyn/content/article/2007/03/06/AR2007030602331.html

Fisher, M. (2007, February). Don't gum up sex-ed; leave instruction to professional teachers." *Washington Post.* Retrieved September 15, 2007, from www.washingtonpost.com/wpdyn/content/article/2007/02/14/AR2007021401477.html

Forhan, S. (2008). *Nationally representative CDC study finds 1 in 4 teenage girls has a sexually transmitted disease.* Presentation given at 2008 National STD Prevention Conference, Chicago, Illinois, March 11, 2008.

Irvine, J. (2004). Talk about sex: The battles over sex education in the United States. Berkley: University of California Press.

John Birch Society. (2008). Political Research Associates. Retrieved December 20, 2008, from http://www.publiceye.org/tooclose/jbs.html

Kempner, M. (2001). Toward a sexually healthy America: Abstinence-only-until-marriage programs that try to keep our youth scared chaste. New York: The Sexuality Information and Education Council of the United States.

Kempner, M. (2003). A controversial decade: 10 years of tracking debates around sexuality education. *SIECUS Report, 31*(6), 33–48.

Mast, C. K. (2001). Sex respect: The option for true sexual freedom, student workbook. Bradley, IL: Sex Respect.

Price, C. (1999, October 14). Debate runs hot over school agenda," *Taunton* (MA) *Daily Gazette.*

Quinones, T. (2007, January 31). Parents outraged by "family" video presentation," *CBS3.com.* Retrieved January 31, 2007, from http://cbs3.com/topstories/local_story_030235258.html

School district bans diversity video because it includes gay couples. (2007 September). *365gay.com.* Retrieved September 4, 2007, from www.365gay.com/Newscon07/09/090307video.htm

Seay, B. (2007, May). Sexy Abs' shot down by Superintendent Brigman. *The Macon County News & Shopping Guide.* Retrieved May 22, 2007, from http://maconnews.com/index.php?option=com_content&task=view&id=659&Itemid=34

Sex in the classroom. (1969, July 25). *Time Magazine.* Retrieved January 7, 2009, from http://www.time.com/time/magazine/article/0,9171,901130-2,00.html

Trenholm, C., Devaney, B., Fortson, K., Quay, L., Wheeler, J., and Clark, M. (2007). *Impacts of four Title V, Section 510 abstinence education programs: Final report.* Trenton, NJ: Mathematica Policy Research, Inc.

Underhill, K., Montgomery, P., & Operario, D. (2007, July). Sexual abstinence only programmes to prevent HIV infection in high income countries: Systematic review. *British Medical Journal.* Retrieved August 13, 2007, from http://bmj.com/cgi/content/full/335/7613/248

Ventura, S. (2007). *Statcast: Teen unmarried births on the rise.* Atlanta: National Center for Health Statistics. Retrieved June 19, 2008, from http://www.cdc.gov/nchs/pressroom/07newsreleases/teenbirth.htm

Yarber, W. (1994). Past, present and future perspectives on sexuality education. In J. C. Drolet & K. Clark (Eds.), *The sexuality education challenge, promoting healthy sexuality in young people* (pp. 3–28). Santa Cruz, CA: ETR Associates.

# Chapter Nine

# VALUES-FREE SEXUALITY EDUCATION: MYTH OR REALITY?

*John P. Elia and Mickey J. Eliason*

It is not surprising that [school-based] sex education has become one of the most contentious areas of the curriculum, with disagreements surfacing at the most fundamental level.

> J. Mark Halstead and Michael J. Reiss, 2003, p. 15

Essentially, the debate about sex education right now is a debate about values, but as often the case in America, questions about values get obscured in the public arena by questions about practicalities.

> Kristin Luker, 2006, p. 243

Sexuality education is perhaps the most hotly debated curricular issue in American schools. The arguments about it range from advocating not including sexuality studies in the elementary or secondary school curriculum at all, or teaching youth to postpone sexual activity with others until marriage, to teaching about human sexuality from a comprehensive perspective including a wide range of topics from abstinence to variations in sexual and gender expression. These are only three approaches to sexuality education among many forms. However, no matter what form of sexuality education one advocates or opposes, the arguments for or against are based on the values held by individuals, groups of individuals, or communities about what is in the best interest of youth and perhaps of society at large regarding sexual matters. In general, however, the dispute is often framed as one between the abstinence-only-until-marriage (AOUM) advocates versus the comprehensive sexuality education proponents. This debate is hardly new as it has been raging to lesser and greater degrees for about a century. As the quote from Kristin Luker's (2006) book *When Sex Goes to School* suggests, the dispute about sexuality education falls squarely in the arena of values. The questions about "practicalities" (also framed as "effectiveness" or the need to "fix" some problem, such as teen pregnancy) reflect various values about what school-based sexuality education ought to achieve attitudinally and behaviorally. There is an intense national debate about what the outcomes of sexuality education should be. For instance, proponents of AOUM sexuality education suggest that youth ought to postpone sexual activity with others until marriage. Furthermore, they claim that premarital sexuality will likely lead to physical and psychological harm (see E below in the A-H criteria of Title V), yet there is no evidence from research to support this claim. Section 510 of Title V's Social Security Act states that:

> For purposes of this section, the term "abstinence education" means an educational or motivational program which—(A) has as its exclusive purpose, teaching the social, psychological, and health gains to be realized by abstaining from sexual activity; (B) teaches abstinence from sexual activity outside marriage as the expected standard for all school age children; (C) teaches that abstinence from sexual activity is the only certain way to avoid out-of-wedlock pregnancy, sexually transmitted diseases, and other associated health problems; (D) teaches that a mutually faithful monogamous relationship in context of marriage is the expected standard of human sexual activity; (E) teaches that sexual activity outside of the context of marriage is likely to have harmful psychological and physical effects; (F) teaches that bearing children out-of-wedlock is likely to have harmful consequences for the child, the child's parents, and society; (G) teaches young people how to reject sexual advances and how alcohol and drug use increases vulnerability to sexual advances; and (H) teaches the importance of attaining self-sufficiency before engaging in sexual activity. (Social Security Online, 2008)

On the other side of the debate are advocates of what is called "comprehensive sexuality education" who claim that while abstinence is an acceptable sexual lifestyle choice, a broad array of topics need to be covered in sexuality education, including biological aspects of sexuality, sexual health, contraception, psycho–social aspects of sexuality, various sexual lifestyles and choices, and other sexual topics.

These two approaches to sexuality education represent two quite divergent value positions. As such, they are usually the only ones represented in the media and popular culture in general, presenting a debate on the issues. However, there are other sexuality education paradigms that represent other value systems; we will explore these later in this chapter. As a potential way of getting past the debate, some have suggested approaching sexuality education from a *value-free* perspective. In the very public sexuality education debates, some have weighed in, declaring that a value-free sexuality education is the way to proceed to transcend the debate. Inherent in this solution is that it is possible to teach sexuality in a value-free way, based on presentation of neutral scientific facts, and that it is possible to reach consensus about what the facts are and what they mean. We argue in this chapter that there is no such thing as value-free or objective sexuality education. Even if it were possible to teach in a value-free or neutral fashion, would that be somehow more prudent, advantageous, or even ethically responsible? We believe the goals of schooling, in part, are to produce responsible and productive citizens, and schools do this by instilling values.

In this chapter, we will review the most common forms of sexuality education and discuss the underlying value systems that inform each one. Before engaging in a discussion about various forms of sexuality education, however, we consider evidence making it unequivocal that sexuality education can never be value-free. Some might suggest, for example, that sexuality education just stick to the "facts." For instance, here are a few "facts":

1. Condoms are 98 percent effective in preventing pregnancy.
2. The clitoris' only function is female sexual pleasure.
3. The Bible says masturbation is sinful.

Even within these "facts" there is controversy. The first fact is based on many years of research and has been confirmed scientifically (see, for example, Hatcher, Trussell & Nelson, 2007). Yet, some people state that this is a belief, not a fact, and ignore the scientific proof altogether. Another fact open to controversy is that condoms are 98 percent effective in preventing pregnancy, whereby critics emphasize the 2 percent failure rate in preventing pregnancy and note that this risk is unacceptably high. Proponents of comprehensive sexuality education claim these percentages are used as scare tactics to support the AOUM approach on the topic as well as to discredit those who oppose AOUM. Some proponents of AOUM sexuality education programs have declared that the failure rate of condoms is much higher, leading some critics to try to hold these programs to "medically accurate" information (U.S. House of Representatives Committee on Government Reform, 2004), however, the concept of "medically accurate" has no power for those who declare that science is merely one belief system among many.

The second widely accepted fact—that the only purpose of the clitoris is for female sexual pleasure—would rarely be part of most sexuality education curricula because of a belief (value judgment) that children do not need to know or learn about the pleasure aspects of sexuality, or a belief that that kind of information may lead to premature sexual activity. Finally, the third fact is true if one is a believer in the literal truth of the Judeo-Christian Bible, but not if one is not Jewish or Christian, or if one believes that the Bible must be inter-preted within its historical context. This third example points out that "facts" are not limited to "science" but to other belief systems as well. People some-times assign values to "facts," and posit facts based on values and beliefs. Even if individuals stick to facts generated from rigorous scientific studies, science does not exist in a vacuum devoid of cultural influences. For that reason, it is important to make such values transparent so that parents, teachers, and other concerned individuals can make informed choices about sexuality education.

## MORE EVIDENCE THAT SEXUALITY EDUCATION IS VALUE-LADEN: FUNDAMENTAL CONTROVERSIAL QUESTIONS

The following fundamental questions are often posed in response to sexual-ity education and reveal some of the cultural anxieties that underlie the con-sequences of sexuality education, and therefore inform the issue of values in sexuality education.

- The decision to teach/include any form of sexuality education in schools a declara-tion of values?
- What constitutes the content of sexuality education? Does it refer only to repro-ductive anatomy and physiology? Does it include teaching abstinence or telling people how to have sex or how to build intimate relationships? Does it include dis-cussions of gender and sexual identity? Does it present both the potential positive and negative consequences of various sexual activities in a balanced and rational way?
- Who is the arbiter who determines the content of sexuality education?
- Do children need sexuality education? If yes, why? Is it for their protection, to have a satisfying and fulfilling life, to make responsible decisions? If yes, at what age or grade should sexuality education begin?
- Who is—and should be—responsible for sexuality education? Parents, schools, religious leaders, the media, or others?
- How should sexuality education be taught in terms of pedagogical practices? What materials should be used?
- How should sexuality education include issues of sexual preference/orientation and identity, same-sex behaviors, and gender identity and expression, diverse relation-ship structures and sexual behaviors? Or should it not include these issues at all?
- What are the desired outcomes of sexuality education? Should those outcomes include abstaining from sex until marriage, abstaining from sexual activity with others until adulthood, having sex in a safe and responsible manner, giving and receiving pleasure, and experiencing sex/sexuality as an integral aspect of one's life?

These questions about sexuality education represent only the tip of the prover-bial iceberg when considering the plethora of questions that might be raised about this topic.

## SEXUAL VALUES IN CONTEXT

U.S. society cannot even collectively agree on a definition of *sex*, as the debate over former President Bill Clinton and Monica Lewinsky so painfully highlighted in 1998 when Clinton declared, "I did not have sex with that woman" (referring to the fact that he did not engage in penis–vaginal intercourse even though he received oral sex from her; Crooks & Baur, 2008). The term *sex* is often misunderstood to be synonymous with penis–vaginal intercourse as the national debate about their affair revealed. Agreement about such a definition—of what constitutes sex—and a common understanding of concepts in human sexuality will likely only emerge after long and painful public discussions, as sexuality in general remains a highly value-laden and taboo topic. If there was such a thing as values-free sexuality education, there would be more dispassionate clarity about sexual matters. But obviously, this is not the case.

Historically, sexuality education has been in response to a series of sex panics over the past century, and all of them were motivated by religious, political, and cultural ideologies when it was perceived that societal sexual mores were departing from culturally dominant expectations of sexual attitudes and behaviors. For instance, sexuality education was initially offered in U.S. schools in the early twentieth century largely because of the social hygiene movement that, in part, sought to educate students about the deleterious effects of "venereal diseases," and embodying the virtues of a socially and sexually respectable lifestyle based on Victorian values (McKay, 1999; Moran, 2000). Other factors during the late nineteenth and early twentieth centuries sparked a sex panic, which included rising divorce rates, in addition to many women deciding to postpone marriage or forego getting married altogether (Luker, 2006). In part, this led to sexuality education being used as a corrective force. Another example of a sex panic occurred in the mid-1990s with the Welfare Reform legislation that resulted in federal funding of AOUM sexuality education in schools and community-based organizations, which was fueled by the worry about the incidence and prevalence of sexually transmitted infections (STIs) and teen pregnancy. The AOUM approach has been, and continues to be, a deeply contested issue. Table 9.1 shows a timeline of some historical events that impacted how members of our society thought and continue to think about sexuality education of children and adolescents.

This table provides a historical timeline of a few of the major events in the history of sexuality education and of sexuality in general in the United States from the early twentieth century to the present. Each event resulted in societal debates that highlighted clashing value systems.

Sexuality education was originally taught in schools to reinforce Victorian morality, stem the tide of sexually transmitted infections (Brandt, 1987;

**Table 9.1**
**Timeline of Selected Historical Events Related to Sexuality Education**

| Historical Time Period | Key Value-laden Events |
| --- | --- |
| Early 1900s | Venereal disease |
| | Social Hygiene Movement at end of Victorian Era |
| | Development of the concept of the adolescent |
| 1940s | WWII led to greater independence of women |
| | Urbanization and sexual cultures |
| | Kinsey's report on male sexuality |
| 1950s | Kinsey's report on female sexuality |
| | McCarthyism and witch hunts of gays and lesbians |
| | Homophile movement |
| 1960s/70s | Birth control pill separates sex and reproduction |
| | Sexual revolution |
| | Liberation movements: women, civil rights, gay |
| 1980s | HIV/AIDS |
| | Rise in fundamentalism worldwide |
| | 1981: Adolescent Family Life Act (AFLA) |
| 1990s | Viagra and the marketing of sex |
| | Clinton/Lewinsky hearings and defining sex |
| | Defense of marriage act |
| | Welfare reform and rise of abstinence-only education |
| 2000s | Community-based abstinence-only funding |
| | Debates about same-sex marriage |
| | HPV vaccine |

Campos, 2002; D'Emilio, & Freedman, 1988; Elia, 2000), and shore up the institution of marriage, which was on the decline for a number of reasons during the late nineteenth and early twentieth centuries (Luker, 2006). The reasons why sexuality education was offered were steeped in values. The values that were being taught both implicitly and explicitly were to uphold the sexual morality espoused by Victorianism in general, promote sexual health, and strengthen heterosexual marriage. Remarkably, not much has changed in the century that sexuality education has been a part of the public school curriculum. Currently, the most publicly funded sexuality education in the United States is the AOUM approach, which echoes much of what constituted the initial school-based sexuality education in the early twentieth century. Sexuality education in the twenty-first century is still aimed at upholding Victorian standards of morality, but the major difference between the early 1900s and recent times is that the federal government is now in the business of funding and regulating sexuality education and promoting heterosexual marriage.

## CURRENT MODELS OF SEXUALITY EDUCATION

Most of the discussion about sexuality education programs in the United States might lead one to believe that there are only two forms: AOUM and comprehensive sexuality education.

This simplistic classification obscures some of the more subtle differences in the wide variety of programs that are available today. In the remainder of this chapter, we categorize current sexuality education models/philosophies into four types that fall along an information continuum, from providing no information about sexuality to providing a comprehensive coverage of sexuality topics. We recognize that the continuum is broader than these four types and that there are approaches/programs/models that fall between the four main types we outline. These points on the continuum represent a variety of values about sexuality education, political battle lines, pedagogical differences, and culture wars that have been waged over the past century. The four models include:

- *No School-Based Sexuality Education:* This model holds that children need to be protected from sexuality, thus sexuality education in the schools is deliberately avoided. Such advocates for no sexuality education believe that sexuality is inherently a private adult matter and has no place in the classroom. Additionally, these individuals believe that sexuality is a natural part of life and that nature will take its course, without the benefit of explicit instruction.
- *Abstinence-Only-Until-Marriage (AOUM) Sexuality Education:* This view maintains that sexual behavior belongs only within heterosexual marriage, thus no education is necessary except that which emphasizes refusal skills. This form of sexuality education is currently sanctioned and funded by the U.S. government and found in countless public schools.
- *Abstinence-Based Sexuality Education:* In this approach, sexual abstinence is presented as the best option for youth, but proponents recognize that in reality, many teens are sexually active so they need information to reduce their risks (therefore this is often referred to as the "harm reduction model"). This model is often touted as values-free sexuality education, and before the late 1990s, it was the most common form of sexuality education in the United States.
- *Comprehensive Sexuality Education (CSE):* This approach contends that sexuality has to do with much more than sexual behaviors and is a core element of human life. Therefore, children and adolescents need age-appropriate and developmentally appropriate education about a wide range of topics related to sexuality, and they need to learn about both risks and pleasures/privileges of sexual behavior. Because of its inclusion of anything other than abstinence only, CSE is sometimes labeled as liberal sexuality education.

We will describe these four models, which vary on several dimensions, but we would like to first acknowledge that there are many additional points along this continuum where sexuality education programming may fall. We present values inherent in each level of the model, which can be characterized as representing a political continuum ranging from very conservative to liberal. Admittedly, these terms are somewhat limited in relation to human sexuality, having different meanings than strictly falling along political party identifications because sexuality education curriculum can be viewed through many lenses: religion, politics, moral/ethical perspectives, feminism, queer theory, critical theory, critical pedagogy, scientific (biomedical), and human rights/social justice, to name just a few. Some of these perspectives can be categorized as essentializing (meaning that sexuality is a fixed biological phenomenon that is universal), social constructionist (whereby sexuality is dependent on the historical, cultural, political, and geographic contexts; De Cecco & Elia, 1993), or interactionist (considering sexuality a combination of biological and sociocultural factors). Alternatively, the continuum could be viewed along a continua ranging from danger to pleasure—depending on whether or not the curriculum focuses on the degree to which sex is portrayed as risky and dangerous or as a source of pleasure and life satisfaction. These various perspectives or worldviews can be placed imperfectly along the continuum outlined in the models 1 through 4 of sexuality education discussed later. Within each model, we need to consider issues of content and interpretation of the meanings of sex, gender, and sexuality, and we summarize some of the values found in each model in Table 9.2.

## Model 1: No Sexuality Education

This model is based on the idea that children need to be protected from sexuality because sexuality marks an essential border between child and adulthood that must be maintained (Renold, 2005). Gilbert (2004) proposed that sexuality precedes language and is ever-present, but our contemporary culture has restricted its expression to adults. This boundary is important because some experts pose that sexual knowledge is believed to be dangerous to the child, who is inherently "innocent" and "asexual" (Levine, 2002). While Freud postulated that sexuality is inherent in the individual from the time of birth, his ideas may have created one of the first "sex panics" regarding children, causing caution and warning. For example, Foucault (1978) noted, "children were surrounded by an entire watch-crew of parents, nurses, servants, educators, and doctors, all attentive to the least manifestations of . . . sex" (p. 98). Any sign of sexual knowledge in the supposedly chaste child is thus construed as a sign of pathology. Additionally, Epstein and Johnson (1998) noted, sexual

**Table 9.2**
**Sexuality Education Models and Values about Gender, Sexual Behavior, and Sexual Identities**

| Model | Gender | Sexual Behavior | Sexual Identities |
|---|---|---|---|
| No Education | Status Quo ("traditional" views of male and female as opposites that are biologically and psychologically distinct) | The only acceptable behavior is heterosexual missionary style married vaginal intercourse. Children must be protected from any sex talk. | LGBTQ people and issues are unacceptable, unspeakable. |
| Abstinence-Only-Until-Marriage | Status Quo | Same, except adolescents need to learn refusal skills. | LGBTQ unacceptable |
| Abstinence-Based | Status Quo | Recognizes that the majority of people engage in premarital sex; that sexual activities are varied, but focus on the risk aspects of sex | Recognizes that some people are LGBTQ, but focus on risk behaviors rather than identities. |
| Comprehensive Sexuality Education | Challenges the status quo by introducing gender socialization, gender discrimination, and gendered sexual violence. | Proposes that people engage in a wide variety of sexual activities for a diverse number of reasons. Recognizes marriage as a social construct, one form of relationship. | Teaches about sexual and gender identities and behaviors as normal variants of human expression. |

innocence is "something that adults wish upon children, not a natural feature of childhood itself" (p. 97).

In present-day discourses, attempts to keep sexual knowledge from children have manifested in several forms, such as in the political arena when former U.S. Surgeon General Jocelyn Elders was fired for mentioning that children should learn about masturbation; in attempts to regulate what children see on television, in movies, and on the Internet (via parental controls and rating systems); through laws (age of consent, laws prohibiting adult/child sexual contact); and in restrictions on sexual content in sexuality education programs and the types of books contained and available in school libraries. In spite of this policing and attempt to control access to sexual information, such information is still easily accessible to children and adolescents.

Ironically, the attempts to control sexual content are much more intense than attempts to control violent content in the media. Renold (2005) demonstrated how imbedded heteronormativity is in our culture. Yep (2003) identifies heteronormativity as a process that "makes heterosexuality hegemonic through the process of normalization...[which] is a site of violence in the lives of women, men, and transgenders—across the spectrum of sexualities—in modern Western societies" (p. 18). Gendered sexuality is in the life of even primary school children as part of the "hidden" curriculum of schools. Regarding gender, this model upholds the status quo of gender stereotypes and even promotes the "treatment" of children with "gender-atypical" behaviors (that is, when boys are not perceived to be sufficiently masculine or girls not sufficiently feminine or either sex is perceived to be potentially bisexual, gay, or lesbian). This model discounts the possibility that children or even adolescents could possibly know that they are lesbian, gay, bisexual, transgender, questioning, or queer (LGBTQ) and that if they express these identities, it is because of corrupting influences (of "gay" culture). Janice Irvine (2000) discussed how members of the Christian right attempt to ban any talk of LGBTQ issues in schools by suggesting that speech acts are per formative (the same as action) and that talk about LGBTQ issues and sexuality in general to innocent children constitutes a form of child sexual abuse. While this is the most extreme viewpoint, some of these ideas underlie the AOUM model as well.

## Model 2: Abstinence-Only-Until-Marriage (AOUM) Sexuality Education (The Only Good Sex Is within the Marital Bedroom)

These are state-sanctioned sexuality education programs supported by a combination of federal and state funding as a result of the Welfare Reform Bill of 1996 and other recent federal legislation.

For schools or community-based organizations to receive abstinence-only funding from the federal government, they must adhere to strict regulations and guidelines requiring teaching that:

(1) physical, social, and psychological health are best achieved by abstaining from sexual activity before marriage;
(2) sexual abstinence is the expected norm of school-aged youth;
(3) a mutually faithful relationship within the context of marriage is the expected norm;
(4) sexual activity outside of marriage is likely to cause physical and psychological harm;

(5) the only guaranteed way of preventing pregnancy and sexually transmitted diseases, and other forms of harm resulting from sexual activity is to be sexually abstinent;

(6) pregnancy out of wedlock is deleterious to the child, parents, and to the society at large;

(7) rejecting sexual advances is expected behavior, and the use of alcohol and drugs increases vulnerability of not being able to uphold sexual abstinence; and

(8) it is critical to achieve self sufficiency prior to getting involved in sexual activity. (Halstead & Reiss, 2003)

This model, like the "no education" model described previously, is based on the idea that any sexual behavior is inappropriate for children/adolescents (and even for adults who are not heterosexually married). Sexual behavior is the domain of married heterosexuals only, but there is recognition that children will be exposed to sexual messages and pressures, thus must be given some information and skills to protect themselves. Abstinence-only-until-marriage (AOUM) programs often include lectures about the dangers of sexually transmitted infections (STIs) and teen pregnancy as scare tactics and include instruction on avoiding sexual temptation and developing refusal skills. In most locales, same-sex couples are not allowed to marry, so this model ignores any education addressed to concerns of LGBTQ youth, and because the emphasis is on the prevention of risk factors (STIs, pregnancy), transgender identities are generally not even considered noteworthy because all people are assumed to have been born clearly male or female and stay that way throughout life. Because LGBTQ youth are systematically and purposefully missing from the curricula, the hidden agenda or message is that LGBTQ youth are not worth consideration (Lipkin, 1999; Owens, 1998; Sears, 1999).

One example of an AOUM textbook is a more than 600-page volume titled *Sexuality and Character Education, K–12* (Meeks & Heit, 2001). This book, which is a detailed curriculum with lesson plans, contains no mention of sexual orientation or gender identity and focuses more attention on the character building (generic communication skills and manners) than sexuality information. The content of this book is reminiscent of early twentieth-century sexuality education.

Another example is Focus on the Family's curriculum titled "No Apologies: The Truth about Life, Love, and Sex," which is being used widely in the United States as well as in seven African countries, with over 100,000 participants, and China, with over 6,000 youth. Scrutiny of evaluations of these AOUM curricula has found them to be ineffective in terms of their stated outcomes, which are generally to reduce teen pregnancy and STI rates among youth (Hauser, 2004; Santelli et al., 2005; Trenholm, 2007). LGBTQ people simply do not exist in this model, and there is no research that explores how an AOUM approach might impact LGBTQ youth in the short or long term.

What do LGBTQ youth learn from these silences? How are they harmed by these silences? In this model, homophobia and heterosexism are not challenged, bullying and taunts go unchecked, and students learn that same-sex behaviors, attractions, and identities are taboo—so negative that they cannot be spoken about in school. It is interesting to note, however, that there is a recent trend of states returning the AOUM funding as a rejection of the AOUM approach.

## Model 3: Abstinence-Based Sexuality Education (Just the Facts)

The goal of abstinence-based sexuality education is to reduce the harmful outcomes of early sexual activity by providing "medically accurate" facts. This model proposes that abstinence is the best message for youth, but because many young people are sexually active, they need information to reduce their risks of teen pregnancy and contracting STIs. These models may be called "harm reduction," "abstinence-but," or "abstinence-plus" education. This model, like the AOUM, focuses on the dangers of child or adolescent sexuality, but it also provides information to reduce the risk factors for STIs and pregnancy. These programs generally do not provide much, if any, information on sexuality as a source of identity or pleasure or critique gender stereotypes and bias. Abstinence-based education may or may not include information on sexual or gender identities, attractions, or behaviors as they tend to focus on sexual health from a biomedical approach. An example is a program developed from government funding called "Reach for Health" (Administration for Children and Families [ACF], 2007), aimed at 7th- and 8th-grade urban minority youth. It contains 40 lessons given over 2 years that focus on prevention of HIV and STIs. A content analysis by ACF (2007) revealed only two mentions of sexual orientation (compared to 113 mentions of pregnancy, 48 mentions of refusal skills, and 15 mentions of abstinence).

Often abstinence-based education is pragmatic and claims to present only the scientific facts about sexuality. Facts, however, are never neutral and need to be considered within their sociocultural context. In fact, they are value laden. Conservative right-wing critics have pronounced that science is "just a belief system" replacing a religious ideology with empirical science (Irvine, 2000), making it possible for them to create their own "facts" based on a religious/moral belief system. Even if this model focused only on medical facts about sexuality, the values of science would prevail—objectivity, reliance only on facts that stem from methodologically sound research, and caution in interpreting what the facts mean. Many critics have challenged the idea of objectivity—no one exists outside of a cultural context and everyone is socialized within specific value systems that affect how one views the world, frames research questions, and interprets the findings. Thus, science is one imperfect method of understanding the world, but it is not the only philosophical framework and is limited in answering certain types of questions.

## Model 4: Comprehensive Sexuality Education (CSE)

The goals of this model are to provide young people, from grades K–12, with knowledge and skills to be productive and responsible sexual citizens, exercising their rights to sexuality. This model suggests that children and adolescents need age-appropriate and developmentally appropriate education about abstinence as an individual choice, but they should also be educated on the full range of other options related to the risks and pleasures/privileges of sexual behavior. Examples of comprehensive sexuality education guidelines can be found in the United States through the Sexuality Information Education Council of the United States (SIECUS) guidelines and internationally through the International Planned Parenthood Federation (IPPF, 2005), the World Health Organization (WHO) guidelines, and organizations such as the Canadian SIECCAN (Health Canada, 2003). International organizations tend to advocate for sexuality education as a human right (e.g., Pan American Health Organization & WHO, 2000). The SIECUS *Guidelines for Comprehensive Sexuality Education: Kindergarten Through 12th Grade* (2004) note, "Sexuality education is a lifelong process of acquiring information and forming attitudes, beliefs and values about such important topics as identity, relationships, and intimacy . . . all people have a right to comprehensive sexuality education that addresses the socio-cultural, biological, psychological, and spiritual dimensions of sexuality" (p. 13). Some of the elements of the SIECUS guidelines are presented in Table 9.3.

Comprehensive sexuality education (CSE) tends to be more interdisciplinary with biomedically oriented sexual health as one component of the program and information about gender stereotypes, sexual identities, same-sex behaviors, media literacy, and cultural values about sexuality throughout. Most CSE programs also include discussions of abstinence as the only sure way to prevent pregnancy and STIs, but they provide a balanced discussion of other options. One limitation of some CSE programs in many countries is their focus on sexual health, resulting from placing the content within the health curriculum and focusing on disease prevention. A more balanced interdisciplinary approach would reduce what's called "medicalizing" of sexuality, which means that it is generally focused on sexual disease and abnormality, implying that medicine/science is the proper authority on sexuality and the best place to address all sexual matters. In addition, SIECUS contains some excellent principles for teaching about sexual orientation, but the focus on orientation rather than sexual identity tends to essentialize behaviors/identities that are in reality

Table 9.3
**Guidelines from the Sexuality and Information Council of the United States**

| Key Concepts | Examples of Topics |
| --- | --- |
| Human Development | Reproductive and sexual anatomy and physiology |
| | Puberty |
| | Body Image |
| | Sexual Orientation |
| | Gender Identity |
| Relationships | Families |
| | Romantic relationships and dating |
| | Marriage and lifelong commitments |
| Personal Skills | Values |
| | Decision making |
| | Communication |
| | Negotiation |
| Sexual Behavior | Masturbation |
| | Shared sexual behavior |
| | Sexual abstinence |
| | Human sexual response |
| Sexual Health | Reproductive health |
| | Contraception |
| | Pregnancy/prenatal care |
| | Abortion |
| | STDs |
| | Sexual abuse/violence |
| Society and Culture | Gender roles |
| | Sexuality and the law |
| | Diversity |
| | Sexuality and the media |

fluid and contextual. Another limitation of the CSE programs is the lack of research on developmentally appropriate lessons. How do we determine when a child is ready to learn about certain topics? There is an implication that wise adults know when to deliver what information; but in reality, there is little evidence to guide this assumption. Information on sexual identity is often delayed until adolescence, yet much research shows that first same-sex attractions and feelings emerge before the age of 10. It is important to provide such information to youth regardless of their eventual sexual orientation. Other guidelines from international organizations such as WHO and IPPF propose that teaching topics when students ask about them is more respectful of students' rights and more relevant than following a lock-step age-appropriate curriculum.

These four models share one value in common. They all assume that knowledgeable adults know what is best for innocent children, thus the flow of information is tightly controlled from the adults to the minors. Children and adolescents are given no power over what they learn. Now that we have identified and described the various current models of sexuality education, we turn to an exploration of the most appropriate and sensible sexuality education.

## THE MOST SENSIBLE AND ETHICALLY DEFENSIBLE FORM OF SEXUALITY EDUCATION

As we have already indicated, sexuality has always been and will continue to be a controversial topic regarding whether or not it should be taught, what should be taught, and who should teach it. Its contentiousness has resulted in public schools having avoided giving it a solid position in the curriculum, opting instead for the federally sanctioned abstinence-only approach. Also, sexuality education has not been viewed as part of an academic curriculum but as something extracurricular and, hence, more suspect. In fact, not only have school boards and other policymaking entities not accepted that sexuality education enjoy a curricular priority, but they have actively resisted providing responsible sexuality education (Irvine, 2002). To not offer—or discuss—a subject or a topic because it is controversial is antithetical to democratic ideals. If for no other reason than this, sexuality education, along with all of the other "unmentionables," deserves coverage, discussion, and exploration.

## ARGUMENTS FOR OFFERING SEXUALITY EDUCATION

Upholding democratic ideals is not the only reason for offering sexuality education. It is only one among many reasons for offering such a program of study. Before we go on to explore arguments for why a rational and critical sexuality education ought to have a prominent place in the schools, we need to examine what is it that we are referring to as "responsible or rational sexuality education." What does it include? This question may be best answered in terms of structural considerations, curricular interventions, and pedagogical practices.

### Structural Considerations

From our perspective, the optimal form of sexuality education would consist of an antioppressive and inclusive model, which we will describe later. In terms of structural considerations, we believe that sexuality education should be taught across the curriculum and that relegating it to a single class or single topic area (e.g., a health education class or a biology class—the most common disciplinary sites for such instruction) would be misguided for a few reasons. In terms of the implicit values taught in the health education arena, usually the disease model is used to anchor sexuality education. Often, even the most well-intentioned health education teachers teach from this perspective, which may induce fear about sexual matters (fear of contracting a sexually transmitted infection, fear of pregnancy, fear of criminal sexual assault, etc.). In a biology curriculum, reproductive anatomy and physiology would be the bulk of what gets covered, and the values taught—both implicitly and explicitly—would emphasize and favor reproductive or biomedical sexuality content. In both conventional health education and biology classes, sexuality is studied focusing on its physical, mechanistic features. Historically, these are the locations in the secondary school curriculum where sexuality was and continues to be taught. If sexuality was taught more broadly across the curriculum, students would value not only the complexity of sexuality, but also, they would appreciate its interdisciplinary and multidisciplinary aspects. They would learn that sexuality has biological components but also has a history, a politic, a sociology, psychology, and artistic expression, just to mention a few possible applications.

## Curricular Considerations

It is extremely important that sexuality be taught throughout the curriculum to provide students with the benefit of learning about sexual matters from a multidisciplinary—and in some instances, an interdisciplinary—perspective. This applies to nearly every subject. For instance, from an antioppressive and inclusive perspective, teachers, no matter what their field, could focus on sexual and social justice issues. Some might argue that teachers have too much to do and that adding more is untenable, or that sexual matters have no place in particular areas of study. However, infusing sexuality education content could enhance the subject matter and potentially make it more interesting for students. Perhaps students would find such an infusion interesting and intrinsically valuable; therefore, they might retain what they learn more readily and apply what they learn to their lives. Some examples of subject matter within sexuality education might include:

- *Gender education.* Education about gender is tied to sexuality education in the sense that people explore assumptions about gender and gender role stereotypes. An important discussion about various aspects of gender ranges from sexism to the notion that females and males are not opposites of each other. Many scholars raise questions about the social construction of the binary notion of the *opposite* sex.

Even the issue of how girls are treated differently from boys in school settings is a worthwhile topic. Transgender individuals along a broad spectrum exist in and out of schools. Practices and expressions of those who do not conform to traditional gender role stereotypes (in everything from mannerisms to dress) ought to be critically examined, if for no other reason than to expose the hegemony and consequences of traditional notions of gender. Conceptions of gender and how the socialization process influences how we relate to one another are in need of much examination. Also, the ways that gender is portrayed in the media deserve attention and close, critical scrutiny.

- *Intimate and sexual relationships need to be explored in a sexuality education program.* This includes such aspects as barriers to forming relationships, initiating relationships, building social confidence and skills, sexual decision making, compatibility, conflict resolution, sexual consent, and communication about sexual matters (from perceptions to individual preferences and limits). Additionally, assumptions about what constitutes a "valid" relationship need to be explored. In a pluralistic society, youth need to know the numerous forms of sexual relationships, for example, monogamous, nonmonogamous, bisexual, heterosexual, homosexual, open, and closed relationships. While it is important to learn how to relate to others in sexual situations, it is also important to learn about oneself, sexually speaking. This is often done by exploring not only one's thoughts about sexual matters but also exploring one's body by autoeroticism or masturbation. Masturbation is perhaps the most common form of sexual activity. Yet, old myths about mental and physical illness as a result of this act (e.g., going blind, etc.) and bodily changes (e.g., growing hair on the palms of hands, etc.) persist. These myths are likely to create questions and anxiety among adolescents. Other issues that teens have, such as body concerns and fantasies, deserve attention (Kuriansky, 1996).

- *Sexual anatomy and physiology.* Students ought to be prepared for the physical changes they will experience as they enter and go through puberty and their adolescent years. For example, Crooks and Baur (2008) report that many young women are not well prepared for menstruation, and young males are not usually informed about this topic. Young boys are often not prepared for first ejaculation and wet dreams, and young girls are subject to horror stories about menstruation rather than the facts. Sexuality education needs to be inclusive and not gender-segregated. It needs to address the biological and mechanical aspects of sexuality and at the same time consider their sociocultural considerations. The main point is that it should be done intelligently, sensibly, and inclusively.

- *The issue of sexual diversity ought to be addressed in sexuality education.* This includes the sexuality of those who are physically or mentally challenged (e.g., recent sufferers of spinal cord injuries) or those suffering from various medical conditions; injured or disabled individuals are all too often discounted sexually, are sexually invisible, and tend to be perceived as sexless. Myths such as these need to be exploded, and sexuality education is an appropriate forum to examine these issues.

- *Including LGBTQ persons.* Those who do not fit the typical conception of what is considered "normal" are invisible. Lesbian, gay, bisexual, transgender, and queer identified or questioning students are often mistreated. Even though thousands upon thousands of nonheterosexual individuals have made societal contributions (literary prominence, historical recognition, scientific advancements, etc.), their sexual identities and expressions continue to be ignored in both the traditional curriculum and sexuality education curriculum. One might argue that if one is studying achievements of prominent writers, artists, and historical figures, there is no reason to discuss their sexual or gender identities and expressions. But it is of paramount importance that their sexualities be known. To the extent that their works reflect and are a part of their sexuality, this provides us with lenses through which they viewed and related to the world. Most importantly, these significant people can serve as role models for LGBTQ people. Famous people such as Leonardo Da Vinci and Michelangelo have a "more complete" visibility in the curriculum. When literature is taught at the high school level (and more than occasionally at the college and university levels), the fact that James Baldwin, E. M. Forster, Audre Lorde, Mary Renault, Gore Vidal, and Walt Whitman were other than heterosexual is often glossed over, not to mention that the homosexually significant overtones of their work often remain unexamined. This issue is even more poignant and important given incidents where LGBTQ youth are verbally, emotionally, and physically assaulted in the schools (Elia, 1993/1994; Kuzma, 2007). Heterosexism and sexual prejudice (e.g., biphobia and homophobia) and gender normativity are rampant and need to be addressed as human rights issues. The issue of the marginalization and subsequent discrimination against nonheterosexuals needs serious attention in the schools. Sexuality education across the curriculum would address discrimination by using a democratic educational framework, emphasizing such qualities as justice, equity, freedom for all, and protection of minority rights. This becomes another opportunity to explore the nature of democracy.

- *Sexual desire, sexual fulfillment, and the pleasurable aspects of sexual activity.* These aspects need to be acknowledged and substantively addressed. Historically, these topics have not been included in most school-based sexuality education efforts except when linked to difficulties associated with them. The merits of sexual desire, sexual fulfillment, and pleasure as elements that ultimately enhance the quality of life need to be covered. Youth get these messages of pleasure from the media, often in unrealistic ways, and if the schools do not address these messages, they may be uncritically adopted by youth.
- *Medical consequences.* Along with the fulfilling and pleasurable aspects of sexuality are the potential consequences of unprotected sexual behavior. Sexually transmitted infection (STI) prevention and contraception are part of sexuality education. Traditionally, scare tactics have been the primary educational modality.
- *Sexual Health.* Along similar medical lines, boys ought to be taught to do testicular self-examinations, and girls should learn how to perform monthly breast self-examinations. Young males between the ages of 15 and 35 are at the highest risk for testicular cancer (Crooks & Baur, 2008). Women, both younger and older, run risks of breast cancer, depending on genetics and lifestyle (Boston Women's Health Book Collective, 1992). Also, young women ought to learn about the importance of annual Pap smears and detection of cervical cancer. Female and male adolescents should be encouraged to look after their sexual health. Transgender youth need accurate information on short- and long-term hormone use and other medical/health-related aspects of transitioning.
- *Sexual Disorders.* Sexuality education programs should explore sexual dysfunctions and demystify them. Whether a lack of lubrication or absence of orgasm in women or a premature ejaculation or erectile difficulty in men, these issues

deserve exploration, particularly in youth where incidences of these behaviors are not uncommon. Also, an examination of inhibited sexual desire (ISD), a common sexual complaint, deserves attention, particularly for youth where these issues are confusing. The etiologies of these dysfunctions need close examination so people can either prevent or manage sexual difficulties and have fulfilling sex lives. Sexual disorders can be studied from a historical standpoint, such as discussion of the development of the *Diagnostic and Statistical Manual* and how it has characterized sexual disorders over time, or the sociopolitics of the pharmacological treatments (e.g., for men, including Viagra, Levitra, and Cialis).

• *Sexual Violence.* The media now commonly report on issues of sexual harassment, not only in and out of the workplace, but also in the schools. Akin to sexual harassment, as a form of sexual violence, are sexual coercion and rape. Hate crimes directed at people based on their gender expression or perceived sexuality occur but are often not mentioned in schools today. Internet connections and e-mailing has led to increased sexual violence and even rape. These very serious issues focus attention on the issue of sexual consent. Because these behaviors are illegal, it is important that students become informed about sex and the law.

## Pedagogical Considerations

Even though the issues just discussed are crucial and should be integral to any sexuality education program that is inclusive and antioppressive, such an endeavor ought to be derived from student interest coupled with guidance from a sexuality educator. These can be in a variety of forums, including a sexuality education class, a class from the standard curriculum (biology, English, history, and social studies), or an after-school program. This is in keeping with the philosophical underpinnings of progressive education. Moving into a completely student-centered approach may not be possible in contemporary times given the constraints of today's schooling regarding, for instance, the push for standardized testing and how that has regulated the curriculum and pedagogical practices. But students and teachers could work out a curriculum in which students could pursue what they find most interesting and personally relevant. If sexuality education has any chance of being successful, we must pay attention to and respect the students' curiosities, interests, hopes, fears, and needs.

In addressing what and how sexuality education should be taught, considerable attention must be paid to the underlying philosophy of instruction. To date, most sexuality education teachers have used the "disease model," otherwise known as the "crisis intervention approach" (Biehr, 1989). That is, whenever a problem is perceived at the societal level—such as the rise in the rate of teenage pregnancies or an increased incidence of STIs—there is often a concerted effort to eradicate such problems. For everyone involved in this process—from policymakers and school administrators, to teachers and even the students themselves—the message purposefully conveyed is one of alarm: Sexuality is perceived as problematic and unhealthy. In contrast to this approach, a viable alternative to this traditional approach has come to be known as the "health promotion model," which emphasizes that sexuality can be part of a healthy and rewarding life rather than educating only to prevent disease (Carroll & Wolpe, 1996).

## THE VALUES AND QUALITIES OF SEXUALITY EDUCATION TEACHERS

Besides what to teach, the question of *who* will teach the topic remains. This presents another level of challenge. The quality of instruction in schools is of critical importance. In the schools we find certified, credentialed professional educators. However, to date, there are several problems: Very few teachers are prepared to deal with sexuality. As a result, there needs to be a concerted effort to train teachers in this area. Despite the lack of teacher training in this area, schools have professionally trained educators who make excellent teachers based on their approach to the subject as well as positive characteristics and the values they embody.

It is important to turn to an exploration of various characteristics that sexuality educators should possess. It takes a special kind of teacher to teach sexuality education effectively and intelligently. According to Malfetti and Rubin (1967), there are six desirable characteristics of sexuality educators. Among them are: (1) *acceptance of human sexuality*, which includes a positive regard for one's own sexuality and being accepting and respectful of others' sexualities; (2) *respect for youth*, including but not limited to treating students with dignity and addressing their questions and concerns warmly, honestly, openly, sensitively, and clearly. This also includes building a trustful relationship with students; (3) *ability to communicate*, which includes the ability to not only discuss sensitive and potentially embarrassing topics but also to communicate the genuineness with which one is treating their concerns, interests, and questions; (4) *empathy*, which includes putting one "in the shoes of students" in an effort to understand fully students' experiences. This also includes availability to students, being sensitive to the needs of students, and a desire to assist students; (5) *nonauthoritarian teaching techniques*, which includes utilizing a nonthreatening teaching style. It is important that sexuality educators approach their students warmly and compassionately; and (6) *knowledgeable about sexuality*, including not only factual knowledge but also an appreciation of the interdisciplinary nature of human sexuality studies and the ability to facilitate student learning in an interdisciplinary fashion.

To this list, we would add teacher reflexivity; that is, the commitment to scrutinize one's own value system and assumptions and consider pedagogical strategies that will allow students to express their opinions safely, that will reduce bias stemming from teacher's values, and that will encourage students to form their own values after being provided with multiple perspectives on any issue.

Also, sexuality educators should be cognizant of community resources as this familiarity will undoubtedly be of use to students much of the time. It is extremely important that sexuality educators do not shy away from sensitive or controversial topics. Academic freedom needs to be used to ensure a worthwhile educational process. To the extent possible, teachers need to defend their own and students' rights to pursue unconventional or unpopular areas of inquiry. If educators and school administrators are not willing to embrace this kind of education—even if it involves "pushing the envelope"—then authoritarian and conventional educational techniques will prevail. Thus, fruitful and effective sexuality education will be precluded. We cannot afford to reproduce the standard, old-fashioned approach to sexuality education if we are to provide students with a relevant, meaningful, rich educational experience, not to mention one that is timely, engaging, ethical, and inclusive.

## POSSIBILITIES FOR THE FUTURE: ANTIOPPRESSIVE, INCLUSIVE SEXUALITY EDUCATION

While some of the models of sexuality education mentioned earlier are better than others, none of them are ideal. We believe that a positive future direction of sexuality education ought to include an antioppressive, inclusive approach to sexuality education. This approach would characterize sexuality as contextual and as a source of power. As such, sexuality education would need to be imbedded within a context that equally honors other diverse and contested identifications, such as various sexual identities, lifestyles, and relationships; racial/ethnic background; class status; educational level; gender-based discrimination; ability/disability status; and other forms of oppression.

This model would recognize that sexuality is a commodity and a sociocultural, political concept. This interdisciplinary model would be based on a social construction model that acknowledges that human sexual desires, fantasies, thoughts, and behaviors are not always consistent or easily labeled, and much of human gendered and sexual behavior is characterized by change and fluidity. This model critically examines the power dynamics (e.g., sexism, racism, heterosexism) that create oppression and social and sexual injustice. The goals of the program would be to provide learners with the knowledge and skills to identify and challenge injustice based on Foucault's (1978) idea that knowledge about sexuality is empowering.

The qualities of antioppressive sexuality education programs are rare in public education, but they may be found in colleges and universities and in select secondary classrooms (depending on the teacher). An example of this model is found in Kevin Kumashiro's work (2001, 2002) and is based on a theoretical perspective that stems from critical pedagogy and theories labeled queer, critical, and feminist. *Antioppressive, inclusive sexuality education* would include but is not limited to the following characteristics/qualities: (1) it would be democratic, (2) it would promote critical thinking and sexual and gender health and well-being in the broadest sense, (3) it would promote social and sexual justice, (4) it would increase sexual and gender self-efficacy and empowerment, and (5) it would be integrated throughout the curriculum rather than exist as a single, stand-alone course on sexuality education.

## CONCLUSIONS

It is clear that the decision to teach about sexual matters is a declaration of values. It is impossible and even imprudent to offer a value-free sexuality education. The four models of sexuality education described in this chapter are imbued with values in one way or another. Even if it were possible to offer a value-free sexuality education, we are advocating that sexuality education be taught from an antioppressive and inclusive perspective, reflecting a social justice value system.

An antioppressive and inclusive perspective would necessarily involve actively working to shed light on a variety of sexual matters and do so with critical consciousness and deliberation. This approach to sexuality education would specifically require that:

- All sexual topics are open to critical exploration (in an age appropriate fashion) and from a variety of disciplinary perspectives (e.g., there would not be one class designated as the sex-ed class);
- The learning environment is safe—emotionally and physically—for everyone in the school environment (both in classrooms and in the larger school environment);
- Teachers are self-reflexive about their own sexual values and sexual value judgments, biases, and even prejudices. Students should be encouraged to do the same;
- There would be a commitment to identifying, examining, and dismantling sexual and gender injustices by studying issues of power and hegemony (e.g., sexual prejudice, sexism, transphobia);
- An ethic (or disposition) be promoted to help engender an environment of caring about people and ideas (Noddings, 1992); and
- Students help to cocreate the curriculum to study what they find relevant and interesting.

It has been suggested that one of the values that should result from a thoughtful sexuality education is having *good* sex. Jan Steutel and Ben Spiecker (1996), philosophers of education, suggest that *good* sex ought to be both the aim of sexuality education and a chief reason why it ought to be offered. They refer to *good* in two ways: in the moral and nonmoral senses of the term. In the moral sense of *good* they refer to the types of sexuality that can withstand moral criticism. In other words, such issues as consent, keeping one's integrity intact, and being mindful of one's and others' physical and emotional well-being are a part of morally *good* sex. On the other side, the nonmoral sense of *good* has to do with the pleasurable, gratifying, and generally enjoyable sexual encounters that lead to being fulfilled "in a flourishing life" (p. 2). These writers argue forcefully that both the moral and nonmoral aspects of good sex need to be integral in sexuality education to lead a moral/ethical sexual life coupled with one that takes sexual pleasure into account in aiming at personal growth and happiness. An antioppressive and inclusive approach to sexuality education meets these criteria and, in our view, would be the most ideal and forward-thinking form of school-based sexuality education.

## REFERENCES

Administration for Children and Families (ACF). (2007, May). *Review of comprehensive sex education curricula.* Washington, DC: Department of Health and Human Services.

Biehr, B. (1989). Problem sexual behavior in school-aged children and youth. *Theory into Practice, 28,* 221–226.

Boston Women's Health Book Collective. (1992). *The new our bodies ourselves: A book by and for women.* New York: Touchstone Books.

Brandt, A. (1987). No magic bullet: A social history of venereal disease in the United States since 1880. New York: Oxford University Press.

Carroll, J. L., & Wolpe, P. R. (1996). *Sexuality and gender in society.* New York: HarperCollins.

Crooks, R., & Baur, K. (2008). *Our sexuality* (10th ed.). Belmont, CA: Thomson Wadsworth.

De Cecco, J. P., & Elia, J. P. (1993). A critique and synthesis of biological essentialism and social constructionist views of sexuality and gender. In J. P. De Cecco & J. P. Elia (Eds.), *If you seduce a straight person can you make them gay? Issues in biological essentialism versus social constructionism in gay and lesbian identities* (pp. 1–26). New York: The Haworth Press.

Elia, J. P. (1993/1994). Homophobia in the high school: A problem in need of a resolution. *The High School Journal, 77*(1 & 2), 177–185.

Elia, J. P. (2000). Democratic sexuality education: A departure from sexual ideologies and traditional schooling. *Journal of Sex Education and Therapy, 25*(2 & 3), 122–129.

Epstein, D., & Johnson, R. (1998). *Schooling sexualities.* Buckingham: Open University Press.

Foucault, M. (1978). *The history of sexuality.* New York: Pantheon Books.

Gilbert, J. (2004). Between sexuality and narrative: On the language of sex education. In M. Rasmussen, E. Rofes, & S. Talburt (Eds.), *Youth and sexualities: Pleasure, subversion, and insubordination in and out of schools.* New York: Macmillan.

Halstead, J. M., & Reiss, M. J. (2003). *Values in sexuality education: From principles to practice.* New York: RoutledgeFalmer.

Hatcher, R. A., Trussell, J., & Nelson, A. (2007). *Contraceptive technology* (19th. ed.). New York: Ardent Media, Inc.

Hauser, D. (2004). Five years of abstinence-only until marriage education: Assessing the impact. Washington, DC: Advocates for Youth.

Health Canada. (2003). *Canadian guidelines for sexual health education.* Ottawa, Ontario: Ministry of Public Works and Government Services.

International Planned Parenthood Federation [IPPF]. (2005). IPPF *framework for comprehensive sexuality education.* London: Author.

Irvine, J. M. (2002). Talk about sex: The battles over sex education in the United States. Berkeley: University of California Press.

Irvine, J. M. (2000). Doing it with words: Discourse and the sex education culture wars. *Critical Inquiry, 27*(1), 58–76.

Kumashiro, K. (Ed.). (2001). Troubling intersections of race and sexuality: Queer students of color and anti-oppressive education. Lanham, MD: Rowman & Littlefield.

Kumashiro, K. (2002). Troubling education: Queer activism and antioppressive pedagogy. New York: RoutledgeFalmer.

Kuriansky, J. (1996). *Generation sex.* New York: Harper Books.

Kuzma, C. (2007). Teaching homophobia: Abstinence-only sex education programs. *Teenwire.com.* Retrieved January 2, 2007, from http://www.teenwire.com/infocus/2007/if-20070313p479-homophobia.php

Levine, J. (2002). *Harmful to minors: The perils of protecting children from sex.* Minneapolis: University of Minnesota Press.

Lipkin, A. (1999). Understanding homosexuality, changing schools: A text for teachers, counselors, and administrators. Boulder, CO: Westview Press.

Luker, K. (2006). When sex goes to school: Warring views on sex and sex education since the sixties. New York: W.W. Norton.

Malfetti, J. L., & Rubin, A. M. (1967, December). Sex education: Who ought to be teaching the teachers? *Teachers College Record,* 213–222.

McKay, A. (1999). Sexual ideology and schooling: Towards democratic sexuality education. Albany: State University of New York Press.

Meeks, L., & Heit, P. (2001). *Sexuality and character education, K–12, Abstinence Edition.* Chicago, IL: Everyday Learning Corporation.

Moran, J. P. (2000). Teaching sex: The shaping of adolescence in the 20th century. Cambridge: Harvard University Press.

Noddings, N. (1992). *The challenge to care in schools.* New York: Teachers College, Columbia University Press.

Pan American Health Organization & World Health Organization. (2000, May 19–22). *Promotion of sexual health: Recommendations for action.* Proceedings of a regional consultation convened by PAHO and WHO in collaboration with the World Association for Sexology, Antiqua, Guatemala.

Owens, R. E. (1998). Queer kids: The challenges and promise for lesbian, gay, and bisexual youth. New York: The Haworth Press.

Renold, E. (2005). Girls, boys and junior sexualities: Exploring children's gender and sexual relation in the primary school. New York: Routledge.

Santelli, J., Ott, M., Lyon, M., Rogers, J., Summers, D., & Schlefer, R. (2005). Abstinence and abstinence-only education: A review of U.S. policies and programs. *Journal of Adolescent Health, 36*(1), 72–81.

Sears, J. T. (1999). Teaching queerly: Some elementary propositions. In W. Letts & J. T. Sears (Eds.), *Queering elementary education: Advancing the dialogue about sexualities and schooling* (pp. 3–14). Lanham, MD: Rowman & Littlefield.

Sexuality Information Education Council of the United States (SIECUS). (2004). *Guidelines for comprehensive sexuality education: Kindergarten through 12th grade* (3rd ed.). New York: National Guidelines Task Force, Author.

Social Security Online. (2008). Separate program for abstinence education. *Compilation of the Social Security laws.* Retrieved June 24, 2008, from http://www.ssa.gov/OP_Home/ssact/title05/0510.htm

Steutel, J., & Spieker, B. (1996, March 29). *Good sex as the aim of sexual education.* Paper presented at the Annual Meeting of the Philosophy of Education Society, Houston, Texas.

Trenholm, C. (2007). Impacts of four Title V, Section 510 abstinence education programs, Final Report. Princeton, NJ: Mathematic Policy Research.

U.S. House of Representatives Committee on Government Reform. (2004, December). *The content of federally funded abstinence-only education programs.* Prepared for Rep. Henry A. Waxman.

Yep, G. A. (2003). The violence of heteronormativity in communication studies: Notes on injury, healing, and queer world-making. In G. A. Yep, K. E. Lovaas, & J. P. Elia (Eds.), *Queer theory and communication: From disciplining queers to queering the disciplines* (pp. 11–60). New York: Harrington Park Press.

Chapter Ten

# REACHING CONSENSUS: A CALL TO ACTION TO PROMOTE SEXUAL HEALTH AND RESPONSIBLE SEXUAL BEHAVIOR

*Christian J. Thrasher*

In the current quagmire of the national dialogue regarding sexual health, the Surgeon General's Call to Action to Promote Sexual Health and Responsible Sexual Behavior (2001) provides the vision and the National Consensus Process provides a model for a new way toward implementation of sound public policy regarding sexual health. The Call to Action and the Interim Report of the National Consensus Process on Sexual Health and Responsible Sexual Behavior (2006) can be accessed online at www.surgeongeneral. gov/library/sexualhealth/call.pdf and www.msm.edu/Documents/Research/ CESH_NCP_InterimReport.pdf. There is hope for sexual health and public policy within a productive democracy.

## QUAGMIRE CONDITION

For a number of years, there has been a quagmire of public discussion of sexual health in the United States. It is an awkward, complicated, and dangerous situation from which it is difficult to escape. In this predicament, there has been a lack of clarity about how to move forward.

In 2001, the then Surgeon General of the United States, Dr. David Satcher, initiated a mechanism to bring sexual health to a new level of public visibility and to provide a vision for moving forward toward sound public policy based on broad public participation in sustained dialogue. This was the Call to Action.

In the Call to Action, the Surgeon General identified the importance of increasing awareness of sexual health, implementing and strengthening sexual health interventions, and expanding the sexual health research base. Dr. Satcher emphasized the importance of promoting sexual health and responsible sexual behavior that is consistent with the best available science and deeply held values.

Most importantly, he set the challenge to raise the level of national dialogue throughout the country on human sexuality, sexual health and well-being in a sustained, informed, mature, and respectful way and to link it to actions that reflect both the expanding scientific evidence and deeply held beliefs.

## CALL TO ACTION

The U.S. Surgeon General's 2001 Call to Action document is itself the result of an innovative process to bring leaders together to focus attention on the state of sexual health in the United States and to set the context for future progress in sexual health. As U.S. Surgeon General, Dr. David Satcher gathered together scientific and constituency leaders of diverse interpretive viewpoints to work on a document to develop a national recognition for the role of sexual health within public health in the United States. They used the public health approach to describe the state of sexual health, to identify the areas of need for sexual health, and to suggest the mechanism for building a common public policy regarding sexual health in the United States. This approach has four central components: (1) identifying the problem; (2) identifying risk and protective factors; (3) developing and testing interventions; and (4) implementing, and further evaluating, those interventions that have demonstrated effectiveness. The Call to Action was based on the refinement of diverse views on sexual health and responsible sexual behavior. The Call to Action document reflected an important step in developing a collaborative process for building sound public policy in an area of multiple and chronic controversies.

The Call to Action was the first U.S. government recognition of sexual health as part of public health. The U.S. Surgeon General went further and called for a mature and thoughtful national discussion about sexuality based on the Call to Action. The Call to Action was the beginning of a powerful and productive process toward developing shared public policy.

## TRANSITION

When Dr. Satcher left government services, he was named Director of the National Center for Primary Care at Morehouse School of Medicine in Atlanta, Georgia. Within that framework, he established the Center of

Excellence for Sexual Health as a mechanism for pursuing that national discussion about sexual health and responsible sexual behavior. Through the Center of Excellence for Sexual Health, he set the strategic direction for bringing people together. He fashioned a new model of bringing leaders together to build practical agreements on difficult issues of public policy regarding sexual health. From this initiative came the National Consensus Process.

## PRODUCTIVE INNOVATION

The National Consensus Process is an initiative with potential for establishing a hopeful, new infrastructure for democratic participation in public health policy. First came the identification of a broad recognition of the task in the Call to Action and need for practical structure and process for implementation. Then came the practical process, including the offering of respected convening service, experienced meeting facilitation and documentation services, a framework of ground rules for the deliberations, logistical staff services, and provision of a confident space for conversation and shared meals together. These services support participant control of the process and provide for translation of agreements into initiatives for practical implementation. A rule of decision of unanimity relieves the pressures of caucusing and coercion and permits a creative exchange that reflects productivity.

## PRODUCTIVITY

The Interim Report of the National Consensus Process demonstrates the potential for creative agreements in the national dialogue on sexual health and responsible sexual behavior. From the leaders of the participating national constituency organizations, they developed a shared vision for sexual health, a shared approach to sexual health research methodology, a shared parental sexual health education program, and a start for a shared scientific research agenda.

Nonagreement is a form of agreement if it results in a deeper understanding of the nonagreement. These identifications of clarified nonagreement become a significant basis and support for setting components of a national research agenda to clarify the elements of current nonagreement and opportunities for further consultation. In each consensus process, those issues of current nonagreement are clarified for future work together. For example, in the National Consensus Process, the areas of then current nonagreement included the scientific questions of the demographic frequency and cause of sexual orientation and the timing and emphasis of sexuality education.

Further work is underway within the National Consensus Process, and there are many aspects of sexual health that are amenable to future consensus processes. For example, the participants in the National Consensus Process have focused on the role of faith in sexuality and sexual health, HIV/AIDS, HPV, and sexual health vaccine introduction guidelines. These are continuing subjects, based on developing professional relationships, while exploring joint and parallel projects with new clarity.

The vision for the future of sexual health within the Call to Action is reflected in the initiatives pioneered by Dr. Satcher through the National Consensus Process. This experience reaffirms the vision of the Call to Action and points in practical ways to the strategic methodology for developing sound public policy in the United States.

Public health leaders can build on the experience of the National Consensus Process to improve the services to national constituencies in building agreements regarding sexual health and other public health issues. It is important to affirm the leaders in initiating and participating in these initial consensus processes. When the time is right and the will is expectant, areas for work for future consensus processes may include abortion, stem cell research, circumcision, gender change and social policy, and the role of vaccines in preventing sexually transmitted diseases.

What we need to do is to bring people together. To paraphrase Dr. Satcher from his letter in the Call to Action six years later: Finding common ground is not easy, but it is possible, and essential for our field in developing sound public policies. The process leading to this Call to Action has shown that persons with very different views can come together and discuss difficult issues and find broad areas of agreement. The process of the National Consensus Process has shown that leaders of national constituencies of diverse interpretive viewpoints can come together, discuss difficult issues, find broad areas of agreement, clarify areas of continuing nonagreement, and establish mechanisms for their resolution.

Approaches and solutions will be complex, but we do have evidence of success. We need to appreciate the diversity of our culture; engage in mature, thoughtful, and respectful discussion; be informed by the science that is available to us; recognize deeply held beliefs; and invest in continued research. This is a call to action. We cannot remain complacent. Doing nothing is not an acceptable strategy in a productive democracy. Our efforts not only will have an impact on the current health status of our citizens but also will lay a foundation for a healthier society in the future. In these processes, we contribute to productive democracy.

## SUMMARY CONCLUSION

In the current quagmire of the national dialogue regarding sexual health, the Call to Action provides the vision and the National Consensus Process provides a model for a new way toward implementation of sound public policy regarding sexual health. Public dialogue can be improved and encouraged. Consensus processes are essential and will become increasingly visible and indispensable to public policy in a productive democracy. Bringing people together is an important and needed service for public health. The consensus process model is practical and replicable. With creative models like that provided by the Center of Excellence for Sexual Health, with Dr. Satcher's vision and leadership, nonprofit organizations will stand ready to provide this service to leaders for building agreements on difficult areas of sexual health policy. We need to work together. We need to respect our differences. We need to acknowledge our diversity. We need to find common ground. Doing nothing will forever continue to be unacceptable!

### Questions for your consideration:

- Why do we need to think *strategically* about improving sexual health in the United States?
- How can U.S. sexual health leaders *contribute to global sexual health* through U.S. public policy?
- What *other* options are available to U.S. sexual health leaders?
- What are the *alternatives* to providing forums and assistance to leaders in building agreements to improve sexual health?

For further information on Consensus Building, contact:

Christian J. Thrasher
Director—The Center of Excellence for Sexual Health
Morehouse School of Medicine
720 Westview Drive SW, Suite 233
Atlanta, Georgia 30310–1495
P: 404-756-8800
F: 404-756-5709
E-mail: Cthrasher@msm.edu
Web site: http://cesh.msm.edu

Part IV

# GOING BEYOND (ADDING TO) THE BASICS

## Chapter Eleven

# WILL THE GOOD SEXUALITY EDUCATORS PLEASE STAND UP?

*Gary F. Kelly*

Planning for the training of teachers to be sexuality educators in the United States extends back 100 years. It was at that time that some educators, physicians, and moralists wanted to wipe out the threat of what was then called venereal disease, and informing public school students about the risks of sex seemed a reasonable course of action. This chapter will examine the evolution of ideas since that time regarding the qualities that effective sexuality educators should have. Naturally, opinions on the matter tend to be based in the philosophical underpinnings of particular approaches to sexuality education, and these concepts have evolved over time as well. The chapter favors the goals and objectives of comprehensive sexuality education, while recognizing the value for people at any age of abstaining from sex until they are prepared for the emotional implications, responsibilities, and obligations that accompany the choice to share sexual activity.

## THE EARLY DAYS: 1900–1948

In 1912, the National Education Association (NEA) called for programs that would prepare teachers for what was already recognized to be a sensitive and rather personal subject matter in the schools. Opinions began to emerge about what factors would be critical in teaching human sexuality. Assessing how the training of sexuality educators was progressing in 1916, one of the leaders of the movement at the time, Dr. Max Exner, wrote:

In the past there has been a shrinking attitude on the part of the public with respect to the subject of sex. Special lectures on the "hard cold facts" or the sentimentality and exaggeration of the moralists marked the next stage of development. The distinguishing characteristic of the present-day attitude is the insistence on the normal side of sex education. The growing demand for the training of teachers in methods of sex education is the most significant trend in recent times. (p. 2)

Although attempts to "normalize" sex education and meet the growing need for qualified teachers may have been progressing, the identification of the qualities of an effective sexuality educator was apparently slow to develop. Little was published on the topic until the 1930s, when the American Social Hygiene Association (ASHA) determined that sexuality educators should be of "good character" and "well versed" in their subject matter, seemingly general enough qualities to be expected of a teacher of any subject. But it was also stated that those who are "embarrassed, abnormal, unhappily married, or pessimistic" should not be allowed to be sex educators (Bigelow, 1936). One can only wonder how such qualities of life and personality were to be evaluated.

By the 1940s, it had been realized that it would be unrealistic to expect sexuality educators to have had thorough preparation in all of the multidisciplinary academic fields that relate to human sexuality. As a result, the recommendations for qualities of a sexuality educator slid to the opposite side of the spectrum, with one expert at the time writing that sexuality educators would need only "the meagerest academic knowledge" about the body, behavior, and human development but should possess personal attributes such as a sense of humor, freedom from embarrassment, an understanding of children, honesty, sensitivity, broad mindedness, and tolerance (Bibby, 1946). While the expectations of factual knowledge shrunk, the stakes were getting higher in terms of personal qualities.

## PRE-SEXUAL REVOLUTION: 1948–1960

Following the publication of the first scientific study by Alfred Kinsey and his colleagues on sexual behavior in males in 1948—a development that would set the stage for the eventual sea change in sexual information and attitudes that would be called the sexual revolution—more clearly defined objectives for the preparation of sexuality educators began to emerge. There was a new appreciation for the fact that human sexuality could indeed be studied scientifically. As the importance of personal psychology and human development theory emerged in the social sciences, Lester Kirkendall (1950), a teacher educator at Oregon State University, was among the first to point out the need for sex educators to have a good balance of academic preparation, methodological skills, and an opportunity to evaluate one's own attitudes and values regarding sexuality. This was in many ways a revolutionary perspective on teacher preparation because it encompassed personal characteristics that had seldom received particularly serious consideration in education.

## THE GOLDEN TRIAD OF ORGANIZATIONS IN THE 1960s AND 1970s

During the 1960s, as the nation became increasingly preoccupied with concerns about the sexual behavior of the younger generation, and an anti-establishment counterculture movement was building on several fronts, three national organizations appeared that would further highlight the need for effective sexuality education. The Sexuality Information and Education Council of the United States (SIECUS) advocated scientifically-based sexuality education for people of all ages and preparation of educators in schools and religious institutions and for the preparation of parents to do a more thorough job at home with talking about sexuality with their kids (Schulz, Calderwood, & Shimmel, 1968). The National Council on Family Relations (NCFR) and the American Association of Sexuality Educators, Counselors, and Therapists (AASECT) promulgated similar guidelines for curricula and the preparation of sexuality educators (Schiller, 1973; Somerville, 1970).

By this time, Lester Kirkendall had become a preeminent figure in sex education, and following his lead, all three national organizations embraced three essential dimensions for the preparation of sexuality educators:

1. *Knowledge of subject matter.* The field of human sexuality encompasses disciplines ranging from biology and psychology to anthropology and sociology, and it is agreed that educators should have a fundamental understanding of the well-researched, scientifically-based factual information that is available on the subject.
2. *Skills in communicating with students and facilitating meaningful discussion.* Because human sexuality is such a deeply personal subject, it is crucial for sexuality educators to be able to help students sort through the complexities of the subject matter and their own attitudes in order to develop clear sets of values and guidelines in the students for making responsible personal decisions. This skill set requires an awareness of age- and developmentally appropriate ways of reaching different learners.
3. *Attitudes.* It has been assumed that effective sexuality educators require a level of awareness about their own sexuality and sexual attitudes in order to help students clarify their attitudes and values. Educators need to have had the opportunity to understand themselves as sexual beings and to achieve a degree of comfort with their sexuality. This is also important in helping them develop the skill to avoid allowing their own attitudes and values from coloring the learning process in unfair or biased ways.

In 1968, as the qualities of sexuality educators were further clarified, New York University received a grant from the U.S. Office of Education to begin a training program for teachers of sexuality education. In 1970, the university became the first in the nation to offer a Master's degree in sexuality education and subsequently a doctorate (Calderwood, 1981). It looked as though the preparation of sexuality educators would be taken seriously and become a reality at schools of education throughout higher education. However, that was not the case.

As fears intensified in the late 1980s about the dangers of HIV and AIDS, states began to create recommendations and requirements regarding sexuality and HIV/AIDS education in their public schools. Nonetheless, as a reflection of the pervasive hesitancy on the part of legislators to take stands that might alienate either their conservative or liberal constituencies, these mandates were vague about things such as classroom contact hours, curricular content, and requirements for teacher preparation (Rodriguez, Young, Renfro, Asencio, & Haffner, 1997).

## TOWARD THE PRESENT

In 1985, a special issue of the *Journal of Sex Education and Therapy* examined the past, present, and future of sex education. Educators Kenneth George and Andrew Behrendt (1985) stated in an article on research priorities in sex education that research about the teacher characteristics that would establish the proper learning climate for sexuality education should be a top priority. Little has happened in this regard in the ensuing quarter century. How curious it is that an academic field having such a comprehensive and solid base of substantive research, and obvious relevance to the lives of human beings at all age levels, has received such scant attention as a valid scholarly field for either teaching or learning. It may well reflect the reticence we seem to have in our culture about addressing sex-related issues openly and honestly.

In fact, there have never been specific teacher certification requirements for sexuality educators. Most states allow parents to opt out of sexuality education for their children. Most teachers who teach anything about sexuality have had little or no training or preparation in methodologies for doing so. It is still not all that unusual, in order to satisfy minimal state or local school "health education" requirements, for physical education teachers and school nurses to gather the boys and girls into separate rooms for a one-time lecture or film about the "birds and the bees." Not surprisingly, there has also been no strong motivation for teacher training institutions to add well-conceived, thorough, sexuality education training programs to their curricula. While there are well-established health education programs, and most colleges now offer a course in human sexuality, there are almost no institutionalized requirements to learn about methods for teaching sexuality education (Rodriguez et al., 1997).

## ENLARGING THE SCOPE OF THE GOLDEN TRIAD

Although little research has examined what teacher characteristics yield the most desirable outcomes in sexuality education, there are a few studies and some anecdotal evidence from experts in the field that confirm the importance of having certain qualities in a sexuality educator. For example, Haignere and Culhane (1996) recognized that educating about human sexuality can be difficult because it is such a personal subject and can cause embarrassment or anxiety for teachers and students alike.

### Key Concepts and Content Areas

Over the years, SIECUS has brought together a number of experts who have developed guidelines for comprehensive sexuality education at various grade levels. These experts have identified six key concepts around which topics, activities, and learning objectives could be constructed in a curriculum. The key concepts are as follows:

1. *Human Development.* Human development is characterized by the interrelationships among physical, emotional, social, and intellectual growth.
2. *Relationships.* Relationships play a central role throughout all developmental stages of the human lifespan.
3. *Personal Skills.* Healthy sexuality requires the development and use of specific personal and interpersonal skills.
4. *Sexual Behavior.* Sexuality is a central part of being human, and individuals express their sexuality in a variety of ways.
5. *Sexual Health.* The promotion of sexual health requires specific information and attitudes to avoid unwanted consequences of sexual behavior.
6. *Society and Culture.* Social and cultural environments shape the way individuals learn about and express their sexuality. (National Guidelines Task Force, 2004)

These concepts provide a useful outline for the knowledge areas that should be covered in preparing to be an effective sexuality educator.

Since the mid-1980s, a number of more specific personal qualities have been identified by educators and researchers as being essential for sexuality educators, in addition to the obvious need for a thorough knowledge base about the key concepts described previously. Here are some of those qualities:

• *Comfort with the subject matter.* It is one thing to study the details of sexual anatomy and physiology and the sometimes stark information about a spectrum of sexual behaviors. It is quite another to be able to talk about these things in a relaxed, nonthreatening, and enthusiastic manner or to respond to blunt questions from students. Yet, the latter is surely a central requirement for a sexuality educator (Harrison & Hillier, 1999).

- *Respect for students.* It is critical for students to have input for the development of sexuality education curricula and to be able to share the fears and concerns they face in making decisions about their own sexuality. Only too often that input is ignored, and adults make all of the decisions about content, philosophy, and methodology (Rodriguez, 2000). Teachers who respect their students enough to listen to them and heed their suggestions will be more effective in helping those students take sex information seriously and make better sexual decisions (Daria & Campbell, 2004).

- *A sense of humor.* While the ability to convey sexuality information in a matter-of-fact way is important to the creation of a classroom atmosphere where students take the subject matter seriously, this can be balanced with the ability to see the humor in sex, student questions, and classroom situations. While most of us in the field aren't entertainers, and too much wittiness can surely dilute the message, appropriately placed humor can relieve tension, bring a more human face to important topics, and remind us that life can be fun as well as serious (Greenberg, 1989).

- *Respect and acceptance for a variety of beliefs and values.* While there is often pressure on sexuality educators from school and community forces to proselytize certain beliefs, it is important for them to understand the many different perspectives relating to sexual choices and behaviors. Researchers who conducted the National Health and Social Life Survey found that there are several distinct attitude systems regarding sexuality within the U.S. population. They range from traditional ideas about sex being primarily for procreation, through the importance of sex within committed relationships, to sex as a recreational pleasure between consenting adults. However, there is no single set of American sexual values (Laumann, Gagnon, Michael, & Michaels, 1994). Sexuality educators can hope to be respected and taken seriously by their students only if they clearly recognize and accept the spectrum of sexual belief systems that surround them (Daria & Campbell, 2004).

- *Acceptance of sexual feelings, fantasies, and desires.* Human sexual nature encompasses a variety of thoughts, emotions, fantasies, and desires, some of which may even seem bizarre or inappropriate at times. Sexuality educators should have had the opportunity to learn about these phenomena, while also increasing their understanding and acceptance of their own inner sexual lives (Yarber & McCabe, 1984). It is generally accepted within the field of sexology that these inner cognitive experiences need not be considered wrong; it is their translation into antisocial, self-destructive, or illegal behavior that causes problems. It is crucial for students to be able to understand this distinction and learn how to make responsible choices about their actions, rather than their imaginatively colorful fantasy lives over which they can exert only minimal control.

- *Tolerance of ambiguity.* The complex issues and questions surrounding human sexuality do not always lend themselves to simple or absolute answers, even though we may be tempted to find a black or white resolution for them. Instead, sexuality education is fraught with gray areas. Ethical dilemmas, determination of values, and questions of appropriateness often must be analyzed and discussed with the realization that not everyone sees them in the same way. Being able to balance all of this ambiguity without stripping the issues down to simplistic aphorisms or incorrect answers takes a good deal of intelligence, tact, and tolerance of human differences. Yet, in many ways, this is one of the most important qualities for a sexuality educator to exhibit (Greenberg, 1989).

- *Desire to be a sexuality educator.* Only too often, when an educational institution begins offering some instruction regarding sexuality, the administration chooses someone who is thought to have the right academic background and personal characteristics to do the teaching. However, if the individual does not want to teach this material, the choice is most likely not a good one. The job may require a significant amount of additional training and preparation, and there may be political concerns from parents or the community that place pressures on the teacher. Dealing with all of these demands requires commitment to the goals of sexuality education and a degree of personal fortitude, as well as an ability to articulate clearly the principles and purposes behind what is being taught (Greenberg, 1989).

So our list of qualities lengthens, but I would venture that for the most part, these characteristics are not all that different from what we would want for teachers of any subject matter. Surely we hope for all teachers to be comfortable with their subjects, respectful of their students, able to laugh at times, conscious of the need to honor the beliefs and values of others, tolerant of ambiguity, and wanting to teach what they're teaching. We expect our science teachers to tell students about the latest findings of research. We trust our mathematics teachers to be true to the laws of numbers and theorems of shapes and angles. We would not want our social studies teachers to be forcing the beliefs and political platforms of one party or another on their students. We would expect teachers of English and the arts to be open to and encouraging of the differing interpretations and creative capacities of their students. These things are not too much to expect, but gearing up to identify the individuals who possess the qualities of a good sexuality educator, and training others to have them, can be more daunting. And then, there are broader political movements that can make identifying the appropriate candidate even more complicated.

## WHAT WORKS AND WHO DECIDES?

In order to understand the complexities of identifying the best qualities for sexuality educators, to develop appropriate training for them, and to encourage them to deal with the many dimensions of sexuality education, it is necessary to understand where we stand in terms of national trends and opinions regarding sexuality and sexuality education. In the United States, sexuality has become firmly entangled with politics in ways that have further complicated the issues surrounding sexuality education. As sociologist Janice Irvine (2004) observed in her book *Talk About Sex: The Battles over Sex Education,* "Sex education's story is part of long-standing efforts to regulate sexual morality through control of sexual speech." In its early efforts to provide the contexts for meaningful sexuality education in the 1960s and 1970s, SIECUS strongly advocated the need for recognizing that America incorporated many different values regarding sexual activities, orientations, and lifestyles and that this plurality of belief systems necessitated a largely values-neutral approach on the part of sexuality educators (McKay, 1997).

The concept of pluralism gradually became incorporated into the larger diversity movement that swept through corporations and educational institutions during the 1990s. It recognized the changing ethnic demographics of the American population, as well as the need for cross-cultural understanding in a shrinking world with burgeoning international business connections. Textbooks were more careful to use photographs and drawings that represented multiple ethnicities and the customs and beliefs of many cultures. Sexuality educators presumably were to do the same, although it is unclear how responsive they actually were to such initiatives (Hemingway, 2006).

As the political pendulum was forcibly pushed back from its more liberal swing of the sixties and seventies, emergent conservative voices raised serious misgivings about the emphasis on neutral values and diversity within sexuality education. People were choosing sides for what we now call the "culture wars." During the decades when access to effective birth control and legal abortion had made it possible to separate sex from reproduction, a divide developed between what Kristin Luker (2006), a sociologist at University of California, Berkeley, calls "sexual conservatives" and "sexual liberals." While the liberals wanted to build on the openness, tolerance, and freedoms of the sexual revolution, the conservatives wanted to power a counterrevolution that would return things to a world where sex was considered "sacred," appropriate only within marriage, and to be shared only within male–female partnerships. Value neutrality was thought to mitigate against such attitudes and to encourage far too much personal latitude for youthful decision making. Acceptance of pluralism was seen simply as a way to legitimize what the conservatives perceived as inappropriate beliefs and immoral sexual behaviors.

As local disputes over the content of sexuality education programs helped people involved in the struggles to identify more clearly their own positions, the divide between these two political forces widened into a chasm (Luker, 2006). After Ronald Reagan's election as president, the Adolescent Family Life Act (AFLA), sometimes dubbed the "Chastity Act," denied federal funding to any programs that provided abortion counseling or education and mandated an abstinence-only approach in any funded sexuality education programs. New curricula began to emerge from conservative religious groups. The Clinton administration's 1996 Welfare Reform Act subsequently provided $250 million to states for sexuality education that promoted sexual abstinence until marriage. Over the past quarter century, in fact, Congress has spent over $1.5 billion on abstinence-only-until-marriage programs. With the lure of such financial enticements, the face of sexuality education began to change.

SIECUS, AASECT, and other national organizations that had been involved for years in the development of guidelines for what they considered to be *comprehensive* sexuality education, argued that the more thorough approach was essential, given the available data that showed at least 85 percent of youth had experienced sexual intercourse by the time they were 19 years old (SIECUS, 2007). Unprotected oral sex was also increasing in frequency, and teenagers often did not seem to consider this to be "sex" per se, even though the practice has both emotional implications and risks for transmitting disease. The comprehensive approach is meant to provide young people all of the information they need to make decisions about sex and to protect themselves from pregnancy or disease if they decide to participate.

A few studies emerged showing the abstinence-only programs to be filled with inaccuracies and exaggerations, and U.S. Representative Henry Waxman asked for a study to be done on the merits of these curricula. The resulting meta-analysis demonstrated that many of these programs contained medical inaccuracies, blurred lines between religion and science, and stereotypes about gender differences being presented as fact (U.S. House of Representatives Committee on Government Reform, 2004).

What has become even more clear is that, generally speaking, the priority of sexual conservatives is to protect youth from sexual information; encourage them to avoid sex until marriage or at least until "later"; discourage discussion of condom use or any other protective measures that they believe will make it easier for them to decide to have sex; and advocate for heterosexual marriage as the only acceptable direction for their futures. As Luker (2006) observed, the sex-related problems of which teenagers are perceived to be part are not so much because they are teenagers; it is because they are American. Citizens of this country, including the adults, more than most other developing countries, have tremendous difficulties managing their sexualities, marriages, and children, as rates of sexually transmitted disease, unintended pregnancy, abortion, and divorce outstrip the rates in nearly all other nations. Naturally, young people are going to have some problems.

The question remains as to what educational approaches could help reverse this state of affairs. However, it is worth noting that among teenagers in the United States, the rates of sexual intercourse, unintended pregnancy, and abortion have in fact decreased over most of the last 20 years, largely because of greater access to birth control and its more consistent use (National Center for Health Statistics, 2007; Underhill, Montgomery, & Operario, 2007).

Another of the concerns that emerged with regard to abstinence-only educational approaches was whether or not they were accomplishing the goals for which they were designed, namely, reducing sexual activity and its negative consequences among teenagers. Given that some states (16 by the end of 2007) were refusing the funding for abstinence-only-until-marriage programs or stipulating that they would use it for comprehensive sexuality education, and Congress was getting increasingly concerned about the value of the programs, the U.S. Department of Health and Human Services funded a study to examine these questions. The study found that the abstinence-only-until-marriage programs did not prevent teenagers from engaging in sexual intercourse. In fact, students in these programs were just as likely to have sex as students who were not part of the programs, they started having sex at about the same age (just under 15 years), and they tended to have the same numbers of sexual partners (Trenholm et al., 2007). In other words, the programs weren't fulfilling the objectives for which they were being funded.

Two other extensive studies have supported these conclusions. One report analyzed data on 1,719 students aged 15 to 19 from the National Survey of Family Growth in order to compare those who had participated in abstinence-only, comprehensive, or no sexuality education at all (Kohler, Manhart, & Lafferty, 2008). The other report analyzed data on a number of abstinence-only-until-marriage programs that involved nearly 16,000 students (Underhill et al., 2007). The combined findings of these studies may be summarized as follows:

1. Abstinence-only programs were not significantly associated with a risk reduction for teen pregnancy when compared with no sex education.
2. In comparing abstinence-only programs with comprehensive sex education, comprehensive sex education was associated with a 50 percent lower risk of teen pregnancy.
3. After adjusting for demographics, abstinence-only programs were not significantly associated with a delay in the initiation of vaginal intercourse.
4. Comprehensive sex education was marginally associated with reduced reports of vaginal intercourse.
5. Neither abstinence-only programs nor comprehensive sex education were significantly associated with risk for an STD when compared to no sex education.

## THE VALUE OF ABSTINENCE PLEDGES

Asking students to sign pledges promising that they will abstain from sex until they marry is a common practice in abstinence-only-until-marriage programs, but the research evidence suggests that these pledges are not only ineffective, but also may increase the risks for negative consequences once teenagers decide to engage in sexual activity. While the pledges may delay students from having vaginal intercourse for somewhat over a year, the teenagers who had taken the pledges were one-third less likely to use condoms or other forms of birth control when they eventually did have sex (Bearman & Bruckner, 2001). Those who had taken virginity pledges had the same rate of STDs as those who had not and were in fact six times more likely to have engaged in oral or anal sex than their nonpledging peers, probably as ways to avoid vaginal intercourse (Bearman & Bruckner, 2005). These findings indicate that the sexuality education programs that are most intended to protect young people may actually set them up for even more sexual health risks.

## WHAT IS EFFECTIVE?

Researcher Douglas Kirby and his colleagues at ETR Associates, a private research organization, have been conducting systematic research on the effectiveness of various approaches to sexuality education. Their findings have highlighted the complex nature of developing and implementing a sexuality education program that accomplishes desired behavioral goals, including the reduction of risky sexual activities. Here are some of the characteristics of the effective programs that speak specifically to the qualities a sexuality educator would need to bring to the program:

1. Effective programs focus on reducing one or more sexual behaviors that lead to unintended pregnancy or HIV/STD infection and are based on proven theoretical approaches that have been demonstrated to influence other health-related behavior.
2. They deliver and consistently reinforce a clear message about abstaining from sexual activity and/or using condoms or other forms of contraception. This appears to be one of the most important characteristics that distinguish effective from ineffective programs.
3. They provide basic, accurate information about the risks of teen sexual activity and about ways to avoid intercourse or use methods of protection against pregnancy and STDs.
4. They include activities that address social pressures that influence sexual behavior.
5. They provide examples of and practice with communication, negotiation, and refusal skills.
6. They employ teaching methods designed to involve participants and have them personalize the information.
7. They incorporate behavioral goals, teaching methods, and materials that are appropriate to the age, sexual experience, and culture of the students.
8. They often include people with different backgrounds and expertise especially in the areas of theory of health behavior and research.
9. They assess the relevant needs and assets of the young people they are targeting.
10. They specify the health goal(s) they are trying to achieve, identify the particularly important behaviors that lead to HIV/STD transmission or pregnancy or their prevention (e.g., abstaining from sex or using condoms or contraception), and identify psychosocial sexual risk and protective factors affecting those behaviors.
11. They design activities consistent with community values and available resources (staff time, staff skills, facility space, and supplies).
12. They focus narrowly on specific behaviors leading to these health goals, give clear messages about these behaviors, and address situations that might lead to them and how to avoid them.

13. They attempt to create a safe environment for youth to participate. Virtually all of the effective programs start by creating a set of ground rules for class involvement. Some programs try to create a safe environment by separating the class into same-sex groups for certain topics or occasionally limiting the entire course to only one sex.

14. They employ instructionally sound teaching methods that actively involve the participants, that help participants personalize the information, and that are designed to change each group of risk and protective factors.

15. They implement needed activities to recruit and retain youth. For example, if appropriate, they obtain parental notification, provide transportation, implement activities at convenient times, and assure safety. (Kirby, 2001; Kirby, Laris, & Rolleri, 2006)

A number of these findings underscore some of the educator qualities listed earlier: strong communication skills for facilitating student discussion and personal integration of the material; respect for students and what *they* need; and respect and acceptance for a variety of value systems. Based on the current political confusion over sexuality education and this empirical evidence about what makes programs effective in meeting their goals, a few additional criteria can be added to the list:

- A willingness to weigh all sides of the issues and make a decision about a personal philosophy that will provide a backdrop for one's work. Ultimately, in a political environment such as this, we must sort out where we stand, even as we are cautious not to force that stand on others.

- *Openness to balancing the concepts of abstinence and protection.* Because it is clear that calling for complete sexual abstinence until some point in life ultimately does not remain effective for long, young people also need to understand the various ways, including condom use, by which they may reduce their risks for disease and pregnancy. An effective sexuality educator needs to understand how to reach this balance without conveying a confusing dual message that becomes lost on students (Walters & Hayes, 2007).

- *The ability to define program goals behaviorally.* It makes sense to establish behavioral goals and outcomes for any sexuality education setting within the context of health and a desire to assist young people in avoiding risky sexual activity.

- *Recognition of the developmental stages of children, adolescents, youth, and adults with regard to sexual development.* Sexuality education is most effective when it addresses the developmental stages of learners and the opportunities for sexual experiences available to the learner population.

- *Willingness to share the responsibility.* Effective programs seem to be able to take advantage of the strengths and specialized knowledge of more than one educator. While resources may sometimes make this option limited or impossible, using guest speakers or local experts may help improve the effectiveness of the program. Being willing to let go of "center stage" may be necessary to accomplishing this.

- *Sensitivity to community values.* Framing the sexuality education within prevailing community standards and values may be important to the program's ultimate acceptance and success. With some careful planning and consultation, this can usually be accomplished without compromising one's standards of honesty or the goals of the program (Gawlinski, 2007).

• *The ability to create a safe and comfortable environment for students and providing aid to keep them in the program.* It is essential for sexuality educators to care enough about their students to help them feel safe enough to deal with relevant issues in their lives and to make it as easy as possible for them to take advantage of the opportunity to receive education about human sexuality.

There is no way to predict where the political winds will blow next and how they will affect our perceptions of sexuality education. Luker (2006) has even suggested that because it may well be impossible to find a compromise curriculum, the solution might well be to offer both types of sexuality education—abstinence-only-until-marriage *and* comprehensive—side-by-side in the same schools. She has also recommended that schools teach about the conflict over the two approaches, explaining what the differences in positions are and the reasons behind them. Realistically, it seems unlikely that these approaches would satisfy what Luker calls sexual conservatives or sexual liberals.

Given the social and political pressures between conservative and liberal ideals, sexuality educators may well have to choose sides and make some decisions about how far they are willing to ignore scientific facts or bend their own beliefs and integrity. It's not that choosing to abstain from sexual activity doesn't represent a valid and sensible decision for the young. It makes a great deal of sense to avoid the physical and emotional risks and entanglements until one is properly ready. All sexuality educators would probably want to give the concept of abstinence its due by including it as one of the safe and rational choices available. However, the facts remain that most people do not wait until marriage to have sex and that there are gay, lesbian, and bisexual people who do not yet even have the right to marry one another in all but a couple of the United States. Can sexuality educators really ignore these facts? Should educators who believe in one approach or another to sexuality education be asked to teach value issues that are not consistent with their beliefs? Should we encourage any educator to teach one thing while believing another, an approach that is surely destined to offer confusing mixed messages to young people?

There is another interesting dimension to the question of sexual activity among teenagers that rarely gets mentioned—one that sexuality educators should also consider. The many potential negative outcomes associated with early sexual intercourse have surely been documented, including STD rates and the consequences of unintended pregnancies, but there is also evidence to show that many young people feel quite positively about their early sexual experiences. The National Health and Social Life Survey found that 71 percent of adult women and 92 percent of adult men who had intercourse during their teen years reported that they wanted it to happen and were not pressured into it (Laumann et al., 1994). When older teenagers share their first sexual intercourse and other intense forms of sexual activity, and it is not forced or associated with drugs or alcohol, they often feel better about themselves (Else-Quest, Hyde, & DeLamater, 2005).

## ADAPTING TO CHANGE

As a relatively new part of any curriculum, sexuality education has naturally had to face its share of tweaking and adapting. Terms and definitions change; sexual topics come and go in the media and sometimes see a sudden burst of attention; television talk shows introduce people representing some relatively obscure sexual interest. There are plenty of things to which sexuality educators have had to adjust. Here are some examples, followed by another set of recommended qualities for sexuality educators:

*Impact of the Entertainment Media.* As a sexuality educator for over four decades, I have witnessed the gradual evolution of sexual openness and explicitness in television, movies, music lyrics, advertisements, and the news. Despite governmental attempts to clean up the media and sanction any offenders, children and adolescents are now bombarded with sexual messages and terms in ways that are, in my opinion, neither subtle nor tasteful. Short of parents making drastic choices to isolate their children from media exposure by moving to a wilderness bare of conveniences or amenities (which ultimately might not be doing the children any favors), there is really no way of protecting kids from the media, including by Internet filters and locks on certain television channels. When youngsters are limited from access at home, they only become more wily about seeking it out from friends.

There truly isn't much about human sexuality to which most young people haven't had at least some exposure. Having worked with college students for most of my career, I find it particularly interesting that these young adults—despite the wide range of sexual topics about which they have knowledge—have not become markedly more adept at integrating what they personally need to live healthy, responsible, and satisfying sexual lives. They are perhaps a bit less guilty about their bodies and sexual activities and more willing to talk openly about sex. Beyond that, young people seem to be facing the same personal dilemmas, confusions, fears, and problems as did the youth of 50 years ago. They are simply more sophisticated about accessing information and therefore that much more obligated to appear cool.

*Advances in Information Technology.* Surely the most startling advances of contemporary life in recent times have been in the ease and speed with which we can access information and images regarding any subject imaginable. There is evidence that some of the most accessed sites on the Internet are those related to sexuality, and Internet pornography brings in billions of dollars each year. In a way never before paralleled, the sexuality genie is out of the bottle; a sexual Pandora's box has been opened, and it will not be closed (Kelly, 2005). It is no longer possible to prevent access to all kinds of sexual information.

*International Attention to Sexuality.* Increasing openness about human sexuality and a willingness to examine sex-related issues more closely have been worldwide phenomena. As professionals in the field of sexology have developed international connections, some important concepts have emerged that have an impact on how sexuality should be viewed. The first of these grew from a conference of the World Health Organization in 1975 and represented the first time global attention had been paid to the concept of *sexual health*. It recognized the public health issues surrounding sexuality and led to the formation of some basic principles for the prevention and treatment of unintended pregnancies, STIs, and HIV/AIDS. It also made it clear that sexual behavior as a force of human nature was not particularly amenable to outright "control" (Giami, 2003).

Twenty-five years after the World Health Organization Conference, and following five years of deliberation, the World Association for Sexual Health (WAS) adopted a *Declaration of Sexual Rights* hat has established some clear principles by which people should be allowed to lead and control their own sexual lives (Lottes & Adkins, 2003). The WAS has over 100 member organizations representing over 30 countries. Its *Declaration* has not been given wide publicity in the United States, perhaps because the idea of young people having "rights" to their sexuality makes most people uneasy. Among the rights that are declared are the right to sexual pleasure, including autoeroticism (masturbation); the right to sexual information based upon scientific inquiry; and the right to comprehensive sexuality education.

*Changing Generational Characteristics.* Many educators, like other adults, still harbor a perception of adolescents as being troubled, unfocused, rebellious against adults, and in need of careful supervision. The books *Millennials Rising: The Next Great Generation* and *Millennials Go to College* by Neil Howe and William Strauss (2000, 2003) tell us a very different story in their analysis of what they have called the *millennial generation*, the cadre of people born since 1982 who continue to move through our educational systems. These are not undisciplined or disinterested kids just waiting to get into trouble, but instead, they are pretty responsible individuals trying to do the right thing. They have been shown in general to have the following characteristics (Howe & Strauss, 2003):

1. They are close to their parents, respectful of their parents' values even if they may not entirely agree with them, and appreciative of the many advantages they recognize they have been afforded while growing up. They are used to being involved in group activities designed and led by adults.

2. They recognize the importance of education and tend to be very focused on grades and personal achievement, while being extremely active in extracurricular activities. As a generation that spent a good deal of time in daycare, they value teamwork.

3. They see the value of community service and believe that they can work to make the world a better place.

4. They are skilled in technology and more interested in math and science than they are the humanities.

5. They tend toward conventional thinking and are quite respectful of institutional and cultural norms.

6. They expect a safe, secure, and regulated environment where the rules are enforced and peer pressures are exerted on those who fail to conform.

7. They are ethnically diverse and understand the importance of equality of the sexes, but they are less concerned than their elders about questions of racial or gender identity.

So as a group, this generation is thought to be quite open to the ideas that adults share with them and anxious to work toward a world that is more fair and orderly.

## MORE QUALITIES FOR GOOD SEXUALITY EDUCATORS

Given these social developments that have relevance to sexuality education, I offer a few more qualities of importance to sexuality educators:

• *An understanding of the vast array of sex information and sexually explicit images available to youth today, and a willingness to help them interpret its meaning.* It is naïve to imagine that kids today can actually be protected from the pervasive sexuality that surrounds them. Sexuality is there for them to absorb, and there is not much anyone can do about that. I believe that teens take it all in stride, although the unfiltered information they receive surely makes for a confusing mix of feelings and reactions: intrigue and disgust; titillation and fear; curiosity and satiation; sexual interest and disappointment. It is not appropriate for any sexuality educator to ignore the impact of sexually explicit material on teens or to pretend that the material does not exist. It is precisely these influences that young people need to discuss and understand better as they struggle to integrate the meaning and value of the material for their own lives and sexualities.

• *A willingness to see the broader global contexts into which sexuality fits and to accept the need to address the sexual health needs of students, as well as the possibility that they have certain sexual rights.* It will not be possible to make progress on solving the health problems associated with sex, or to be able to connect effectively with youth about their own lives, until fundamental concepts of sexual health and sexual rights that have been agreed upon internationally are integrated into our consciousness and into our curriculum planning.

• *An acceptance that every generation and every individual has unique characteristics.* This broadens the qualities already discussed concerning respect for students and a variety of value systems. Educators must always wrestle with our very human impulses to categorize and stereotype the students with whom we work, but those very students need to feel that they are recognized and valued for being individuals and for having worthwhile qualities. An important component of professional training for sexuality educators is offering the most up-to-date information about the populations of learners with whom they will be working.

## POLITICIAN, DIPLOMAT, PUBLIC RELATIONS EXPERT, INTERPRETER, AND ETHICIST

As the list of qualities for an effective sexuality educator continues to lengthen, perhaps we have inadvertently revealed a set of characteristics that are beyond the capabilities of any mortal being. I fear that some potential sexuality educators might consider this list and decide that anyone would have to be naïve or a fool to pursue a career with such daunting qualifications. I would counter by saying that our greatest challenges can yield the most satisfying rewards.

It is important, however, for those who venture into this field to accept that sexuality education is presently fraught with more controversy than any other academic endeavor. The sides of the debate have been drawn along political and religious battle lines, representing various agendas. This is an inescapable fact. To be a sexuality educator today typically will require choosing up sides. A middle ground, from either a political or religious perspective, has not yet been clearly established or mutually valued.

Sexuality educators may also find themselves called upon to help develop a curriculum or program, or to defend a curriculum that is in place but has created criticism or controversy within the community (Harrison, Hillier, & Walsh (1996). These efforts will require the building of alliances with others and interaction with representatives of the institution and the community. Such situations demand clear-headedness, an ability to express the scientific reasoning behind curricular decisions, and keeping one's balance between articulate assertiveness and angry defensiveness. To convince others of the worthiness and ultimate value of any project takes some skill in public relations. Yet, never must these challenges be met alone. There are others with whom ideas can be tested and from whom knowledge and expertise can be gained. There are always helpful kindred spirits to share the burden and the frustration. And there is always room for compromise.

Just as challenging can be the tasks that are encountered in the classroom. The need to help young people interpret and integrate the sexual images and bytes of information to which they are exposed can be daunting and, at times, seem overwhelming. Sexuality educators find themselves confronted with ethical questions and dilemmas to be sorted out, and learning to approach such things with intellectual balance and emotional poise takes practice. However, these can be the truly rewarding aspects of playing a role in the education of the young.

## CHALLENGING QUESTIONS FOR THE FUTURE

So where do we go from here? It is clear that sexuality education as a professional field is in a state of flux and surrounded by controversy. Sometimes the public pays attention to the research evidence, and sometimes not. Being an effective sexuality educator calls for a long list of qualities, but it is not an unrealistic or impossible list. The best qualified people will be more amenable to accepting the responsibilities of being a sexuality educator when they are offered the most thorough training and preparation possible for the complexities of the job.

There also needs to be further clarification about the role of educational institutions in our culture. While schools and colleges should be expected to establish and enforce certain fundamental standards of good character and personal responsibility, it has generally not been assumed that they should shade or edit scientific facts or adopt particular religious dogma or political stands in an effort to promote some group's beliefs about the proper way to live one's life.

People today are fully aware of the existence of varying sexual orientations and gender identities and generally accepting of them, but there is also much they do not understand. In any group of students, there will almost certainly be one or more who is experiencing personal questions and confusions regarding these things. To ignore, demonize, or otherwise marginalize such young people not only does a disservice to them, but to their peers in the group. It is important for sexuality educators to discuss the fact that the "American Family" no longer consists of mom, dad, and their kids who are going to perpetuate the same pattern. In fact, that is no longer the most typical demographic of family configurations.

Dr. Mary S. Calderone, the cofounder and first leader of SIECUS who was primarily concerned about the health aspects of sexual decision making, once told me that she sought only to tell young people the truth about sexuality. I know of no better goal for any educator. That brings me to one of my central concerns about sexuality education and where it has been heading. Because it has so often been co-opted as a venue for proselytizing various moral and political beliefs, sexuality education has lost its focus as an academic enterprise. While I have stated previously that any educator has some responsibility to help young people construct a mature set of moral principles and decision-making skills, *based on widely-accepted and agreed-upon codes of conduct and social interaction,* this is not a license to proselytize one's own particular values on the political controversies of the day (Kelly, 2005).

Professional organizations such as SIECUS and AASECT have made remarkable progress in bringing outstanding professionals together and establishing meaningful standards and guidelines for sexuality education. There is much yet to be done, however, as their elucidation of the qualities for educators themselves has not been as comprehensive. Another problem is that these organizations have generally been perceived by more conservative political groups as purveyors of an ultra-liberal approach to sexuality. Their positions and statements are oft-times quoted out of context as examples of outrageous things that will be conveyed to the young. It will require more political clout on their part to bring their standards and substance into the American mainstream.

Until states are under real pressure to develop and maintain high standards for the training and certification of sexuality educators for their public schools, colleges and universities that prepare teachers for their professions will have little motivation to establish effective programs for that specialized kind of training. Out of such motivation will grow more research about the qualities that are necessary to be an effective sexuality educator and the further honing of teacher training curricula.

For all of these reasons, I hold that those who believe in the value and significance of high-quality sexuality education taught by effective sexuality educators have little choice but to become politically interested and involved. At its roots, this remains a political debate and a political struggle. Yet, it is also an area of life that is deeply personal and meaningful.

Of all the responsibilities and duties I have encountered during my career as a high school teacher, university administrator, counselor, and faculty member, I can say that one of the most interesting and rewarding has been educating young people about human sexuality. It has not been unusual for students to tell me that a course in human sexuality has been one of their most valuable college courses. Some of them have gone on to pursue graduate work in sexuality education or sex therapy. I have observed quite clearly how necessary and valuable it is for youth to have the chance to explore the body of knowledge in sexology, figure out where they stand on some of the critical issues, and move on a bit more confidently and clear-eyed with their own sexual lives. If we are really serious about creating a society in which sex is less of a focal point and people are responsible and considerate in their sexual decision making, well-prepared sexuality educators can go a long way toward making the difference.

## REFERENCES

Bearman, P., & Bruckner, H. (2001). Promising the future: Virginity pledges and the transition to first intercourse. *American Journal of Sociology, 106*(4), 859–912.

Bearman, P., & Bruckner, H. (2005). After the promise: The STD consequences of adolescent virginity pledges. *Journal of Adolescent Health, 36*(4), 271–278.

Bibby, C. (1946). Sex education: A guide for parents, teachers, and youth leaders. New York: Emerson Books.

Bigelow, M. (1936). *Sex-education.* New York: American Social Hygiene Association.

Calderwood, D. (1981). Educating the educators. In L. Brown (Ed.), *Sex education in the eighties: The challenge of healthy sexual evolution* (pp. 191–201). New York: Plenum.

Daria, M. P., & Campbell, K. J. (2004, October 10). Schools need sexuality education programs. *Electronic Journal of Human Sexuality, 7.* Retrieved March 31, 2008, from http://www.ejhs.org

Else-Quest, N., Hyde, J. S., & DeLamater, J. (2005). Context counts: Long-term sequelae of premarital intercourse or abstinence. *Journal of Sex Research, 42*(2), 102–112.

Exner, M. J. (1916). *Problems and principles of sex education.* New York: Association Press.

Gawlinski, J. R. (2007). A teacher's point of view on family life (sex) education. *American Journal of Sexuality Education, 2*(2), 73–78.

George, K. D., & Behrendt, A. E. (1985). Research priorities in sex education. *Journal of Sex Education and Therapy, 11*(1), 56–60.

Giami, A. (2003). Sexual health: The emergence, development, and diversity of a concept. *Annual Review of Sex Research, 13,* 1–35.

Greenberg, J. S. (1989). Preparing teachers for sexuality education. *Theory Into Practice, 28*(3), 227–232.

Haignere, C. S., & Culhane, J. F. (1996). Teachers' receptiveness and comfort teaching sexuality education and using nontraditional teaching strategies. *Journal of School Health, 66*(4), 140–144.

Harrison, L., & Hillier, L. (1999). What should be the "subject" of sex education? *Discourse: Studies in the Cultural Politics of Education, 20*(2), 279–288.

Harrison, L., Hillier, L., & Walsh, J. (1996). Teaching for a positive sexuality: Sounds good, but what about fear, embarrassment, risk, and the "forbidden" discourse of desire?" In L. Lasky & C. Beavis (Eds.), *Schooling and sexualities: Teaching for a positive sexuality* (pp. 69–82). Geelong: Deakin University Press.

Hemingway, J. (2006). Reframing sex education. *Sex Education: Sexuality, Society and Learning, 6*(4), 313–315.

Howe, N., & Strauss, W. (2000). *Millennials rising: The next great generation.* New York: Vintage Books.

Howe, N., & Strauss, W. (2003). *Millennials go to college.* Washington, DC: American Association of Collegiate Registrars and Admission Officers, and LifeCourse Associates.

Irvine, J. (2004). Talk about sex: The battles over sex education in the United States. Berkeley: University of California Press.

Kelly, G. F. (2005). Re-Visioning sexuality education: A challenge for the future. *American Journal of Sexuality Education, 1*(1), 5–21.

Kinsey, A. C., Pomeroy, W. B., & Martin, C. E. (1948). *Sexual behavior in the human male.* Philadelphia: W. B. Saunders Co.

Kirby, D. (2001). *Emerging answers: Research findings on programs to reduce teen pregnancy.* Washington, DC: The National Campaign to Prevent Teen Pregnancy.

Kirby, D., Laris, B. A., & Rolleri, L. (2006). The impact of sex and HIV education programs in schools and communities on sexual behavior among young adults. Research Triangle Park, NC: Family Health International.

Kirkendall, L. (1950). *Sex education as human relations.* New York: Inor.

Kohler, P. K., Manhart, L. E., & Lafferty, W. E. (2008). Abstinence-only and comprehensive sex education and the initiation of sexual activity and teen pregnancy. *Journal of Adolescent Health, 42*(4), 344–351.

Laumann, E. O., Gagnon, J. H., Michael, R. T., & Michaels, S. (1994). *The social organization of sexuality.* Chicago: University of Chicago Press.

Lottes, I. L., & Adkins, C. W. (2003). The construction and psychometric properties of an instrument measuring support for sexual rights. *Journal of Sex Research, 40*(3), 286–295.

Luker, K. (2006). When sex goes to school: Warring views on sex and sex education since the sixties. New York: W. W. Norton.

McKay, A. (1997). Accommodating ideological pluralism in sexuality education. *Journal of Moral Education, 26*(3), 285–300.

National Center for Health Statistics. (2007). Advance data from vital and health statistics. *Sexual behavior and selected health measures: Men and women 15–44 ears of age, United States.* Washington, DC: National Center of Health Statistics.

National Guidelines Task Force. (2004). *Guidelines for comprehensive sexuality education* (3rd ed.). New York: Sexuality Information and Education Council of the United States.

Rodriguez, M. (2000). Working together for a sexually healthy America. *Educational Leadership, 58*(2), 66–69.

Rodriguez, M., Young, R., Renfro, S., Asencio, M., & Haffner, D. W. (1997). Teaching our teachers to teach: A study on preparation for sexuality education and HIV/AIDS prevention. In J. W. Maddock (Ed.), *Sexuality education in postsecondary and professional training settings* (pp. 121–141). New York: Haworth Press.

Schiller, P. (1973). *Creative approach to sex education and counseling.* New York: Association Press.

Schulz, E., Calderwood, D., & Shimmel, G. (1968). A need in sex education: Teacher preparation. *SIECUS Newsletter, 3*(4), 1–2.

Sexuality Information and Education Council of the United States (SIECUS). (2007). Sexuality education and abstinence-only-until-marriage programs in the United States: An overview. Retrieved March 12, 2008, from http://www.siecus.org/policy/states/2006/analysis.html.

Somerville, R. (1970). Family life and sex education: Proposed criteria for teacher education. *The Family Coordinator, 19*(2), 183–186.

Trenholm, C., Devaney, B., Fortson, K., Quay, L., Wheeler, J., & Clark, M. (2007). *Impacts of four Title V, Section 510 abstinence education programs: Final report.* Princeton, NJ: Mathematica Policy Research Group.

Underhill, K., Montgomery, P., & Operario, D. (2007). Sexual abstinence only programmes to prevent HIV infection in high income countries: Systematic review. *British Medical Journal.* Retrieved April 7, 2008, from http://bjm.com/cgi/content/full/335/7613/248

U.S. House of Representatives Committee on Government Reform, Special Investigations Committee. (2004). The content of federally-funded abstinence-only education programs. Retrieved April 7, 2008, from http://oversight.house.gov/documents/20041201102153–50247.pdf

Walters, A. S., & Hayes, D. M. (2007). Teaching about sexuality: Balancing contradictory social messages with professional standards. *American Journal of Sexuality Education, 2*(2), 27–49.

Yarber, W. L., & McCabe, G. (1984). Importance of sex education topics: Correlates with teacher characteristics and inclusion of topics in instruction. *Health Education, 15*(36), 41.

# Chapter Twelve

# OH, GOD: THE MORAL AND SCRIPTURAL IMPLICATIONS OF SEXUALITY EDUCATION AND RELIGION

*William R. Stayton and Sabitha Pillai-Friedman*

In this chapter we will consider the moral and scriptural implications of what each of the major world religions teach about sexuality education in their own moral and scriptural context. Because there are so many religions practiced throughout time, we will focus on the current world religions that are commonly practiced, including Hebrew, Christian, Islam, Hindu, and Buddhism.

*Religion* can be defined as "a set of beliefs concerning the cause, nature, and purpose of the universe, especially when considered as the creation of a superhuman power or authority, usually involving devotional and ritual observances, and often containing a moral code governing the conduct of human affairs" (Random House Unabridged Dictionary, 2006). In considering moral implications, we will be relating the principles of each religion regarding the right and wrong in sexual behavior. The scriptural implications are the body of writings considered sacred or authoritative in the teachings and practices that offer followers a sexual code of conduct (Webster's Revised Unabridged Dictionary, 1998).

## RELIGION'S SEARCH FOR SEXUAL MEANING: THE ART OF ETERNAL LOVE

Religion has a strong influence on an individual's interpretation of sexuality. The questions raised by religion regarding sexuality are: What is sexuality? How is it practiced? and Who has the right to practice it? The answers to these questions are often determined by the sexual norms of each society. According to sociologist Jeffrey Weeks (1981), there are two sociological approaches to the interpretation of sexuality, namely, essentialism and constructionism. First, essentialism interprets sexuality as a basic and fundamental part of being a human. This approach suggests that sexuality is almost instinctual and totally free from all influences. Constructionism interprets sexuality as a learned way of thinking and acting. The social construction theory postulates that all aspects of sexuality, including fantasies, behaviors, taboos, and responses, are socially constructed. The wide variation in sexual forms, beliefs, ideologies, and behaviors around the world suggests that sexuality is indeed socially constructed. Sexuality of individuals derives from both essentialism and constructionism. However, the impact of religion on sexuality is better explained by constructionism.

Sexual scripts serve to embody society's construction of sexuality, and they operate on three levels: the cultural, the interpersonal, and the intrapsychic (Simon & Gagnon, 1986). The cultural scripts are the societal norms and narratives that provide guidelines for various aspects of sexual conduct. Who a person picks as a sexual partner, what sexual acts are appropriate, and where and when to perform these sexual acts are guided by cultural scripts. Cultural scripts are often abstract and general. The interpersonal scripts translate abstract cultural scripts into scripts appropriate for individual situations. Interpersonal scripts involve negotiating sexual wishes with relation to another person's anticipated or actual responses. Intrapsychic scripts are one's internal thoughts, expectations, and fantasies about their sexuality.

Religion impacts sexual scripts on all three levels and, hence, every aspect of sexuality. A good example is in the case of a sexual dysfunction called vaginismus, which clearly illustrates the impact of religion and culture of sexual scripts on all three levels. *Vaginismus* is the involuntary tightening of the muscles around the entrance of the vagina, which does not allow for anything to be introduced into the vaginal canal. On a cultural level, most religions, Hinduism, Islam, and Christianity, to name a few, are against premarital sex. This taboo is imprinted in the minds of men and women overtly and subliminally. On an interpersonal level, a woman may fear that she will be ostracized or will lose her "purity" if she engages in premarital sex. Men who subscribe to these sexual scripts may, in fact, look down upon women who engage in premarital sex as unworthy of spousal status. Hence, the conflict within gets heightened by the interpersonal dynamics between men and women in these cultures. On an intrapsychic level, a woman who subscribes to these repressive cultural scripts may manifest her internal conflict in the form of vaginismus or another sexual dysfunction. A man who subscribes to the same repressive sexual script may marry a sexually repressive woman and seek sexual pleasure outside of marriage and, therefore, manifest his internal conflict as a split. Religion is a powerful force that can impact sexuality in many ways. It is important to understand how the major religions around the world interpret sexuality.

## SEXUAL VALUE SYSTEMS

In all of the major world religions, there are at least three distinct sexual value systems (Stayton, 1985, 1992, 2007). The first sexual value system is based on the actual sexual behaviors. It is described as an *Act*-based sexual value system and can be referred to as "A" because there is no emotional connection to the letter "A" as there would be to a label such as liberal, conservative, evangelical, or fundamentalist. It is the act itself that defines what is moral or immoral regarding behavior. This system is also based on male sexuality. It is believed that the male sperm is the basis of life, therefore, not only is the sperm the biological basis of life, it also defines the role of males in a society. Males are to be the leaders in society. In this sexual value system, females also have a biological and social role. They are the supporter and nurturer of the sperm, which is their biological role. Their social role is to be the supporter and nurturer of the male, not the leader. If the male sperm is the basis of life, it has two purposes: procreation and responsibility. Procreation, however, requires sexual intercourse with another person of the opposite sex and in an appropriate manner. Male sperm also requires responsibility for the upbringing of offspring.

This formula for human sexuality is actually connected to religion by means of the Canon Law of 1918 of the Roman Catholic Church. It is, however, the same formula used in most all religions. This formula also outlines what is not acceptable in sexual behavior. If male sperm is for procreation, then birth control, abortion, and same-sex marriage are not allowable. If male sperm requires sexual intercourse, then masturbation will not be allowed. If male sperm requires another person, then many of the fetishes and bestiality will not be allowed. If male sperm requires sexual intercourse with another person of the opposite sex, then homosexuality and bisexuality will not be allowed. If male sperm requires sexual intercourse with another person of the opposite sex, then it must be in an appropriate manner. Thus, for the purist, oral sex, anal sex, and many of the erotic positions for sexual intercourse, as well as sex toys, will not be allowed because these do not result in procreation.

Male sperm is not only for procreation, but it carries with it responsibility for the upbringing of offspring from that procreation. This means that premarital sex, extramarital sex, heterosexual alternative sexual lifestyles, same-sex marriage, or even divorce will not be acceptable. Sexual lifestyles are patterns around which persons organize their life for daily living, thus the same lifestyle may be heterosexual, bisexual, or homosexual. Examples of alternative sexual lifestyles could include swinging, group marriage, open sexual living, and cohabitation.

To summarize in sexual value system "A," the focus of concern is on "Sexual Acts" as determining what is moral or immoral. The location of authority is external, such as Scripture, parents, or religious authorities. Moral responsibility is proclaimed by an outside person who is often detached and aloof. The purpose of this value system is to maintain tradition, and the reward is Divine favor and heaven.

Regarding sexuality education, system "A" advocates for "abstinence-only-until–marriage," which fosters ignorance, secretiveness, and trauma. Because the act of sexual intercourse is to be saved until marriage, the sperm is to not be wasted in any way. Abstinence-only-until-marriage is currently the official government-sponsored program in the United States. First, ignorance is valued because it is feared that knowledge about sexuality will encourage sexual acting out and promiscuity. Second, secretiveness is valued because youth are not encouraged to ask specific questions about sex, such as masturbation, any sexual shared behaviors, homosexuality, abortion, contraception, safer sex, or condom use, without getting negative, fearful, or disapproving responses. Trauma can occur because sexual feelings and curiosity are natural to human beings, and this value system discourages discussion about most sexual behaviors except those that promote procreation within the context of marriage between a man and a woman. Guilt and shame are the result of allowing other sexual thoughts, fantasies, or questions if they are not related to marriage and procreation.

A second sexual value system of the world's major religions—which can be called "B"—is based on the nature of relationships. Morality and immorality are not based on the acts of sex, but rather on the motives and consequences of those acts. In other words, there is nothing inherently moral or immoral about any of the acts of sex. To discern the motives and consequences of the acts, one must take into account what we have learned from human experience, what research has shown us, as well as what we have learned from scientific inquiry. This value system requires equipping persons with good decision-making skills. It also requires helping persons to develop loving, intimate, and appropriate ways of developing their relationships based on responsible sexual behaviors.

To summarize, sexual value system "B" is relationship-centered. God's creation, the Scriptures, and great religious leaders, such as the Hebrew prophets, Jesus, or Mohammed, teach about the nature of relationships. The importance in this value system is on one's relationship with God, with self, with others, and with the things in our life and environment, such as material possessions, use of money, and justice issues. This value system teaches that all of society is involved in the moral climate. It is believed that values promote growth, better people, and a better society. The reward for holding responsible sexual values is creating a better, more meaningful life in the here and now.

*Comprehensive sexuality education*, which is age-appropriate, would be fostered by this sexual value system. It is believed that sexuality education produces knowledge, and knowledge results in responsible sexual behavior (Office of the Surgeon General, 2001). Much sexual acting out with adolescence is out of curiosity and ignorance. When questions are answered, without producing guilt and shame, it is believed that young people will put more thought into their sexual decisions and behaviors. Because this value system encourages communication about sexuality, questions are encouraged, and sexual behaviors are framed in a more natural perspective. Issues, such as masturbation, homosexuality, contraception, abortion, safer sexual practices, and condom use are explained as natural and not condemned. Decision-making skills are often taught and practiced. Premarital, extramarital, or alternative sexual lifestyles are seen as personal decisions. Gay, lesbian, bisexual, transgender, and intersex persons are fully accepted and affirmed. Marriage has to do with the nature of a loving relationship and not gender biased as being only between a male and a female.

A third sexual value system—which can be labeled "C"—is the value system seemingly held by most people. This occurs when persons get caught between their religious teachings and their nature to be sexual. It takes from both the first and second value systems depending on the issue and comfort level with a particular sexual behavior. It often becomes confusing because there is no consistent theological or scriptural basis. For example, a person may accept masturbation, contraception, and oral sex from value system "B" because it enhances their relationship. They may reject abortion, homosexuality, and anal sex, using value system "A," because of their discomfort with the subjects.

Religious institutions may also operate from a combination of both "A" and "B" value systems. For example, a faith community may publicly take a stand against a particular sexual behavior but operate from a "don't ask, don't tell" or a "love the sinner, hate the sin" philosophy. Religions holding this value system might be negative toward premarital sex, extramarital sex, homosexuality, and same-sex marriage but be silent, or give limited approval, to such practices as masturbation, non–marital sex between consenting adults, abortion, or safer sexual behaviors.

As we look at the world's major religions, the reader will see how these three sexual value systems are found in each religion.

## HINDUISM

The Hindu values are based on the Vedas. The *Vedas* are a large corpus of texts originating in Ancient India. They are the oldest scriptural texts of

Hinduism. In the life of a Hindu, there are a set of goals and orientation that are to be reached at each stage of a person's life, namely, pleasure (*Kama*), achievement (*Artha*), virtue (*Dharma*), and release from worldly attachments (*Moksha*). Although all the goals are important, *moksha* is the most desirable one even if it is unattainable in one's present life.

*Kama*, sexual pleasure, according to the Hindu scriptures should be enjoyed in the context of *samskara*, the sacrament of marriage. Kamasutra, however, speaks about sex outside of wedlock with other men's wives and courtesans. In most cases, sexual activity before marriage is strongly proscribed in Hinduism, and precautions are commonly taken to limit such opportunities. It is generally understood that sexual impulses need external controls because the internal controls are not reliable. Parents take precautions against having young men and women meet privately by the same logic. A man and a woman meeting privately are assumed to be sexually involved. Marriages based on romantic attraction rather than interfamily arrangement is particularly discouraged.

Hinduism places a lot of emphasis on the sanctity of marriage, and it is considered too important to be left merely to the devices of the individuals involved. This belief has justified the practice of arranged marriages. When children reach marriageable age, the parents of the bride and the groom have the obligation to arrange the marriage on behalf of the family. The chief criterion for such a selection is compatibility, that is, the husband and wife need to be from similar backgrounds as far as caste and community are concerned. However, they need to be from different lineages so as to avoid incest.

The tradition of arranged marriages is slowly declining. As India is becoming more global, some of the ancient Indian traditions are becoming obsolete (Deresiewicz, 2004). Concepts of female sexual purity and arranged marriages were relevant when women gave up education and married early. In recent years, more and more men and women are delaying marriage in favor of career advancement. Men and women of marriageable age work closely in the work environment and often form intimate connections that result in love relationships and marriages. Premarital sex, strongly prohibited by Hindu scriptures, is becoming more common. These shifts in values do come with a price. Young men and women who have grown up with traditional sexual scripts struggle to integrate the newer, more liberal, sexual standards with their own scripts. For example, Hindu women who have come to the United States and started dating American men, and then decided to become sexually involved with these men, do it with mixed feelings. Although their mind says "yes," their body says "no," and they often suffer from a sexual dysfunction.

Because dating and premarital sex is prohibited, legislators, educators, and parents do not support sex education in middle and high schools. There is widespread denial at all levels. In May 2008, the Indian Supreme Court, which considers education as a fundamental right of children, denied sex education the same protection. There is a widespread belief that sex education is a Western import and can negatively influence "the Indian values" (The birds, the bees and the taboos, 2007). Hence, attempts to provide sex education in Hindu communities may be faced with monumental hurdles with minimum support from the government, educators, or parents.

The Hindu tradition has also become less tolerant of homosexuality (Laurent, 2005). Over the past century in the classical Vedic period, homosexual activity was not seen as a particularly serious infraction of religious codes. In the medieval, post-Vedic period, it came to be punished in both religious and secular law, often by exclusion from the higher castes. Female homosexuality was punished more severely than male homosexuality, out of concern for the protection of women's virginity and sexual purity. Although Kamasutra is often seen as legitimizing homosexuality, it is associated with lower castes in the text. Homosexuality has in fact become less acceptable over time, particularly among Hindu conservatives today. For example, when the Indian movie *Fire*, which portrayed a lesbian relationship, was released, a conservative Hindu mob vandalized a few movie theaters that screened the movie (Guinevere, 1998).

Hinduism does not condemn contraception. The practice has ancient precedents within the tradition. The Hindu tradition does, however, distinguish between family planning, which aims at proper timing and limitation of procreation, and birth control, which seeks to avoid conception altogether. It permits the former, but frowns upon the latter. The Hindu tradition regards conception as the beginning of life as in system "A," the termination of which constitutes murder. In fact, the Hindu word for abortion is *bhruna-hatya*, the same term used to refer to the killing of the Brahmin, a member of the highest social caste.[1] Conception is not merely seen as the material union of sperm and ovum but as something that involves life principle or spirit, the *atman*. The *atman* is a philosophical term used within Hinduism and Vedanta to identify the soul. Hindus believe in reincarnation.[2] Because the atman will be reentering the world through birth, the fetus is endowed with spirit, dignity and a previous history. Hence, abortion is viewed as a severe offence.

However, abortion has been legal in India since 1971 with the passing of the Medical Termination of Pregnancy Act. Abortion has few restrictions and is available on demand in most major medical establishments and in clinics around the country. Due to severe overpopulation, abortion and contraceptive methods are now easily available through government sponsorship. Indian government has invested a lot of resources on educating its adult population about contraception and safe ways to terminate pregnancy. This aspect of sex education is encouraged at all levels, and there is a lot of support on all levels. This shows how value system "C" can be dependent on cultural realities and override traditional religious values. Although abortion is condemned as a heinous act according to the Hindu scriptures, the problem of overpopulation has rendered the Hindu scriptural sanctions against abortion impractical and obsolete.

## JUDAISM, CHRISTIANITY, AND ISLAM

Three closely related religions are Judaism, Christianity, and Islam. They are called the Abrahamic religions because they all consider Abraham their spiritual ancestor. Judaism is based on the Hebrew Bible. The Hebrew Bible is accepted by both Christianity and Islam. Islam accepts both the Hebrew Bible and the Christian Testament but includes the Qur'an. Although the sources seem to be similar, the three religions are very different from each other. Each religion interprets sexuality in myriad ways as well.

### Judaism

Jewish religious laws are based on the Torah and the Talmud. The *Torah* is the most important document in Judaism, revered as the inspired word of God, traditionally said to have been revealed to Moses. The word *Torah* means "teaching," "instruction," or "law" in Hebrew. The *Talmud* is a record of rabbinic discussions pertaining to Jewish law, ethics, customs, and history. There are a few versions of Judaism, namely, Orthodox, Conservative, Reform, and Reconstructionist. Each of these versions has different interpretations of sexuality.

In Jewish law, sex is considered a basic need like hunger or thirst. When sexual desire is satisfied between a husband and wife under the right circumstances with mutual love, it is considered a *mitzvah*. In Christian law, procreation is considered the primary purpose of sex. In Jewish law, however, the primary purpose of sex is to reinforce the loving marital bond between husband and wife. Jewish law asserts that although sex within the context of marriage is an act of immense significance, sex outside of the context of marriage is strongly forbidden. Sexual contact short of intercourse, such as petting, is also forbidden. This particular aspect of Jewish law is not observed by most Jewish groups. Similarly, Jewish law forbids male masturbation. Destruction of the seed, *ha-sh'cha'tat zerah*, ejaculation outside of the vagina, is strictly forbidden. The Torah does not forbid female masturbation, although fantasies and "impure thoughts" are forbidden. Petting, premarital sex, cohabitation, and masturbation are commonly practiced by present-day Jewish lovers. Here is an example of value system "A" being rejected in favor of value system "B."

Jewish law favored women's rights in the discussion about sexuality. The Talmud offers strict guidelines about the quality and quantity of sex that a woman is entitled to. It specifies that the frequency of sexual obligation should be based on the husband's occupation. The obligation can be modified in the *ketubah* (the marriage contract). The woman's right to sexual intercourse is referred as an *onah,* and it is a basic right as food and clothing. A wife who is deprived of sexual satisfaction for prolonged periods of time can choose to divorce her husband. Most Jewish men and women seem to be unaware of these special rights bestowed upon women. In this situation, the Jewish sexual value has been influenced or completely replaced by cultural and religious laws that do not honor women with any sexual rights.

Orthodox Jews observe certain traditions that are no longer observed by the more liberal Jewish groups. Orthodox Jews reject premarital dating and intimacy. Usually, bride and groom consummate their relationship on the wedding night. Also, premarital counseling and sex education is limited to information about basic mechanisms of sexuality and menstrual taboos. However, there is a movement within the community to provide better sex education to brides (Sherman, 2008). The Orthodox Jews observe menstrual taboos as do upper caste Hindus and Muslims. In Judaism, the menstrual taboo derives from the priestly codes of the Hebrew Bible and from rabbinic law. The rabbis reinforced the injunctions of Leviticus 12:1–5 and 15:19–32 by ruling that a menstruant is impure for the five or so days of her menses and for at least seven days afterwards. After this time has elapsed, the menstruant (*niddah*) visits a ritual bath (*miqveh*), and after immersion, physical relations with her husband can be resumed. Although this practice is viewed by more liberal Jews as backward and old-fashioned, increasingly sex therapists are recommending periods of abstinence in relationships as a way to rejuvenate sexual energy. Kerner (2008) claims that sex or dating detox impacts one's mind and body and rejuvenates one's love life the same way a physical fast alters metabolism and natural body chemistry. This is a situation where the benefit of value system "A" is rediscovered by mainstream society.

Sexual relations between men are strongly forbidden according to the Torah (Lev. 18:22). However, Jewish law differentiates between homosexual acts and homosexual orientation. Although homosexual acts are forbidden, homosexual orientation is not considered a sin. In other words, a man can desire sexual relations with another man as long as he does not act on it. There is very little discussion about lesbianism in the Talmud or Torah. Hence, the taboo on male homosexuality may be explained as a way to prevent *ha-sh'cha'tat zerah,* destruction of the seed. In modern society there are various degrees of acceptance of homosexuality. Most Jewish individuals subscribe to value system "C," a combination of "A" and "B." Their acceptance level may fluctuate with the society's general attitudes toward gay men and lesbians, but their deep discomfort with homosexuality may be related to value system "A."

Birth control is permitted as long as the couple is committed to procreation at a later stage. The Talmud recognizes the importance of contraception use by very young women and nursing women. Contraceptive devices that destroy the seed or block the passage of the seed are not permitted. This value system is not practical in a world that is increasingly threatened by deadly sexually transmitted diseases. Hence, in this case, the value system "A" had been replaced by value system "B" in the interest of safety and well-being of sexually active individuals.

The Talmud recommends abortion in the event the mother's life is in danger. The fetus, "potential human life," is not considered more valuable than a life in existence. Additionally, a fetus is not considered a *nefesh*, a person, until the head emerges in the birthing process. This is a situation where value system "A" is quite liberal and challenges the ongoing legal dilemma around abortion rights.

Overall, Judaism seems to have the most liberal attitudes about sexuality and truly represents value system "C." On the one hand, it has a value system "B" on certain sexual behaviors, while on the other hand, it is has a strong value system "A" on others. Judaism does not emphasize sexual renunciation and generally celebrates sexuality within certain limits. Sexuality educators need to be aware of the differences in the various versions of Jewish religion before proceeding with the development of the syllabus.

## Christianity

Christianity is one of the most difficult religions to discuss because there are so many different Christian denominations. While the Bible is the only recognized scripture, there are at least 110 versions in English. There is a great difference as to the way both Hebrew and Greek words for sexuality are mistranslated and misunderstood in many of these versions. For example, there are basically five verses that discuss same-sex sexual relationships, which is one of the most hotly debated subjects in Christendom today: two verses in the Hebrew Bible and three verses in the Christian Testament. While the term *homosexual* did not come into usage until the nineteenth century, several versions of the Bible use the term. Actually, there is no word for what we define as homosexual sexual orientation in either Hebrew or Greek. Biblical scholars disagree on the translation of these five verses. Some believe that these five verses are a condemnation of homosexual behaviors; some believe that these five verses have absolutely nothing to do with homosexual orientation; and some believe that the Hebrew Bible verses are about sexual practices and rituals within non-Hebrew religions and, in the Pauline letters, about either the practice of pederasty or pagan religious idolatrous rituals. The practice of pederasty was a Roman and Greek practice of an adult male mentoring an adolescent male about sexuality by having sex with that young male. Because of abuses toward adolescent males, the practice of pederasty was being questioned by all parts of the society, including the churches where Paul was visiting and involved.

Not only is there a problem with the translation of sexual issues, there is also a problem with misquoting and misunderstanding scriptural references regarding sexuality. For example, the Bible does not say anything about homosexuality as we understand it today; it says nothing about masturbation, birth control, abortion, premarital sex, or extramarital sex. Yet, many clergy will use the Bible to condemn these sexual practices. The Bible neither proscribes nor prescribes monogamy, yet most clergy will use the Bible as proclaiming monogamy only. In fact, the Bible assumes polygyny, or a male having more than one wife.

Another commonly misunderstood sexual behavior is masturbation. The scriptural story that is usually quoted is the story of the sin of Onan (Genesis 38). To link the story of Onan with masturbation is a gross misunderstanding of this story, which is really about the issue of Levirate marriage. The context for the story of Onan is that when an older brother dies, the next brother is to impregnate the older brother's wife so that the older brother's inheritance line will be continued. In Genesis 38, Onan's brother dies, and Onan is ordered by his father to impregnate his sister-in-law; however, because Onan wanted to keep all the inheritance for himself, he withdraws (coitus interuptus) from his sister-in-law and "spills his seed" on the ground. The Lord kills Onan for breaking the Levirate Law, not for masturbating. Unfortunately, even dictionaries often include *onanism* as a synonym for masturbation.

Women are often brought up that their genitals are dirty and that it is sinful to touch them. There is nothing scriptural to substantiate this message or practice. In fact, one only has to read the "Song of Songs" to find a very positive view of both the male and female body, including genitals.

Within all churches and Christian denominations one can find all three sexual value systems represented. One recent interdenominational study, funded by the Lilly foundation through Hartford Seminary (Hartford Institute for Religion Research, 2001), surveyed 41 different religious faith communities representing 95 percent of all religious congregations in the United States, including Jewish, Roman Catholic, Protestant, Pentecostal, Mormon, Islamic, and Bahai religions. Only one question on sexuality was asked to the Protestants only. The question was, "to what extent does your congregation encourage abstaining from premarital sex?" There were 11,000 responses. There were three possible answers: little or no encouragement for abstinence; some encouragement for abstinence; and strongly encouraged abstinence until marriage. Twenty-three percent said little or no encouragement for abstinence; 25 percent said some encouragement for abstinence; and 58 percent said strong encouragement for abstinence until marriage. Eighty percent of the evangelical congregations replied strong encouragement for abstinence until marriage, while only 35 percent of moderate congregations and 20 percent of liberal congregations reported strong encouragement for abstinence until marriage (Hartford Institute for Religion Research, 2001).

There are only a few, if any, research studies based on outcomes for religion-based human sexuality programs in Christianity. It is easier to evaluate current programs based on whether or not the program is meeting its goals and objectives related to its professed actual value system (Office of the Surgeon General, 2001).

There are two well-known curricula available in sexual value system "A" programs. They are "Sex Respect" and "True Love Waits." These curricula are similar in that they both teach the importance of remaining "sexually pure" until marriage and thus do not discuss anything about sexual behaviors, other than procreation within marriage. Masturbation, homosexuality, safer sexual practices, proper use of condoms, and premarital sex are not covered. The emphasis is on chastity, virginity, and abstinence until marriage.

There are two denominationally-based comprehensive programs in human sexuality education available in value system "B." They were codeveloped by the Unitarian Universalist Association (Frediani, 1999) and the United Church of Christ (Frediani, 2000) and span the life cycle. The Unitarian Universalist Association (UUA) program is called "Our Whole Lives" and has been successfully field-tested. It is designed for children, youth, and adults. The United Church of Christ (UCC) program, cowritten by UUA and UCC church members, called "Sexuality and our Faith," is the companion piece to "Our Whole Lives." All of these curricula cover the range of sexual behaviors in a positive way along with helping students to develop decision-making skills that will result in high sexual self-esteem.

There are several denominationally-based sexuality programs in sexual value system "C" from the Presbyterian Church USA, the Episcopal Church, the Lutheran Church, the United Methodist Church, and the Roman Catholic Church: Minneapolis/St. Paul Archdiocese. Each of these curricula attempt to be sexually positive, but do not cover difficult or controversial issues that youth are most interested in discussing.

## Islam

Islam is a complex and multifaceted set of religious beliefs and practices. Hidayatullah (2003) advises against any study of sexuality and Islam to avoid the risk of essentialism. She emphasizes, "There is no one Islam" (p. 259). Islam is practiced in several countries around the world with different degrees of rigidity and laxity. In countries where the legal system is based on *Shari'a* there are very clear rules of sexuality.[3]

The basis for the Islamic perspective on human sexuality is found in the Qur'an. There are three issues of particular interest in Islamic scripture: polygyny, interfaith marriage, and arranged marriage. Islamic law allows polygyny but limits the number of wives to four and requires equal treatment of all. Women are not allowed to marry more than one husband. Islamic law permits a Muslim man to take a Jewish or Christian wife but forbids interfaith marriage entirely to Muslim women. Arranged marriages over romantic unions are preferred in most Islamic communities.

Marriage has a spiritual foundation within Islam as a religious duty enjoined by scripture and tradition on all who can undertake its responsibilities. According to Hidayatullah (2003), "marriage is a sacred act and the subject of serious consideration throughout the Quran" (p. 263). The purposes and benefits of marriage from the Muslim point of view include containment of sexual drives within legitimate social bounds, procreation, companionship, and a loving and joyful personal relationship. Islam advocates the permanency of marriage but allows for the realities of divorce.

Traditional Islam prohibits premarital sex, and dating is restricted because of its supposed inducement of sexual activity (Dunne, 1998). The sexual purity and innocence of young unmarried women is highly valued, and any deviation from this norm brings disgrace to the whole family. Unmarried individuals have one of two choices: marriage or total abstinence until marriage. The Qur'an says, "Let those who find not the wherewithal for marriage, to keep themselves chaste till God find them the means from His Grace" (24:33). Most Islamic countries enforce strict laws against dating and premarital and extramarital sex. However, traditional Islamic laws are being challenged by educated and Westernized youngsters (Therborn, 2006).

Traditional Islam's primary source, the Qur'an, is very explicit in its condemnation of homosexuality, leaving scarcely any loopholes for a theological accommodation of homosexuals in Islam. Homosexuality is viewed as unnatural and a deviation from the norm. Special mention is made of its practice in the Qur'an: "What! Of all creatures, do you approach males and leave the spouses whom your Lord has created for you? Indeed, you are people transgressing (all limits)" (26:165–166). Homosexual activity is punishable in Islamic societies as a crime against the laws of God. Despite Islam's condemnation of homosexuality, there are gay and lesbian Muslims who negotiate a complex relationship between their sexuality and religion (Boellstorff, 2005). The Internet has been used by Islamic gay and lesbians to connect and network secretly. A popular Web site called Queer Jihad offers provocative essays and articles by writers worldwide and numerous links to gay Islamic, Arabic, and Asian cultural, legal, and political sites.

Most schools of Islam permit contraception provided that both spouses have given their consent. There is particular emphasis on securing the consent of the woman. In Islam, abortion is forbidden once ensoulment takes place (Kyriakides-Yeldham, 2005). There are various schools of thought on when ensoulment actually takes place, but no school of Islam permits abortion after the fourth month, except to save the life or health of the mother. Abortion may also be justified when there are incurable mental or physical defects in the fetus. Some Islamic scholars have argued that abortion may be justified in cases where a larger family would constitute a hardship for parents.

According to Hidayatullah (2003), the *Shari'a* offers strict rules about men and women's clothing. Most importantly, men and women need to dress in a way that emphasizes masculine and feminine characteristics, respectively. Islamic legal and political authorities strive to preserve the heterosexual order of Islamic societies and condemn any inversion or overlapping of gender roles. The above author also claims that although Islamic theology emphasizes modesty and restricts both men and women from gazing at members of the opposite sex, it does not endorse harem, the *hijab*,[4] or the seclusion of women from public spaces. These practices "are contributions of cultures and social attitudes that have surrounded Islam since its beginning" (p. 279). However, these practices have been seamlessly incorporated into Islamic *Shari'a* and have become mandatory law. In countries practicing *Shari'a*, women who appear in public places without a *hijab*, or who are inadequately covered, may be assaulted in public by law enforcement authorities, and establishments that entertain such women may be fined.

In summary, in Islam, genital intercourse, oral sex, and even masturbation is lawful. Sexual behaviors that are prohibited in Islam are anal intercourse, intercourse during menstruation, adultery, homosexuality, lesbianism, bestiality, rape, child molesting, incest, obscenity, nudism, orgies, wife swapping or open marriages, fetishes, sadism/masochism, enjoyment of filth, necrophilia, celibacy, and castration. Islam encourages birth control and permits coitus interruptus but prohibits permanent measures of birth control. Thus, Islam falls in the sexual value system "A" category, with a few exceptions that would enhance a couple's relationship. There is no formal sexuality education in Islamic countries. Because most conservative Islamic countries do not even allow girls to attend school, providing sex education can be quite a challenge. In more liberal Islamic communities, sexuality education is presented under the title "hygiene." The anatomy and physiology of sexuality may be presented with scarce details. There is a belief in Islamic countries that providing sex education may encourage youngsters to have sex out of wedlock.

## TAOISM, CONFUCIANISM, AND BUDDHISM

Taoism, Confucianism, and Buddhism have influenced most of the Far East Asian countries. All three religions have impacted sexuality and sexuality education in many different ways (Fang, 1991).

Taoism was one of the ancient doctrines that early Chinese dynasties used as a guideline for various aspects of life. Taoism was not structured as a formal religion at that point in history. According to Taoism, men and women were divided into the *yin* and *yang* (Yao, 2003). Women had an unlimited supply of *yin,* and men had a limited supply of *yang.* The doctrine warns men to safeguard their precious *yang,* the depletion of which would cause health problems and death. Men were instructed to acquire plenty of *yin* before using their *yang.* For instance, during sexual intercourse, men were required to make a woman orgasm several times in order to get their *yin* energy before ejaculating, using up their *yang* energy. Similarly, masturbation by men was considered unhealthy and forbidden because it resulted in loss of precious *yang* energy. There were no such restrictions on female masturbation because females were believed to have unlimited *yin.* Sexual intercourse, according to Taoism, had two purposes: to produce male heirs and to strengthen male vitality through the absorption of female *yin* energy. Taoism encouraged elaborate and sometimes complicated sexual techniques, not unlike Indian Tantra.

Confucian teaching, which became more prevalent than Taoism, had a very rigid and negative approach to sexuality. Confucian teaching emphasized the importance of sexual relations in the context of marriage for procreation. However, women were considered inferior beings and were expected to live in segregated quarters except during bedtime. Women's sexual desire was considered unnatural and offensive. Men, on the other hand, were allowed to take concubines if their wife was unable to have a son or if he was no longer attracted to his wife. Confucian and Taoist teachings often merged on some aspects of sexuality, namely, homosexuality. Male friendship was one of the Confucian virtues, but homosexuality was never mentioned in any of the sex manuals. Lesbianism was common and tolerated. Confucian teaching was challenged later by Buddhist teachings that aligned with the pleasure-positive teachings of Taoism.

Chinese sexuality was influenced by the teaching of Taoism, Confucianism, and Buddhism. Political doctrines of communism played an important role in influencing sexuality as well. These teachings often contradicted each other on several aspects. In modern China, sexuality is influenced by ancient religious teachings, political doctrines, and Western influence. Regarding a sexual value system, China presents a true "C" value system.

Sexuality education in modern China has had several ups and downs depending on how liberal or repressive the political climate was. Communist leaders of China saw any form of liberation, political or sexual, as a sign of moral corruption. But in recent years, increased incidence of STDs and overpopulation has served to create a demand for sexuality education.

Masturbation of men is discouraged according to value system "A." It is seen as an act that may deplete men's energy (Chang, 1977). However, a study conducted in 2000 with a nationally representative sample from China found that younger men in their 20s reported masturbating almost as much as their Western counterparts. The researchers found that sexual contact in childhood, early puberty, and early sex were related to adolescent masturbation and liberal sexual values, and sexual knowledge increased the probability of masturbation (Das, Parish, & Laumann, 2007). In this situation, value system "A" seems to evolve into value system "C" due to liberal sexual values and sexual knowledge.

In mainland China, although there are no laws about homosexuality, it is included in the category of "hooliganism." The current Criminal Law of the People's Republic of China Article 106 states that all hooliganism should be subjected to arrest and sentence. Homosexuality is considered a form of sexual offense, and its prevalence is explained as a manifestation of Western influence (Laurent, 2005). The resistance of Chinese culture to homosexuality is because it goes against value system "A." Sexual relations for procreation and male ejaculation in the absence of *Yin* (female) energy can be very harmful for a man's *Yang*.

Contraception and abortion are freely accepted by Chinese political leaders and by the Chinese public. Here, having sexual relations for procreation, as in value system "A," has been modified to control overpopulation. The government's "one child policy," which mandates that all married couples have no more than one child, has several surreptitious opponents. Ancient religious doctrines emphasize the importance of having a son in order to continue the family lineage. The one-child policy allows one child per couple whether the child is male or female. This causes conflict for Chinese couples who have a girl child and are unable to have a boy in accordance with value system "A." Here is a situation where there is a conflict between value system "A" and "B." Despite their opposition to the government-enforced one-child policy, couples follow it grudgingly to avoid imprisonment.

Buddhism is a complex religion, and there are numerous variations or denominations of Buddhism. There is no single scriptural authority in Buddhism. Each denomination has its own canonical scripture. Hence, it is almost impossible to offer a generalized attitude toward sexuality. The central problem that Buddhist teachings address is the problem of suffering and dissatisfaction. The Four Noble Truths set forth by Buddha are as follows: life is dissatisfying; life is dissatisfying because of craving or "thirst"; life does not have to be dissatisfying—dissatisfaction can end; there is a path to the end of dissatisfaction (Wilson, 2003). The path to end dissatisfaction has eight elements, each described as "correct" or "proper": proper understanding, proper intention, proper speech, proper action, proper livelihood, proper effort, proper mindfulness, and proper concentration. Sexual expression falls under the category of proper or improper action.

Sexual desire or longing is considered an obstacle to salvation. Salvation lies at the end of a long painful process of purification. Almost all forms of Buddhism subscribe to this belief of renunciation of family life in pursuit of salvation. Buddhist thought depreciates the body, particularly the female body, which is described as a vehicle for lust and desire (Faure, 1998). Buddhist literature offers models of dharmic lay life in the form of celibate marriages. Mahayana Buddhism presents a more progressive attitude and positive conceptions about desire and passions.

Different forms of Buddhism offer different responses to homosexuality. Generally speaking, Buddhism may be the only world religion that treats homosexuality more favorably than heterosexuality (Conner & Donaldson, 1990). Sexual relations between young novices and senior monks are celebrated in Japanese tales known as *chigo monogatari* (tales of *chigo*). There are a number of openly gay Western Buddhist teachers. Lesbian, gay, bisexual, and trangender Buddhists have established separate mediation centers to cater to the needs of the community. Here is a situation where value system "A" is more progressive and offers a model for society.

A modern development that came out of ancient Hinduism and Buddhism and developed during the fifth to the thirteenth century in the Common Era is Tantra. During the later part of the twentieth century, Tantric sexuality has become popular. While it is too extensive to write in depth about Trantras development, it is an important addition to modern-day Western religions. Tantra is the blending of male and female, masculine and feminine, bigender and transgender, heterosexuality, bisexuality, and homosexuality. It is in this blending that humans gain divinity and are one with God (Barratt, 2006). Two bodies have become one soul. It stresses the equality in nature of male and female. While not a religion, Tantric practices are found in individuals and groups in Christianity and Judaism as well as Hinduism and Buddhism.

## CONCLUSION

In this chapter, we have presented the primary scriptural, literary, and philosophical concepts that guide sexual behaviors around the world. All the world religions and philosophies are presented in the context of three basic value systems. The major value system of the world religions has been based on the "Acts of sex" (sexual value system "A") as defining what are acceptable or unacceptable sexual behaviors.

A second sexual value system, "B," which is just as ancient and philosophically and scripturally defended, is not based on the Acts of sex but rather on the nature of human relationships. In this value system, the motives and consequences of the Acts of sex become the definers of moral behavior and decision making. Every religion and world philosophy has adherents to both value systems.

The majority of people around the world represent the third value system, "C." These people are caught between value systems "A" and "B," which makes their sexual behaviors and decisions random according to what is emotionally comfortable for them.

## NOTES

1. According to the ancient Hindu scriptures, there are four *varnas* or castes: the Brahmins (teachers, scholars, and priests), the Kshatriyas (kings and warriors), the Vaishyas (traders), and the Shudras (agriculturists, service providers, and some artisan groups; Chaudhary, 2007). Although the caste system was legally abolished after India's independence, it is alive and well in most Indian communities (Rajagopal, 2007). Most political leaders vow to end discrimination, and there are several programs in place to benefit the lower castes. However, caste discrimination exists the way race discrimination exists in the United States, mostly insidious and subtle but sometimes overt and violent.

2. This is the *religious* concept of the eternal birth-death-birth cycle, where a soul moves from body to body. The status of each successive body, whether human or animal, is the direct result of the quality of the life the soul led in the previous body. Thus, a *good* life results in rebirth to a higher quality form, and a *bad* life results in rebirth to a lower quality form.

3. *Shari'a* literally means "the path to the watering hole." It is a body of Islamic religious law. *Shari'a* deals with many aspects of day-to-day life, including politics, economics, banking, business, contracts, family, sexuality, hygiene, and social issues.

4. *Hijab* is the Arabic term for "cover." It is mostly used to refer to women's head and body covering. In Islamic scholarship, *Hijab* is given the wider meaning of modesty, privacy, and morality. *Hijab* can vary considerably in different parts of the world. It can range from a simple head scarf to head-to toe cover with holes cut out for the eyes. It is not uncommon for young women in Muslim countries to wear fashionable Western clothes under their *Hijab*.

## REFERENCES

Barratt, B. B. (2006). *What is Tantric practice?* Xlibris: Philadelphia.

The birds, the bees and the taboos. (2007, September 9). *Economist*, pp. 54–54.

Boellstorff, T. (2005). Between religion and desire: Being Muslim and gay in Indonesia. *American Anthropologist, 107*(4), 575–585.

Chang, J. (1977). The Tao of love and sex: The ancient Chinese way to ecstasy. London: Wildwood House.

Chaudhary, L. (2007). Essays on education and social divisions in Colonial India. *Journal of Economic History, 67*(2), 500–503.

Conner, R., & Donaldson, S. (1990). Buddhism. In W. Dynes (Ed.), *Encyclopedia of Homosexuality*, Vol. 1 (pp. 168–171). New York: Garland Press.

Das, A., Parish, W. L., & Laumann, E. O. (2007). Masturbation in Urban China. *Archives of Sexual Behavior* (Online Publication). DOI # 10.1007/s10508–007–9222-z.

Deresiewicz, W. (2004). Letter from India. *Yale Review, 92*(2), 29–37.

Dunne, B. (1998). Power and sexuality in the Middle East. *Middle East Report, 206,* 8–11.

Fang, F. (1991). Sex in China: Studies in sexology in Chinese culture. New York: Plenum Press.

Faure, B. (1998). *The red thread: Buddhist approaches to sexuality.* Princeton, NJ: Princeton University Press.

Frediani, J. A. (1999). *Our whole lives.* Boston: Unitarian Universalist Association.

Frediani, J. A. (2000). *Sexuality and our faith.* Boston: United Church Board of Homeland Ministries.

Guinevere, T. (1998, January, 20). Star of India. *Advocate, 750/751,* 88–90.

Hartford Institute for Religion Research. (2001, March). *Faith Communities Today 2000 (FACT 2000): A Lilly Endowment Funded Project.* Hartford, CT: Hartford Seminary.

Hidayatullah, A. (2003). Islamic conceptions of sexuality. In D. W. Machacek & M. M. Wilcox (Eds.), *Sexuality and the world religions* (pp. 257–292). Santa Barbara, CA: ABC-CLIO, Inc.

Kerner, I. (2008). Sex Detox: Recharge desire. Revitalize intimacy. Rejuvenate your love life. New York: Harper Collins.

Kyriakides-Yeldham. (2005). Islamic medical ethics and the straight path of God. *Islam and Christian-Muslim Relations, 16*(3), 213–225.

Laurent, E. (2005). Sexuality and human rights: An Asian Perspective. *Journal of Homosexuality, 48,* 3 & 4, 163–225.

Office of the Surgeon General. (2001). The Surgeon General's Call to Action to promote sexual health and responsible sexual behavior. Washington, DC: Government Printing Office.

Rajagopal, B. (2007, August 18). The caste system—India's apartheid. *The Hindu* (online edition). Retrieved from http://www.hinduonnet.com/2007/08/18/stories/2007081 856301200.htm

*Random House Unabridged Dictionary.* (2006) New York: Random House, Inc.

Sherman, R. (2008, January, 9). Sex ed, Orthodox style. *The Jewish Week.* Retrieved December 26, 2008, from www.thejewishweek.com

Simon, W. & Gagnon, J. H. (1986). Sexual scripts: Permanence and change. *Archives of Sexual Behavior, 15,* 97–119.

Stayton, W. R. (1985). Alternative lifestyles: Marital options. In D. C. Goldberg (Ed.), *Contemporary marriage: Special issues in couples therapy* (pp. 241–260). Homewood, IL: Dorsey Press.

Stayton, W. R. (1992). Conflicts in crisis: Effects of religious belief systems on sexual health. In R. M. Green (Ed.), *Religion and sexual health: ethical, theological and clinical perspectives* (pp. 203–218). Boston: Kluwer Academic Publishers.

Stayton, W. R. (2007). Sexual value systems and sexual health. In M. S. Tepper & A. F. Owens (Eds.), *Sexual health: Vol. 3. Moral and cultural foundations* (pp. 79–96). Westport, CT: Praeger Perspectives.

Therborn, G. (2006). Families in today's world—and tomorrow's. *International Journal of Health Services, 36*(3), 593–603.

Yao, X. (2003). Harmony of Yin and Yang: Cosmology and sexuality in Daoism. In D. W. Machacek & M. M. Wilcox (Eds.), *Sexuality and the world religions* (pp. 65–99). Santa Barbara, CA: ABC-CLIO, Inc.

Webster's Revised Unabridged Dictionary. (1998). Plainfield, NJ: MICRA, Inc.

Weeks, J. (1981). Sexual politics and society: The regulation of sexuality since 1800. London: Longman.

Wilson, L. (2003). Buddhist views on gender and desire. In D. W. Machacek & M. M. Wilcox (Eds.), *Sexuality and the world religions* (pp. 133–175). Santa Barbara, CA: ABC-CLIO, Inc.

## Chapter Thirteen

# SHIFTING THE PARADIGM: WHAT OTHER COUNTRIES CAN LEARN FROM WESTERN EUROPE ABOUT SEXUALITY EDUCATION

*Barbara Kemp Huberman*

Since the 1980s, data has been available comparing the teen pregnancy and teen birth rates of various countries. The United States has consistently had much higher teen birth rates than almost all other developed countries. While it has been fairly clear that comprehensive sexuality education and easy access to contraception have had a significant impact on reducing rates of teen pregnancy and births in other countries, many other factors have also played significant roles.

In 1998, Advocates for Youth began to offer an annual two-and-one-half-week study tour to Germany, France, and the Netherlands to give American sexual health professionals the opportunity to explore the various cultural, social economic, and policy changes that have led to much lower rates of teen pregnancy and births in these countries.

This chapter addresses some of the most relevant lessons learned from 10 years of observing and listening to experts in these 3 countries talk about what made the difference. It is the result of many conversations, lectures, interviews, and personal experiences of the author while leading the annual study tours.

## BACKGROUND

In the United States, the adolescent birth rate is 9 times higher than that of the Netherlands (4 per 1,000 women ages 15 to 19). The U.S. adolescent birth rate (49 per 1,000) is almost 5 times higher than the rate in France (10 per 1,000) and nearly 4 times higher than that in Germany (12 per 1,000; Ventura, Mosher, Curtin, Abma, & Henshaw, 2001).[1]

The teen abortion rate in the United States (27.5 per 1,000) is nearly 8 times higher than the rate in Germany (3.6 per 1,000 women ages 15 to 19), over 7 times higher than that in the Netherlands (4.2 per 1,000), and over 3 times higher than the rate in France (10.2 per 1,000; Martin, Hamilton, & Ventura, 2001; Rademakers, 2001).

In the United States, the estimated HIV prevalence rate in young women ages 15–24 is 6 times higher than the rate in Germany, nearly 3 times higher than the rate in the Netherlands, and the same as that in France (UNAIDS, 2000).

In the United States, the estimated HIV prevalence rate in young men ages 15–24 is over 5 times higher than the rate in Germany, 3 times higher than the rate in the Netherlands, and about 1.5 times higher than that in France (Panchaud, Singh, Feivelson, & Darroch, 2000).

In the United States, the teen gonorrhea rate is over 74 times higher than that in the Netherlands and France (Darroch et al., forthcoming).

Finally, in the United States, teens begin having sexual intercourse at the same age or even younger age than teens in the other three nations, but U.S. teens have more sexual partners.

## THE PROJECT: AMERICAN SEXUAL HEALTH PROFESSIONALS LEARN FROM OTHERS

Each summer since 1998, Advocates for Youth and the University of North Carolina at Charlotte have sponsored study tours to France, Germany, and the Netherlands. The 35 participants include researchers, funders, policymakers, youth serving professionals, and young people, and they are asked to study: Why are adolescent sexual health indicators so much more positive in the three European countries than they are in the United States?

There have been many "lessons learned" from each 17-day study tour, but the following are some of the consistent observations and findings.

- Research is the basis for public policies to reduce pregnancies, abortions, and STDs.
- Political and religious interest groups have little influence on public health policy.
- The major impetus for each country's improved access to contraception, comprehensive sexuality education, and widespread public education campaigns is a national desire to reduce the numbers of abortions and to prevent HIV infection.
- Adults in the Netherlands, France, and Germany view young people as assets, not as problems. Adults value and respect adolescents and expect teens to act responsibly. Governments strongly support education and economic self-sufficiency for youth.
- Governments support massive, consistent, long-term public education campaigns utilizing television, films, radio, billboards, discos, pharmacies, and health care

providers. Media is a partner, not a problem, in these campaigns. Sexually explicit campaigns arouse little concern.

- Sexually active youth have free, convenient access to contraception through national health insurance.
- Sexuality education is not necessarily a curriculum; it may be integrated through many school subjects and at all grade levels. Educators provide accurate and complete information in response to students' questions.
- Families, educators, and health care providers have open, honest, consistent discussions with teens about sexuality.
- Adults see intimate sexual relationships as normal and natural for older adolescents, a positive component of emotionally healthy maturation. At the same time, young people believe it is "stupid and irresponsible" to have sex without protection and use the maxim "safe sex or no sex." Marriage is not a criterion for intimate relationships.
- The morality of sexual behavior is weighed through an individual ethic that includes the values of responsibility, love, respect, tolerance, and equity.

But how did these countries get to where they seem to be in terms of openness and comfort with sexuality? What changes in policies, systems, and practices have occurred that have produced the public health outcomes that we strive to achieve in terms of adolescent sexual health?

Prior to World War II, the Netherlands, Germany, and France had many similarities to the United States. Religion dominated both individual ethical decisions about sexual behavior and responsibility and sexual health public policy. The role of women in society was homemaker, child bearer, and parent. Divorce and single parenting were rare. Families generally were nuclear and stayed together in one place, and extended family members had an active role in the raising of children. In the 1960s, television was very tame, only a presence for several hours a day, and many homes didn't even have one, much less a VCR/DVD or computer. Condoms, diaphragms, and abstinence were the only contraceptives that were available. Abortion was possible, though costly, and it was difficult to find someone who would perform the procedure. Nonmedical individuals performed abortions that in many cases were unsafe and physically dangerous. Women themselves tried to abort with coat hangers or knitting needles and died or were rendered sterile from infections. The degree of openness about sexuality, tolerance for diversity, and acceptance of sexual relationships as normal and healthy for older adolescents was nominal.

In conversations with social scientists, researchers, public officials, and individuals in each of the three European countries, there appeared to be some critical events, technology changes, or policies that created a significant cultural shift in the areas of sexuality and reproductive health. It was not one event or change but the cumulative effect of many things.

World War II seemed to be a pivotal point in the cultural shift toward openness and a nonjudgmental, individual ethical framework versus the authoritarian or collective model determining ethical behavior primarily taken from religious doctrine. Some experts related "that when you have lost so much as a result of war, not only did you really have to value young people but you had to see them as contributing members of society and capable of making decisions for themselves."

Young people were considered adults at 16 to 17 and treated as adults. With a need to repopulate countries because of war losses, young marriage and childbearing was condoned. "Teenagers" are basically an American invention, and it's only been recently that other developed countries have embraced the concept of this period of development. In Europe, being involved in intimate sexual relationships was not a crisis or problem for adolescents as they transitioned into adulthood. What was important was to teach young people that intimate sexual relationships must be a "choice" by both partners. European youth related over and over again "only do it if you want to do it—not just because someone's pressuring you." One young man related "you Americans make it such forbidden fruit by preaching 'just say no' and only talking about the dangers, it's no wonder that teenagers want to do it."

America is described by Europeans as hypocritical when it comes to sex. We allow sexual violence in our media but won't support positive, healthy messages. We are sex saturated but rarely condone using contraception and protection. Our politicians approve millions of dollars to tell young people they cannot have sex unless they are married, and then every day a politician is revealed to be committing adultery, involved in sexually abusing someone, or has had children out of wedlock in their past. Young people see adults do one thing but tell them to do another.

The shift from the church or religious doctrine being the dominant factor in shaping how a person took responsibility for his/her life and making individual choices certainly occurred after World War II. Many adults related that the churches role or lack of a role in the Holocaust and other atrocities of the war led people to no longer trust the church as the ultimate moral guide for values and for justice issues. Participation in religious activities began to drop, and life no longer revolved around the church.

There were key moments later in the 1960s, 1970s, and 1980s when respected religious leaders spoke out and gave people the freedom to decide how they wanted to live their sexual and reproductive lives. In the Netherlands, a much admired Catholic bishop on a television program said the following, "family planning is just that, the family plans, not the Pope." Women and couples perceived this as tacit permission to use artificial birth control, mainly oral contraceptives, as they became available. In the 1980s, a French bishop condoned the use of condoms to prevent the spread of AIDS, and even today, there are many priests and bishops within the Catholic church in France who have been open and vocal about realistic ways to prevent AIDS, to increase the role of women in the church, and to accept and open the ministry to homosexuals. Other denominations within the three countries have given women equal or significant roles, supported the feminist movement of the 1960s and 1970s, spoken out for realistic and pragmatic approaches to sexuality, and promoted an individual's right to self determination. Even in America, Catholics for Free Choice has emerged today to become a potent force in the debate over abortion.

Though each country's governmental model is different, there appears to be the commonality of "the state or government has no role in people's personal lives as far as their sexual relationships are concerned." We may *think* we have a separation of church and state in America, but when you look at the way the religious right has taken control of reproductive and sexual health policies, systems, and funding, it is clear that we have allowed *some* groups' religious beliefs and values to restrict information and services that young people need as sexual beings, and it is getting worse. The recent federal program, funded at over a billion dollars so far, that only allows states to use the money for abstinence-only-until-marriage education is a good example of this censorship. Policymakers pay no heed to the majority of parents (80–90%) who do not want this to be all the sexuality education their children receive. In survey after survey, the American public views teen pregnancy and sexually transmitted diseases (STDs) as public health issues that demand a comprehensive educational approach. The majority believe adolescents, if they are sexually active, should have access to contraception and condoms. They do not view teen pregnancy and STDs as only religious or moral problems but pragmatically want their young people to have whatever they need to protect themselves from pregnancy and disease.

There is not doubt that technology, especially the introduction of oral contraceptives, and emergency contraception (EC) have given women and their partners the ability to engage in and enjoy intimate relationships without the crisis of unplanned, unwanted pregnancy. In the case of each of these methods, they were available far earlier and with fewer barriers in the Netherlands, Germany, and France than in the United States. Less stringent governmental regulations and national health care plans that pay for all or most of the cost have made it much easier for women to have a positive attitude toward using them. No pelvic exams, over-the-counter access in pharmacies in some countries, and provider education supported a woman's decision if she chose to use contraception or EC.

In the 1970s, when America legalized abortion and controversy arose, these countries experienced opposition and conflict over the right to choose abortion as well. In America, as the debate and hostility brewed, our public policies began to promote "chastity," "Just Say No" messages, and attempts to do away with legal abortion. In these three countries, the same hue and cry occurred, but policymakers, listening to public health experts, went in totally different directions. They acknowledged that intimate relationships were normal and natural expressions of sexuality, and if unplanned, unwanted pregnancy was to be reduced and the need for abortion eliminated, then you had to educate people and you had to give them the capacity, through reliable contraception, to prevent pregnancy in the first place. Physician education campaigns, media campaigns, and public education campaigns were government funded. A popular slogan in the Netherlands that appeared in posters and was often quoted was: "I'm the boss of my belly." The concept of abstinence or pressure to remain virgins was nonexistent and still is today. Family planning services and organizations have never experienced "gag rules" or censorship, and the decision to provide contraception or abortion to teens—no matter what age— is the decision of the medical practitioner and the patient.

The availability of, and access to, contraception was certainly a significant part of the feminist movement of the 1960s in the three countries. Women, now that pregnancy and child bearing could be controlled by them, began to openly express and demand *pleasure* in sexual relationships and demand equality not just in the bedroom but in other facets of life: educational opportunities, careers, children as a choice, and elected office. America experienced the same sexual and feminist revolution, but the cultural reconstruction to a positive, healthy view of sexuality did not cross the ocean. Most Western European societies moved to openness, naturalness, and a focus on the pleasure *and* the responsibility of sexual intimacy. In America, shame, guilt, and fear became the motivator in the chastity movement, directed especially toward women.

The feminist movement in the United States saw a strong backlash as conservative groups organized and preached a return to "family values," meaning women should stay home, be caretakers of children and husbands, and be content with a subservient role. Concerned Women of America, The Eagle Forum, and other conservative and religious groups supported chastity and abstinence-only-until-marriage curricula as the only sexual information that women or young girls should receive. This backlash never had any foothold in Western Europe or most other developed countries.

Social policies and benefits that *support* family life are far more prevalent. Paid maternity/paternity leave for 14 weeks is the minimum, and parents are encouraged to take more. In France, the more children you have, the larger this paid leave extends. The average workweek is shorter. Summer holiday is usually 4 to 6 weeks, and 10 days to 2 weeks vacation at Christmas time is the norm for most. More mothers of young children have the ability to work part time, and preschool is available to all. Head Start in America has been the most successful teen pregnancy prevention program we've ever had, yet only one-third of eligible children have access to it because of lack of funding. All three countries have national health insurance that affords everyone access to preventive as well as crisis care. It is a right, not a privilege. These countries spend far more on public welfare benefits for families and individuals, young and old, than the United States. Parenthood and retiring from work offers income that is livable and realistic.

In the 1980s, HIV once again opened a door for society to acknowledge sexual relationships in a positive healthy way and give people the tools they needed to protect themselves from transmission of this deadly virus. Most Western European countries embarked on massive, government funded efforts to promote responsible risk reduction, embracing "safe sex or no sex" as the primary message, never abstinence alone. Media and public education campaigns that were based on behavioral research, humorous and diverse, made condom usage a given. European teens today, having heard and seen these messages consistently all their lives, having grown up in families where parents gave condoms to their youth, and seeing condom machines on walls in train stations, men's and women's bathrooms, easily available in tobacco shops, boutiques, discos, clubs and schools relate very consistently, "it would be stupid to have sex and not use a condom." The stigma, if there is one, is on the failure to be responsible—not the decision to be sexually intimate. Every teen interviewed, on the streets, in cafes, and at schools, said it is a given; if you have sex, you will always use a condom. In contrast, teens interviewed in America said things like, "if a girl carries a condom, she's considered a slut," "a guy who carries a condom is only out for one thing," or "if I had condoms, it would be a jinx. I wouldn't get any." This is quite a difference in attitude and intolerable in this era of AIDS. Using condoms and the pill, couples sharing responsibility, is the norm in Europe. In Holland, they call it the "double Dutch method."

Sexuality education is a shared responsibility as well. While there may be courses in sexuality, it is considered a vital component of educational institutions and is integrated throughout many subjects. When asked, young people do not always report they had sex education in school. But if you ask them if they learned about contraception—they say "yes, in biology." If you ask them if they explored relationships, love, and respect, they say "oh yes, in life skills class." If you ask them if they discussed decision making, gay/lesbian issues, justice, and responsibility, they say "yes, in civics class." STDs and HIV prevention are incorporated into religion or science classes. Teachers do not fear censorship, irate parents, or intimidation that if they say the wrong thing or answer a forbidden question they will be fired as is happening in America. Parents welcome and hold the schools responsible for educating their children about sexuality.

Another startling contrast between America and Western Europe is the respect and credibility that is afforded to public health scientists and researchers.

If data and evaluation point to specific strategies to reduce sexual risk taking, then politicians, government officials and funding agents accept it and use it to make decisions. This pragmatic, science-based approach is transmitted to the general public, and even though a minority may object, it rarely changes sound public health policies. An individual's right to information and services is paramount. The greater good for society is seen through helping individuals be responsible and healthy. Needle exchange programs, for instance, are seen as critical to public health but place responsibility for safety on the individual. Telling someone *who* they may be intimate with or when it's okay to have sexual relationships is your decision, not the states. The primary message from the family and from society is: "Here's all we know, here's the services. Be safe, responsible, and respectful; pleasure is important to both partners, in a relationship."

Lastly, the role of media has also been a significant factor in shifting the paradigm to a positive, healthy approach to sexuality. Electronic media, TV, radio, and movies have little of the sexual violence toward women that America seems to crave. Media is seen as part of the solution, not always the problem. Large, government-funded public education campaigns based on behavior change research increased the use of contraception (mostly oral contraception) quickly. Dramatic increases in condom usage were well-documented after intensive "safe sex or no sex" campaigns. Special campaigns at vacation/holiday times were directed at young people and focused on using condoms and pills. Movie trailers, fast-paced "safe sex" videos for discos, and contests for print messages about safe sex engaged young people in promoting safer sex. There is, however, concern about the impact of all the American TV shows, such as *Jerry Springer* and *Big Brother*, that are being imported in terms of violence, sexualization of children, and the lack of a positive, responsible view of sexual relationships.

Though the teen pregnancy rate and some specific STD rates are declining, the United States has continued to be schizophrenic in its approach to sexuality. The sexual behavior of adults is the opposite of what is demanded of our youth. Separation of church and state is supposedly valued, but increasingly, religious organizations and leaders dominate public policy decisions and appropriations. Politicians make laws and policies that infringe on an individual's right to make their own reproductive and sexual decisions and then posture that they want to keep government out of people's lives and bedrooms.

Shifting the culture toward a more open, positive, and healthy framework for sexuality in America will not be easy—but it can be done. Our young people deserve a future where being a sexual person is respected and valued, where knowledge is power and society views sexuality as a wonderful and vital component of being human, and an individual's right to be responsible for their sexual and reproductive decisions is a cultural norm.

## SUMMARY AND RECOMMENDATIONS

Many other developed nations have much lower rates of teen pregnancy and births than the United States. While there are many influences and factors, Germany, France, and the Netherlands have successfully shifted the culture to a more positive, relationship-based world of sexual behavior. They have enacted policies and programs that make sexuality education much more open, comprehensive, and reality-based and have created health plans that make obtaining and using contraception and condoms the norm. Research drives public policies in regard to sexual health programs and services, and the society has accepted that young people are sexual beings and have a right to make their own decisions regarding sexual behavior and relationships.

Advocates for Youth envisions a time when the United States is united in its belief that sexuality is a normal, healthy, and positive component of being human. We support a society that:

- values young people and doesn't demonize or condemn them as sexually promiscuous, or "babies having babies," or irresponsible and incapable of sexual expression that is safe, healthy, and responsible;
- recognizes adolescent sexual relationships as normal and healthy; and
- embraces the contributions and resources young people make to our world.

Based on the lessons learned from our work in Germany, France, and the Netherlands, the vision is to build an American society where:

- Adolescents have the *Right* to balanced, accurate, and realistic sexuality education; confidential and affordable health services; and a secure stake in the future.
- Youth have *Respect*. Today, they are perceived only as the problem.
- Valuing young people means they are part of the solution and are included in the development of programs and policies that affect their well-being.
- Society has the *Responsibility* to provide young people with the tools they need to safeguard their sexual health, and young people have the *Responsibility* to protect themselves from too-early childbearing and STDs, including HIV.

This trilogy of values underpins the social philosophy of adolescent sexual and reproductive health in the Netherlands, Germany, and France and is the vision that should guide our adolescent sexual health programs, services, and policies in the United States.

## NOTE

1. Calculations based on Feijoo, A. N. (1999). *Teenage pregnancy, the case for prevention.* Washington, D.C.: Advocates for Youth.

## REFERENCES

Darroch, J. E. et al. (forthcoming). *Adolescent sexual and reproductive health: A developed country comparison.* New York: The Alan Guttmacher Institute.

Martin, J. A., Hamilton, B., & Ventura, S. J. (2001). Births: Preliminary data for 2000. *National Vital Statistics Reports, 49*(5), 1–20.

Panchaud, C., Singh, S., Feivelson, D., & Darroch, J. E. (2000). Sexually transmitted diseases among adolescents in developed countries. *Family Planning Perspectives, 32*(1), 24–32, 45.

Rademakers, J. (2001). *Sex education in the Netherlands.* Paper presented to the European Study Tour, Leiden, Netherlands, NISSO.

UNAIDS. (2000). *Report on the global HIV/AIDS epidemic.* Geneva, Switzerland: Author.

Ventura, S. J., Mosher, W. D., Curtin, S. C., Abma, J. C., & Henshaw, S. (2001). Trends in pregnancy rates for the United States, 1976–97: An update. *National Vital Statistics Reports, 49*(4), 1–10.

Part V

# PRINCIPLES FOR SEXUALITY EDUCATION

Chapter Fourteen

# AMERICAN ASSOCIATION OF SEXUALITY EDUCATORS, COUNSELORS, AND THERAPISTS (AASECT) CODE OF ETHICS

American Association of Sexuality Educators, Counselors and Therapists
P.O. Box 1960 Ashland, Virginia 23005–1960
Prepared by the AASECT Code of Ethics Committee:
Jack S. Annon, Ph.D., (Chair): Douglas Liebert, Ph.D.;
Catherine Ravella, RN, MA; Craig Robinson, Ph.D.
Board approved May 2004

Recognizing its responsibilities to society and given its own national objectives, AASECT has adopted the following Code of Ethics. The Code: (1) is a condition for membership; (2) applies to all AASECT members, regardless of their certification or member status: and (3) embraces *any* activity that directly or indirectly relates to professional identity or training. The Code does not replace or modify the requirements for or purposes of certification as a sex educator, counselor, therapist or Supervisor.

## PUBLIC POLICY

By public policy, AASECT has a duty to promote (and enforce) quality services from and proper conduct/professionalism by its members. Professionalism is a product of society. Professional status is a privilege, not a right earned by holding a degree, certification, or membership. While professional ethics are not law, they are permissive and they establish both aspirational standards and guidelines for professional practice. AASECT accepts that a professional association has a public duty to advocate standards for the services offered by its membership, so as to (ensure) promote both the protection of and benefits to the consumer. Therefore, AASECT promulgates ethical standards that must be honored by its members.

## GOALS AND OBJECTIVES: (OBJECTIVES)

The Code of Ethics is intended to advance the status of sex education counseling, therapy, supervision and research. The Code of Ethics should not be viewed (solely) as disciplinary in intent. The purpose is to provide guidance to AASECT practitioners and to provide an observable code from which society and consumers may derive expected behavior. (The benefits are primarily for the consumer and society, and only secondarily for the practitioner and AASECT.)

## SELF-REGULATION

Integrity, competence, confidentiality, responsibility and other applicable standards are not always subject to finite definitions, descriptions, prescriptions or proscriptions. Virtually every professional situation requires that the practitioner make judgments as to propriety. Through setting forth suggested standards (rules) of ethical conduct for practice-related conditions, qualities, skills and services, the Code of Ethics is intended to assist AASECT members with such judgments. Each member must exercise self-regulation and satisfy governmental regulatory and legal requirements.

## ACCOUNTABILITY TO AASECT

While ethics do not have the same authority as law, membership in AASECT is predicated upon adherence to the Code of Ethics. That is, members of AASECT, in the conduct of all aspects of their life that relates to their professional work and identity, are expected to honor the Code of Ethics, and to act according to general principles of professional ethical practice that may not be directly dealt with in this Code of Ethics.

The Code of Ethics creates accountability for the member to AASECT. It should be underscored that the Code of Ethics is relevant to justifying membership in AASECT, and is not intended to serve as a standard of care for professional practice in legal proceedings.

Membership in AASECT may be terminated for sufficient cause as outlined in the Bylaws, the Membership Application, and the formal Application for Membership and/or Certification. A prerequisite for initial membership and a requisite for continued membership in AASECT is that each potential member or current member must notify the AASECT Board of Directors in writing of any previous or current legal (civil or criminal), ethical or regulatory (licensing) complaints or judgments, relevant to their practice, and provide any documentation or information pertaining thereto that is requested on behalf of the AASECT Board of Directors. The member shall inform AASECT in writing of any adjudicatory outcome relevant to their practice. Such notification must be done within thirty (30) days of the members' knowledge of the complaint and any request from AASECT for information or documentation must be fulfilled within thirty (30) days. Decisions on all applications for AASECT certification or recertification will be suspended until the adjudicatory outcome of complaints have been determined. Termination shall be by two-thirds vote of the entire Board of Directors in accordance with the policies and procedures established by the Bylaws, and the Letter of Application, and the Formal Application for Membership and Certification.

*Disciplinary Action:* The Board of Directors shall determine the appropriateness of continued or terminated membership in AASECT for any AASECT member who is: (1) adjudged to have violated a civil law that is material and relevant to professional practice; (2) convicted of a criminal misdemeanor or felony, (3) disciplined by a professional ethics committee of the State to which the member belongs, (4) disciplined by a State Licensing or Certification Board, (5) disciplined, or expelled by an Institutional Grievance Boards of the University, College, governmental agency, or organization to which the member belongs; and (6) for religious counselors, disciplined by the State Leader of the Religious Denomination or other appropriate leadership group to which the member belongs. The information available to and the deliberations of the Board of Directors shall be deemed confidential by all AASECT sources. The action regarding continued or terminated membership, with concomitant conditions made by the Board of Directors is final. (No appeal right exists). The member will be notified by the Board in writing of any membership or certification termination. There is no appeal to this process.

## ETHICS PROCEDURE

### Inquiries From AASECT Members

The AASECT Ethics Committee-AEC has a duty to respond to inquiries from AASECT members only. Members who contact the AASECT office in need of ethics consultation will be referred to the AEC Chairperson. The AEC Chairperson will assess the inquirer's needs, provide some immediate feedback, and arrange for follow-up consultation if appropriate. Before the follow-up consultation, the Chairperson will collaborate with other AEC members on the issues at hand. Some or all of these meetings may occur by telephone, or through e-mail or other electronic means, with identities concealed. The identity of all inquirers will be held in confidence within the AEC.

The Chairperson will keep a written record using the AEC Inquiry Consultation Form of all inquiries and make special note of the ethical principles and standards relevant to each inquiry. The Chairperson will collaborate with at least one AEC member on each inquiry. Each inquiry will be discussed at the next scheduled AEC meeting. Further contact will then be made with the inquirer, if indicated by committee consensus.

## CODE OF CONDUCT

### Principle One: Competence and Integrity

The AASECT member shall accept responsibility for the consequences of his/her acts, by omission or commission, and make reasonable efforts to ensure that all professional services are appropriate and adequate for the consumer.

The member shall bear a heavy social responsibility because society deems the services as representing specialized expertise and because the consumers using the services are vulnerable. The member shall, therefore, be committed to maintaining high standards of scholarship and practice and shall be accountable as an individual to the standards of the profession. At a minimum, the member shall perform any professional service in accord with the prevailing standards of performance in professional activities when measured against generally prevailing peer performance.

The member shall have training in sex education, counseling, therapy, and/or supervision that is in accord with the standards promulgated by AASECT and the laws relevant to the jurisdiction in which the member practices.

The member shall recognize his/her limits of competence and shall communicate them at the earliest possible time and at any time thereafter to the consumer. When the member's level of competence does not afford optimal benefits to the consumer, the member shall, in a timely and efficient manner, recommend referral to better-qualified sources.

The member shall not knowingly permit any consumer to misunderstand the member's competency and shall clarify credentials, training, affiliations, experiences and skills in an honest and accurate manner.

The member shall recognize the necessity and benefit of professional growth by participating in continuing education.

The member shall not enter into association for professional practice with or assist, aid, or promote in any manner the practice of an unqualified or incompetent person which shall include any person whom the member knows or has reason to believe, does not adhere to the standards of AASECT or is in violation of any law. This shall include, but is not limited to, making a referral to an unqualified or incompetent person. The member shall verify the competence and integrity of the person to whom a consumer is referred.

The member shall not willfully make or file any false report record, or information, or induce another person to make or file any false report, record or information.

The member shall not provide any remuneration, regardless of form, to any source for receiving the referral of a consumer for professional services unless the source of the referral maintains continued involvement in the care of the consumer. Conversely, the member shall not receive any remuneration regardless of form from any source for providing the referral of a consumer for professional services unless the member maintains continued involvement in the care of the consumer. Any such financial arrangement must be disclosed to and approved and acknowledged in writing by the consumer.

The member who becomes emotionally, physically or otherwise impaired or disabled to a degree that it impacts on the best interest of the consumer shall, in a timely and efficient manner, make a referral of the consumer to a qualified and appropriate professional source so as to avoid any undue abandonment of the consumer.

## Principle Two: Moral, Ethical, and Legal Standards

The AASECT member shall accept that the quality of his/her professional services (are) is dependent upon both personal morality and professional ethics and on the ability to maintain legal standards.

The member shall be aware of and monitor the fact that his/her personal needs may influence judgments and actions in the therapeutic relationship and shall, regardless of experience or training, have a qualified review source such as a supervisor available to assist in safeguarding against unwise or inappropriate judgments and acts.

The member shall not enter into any dual relationship regardless of nature that jeopardizes the well-being of the consumer.

The member shall avoid any action that might violate or diminish the legal and civil rights of the consumer.

The member shall not engage in or condone practices by any source that are inhumane or that result in illegal or unjustifiable action relevant to race, handicap, age, gender, sexual orientation, religion or national origin.

The member shall make only factual, honest, and clearly stated (not misleading) public announcements, statements or communications such as (but not limited to) for advertising or promotional purposes.

The member shall not set forth identification with AASECT such as (but not limited to) membership or certification status in an announcement statement, or communication, whatever the form, that also includes a college or university degree, unless that degree is based on academic merit and is from an appropriately accredited higher education institution.

The member shall act in accord with AASECT ethics, standards and guidelines related to education, counseling, therapy, supervision and research.

The member shall act in accord with the standards and guidelines for the protection of consumers promulgated by other professional associations with which the member is affiliated and the laws of the jurisdiction(s) in which the member provides professional services.

The member shall report any ethical, regulatory, or legal complaint or judgment relevant to their practice filed against the member with this report being submitted in writing within thirty (30) days of knowledge to the Chair of the AASECT Ethics Committee.

## Principle Three: Welfare of the Consumer

The AASECT member shall accept that the consumer is in a unique position of vulnerability in respect to services related to sex education, counseling, therapy, research, and supervision, and shall constantly be mindful of the responsibility for protection of the consumer's welfare, rights and best interests and for the rigorous maintenance of the trust implicit in the educational, counseling or therapeutic alliance.

(A) The member shall, from the onset of professional contact with a consumer or a potential consumer, clarify;
　　(1) Professional training, experiences and competencies;
　　(2) The nature of the professional services available to the consumer (with an explanation of mutual roles and duties);
　　(3) The limits of intervention effectiveness;
　　(4) Personal values or professional preferences that reflect biases rather than being responsive to the needs and well-being of the consumer;
　　(5) Any exceptions to confidentiality and privileged communications (e.g. duty to warn, mandatory reporting, etc.); and
　　(6) Any financial issues, especially the payment obligations of the consumer.

(B) The member shall treat all information received about a consumer as confidential, even if some portions of the information appear trivial, irrelevant or not to require confidentiality; even the existence of an educational counseling or therapeutic relationship with the consumer is confidential. Where required by law, the AASECT provider will design a HIPPA policy and follow all legal requirements protecting consumer privacy.

(C) The member shall advocate the consumer's privileged communication, *as granted by the laws of the jurisdiction applicable to the consumer and/or* the member in the event that there is uncertainty about the effectiveness or validity of the consumer's consent to release information that is potentially confidential and/or privileged, the member shall obtain appropriate legal determination.

(D)   The member shall divulge information received from a consumer or prospective consumer to the extent required only in the following circumstances

    (1)   When the consumer provides written and informed consent, which indicates:

        (a)   The type and nature of information to be released;

        (b)   Knowledge of the purpose for which the information will be used;

        (c)   Designation of the source that will receive the information;

        (d)   That the consent is given voluntarily and with competency; and

        (e)   The consumer's name and the date on which the consent is given.

    (2)   When there is clear and imminent danger of bodily harm or to the life or safety of the consumer or another person disclosure shall be made in accord with the laws of the jurisdiction in which the member practices.

    (3)   When applicable law declares that such information may be released.

(E)   The member shall obtain the consumers' written informed consent for using any identifiable information about the consumer for purposes of education, training, research or publication.

(F)   The member shall reveal a consumer's confidential information to a professional source with a limited right to know, such as (but not limited to) a supervisor or consultant in an appropriate manner; it is the member's responsibility to take reasonable steps to assure that the other professional source will properly treat the information in a confidential manner.

(G)   The member shall keep meaningful records relevant to the professional services provided to and contacts (of any nature) with the consumer and shall have a secure system for the preservation of records with the minimal contents and duration of retention being in accord with the laws that are applicable to the jurisdiction in which the member practices: at a minimum:

    (1)   A full record shall be retained intact for no less than three (3) years after completion of the last date of professional services or contact;

    (2)   A full record or meaningful summary of the record shall be maintained for no less than twelve (12) additional years.

(H)   The member shall have a formal (written) arrangement for the preservation of consumer records upon his/her ceasing of practice, death or incapacity. This arrangement must be in accord with the laws of the jurisdiction in which the member practices.

(I)   The member shall, when providing professional services in a group context or to a couple or family make a reasonable effort to promote safeguarding of confidentiality on the part of each consumer in the group, couple or family.

(J)    The member shall orient the minor consumer to the limits of confidentiality pertaining to a parent's right to know as defined by the laws of the jurisdiction in which the member practices.

(K)    The member shall, regardless of the reasons for which the consumer sought professional services and regardless of the theory or technique being used by the member, predicate every sex counseling or therapy intervention upon diagnosis and meaningful consumer(s) treatment plan, which shall be consistently documented in writing, justified academically, evaluated for effectiveness, monitored for strengths and weaknesses and modified accordingly.

(L)    The member shall as needed to protect the best interest of the consumer, seek consultation and/or supervision with special reference to the treatment plan and to the personal elements of the therapeutic relationship.

(M)    The member shall not engage in any dual relationship, regardless of nature or circumstances, with a consumer or with persons who have a primary relationship with a consumer served by the member if such dual relationship could potentially be detrimental to or jeopardize the well-being of a consumer. A dual relationship occurs when a member is in a professional role with a person and (1) at the same time is in another role with the same person, and/or (2) at the same time is in a relationship with a person closely associated with or related to the person with whom the member has the professional relationship, and/or (3) promises to enter into another relationship in the future with the person or a person closely associated with or related to the consumer.

(N)    The member practicing counseling or therapy shall not engage, attempt to engage or offer to engage a consumer in sexual behavior whether the consumer consents to such behavior or not. Sexual misconduct includes kissing, sexual intercourse and/or the touching by either the member or the consumer of the other's breasts or genitals. Members do not engage in such sexual misconduct with current consumers. Members do not engage in sexual intimacies with individuals they know to be close relatives, guardians, or significant others of a current consumer. Sexual misconduct is also sexual solicitation, physical advances, or verbal or nonverbal conduct that is sexual in nature, that occurs in connection with the member's activities or roles as a counselor or therapist, and that either (1) is unwelcome, is offensive, or creates a hostile workplace or educational environment, and the member knows or is told this or (2) is sufficiently severe or intense to be abusive to a reasonable person in the context. Sexual misconduct can consist of a single intense or severe act, or of multiple persistent or pervasive acts. For purposes of determining the existence of sexual misconduct, the counseling or therapeutic relationship is deemed to continue in perpetuity.

(O)    The member shall terminate professional services to the consumer when it is reasonably evident or should be evident that the consumer is not obtaining benefits sufficient to justify continued intervention. Upon termination the member shall make referral to another professional source and/or offer reasonable follow-up to further the best interests of the consumer.

## Principle Four: Welfare of Students, Trainees and Others

The AASECT member shall respect the rights and dignity of students, trainees and others (such as employees), maintain high standards of scholarship and preserve academic freedom and responsibility.

(A)   The member shall, from the onset of professional contact with students, trainees and others over whom the member has administrative, educational or supervisory authority clarify: the member's professional qualifications and competencies; the objectives, responsibilities and duties of all concerned and any financial issues, especially any payment obligations.

(B)   The member shall accord confidentiality to information of a personal or intimate nature obtained in his/her professional role; the provision of confidentiality does not, however, preclude fulfilling a professional responsibility or duty to consumers, educational or training institutions or programs, professional associations or governmental-regulatory or legal sources.

(C)   The member shall maintain high standards of scholarship and present information that is accurate and timely in all administrative, educational and supervisory activities.

(D)   The member shall keep meaningful and systematic records of all administrative, educational and supervisory activities.

(E)   The member shall not coerce or require a student, trainee or other to serve as a subject for a research project.

(F)   The member shall not provide diagnosis, therapeutic counseling or therapy or any other clinical service to students or trainees or those over whom the member has administrative, educational or supervisory authority.

(G)   The member shall not harass in any manner a student, trainee or other person over whom the member *has* administrative, educational or supervisory authority. Members do not engage in sexual relationships with students or supervisees who are in their department, agency, or training center, or over whom members have, or are likely to have, evaluative authority.

(H)   The member shall not, during the administrative, educational or supervisory period enter into any dual relationship, regardless of nature, that jeopardizes the well-being of the student, trainee or other.

(I)   The member shall not, during the administrative, educational or supervisory period, engage, attempt to engage or offer to engage the student, trainee or other in sexual behavior.

(J)   The member shall be cognizant that a dual relationship subsequent to the administrative, educational or supervisory period may potentially jeopardize the well being of the student, trainee or other.

## Principle Five: Welfare of Research Subjects

The AASECT member shall conduct his/her investigations with respect for the dignity, rights and welfare of the subjects. Research must be ethical and legal at its inception and not justified solely by its intended or achieved outcome.

(A)   The member shall be involved only with sex research that is carried out by persons qualified to do such investigations or under the direct supervision of persons so qualified.

(B)   The member shall be involved only with sex research that designates and identifies (in writing) to the potential subjects the names and professional qualifications of the person or persons with ethical scientific and legal responsibility for the conduct of the investigation.

(C)    The member shall be involved only with sex research that provides adequate protection(s) to human subjects at risk. Any research project must:
   (1)  Include the voluntary and informed consent of each subject; and
   (2)  Be in accord with applicable legal prescriptions or proscriptions.

(D)    The member shall be involved only with sex research that protects the confidentiality of research data including the identity of participants or others revealed during the investigation.

(E)    The member shall be involved only with sex research that requires all investigators to be honest and accurate in their dealings with research subjects and all persons receiving information about the research.

(F)    The member shall be involved only with sex research that offers to provide an explanation of the purpose of the investigation and of the individual and collective results to each person who serves as a research subject.

(G)    The member shall be involved only with sex research that has been prefaced by the submission of a research proposal for peer review with special reference to ethical and legal safeguards for the potential research subjects. This peer review may occur in different forms, such as an institutional review board for evaluation for ethical propriety, and must be in accord with all relevant laws.

(H)    The member will not engage in any type of sexual relationship or sexual misconduct with research subjects as defined above in Principle Three (N). (Final revision June 7, 2004)

## NOTE

Reprinted with permission by American Association of Sexuality Educators, Counselors, and Therapists, AASECT.

Chapter Fifteen

# THE "E" IN AASECT: WHY IT MATTERS

*Patti Britton*

I have worn the mantle of AASECT-certified sexuality educator (ACSE) for many years now. I think it was in 1993, sitting at my desk in a New York City apartment, going over what I might submit for certification, that first moved me about the power of our work. I remember that my application was a thick, 4-inch binder containing a record of my professional life. In it were all of the workshops I had attended, trainings I had received, and my entire doctoral program documentation. On the other side were the pages that contained my legacy as a sexuality educator. I was daunted at first to assemble this dossier, but then I got into it.

As I collected and sorted papers, it suddenly occurred to me, "Hey, this is my life!"

I felt so proud and full. I felt full of the life that my work gives me and filled with a sense of pride in what we do as sexuality educators.

My work in sex ed began in the 1970s as what the local Planned Parenthood called "rural family planning outreach." Sort of the American (think Appalachia) version of the barefoot doctor in Asia. There I was, a petite woman alone in her VW bus, tables and chairs stuck crammed in the back, and a ferocious-looking yellow dog on the front seat as my protector. I would drive the back roads of rural New England in search of "poor women or families." My mission then, not unlike now, was to bring the light. That light was information, education, and empowerment about women's fertility to the most suffering families, to let them choose when and whether to have children. I saw poverty that resembles the poorest of undeveloped nations. What we knew about Africa then had nothing on Vermont's rural poor.

So, with my "birth control kit" in tow, bus parked beside the most tumbledown, horrific decay of living conditions, I would haul out the *Beautiful Book* and teach contraception—and refer to social and public health services for those women with the bands of babies and children running about. That was my first pass as a sexuality educator. I graduated to the clinical setting during that period, teaching in groups about sexuality, family planning, and relationships—always with a sense of how fortunate I was to be doing this high work.

I have had the good fortune to know and work with the best of our craft. People like Carol Cassell, Mike McGee, Michael Carrera, Sol Gordon, Konnie McCaffree, Debra Haffner, Peter Scales, and Martha Roper—these have been my compadres on the path.

I served in a variety of roles: as the SIECUS deputy director delivering HIV/AIDS or comprehensive sexuality education sessions; at PPFA as associate director of education, running the clearinghouse, writing the newsletter, and conducting trainings for educators; and as director of the ETR HIV/AIDS prevention program in which I trained school educators around the country. I have also appeared on national television/radio as a sex expert; or giving quotes each month to a barrage of magazines. This is all sexuality education at the core.

My career has spanned three-plus decades and has had many twists and turns. But through it all, I've remained true to my original calling, an educator first; everything else comes next.

I recall doing work in my private practice, opened in 1993 in Manhattan, at that time with a co–sexologist partner. He was always remarking about my style. "You are the consummate educator," he used to say, "While I bring my therapy and counseling skills first, you always educate then do the rest." Yes, education *and* therapy or counseling is a rainbow of many colors. It can be done in myriad ways.

Whether you are a college professor, a high school teacher, an after-school program leader, a social service worker who teaches teens about STDs, a trainer of professionals, a writer of how-to books (or even a good parent who seizes those "teachable moments" with your own kids who share your breakfast table), you are being a sexuality educator. Our work takes on many faces. I know AASECT-certified sexuality educators abound from the family of Planned Parenthood educators, my home team, who offer a plethora of teaching and educational treasures. Lucky us to have them in our midst. Lucky them to have us on their walls.

ACSE after our names means a lot. It says that we are the pros, not just at knowing the facts, ma'am, but knowing how to tell it like it is: in schools, in clinics, in centers, in classrooms, in hotel conference rooms, behind the desk at our computer, on television, and in the trenches—yes, even in a VW bus—wherever and whatever they may be.

I want to be sure that we, as AASECT, honor and embrace the "E" among our ranks. To be an "E" makes me proud to be in AASECT. Without the "E," we would lose a part of our essence. Our soul would shrink. I hope that you will give a compliment, a hug, a salute to an ACSE the next time you meet one. Come to our annual conference and be dazzled by their savvy and style. Come to our regional events and say "hi." Do what you can do . . . or be . . . to let the "E" become a necessary part of our mission. Being a sexuality educator, especially a certified one, lets me wake up each day with a sense of knowing: "I am living my dream."

Join me in sharing the dream. Celebrate the "E" in AASECT in any way you can.

## NOTE

Reprinted with permission by American Association of Sexuality Educators, Counselors, and Therapists, AASECT.

# Chapter Sixteen

# WORLD ASSOCIATION FOR SEXUAL HEALTH (WAS) GUIDING ETHICAL PRINCIPLES

## PREAMBLE

In our endeavors to achieve international recognition as the peak reference group for all matters associated with human sexuality, the World Association for Sexual Health (WAS) is committed to ethical practice in all areas. The Guiding Principles have application for clinicians, researchers, therapists, educators, and administrators. WAS acknowledges that most professions enunciate a specific code of conduct for their members, the WAS Guiding Ethical Principles are designed to enhance existing codes and provide guidance in the sensitive area of human sexuality.

The term *sexologist* implies a professional with specialist knowledge and skills in the area of human sexuality. Sexologists employ their specialist skills as educators, researchers, sociologists, clinicians, counselors, therapists, and administrators. These Principles apply to all Sexologists when working within their professional capacity.

Various terms are used throughout this document to describe those persons, whether they be individuals, couples, groups, societies, or any other entity receiving services from or potentially affected by the professional activities of Sexologists. The terms include *client, patient, student,* and *research participant.* These terms are not exclusive, nor are they intended to be definitive.

These ethical principles are designed to encompass all areas of sexology.

## THE FOUNDATION PRINCIPLES

The Code is founded on those principles recognized internationally through the agency of the United Nations, the World Medical Association and other, professional bodies.

The major principles are:

*Autonomy.* The obligation to support the individual's right to self-governance through free and rational decision making.

*Beneficence.* The obligation to act for the benefit of those who request professional services.

*Non-Malfeasance.* The obligation to do no harm.

*Justice.* The obligation to act on the basis of fair adjudication between competing claims. (Appendix 1)

## THE PRINCIPLES

### Principle 1: Sexologists shall have appropriate professional preparation and maintain an ongoing commitment to continuing education.

*Application:* Sexologists must hold a relevant, recognized professional qualification for their area of practice. It is the Sexologist's responsibility to maintain standards of professional education and knowledge based on current research and the development of procedures and techniques. This should be achieved through regular attendance at continuing professional education programs, professional seminars, meetings, congresses and the reading of appropriate professional literature.

### Principle 2: Sexologists must operate only within their area of professional expertise and competency.

*Application:* Sexologists should recognize the professional boundaries and the limits of their professional competency. They should declare the parameters in which they work and, where appropriate, refer people to another, appropriately qualified sexologist.

### Principle 3: Sexologists should inform clients, patients and research participants of their professional qualifications and affiliations.

*Application:* In their place of work, where applicable, Sexologists should display their qualifications in a manner that is readily observable. Qualifications should be from recognized institutions and organizations.

*Limitation:* The display should be professional in nature commensurate with the dignity of the profession.

### Principle 4: Sexologists should uphold and enhance the integrity of the profession.

*Application:* Sexologists should act in a manner that supports and enhances the integrity of the profession. Thoughtful application of each of these principles achieves this.

### Principle 5: When available, Sexologists should engage in science-based practice.

*Application:* Sexologists should employ techniques and procedures that have demonstrated efficacy, based on appropriate research.

*Limitation:* In behavioral, clinical, or social research, experimental and developing procedures may be employed when the risk/benefit ratio has been carefully assessed and there is full disclosure to the research participant (Cf. Research Principles, Section C).

In education and health promotion, innovative techniques may be used giving due regard to the social and cultural context and participants are appropriately informed.

### Principle 6: Sexologists have a responsibility to maintain and enhance the knowledge, health and welfare of their communities.

*Application:* Actions taken on behalf of a client, patient, or community may have an undesired effect on others, including groups within a society or the society itself. Sexologists should have regard for the impact of their proposed actions and make a decision based on the greater good.

### Principle 7: Sexologists should exercise respect for colleagues.

*Application:* Sexologists should act in a manner that does not bring disrepute upon their colleagues or their profession. They should act on principles of fairness at all times and not take actions that undermine individual colleagues.

*Limitation:* Where a Sexologist has evidence that a colleague has acted unprofessionally, is incompetent, or otherwise acting inappropriately, the matter should be first discussed with that colleague and, if necessary, brought to the attention of relevant authorities.

### Principle 8: Sexologists shall not breach the professional relationship.

*Application:* Within the context of the professional relationship, the Sexologist must act with integrity at all times. A Sexologist must not engage in intimate relations with a client, research participant, student, or patient or otherwise place them in a position where the professional relationship is compromised. When the service is of a psychotherapeutic nature, a Sexologist should not provide services to a close family member.

### Principle 9: The sexologist shall respect and uphold the autonomy and dignity of those receiving their professional services.

*Application:* This principle applies irrespective of age, gender, race, ethnicity, educational level, sexual orientation, social circumstances, or political affiliation. It obliges the Sexologist to facilitate the exercise of autonomy through providing necessary and sufficient information to enable rational decision making.

*Limitation:* Individual autonomy is limited by the recognition of the rights of others and the avoidance of harm. It is also limited through the capacity of an individual to make rational decisions on their own behalf. Under such circumstances an advocate may act on behalf of that person (Appendix 1).

### Principle 10: The Sexologist shall maintain professional confidentiality.

*Application:* Sexologists should maintain confidentiality at all times. Informed consent must be first obtained prior to disclosing information to third parties.

*Limitation:* Under certain jurisdictions there is a legal obligation to report particular activities to certain authorities. The sexologist is morally obliged to make a reasoned decision as to disclosure. Such decisions should be based on the legal and political circumstances and on what is deemed to be the greater good.

### Principle 11: Where appropriate, the Sexologist should obtain informed consent.

*Application:* Prior to implementing any action, the Sexologist should provide sufficient and necessary information on the recommended activities and alternatives. The possible benefits and risks must be disclosed. The Sexologist may disclose which option is, in their professional opinion, the optimum action within a particular context.

*Limitation:* Where the person is not in a position to provide informed consent, an advocate may act on their behalf (Appendix 1).

### Principle 12: Sexologists will maintain appropriate records.

*Application:* Sexologists will maintain records on clients, client groups, patients, or research participants. Such records may be used for research purposes when prior, written consent has been obtained (Section C).

### Principle 13: Sexologists will provide information on their fee schedule to potential clients.

*Application:* Prior to the provision of services, information on fee schedules, insurance rebates, and tax provisions, where relevant.

## PRINCIPLES FOR THE CONDUCT OF ETHICAL RESEARCH

### Principle 14: Sexologists shall employ recognized research protocols.

*Application:* All research activities should follow an acknowledged research protocol that is deemed by peers to be appropriate to the nature of the study.

### Principle 15: Sexologists shall employ recognized protocols in the use of human research subjects.

*Application:* The use of human subjects requires adherence to the Helsinki Declaration, which includes the following:

- Informed consent
- Potential benefit(s) must outweigh potential risk(s)
- Freedom to withdraw without prejudice
- Confidentiality

### Principle 16: Sexologists shall employ recognized protocols in the use of animal research subjects.

*Application:* The use of animal subjects requires adherence to the protocol set down for the humane treatment of experimental animals, which includes the following:

- Appropriate housing of the animal subject
- Minimization of pain and discomfort

• Appropriate disposal at the conclusion of the study

## Principle 17: Sexologists shall utilize peer review to evaluate their work.

*Application:* Research proposals and research reports should be made available for expert and peer review.

## Principle 18: Sexologists have an obligation to provide support for, or to conduct research and to disseminate findings.

*Application:* Sexologists should contribute to the development of the body of knowledge through the conduct of appropriate research and through dissemination of findings. This applies to adverse outcomes as well as positive ones.

## NOTE

Approved by the WAS General Assembly on July 13, 2005, Montreal, Canada.

## APPENDIX 1

### Autonomy and Advocacy

Under certain circumstances an individual may not be in a position to exercise his or her autonomy. Under such circumstances it may be appropriate and ethically desirable to accept an advocate for the client or patient.

Circumstances where an individual cannot exercise autonomy:
• Where the client or patient is a child of an age where he or she cannot be reasonably expected to have fully developed the capacity for abstract reasoning or an ability to evaluate the possible consequences of a particular course of action.
• Where the adult client or patient has congenital or acquired cognitive impairment to a degree where she or he cannot be reasonably expected to evaluate the consequences of a particular course of action.

The nature of advocacy:
• Contract advocacy—This applies where the person has, prior to her or his current situation, contracted with their nominated advocate that the advocate should proceed in a particular way.
• Cognizant advocacy—Where the potential advocate is deemed to be in a position where they would
• Conjunct advocacy—Where the person has never been in a position to develop or express opinions or contracts and the advocate interests are deemed to be conjoint with those of that person.

## JUSTICE

The obligation of justice may be viewed in three categories.

- Distributive justice—concerns the comparative treatment of individuals. Where there are competing interests for limited resources, one strives to develop criteria to maximize fair distribution. For example, establishing criteria to decide whether more funding should go to HIV/AIDS prevention or to erectile dysfunction treatment.
- Compensatory justice—is provided when compensation is made for past wrongs or deprivation of resources. For example, providing special sexuality education programs for indigenous populations.
- Procedural justice—requires ordering resources in a fair manner, for example on a first come, first serve basis.

Chapter Seventeen

# AMERICAN SCHOOL HEALTH ASSOCIATION: QUALITY COMPREHENSIVE SEXUALITY EDUCATION

WHEREAS, sexuality is a natural and healthy part of living and is comprised of biological, sociocultural, psychological, and spiritual dimensions;

WHEREAS, parents and caregivers are responsible for their children's sexuality education, and most parents and families desire that their children receive accurate sexuality education in school, including topics such as abstinence, contraception, safer sex practices, sexual orientation, human growth and development, and emotional and social skills needed for healthy sexual relationships;

WHEREAS, comprehensive approaches to sexuality education that educate young people in the areas of abstinence, contraception, and STI/HIV prevention are more effective at delaying the onset of sexual intercourse and increase contraception use than those that solely teach abstinence;

WHEREAS, sexual behavior is interrelated with other health behaviors;

WHEREAS, Americans live in a pluralistic society in which the educational system is expected to provide scientifically accurate and comprehensive instruction and to support programs that meet the needs of diverse students and that encourage cultural proficiency and that discourage discimination; and

WHEREAS, sexuality education is a complex and sensitive area of study;

THEREFORE, BE IT RESOLVED: that the American School Health Association:

1) supports and advocates for the right of young persons to have quality, comprehensive sexuality education; and
2) expects that sexuality education in schools will be scientifically accurate and based on current medical, psychological, pedagogical, educational, and social research.

## THEREFORE, the American School Health Association recommends:

1) that comprehensive sexuality education address, at a minimum, and as developmentally appropriate, the following topics: human growth and development, healthy relationships, personal health skills (including the skills to communicate effectively, set goals, make responsible decisions, and access resources and support services), sexual behavior, prevention of intimate partner violence, sexual health, and sexuality within society and culture in the cognitive, affective, spiritual, and behavioral domains;
2) that comprehensive sexuality education is taught PK–12 as part of a coordinated school health program within a comprehensive health education curriculum that is planned, sequential, age and developmentally and culturally appropriate;
3) that comprehensive sexuality education avoids stereotypic references about race, gender, ethnicity, family types, sexual orientation, religion, economics, age, and those with special needs; and
4) that teachers be well-trained and competent to teach sexuality education as defined by:

   (a) sound knowledge of scientifically accurate and age-appropriate content;
   (b) skills to integrate findings from relevant disciplines and apply these to healthy sexuality and family life issues;
   (c) knowledge of and identification with the broad philosophical principles of comprehensive sexuality education;
   (d) skill in using a variety of age-appropriate educational methods;
   (e) the ability to work effectively with both individuals and families in an educational context as well as within the broader community and political context;
   (f) insight into and acceptance of their own personal feelings and attitudes concerning sexuality topics so personal life experiences do not intrude inappropriately into the educational experience; and
   (g) skills in planning, implementing, promoting, and evaluating sexuality education curricula.

Chapter Eighteen

# THE NATIONAL COALITION TO SUPPORT SEXUALITY EDUCATION (NCSSE) MEMBER LIST

The National Coalition to Support Sexuality Education (NCSSE) consists of over 140 national organizations committed to medically accurate, age-appropriate comprehensive sexuality education for all children and youth in the United States. Members of NCSSE represent a broad constituency of education advocates and professionals, health care professionals, religious leaders, child and health advocates, and policy organizations.

## NCSSE'S GOALS INCLUDE:

- Providing a forum for networking, resource sharing, and collaboration among national organizations supporting comprehensive sexuality education.
- Holding biannual meetings on key issues in sexuality education.
- Empowering member organizations to advocate for comprehensive sexuality education policies and programs at the national and state level.

For more information about the National Coalition to Support Sexuality Education, or to join, contact:
NCSSE c/o SIECUS
1706 R Street, N.W.
Washington, DC 20009
Phone: 202-265-2405
Fax: 202-462-2340
E-mail: ncsse@siecusdc.org
Web site: http://www.ncsse.org

## NATIONAL COALITION TO SUPPORT SEXUALITY EDUCATION (NCSSE) MEMBERS

- Advocates for Youth
- AIDS Action Council
- AIDS Alliance for Children, Youth and Families
- The Alan Guttmacher Institute
- American Academy of Child and Adolescent Psychiatry
- American Academy of Pediatrics
- American Association for Health Education
- American Association for Marriage and Family Therapy
- American Association of Family & Consumer Sciences
- American Association of School Administrators
- American Association of Sex Educators, Counselors and Therapists
- American Association of University Women
- American Association on Mental Retardation
- American College Health Association
- American College of Nurses-Midwives
- American College of Obstetricians and Gynecologists
- American College of Sexologists
- American Counseling Association
- American Federation of Teachers
- American Jewish Congress
- American Library Association
- American Medical Association
- American Medical Student's Association
- American Medical Women's Association
- American Nurses Association
- American Orthopsychiatric Association
- American Psychiatric Association
- American Psychological Association
- American Public Health Association
- American School Health Association
- American Social Health Association
- Answer
- Association for Sexuality Education and Training
- Association of Reproductive Health Professionals
- Association of State and Territorial Directors of Public Health Education
- Association of State and Territorial Health Officials
- ASTRAEA National Lesbian Action Foundation
- Balm in Gilead
- Blacks Educating Blacks About Sexual Health Issues
- Boston Women's Health Book Collective
- Bridge for Adolescent Pregnancy, Parenting, and Sexuality
- Campaign for Access and Reproductive Equity
- Catholics for Free Choice
- Center for Law and Social Policy
- Center for Policy Alternatives
- Center for Reproductive Health Policy Research

- Center for Reproductive Rights
- Center for Sexuality and Religion
- Center for Women Policy Studies
- Children's Defense Fund
- Child Welfare League of America
- Choice USA
- Coalition on Sexuality and Disability, Inc.
- Education Development Center, Inc.
- EngenderHealth
- Equal Partners in Faith
- ETR Associates
- Exodus Trust Archives of Erotology
- Federation of Behavioral Psychological and Cognitive Sciences
- Feminist Majority Foundation
- Gay and Lesbian Medical Association
- Gay, Lesbian and Straight Education Network
- Gay Men's Health Crisis
- Gender Public Advocacy Coalition
- Girls Inc.
- Hetrick-Martin Institute
- Human Rights Campaign
- The Institute for Advanced Study of Human Sexuality Alumni Association
- International Center for Research on Women
- Jewish Women International
- The Kinsey Institute for Research in Sex, Gender ,and Reproduction
- Lambda Legal Defense and Education Fund, Inc.
- The Latina Roundtable on Health & Reproductive Rights
- The Mautner Project
- Ms. Foundation
- NARAL Pro-Choice America
- National Abortion Federation
- National Alliance of State and Territorial AIDS Directors
- National Asian Women's Health Organization
- National Assembly on School-Based Health Care
- National Association for Equal Opportunity in Higher Education
- National Association of Counties
- National Association of County and City Health Officials
- National Association of People with AIDS
- National Association of School Psychologists
- National Black Women's Health Project
- National Center for Health Education
- National Coalition Against Censorship
- National Coalition of Abortion Providers
- National Coalition of Advocates for Students
- National Coalition of STD Directors
- National Committee for Public Education and Religious Liberty
- National Council of Jewish Women
- National Council of La Raza
- National Council of Negro Women

- National Council of State Consultants for School Social Work Services
- National Council on Family Relations
- National Education Association Health Information Network
- National Family Planning and Reproductive Health Association
- National Gay and Lesbian Task Force
- National Information Center for Children & Youth with Disabilities
- National Latina Health Organization
- National Latina/o Lesbian, Gay, Bisexual & Transgender Organization (LLEGO)
- National Lesbian and Gay Health Association
- National Medical Association
- National Mental Health Association
- National Minority AIDS Council
- National Native American AIDS Prevention Center
- National Network for Youth
- National Organization on Adolescent Pregnancy, Parenting, and Prevention
- National Partnership for Women and Families
- National Resource Center for Youth Services
- National School Boards Association
- National Urban League
- National Women's Health Network
- National Women's Law Center
- National Youth Advocacy Coalition
- Network for Family Life Education
- New York State Department of Health: Bureau of STD Control
- Office of Family Ministries & Human Sexuality, National Council of Churches
- Parents, Families, and Friends of Lesbians and Gays
- People for the American Way
- Physicians for Reproductive Choice and Health
- Planned Parenthood Federation of America
- Population Communications International
- Population Connection
- Presbyterians Affirming Reproductive Options
- Religious Coalition for Reproductive Choice
- Religious Institute for Sexual Morality, Justice, and Healing
- Sexuality Information and Education Council of the United States
- Sexual Minority Youth Assistance League
- Shield Institute
- Society for Adolescent Medicine
- Society for Public Health Education
- Society for the Scientific Study of Sexuality
- Unitarian Universalist Association
- United Church of Christ, Justice and Witness Ministries
- United States Conference of Mayors
- United States Student Association
- Women of Reform Judaism
- YAI/National Institute for People with Disabilities

- the Young Women's Project
- YWCA of the U.S.A.

The Coalition's breadth reflects the widespread public support for sexuality education for the nation's youth. If your national organization is interested in joining, please contact

# APPENDIX: REFERENCES FOR FURTHER INFORMATION ABOUT SEXUALITY EDUCATION

*Lauren A. Antonecchia and Maria D. Ramirez*

The following is a listing of resources that can be used to acquire additional information about issues addressed in this book series. The list is divided by type of resource, including membership and resource organizations, Web sites, journals, articles, sexuality education institutions, curricula, books, newsletters, magazines, videos/DVDs, film companies, sex museums, additional print resources, and innovations in the area of human sexuality education, with a brief description of each resource. Please keep in mind that this list is not comprehensive and that new resources will continue to become available over time.

## MEMBERSHIP ORGANIZATIONS

Membership organizations give educators, counselors, and therapists the opportunity to pursue shared interest and discuss common concerns dealing with human sexuality and sexual health. Membership organizations further provide research and support that allow professionals to be better prepared in the field of human sexuality. Member groups exist for individual countries (e.g., the China Sexology Association, South African Sexual Health Association, Associacion Argentina de Sexologia y Educacion Sexual, Indian Association of Sex Educators, Counselors, and Therapists) or for regions (e.g., the European Federation for Sexology, the Asia-Oceanic Federation for Sexology).

American Association of Sexuality Educators, Counselors, and Therapists (AASECT)
PO Box 1960
Ashland, VA 23005–1960
P: 804-752-0026

The American Association of Sexuality Educators, Counselors, and Therapists (AASECT) is a not-for-profit, interdisciplinary professional organization.
Web site: http://www.aasect.org

American School Health Association
7263 State Route 43
PO Box 708
Kent, Ohio 44240
P: 330-678-1601
F: 330-678-4526
E-mail: asha@ashaweb.org
Unites many professionals working in schools who are committed to safeguarding the health of school-aged children.
Web site: http://www.ashaweb.org

International Society for the Study of Women's Sexual Health (ISSWSH)
Two Woodfield Lake
1100 E. Woodfield Road, Suite 520
Schaumburg, IL 60173
P: 847-517-7225
F: 847-517-7229
Provides opportunities for communication among scholars, researchers, and practitioners about women's sexual function and sexual experience; supports the highest standards of ethics and professionalism in research, education, and clinical practice of women's sexuality; and provides the public with accurate information about women's sexuality and sexual health.
Web site: http://www.isswsh.org

Society for Sex Therapy and Research (SSTAR)
409 12th St., S.W., PO Box 96920
Washington, DC 20090–6920
P: 202-863-1644
Composed of a broad range of professionals who have clinical or research interests in human sexual concerns. SSTAR's goals are to facilitate communications among clinicians who treat problems of sexual function, sexual identity, and reproductive life and to provide a forum for exchange of ideas between those interested in research in human sexuality and those whose primary activities are patient care.
Web site: http://www.sstarnet.org

Society for the Scientific Study of Sexuality (SSSS)
PO Box 416
Allentown, PA 18105–0416
P: 610-530-2483
F: 610-530-2485
The oldest professional society dedicated to the advancement of knowledge about sexuality. SSSS holds annual conferences each year with presentations about the latest research and science about sexuality.
Web site: http://www.sexscience.org

Healthy Teen Network
1501 Saint Paul St., Ste. 124
Baltimore, MD 21202
P: 410-685-0410
F: 410-685-0481
The only national membership network that serves as a leader, a national voice, and a comprehensive educational resource to professionals working in the area of adolescent reproductive health—specifically teen pregnancy prevention, teen pregnancy, teen parenting, and related issues.
Web site: http://www.healthyteennetwork.org

World Association for Sexual Health (WAS)
Tezoquipa 26
Colonia La Joya
Delegacion Tlalapan
Mexico D.F. 14000
WAS has worked in promoting sexual health for all. Sexual health is not a goal for clinicians only. Sexual health is the crystallization of our common goal. Sexuality education has the objective to facilitate sexually healthy lives of those who are being educated. Interventions in clinical sexology have the goal of restoring sexual health. Sex research, although objectively driven, has as its justification the creation of knowledge that supports others to attain and maintain sexual health.
Web site: http://www.worldsexology.org

## RESOURCE ORGANIZATIONS

The main goal of this section is to provide a variety of different resources pertaining to human sexuality. Resource organizations make valuable information available without cost to professionals and all those who are interested in gaining more knowledge in this field.

Advocates For Youth
2000 M Street NW, Suite 750
Washington, DC 20036
P: 202-419-3420
F: 202-419-1448
Dedicated to creating programs and advocating for policies that help young people make informed and responsible decisions about their reproductive and sexual health. Advocates provide information, training, and strategic assistance to youth-serving organizations, policymakers, youth activists, and the media in the United States and the developing world.
Web site: http://www.advocatesforyouth.org

Centers for Disease Control and Prevention National Prevention Information Network
P.O. Box 6003
Rockville, MD 20849–6003

P: 1-800-458-5231
The CDC National Prevention Information Network (NPIN) is the U.S. reference, referral, and distribution service for information on HIV/AIDS, viral hepatitis, sexually transmitted diseases (STDs), and tuberculosis (TB). NPIN produces, collects, catalogs, processes, stocks, and disseminates materials and information on HIV/AIDS, Viral Hepatitis, STDs, and TB to organizations and people working in those disease fields in international, national, state, and local settings.
Web site: http://www.cdcnpin.org/scripts/index.asp

Gay Men's Health Crisis
119 West 24 Street
New York, NY 10011
P: 212-367-1000
An example of a community-based organization, which provides information and services, committed to the fight against AIDS and homophobia. Operates a hotline in Spanish and English.
Web site: http://www.gmhc.org

Girls Incorporated
120 Wall Street
New York, NY 10005
P: 212-509-2000
Girls Inc. develops research-based informal education programs that encourage girls to master physical, intellectual, and emotional challenges. Major programs address math and science education, pregnancy and drug abuse prevention, media literacy, economic literacy, adolescent health, violence prevention, and sports participation.
Web site: http://www.girlsinc.org/girls-inc.html

Health & Science Advisory Board
HSAB.org, LLC
7765 Lake Worth Rd., Suite 341
Lake Worth, FL 33467
The Health and Science Advisory Board is an interdisciplinary team comprised of more than 40 leading academics, educators, theologians, therapists, and medical professionals worldwide. The HSAB's mission is to provide practitioners, educators, and consumers with information and resources related to sexuality, health, and human relationships.
Web site: http://www.hsab.org

Kaiser Family Foundation
2400 Sand Hill Road
Menlo Park, CA 94025
P: 650-854-9400
Provides data and information on vast array of health issues, including HIV/AIDS and teen sexual activity and pregnancy.
Web site: http://www.kff.org

National Education Association Health Information Network
1201 16th Street NW

Washington, DC 20036
P: 202-822-7570
NEA HIN's mission is to improve the health and safety of school personnel
and students by providing the school community with vital and timely health
information that will increase teacher and education support professional (ESP)
quality and student achievement.
Web site: http://www.neahin.org

Planned Parenthood Federation of America
434 West 33rd Street
New York, NY 10001
P: 212-541-7800
Health Center Hotline: 1-800-230-PLAN
The official gateway to the online Planned Parenthood community and to a wealth
of reproductive health and rights information, services, and resources.
Web site: http://www.plannedparenthood.org

The Guttmacher Institute
120 Wall Street
New York, NY, 10005
P: 212-248-1111
F: 212-248-1951
A nonprofit organization focused on sexual and reproductive health research, policy
analysis, and public education.
Web site: http://www.guttmacher.org

The Women's Sexual Health Foundation
PO Box 40603
Cincinnati, Ohio 45240-0603
The Women's Sexual Health Foundation (TWSHF) is a nonprofit corporation
that supports a multidisciplinary approach to the treatment of sexual health issues
and serves as an educational resource for both the lay public and health care
professionals.
Web site: http://www.twshf.org/
E-mail: info@twshf.org

## WEB SITES

These Web sites—as well as many of those organizations already listed—
present useful information for individuals and professionals as well as specific
cultural groups. Through these Web sites all those interested will gain a better
understanding of human sexuality and where they can go to meet their specific needs dealing with all matters of human sexuality.

Advocates for Youth
Dedicated to creating programs and advocating for policies that help young people
make informed and responsible decisions about their reproductive and sexual

health. Advocates for Youth believes it can best serve the field by boldly advocating for a more positive and realistic approach to adolescent sexual health.
http://www.advocatesforyouth.org

Ambiente Joven
Dedicated to the Young Latino/a Gay, Lesbian, Bisexual, and Transgender community in the United States with the goal of providing information about sexual health.
http://www.ambientejoven.org

American Psychological Association
Scientific and professional organization that represents psychology in the United States. References for books, articles, films and videos, organizations, and health information, pertaining to all fields of psychology, including human sexuality.
http://www.apa.org

American Social Health Association (ASHA)
Offers a wealth of information about health, focusing on sexually transmitted diseases.
http://www.ashastd.org/

Answer
A national organization dedicated to providing and promoting comprehensive sexuality education to young people and the adults who teach them. Includes a teen-to-teen sexuality education initiative that features the SEX, ETC Web site and magazine, and a nationwide training programs for youth-serving professionals.
http://answer.rutgers.edu
http://www.sexetc.org

The Birds and Bees Project
Provides comprehensive reproductive health information to youth and adults with specific areas of activity, including Internet-based education, classroom-based education, and community outreach. The message in all materials is positive, respectful, developmentally appropriate, and aims to compliment the education and values that people receive from their families and communities.
http://www.birdsandbees.org

The Body: The Complete HIV/AIDS Resource
The Web's largest source of information on HIV and AIDS. Read and listen to the latest news, research, and resources on HIV prevention, testing, and treatment.
http://www.thebody.com

CDC's Division of Adolescent and School Health (DASH)
Seeks to prevent the most serious health risk behaviors among children, adolescents, and young adults.
http://www.cdc.gov/HealthyYouth/index.htm

Children of Lesbians and Gays Everywhere (COLAGE)
The only national and international organization in the world specifically supporting young people with gay, lesbian, bisexual, and transgender parents.
http://www.colage.org

Education Training Research Associates (ETR) Resource Center for Adolescent
Pregnancy and Prevention (ReCAPP)
Non-profit health education promotion organization known for state-of-the-art
programs, professional training, and research in the area of adolescent pregnancy
prevention as well as for publications and clearinghouse services. ReCAPP
provides practical tools and information to effectively reduce sexual risk-taking
behaviors.
http://www.etr.org/recapp/

Family Pride Coalition
Dedicated to advance the well-being of lesbian, gay, bisexual, and transgender
parents and their families through mutual support, community collaboration, and
public understanding.
http://www.familypride.org

The Gay, Lesbian, and Straight Education Network
The largest national organization of parents, educators, and students working to
end homophobia in K–12 schools.
http://www.glsen.org

Gay Men of African Descent
Developing leadership among black gay men to address issues that they face
including homophobia, isolation, discrimination, and invisibility. This mission is
accomplished through trainings, social marketing campaigns, community forums,
advocacy, and direct client services.
http://www.gmad.org

Go Ask Alice! Columbia University's Health Q&A Internet Service
Question and answers on many topics, with a health focus. From Columbia
University's Health Education Program, with a searchable database.
http://www.goaskalice.columbia.edu

Human Rights Campaign
Works for lesbian, gay, bisexual, and transgender equal rights by lobbying the
federal government, participating in election campaigns, mobilizing grassroots
actions in diverse communities, and educating the public about GLBT issues.
http://www.hrc.org

Intersex Society of North America
Devoted to systemic change to end shame, secrecy, and unwanted genital surgeries
for people born with an anatomy that someone decided is not standard for male or
female.
http://www.isna.org

My Sistahs
Created by and for young women of color to provide information and offer support
on sexual and reproductive health issues through education and advocacy.
http://www.mysistahs.org

The National Campaign to Prevent Teen and Unplanned Pregnancy
Seeks to improve the lives and future prospects of children and families and, in particular, to prevent teen pregnancy and unplanned pregnancy among single, young adults. Supports a combination of responsible values and behavior by both men and women and responsible policies in both the public and private sectors.
http://www.teenpregnancy.org

National Gay and Lesbian Task Force
A national organization that advocates for the civil rights of GLBT individuals. Building the grassroots power of the lesbian, gay, bisexual, and transgender (LGBT) community by training activists, equipping state and local organizations with the skills needed to organize broad-based campaigns to defeat anti-LGBT referenda and advance pro-LGBT legislation, and building the organizational capacity of our movement.
http://www.ngltf.org

The National Latina/o Lesbian, Gay, Bisexual, & Transgender Organization
This site is designed to build and strengthen the national network of Latina/o GLBT community based organizations. Information on over 170 affiliated organizations nationally.
http://www.llego.org

National Sexuality Resource Center
The National Sexuality Resource Center gathers and disseminates the latest accurate information and research on sexual health, education, and rights in the United States. The Web site has a news feed about sexuality, sexual health, and gender issues; rotating slideshows about topical issues; and links to *American Sexuality* (targeted to consumers), the *Journal of Sexuality Research and Social Policy* (empirical research), and the University Consortium for Sexuality Research and Training (online networking tool for researchers).
http://www.nsrc.sfsu.edu

Outproud
Serves the needs of GLBT young men and women by providing advocacy, information, resources, and support. Goal is to help queer youth become happy, successful, confident, and vital gay, lesbian, and bisexual adults.
http://www.outproud.org

Renaissance Transgender Association
Support and information for transgendered individuals. Provides comprehensive education and caring support to transgendered individuals and those close to them. This is accomplished through offering a variety of carefully selected programs and resources focused on the factors affecting their lives.
http://www.ren.org

Sex, Etc.
Web site by and for teens; teens and parents can submit questions to a sexuality expert and receive a personal response. A program of Answer at Rutgers University (see previous entry).
http://www.sexetc.org

SexEDLibrary
A highly acclaimed and comprehensive online sex-ed resource by SIECUS (the
Sexuality Information and Education Council of the United States) for educators,
counselors, administrators, and health professionals seeking the latest in human
sexuality research, lesson plans, and professional development opportunities.
http://www.sexedlibrary.org

Sexuality Information and Education Council of the United States (SIECUS)
Develops, collects, and disseminates information; promotes comprehensive
education about sexuality; and advocates the right of individuals to make
responsible sexual choices.
http://www.siecus.org

Talking with Kids about Tough Issues
A national initiative by Children Now and The Kaiser Family Foundation to
encourage parents to talk with their children earlier and more often about tough
issues such as sex, HIV/AIDS, violence, alcohol, and drug abuse.
http://www.talkingwithkids.org

Teenwire
The Planned Parenthood Federation of America Web site for teens, staffed
by professionals who are dedicated to providing the information you need on
relationships and sexuality.
http://www.teenwire.com

Transfamily
Homepage includes many resources for family members of transgender persons. A
Trans 101 written with children of Trans people in mind.
http://www.transfamily.org

Transproud
OutProud's home on the Web for transgender youth. Includes resources and
information, including news, questions and answers, related links, message board,
support, referrals, and more.
http://www.transproud.com

## JOURNALS

Professionals can submit research, reviews, commentar, and other contributions. Some countries have journals open to worldwide readership and sub-
missions (e.g., the *British Journal of Sexual Medecine*) or in local language (e.g.,
the *Chinese Journal of Human Sexuality*). These publications provide current
research, practice methods, and information on a plethora of human sexuality
material.

American Journal of Sexuality Education
Editor: William J. Taverner, MA

Publisher: Taylor & Francis
This peer-reviewed journal provides sexuality educators and trainers at all skill levels with current research about sexuality education programming and "best practices," sample lesson plans, reports on curriculum development and assessment, literature reviews, scholarly commentary, educational program reports, media reviews (books, videos, Internet resources, and curricula), and letters to the editor.
Web site: http://www.tandf.co.uk/journals/titles/15546128.asp

The Canadian Journal of Human Sexuality
Editor: Alex McKay
Quarterly peer-reviewed academic journal focusing on the medical, psychological, social, and educational aspects of human sexuality.
Web site: http://www.sieccan.org/cjhs.html

Electronic Journal of Human Sexuality
Editor: David S. Hall, PhD
To disseminate knowledge about all aspects of human sexuality to the widest possible international community at moderate cost.
Web site: http://ejhs.org/

Journal of LGBT Youth
Editor: James T. Sears, PhD
Publisher: Haworth Press
Covers the latest international perspectives on the issues that impact GLBT students and educators.
Web site: http://www.haworthpress.com/store/product.asp?sku=J524&sid=0HEW LLMQK2BF9HJ7AM27SKKVD1TQ6VH4&

Journal of GLBT Family Studies
Editor: Jerry J. Bigner, PhD
Publisher: Haworth Press
The *Journal of GLBT Family Studies* is the first journal to address family issues and concerns important to GLBT individuals and their families of origin, as well as families formed in adulthood.
Web site: http://www.haworthpress.com/store/product.asp?sku=J461

Journal of Psychology & Human Sexuality
Editor: Eli Coleman, PhD
Publisher: Haworth Press
Encompasses clinical, counseling, educational, social, experimental, psycho-endocrinological, and psycho-neuroscience research devoted to the study of human sexuality. It fills an existing gap in the psychological literature by specifically covering issues in the field of sexual science.
Web site: http://www.haworthpress.com/store/product.asp?sku=J056

The Journal of Sex Research
Editor: Cynthia A. Graham, PhD
A scholarly journal devoted to the publication of articles relevant to the variety of disciplines involved in the scientific study of sexuality. *JSR* is designed to stimulate

research and to promote an interdisciplinary understanding of the diverse topics in contemporary sexual science.
Web site: http://www.sexscience.org/publications/index.php?category_id=439

Sex Education: Sexuality, Society and Learning
Publisher: Routledge
An international refereed journal concerned with the practice of sex education and its underpinnings from various disciplines.
Web site: http://www.tandf.co.uk/journals/carfax/14681811.html

Sexuality Research and Social Policy
Editor: Gilbert Herdt
Official online journal of the National Sexuality Resource Center, publishes multidisciplinary state-of-the-art empirical research on sexuality, theoretical and methodological discussions, and implications for U.S. and international policies regarding sexual health, sexuality education, and sexual rights in diverse communities. Also includes brief research and conference reports, white papers, book, film, and other reviews, along with guest editorials and commentaries.
Web site: http://nsrc.sfsu.edu/sexuality_research_social_policy

## SEXUALITY EDUCATION HIGHER EDUCATION INSTITUTIONS

Below are examples of undergraduate and graduate programs that focus on or result in a degree in fields most directly related to human sexuality. These are recognized institutions throughout the United States and Canada. Most colleges have courses, if not degrees, in subjects like Women's Studies and Gender and Sexuality, which can be found by searching on the web or at sites like http://userpages.umbc.edu/~korenman/wmst/programs.html.  Programs of such study also exist in other parts of the world.

### Undergraduate

California State University-Northridge
Undergraduate Interdisciplinary Minor in Human Sexuality
18111 Nordhoff Street
Northridge, CA 91330
P: 818-677-4830
F: 818-677-4778
Web site: http://www.csun.edu/~sr2022/minor.ht

New York University
Undergraduate Program in Gender and Sexuality Studies
Center for the Study of Gender and Sexuality
41 East 11th Street, Seventh Floor
New York, NY 10003
Phone: 212-992-9540

Fax: 212-995-4433
E-mail: gender.sexuality@nyu.edu
Web site: http://www.nyu.edu/csgs/

Ohio State University
Interdisciplinary Minor in Sexuality Studies
Graduate Interdisciplinary Specialization in Sexuality Studies
186 University Hall
230 North Oval Mall20
Columbus, OH 43210
P: 614-292-1882
F: 614-292-8666
E-mail: humanities@osu.edu
Web site: http://sexualitystudies.osu.edu

San Francisco Sate University
Undergraduate Minor / Graduate Program in Human Sexuality Studies
1600 Holloway Avenue
San Francisco. CA 94132
P: 415-405-3570
F: 415-405-0411
Web site: http://hmsx.sfsu.edu

University of Iowa
Undergraduate Interdisciplinary Program in Sexuality Studies
120 Schaeffer Hall
Iowa City, IA 52242
P: 319-335-2633
F: 319-335-2439

University of Minnesota
Undergraduate Program in Gender, Women, and Sexuality Studies
Minneapolis, MN 55455
E-mail: gwss@umn.edu

University of Pennsylvania
Undergraduate Program in Gender, Culture, and Society
(Specialization in Sexuality Studies)
411 Logan Hall
249 South 36th Street
Philadelphia, PA 19104–6304
P: 215-898-8740
Web site: http://www.sas.upenn.edu/wstudies/

## Graduate/Professional Training

The American Academy of Clinical Sexologists
Ph.D. Program in Clinical Sexology

3203 Lawton Road, Suite 170
Orlando, FL 32893
P: 407-645-1641
Web site: http://www.esextherapy.com

Answer
Online Professional Development Programs
Rutgers University
41 Gordon Road, Suite C
Piscataway, New Jersey 08854–8067
P: 732-445-7929
F: 732-445-7970

California State University, Northridge
College of Social and Behavioral Sciences
Human Sexuality Program
Center for Sex Research
18111 Nordhoff Street
Northridge, CA 91324

Columbia University School of Public Health
Center for Gender Sexuality and Health
Graduate Degree in Sexuality and Health Allan Rosenfield Building
722 West 168th Street
New York, New York 10032
P: 212-305-5656
E-mail: ph-admit@columbia.edu
Web site: http://www.mailman.hs.columbia.edu/sms/programs/sexhealth-track.html

Curtin University of Technology
Graduate Program in Sexology/Doctoral Program in Sexology/Forensic Sexology
School of Public Health
P: +61 (08) 9266 7819
F: +61 (08) 9266 2958
E-mail: enquiry@health.curtin.edu.au
Web site: http://www.publichealth.curtin.edu.au/html/areasofstudy_s.htm

Engender Health
Online Self-Instructional Mini-course on Sexuality and Sexual Health
440 Ninth Ave. New York, NY 10001
P: 212-561-8000
E-mail: info@engenderhealth.org
Web site: http://www.engenderhealth.org/pubs/courses/

The Fogel Foundation
Human Sexuality Institute
Continuing Education, Training Programs and Workshops in Human Sexuality
7920 Old Georgetown Road
Bethesda, MD 20814

P: 301-907-8777
Web site: http://www.thefogelfoundation.org

HIV Center for Clinical and Behavioral Studies
Postdoctoral Behavioral Science Research Training Program in HIV Infection
1051 Riverside Drive, Unit 15
New York, NY 10032
P: 212-543-5969
F: 212-543-6003
Web site: http://www.hivcenternyc.org/training/nrsa.html

Indiana University/Kinsey Institute for Research in Sex, Gender, and Reproduction
Graduate Program in Human Sexuality
Bloomington, IN 47405
P: 812-855-8853
E-mail: kinsey@indiana.edu
Web site: www.kinseyinstitute.org

The Institute for Advanced Study of Human Sexuality
Graduate/Doctoral Programs in Human Sexuality
1523 Franklin Street
San Francisco, CA 94109
P: 415-928-1133
F: 415-928-8061
E-mail: registrar@iashs.edu
Web site: http://www.iashs.edu

The Magnus Hirschfeld Archive for Sexology
Online Courses in sexual health, offered not-for-credit, covering the topics of
Human Sexual Anatomy and Physiology, Human Reproduction, Physical Problems
in Females and Males, Sexually Transmitted Diseases, Sexual Dysfunctions and
Human Sexual Behavior. These open access curricula in sexual health are offered in
Spanish, German, English, Hungarian, Mandarin, and Yugoslavian.
Web site: http://www2.hu-berlin.de/sexology/index.html

Masters and Johnson Institute
Trauma, Dissociative Disorders and Sexual Compulsivity Programs
River Oaks Psychiatric Hospital
1525 River Oaks Rd. West
New Orleans, LA 70123
P: 504-734-1740
For program information: 1-800-598-2040

Medical College of Wisconsin
Postdoctoral Fellowship Program in HIV Behavioral Research
Center for AIDS Intervention Research (CAIR)
Department of Psychiatry and Behavioral Medicine

2071 North Summit Avenue
Milwaukee, WI 53202
P: 414-955-7700
F: 414-287-4206
Web site: http://www.mcw.edu/display/docid215.htm

Universite du Quebec, Montreal
Graduate Program in Sexology
Département de sexologie
P: 514-987-3504
F: 514-987-6787
Web site: http://www.regis.uqam.ca/prod/owa/pkg_wpub.affiche_prog_desc?P_
prog=3713

University of Arkansas
Graduate/Doctoral Programs in Health Science
Program in Health Science
HP 326A
University of Arkansas
Fayetteville, AR 72701
P: 501-575-5639
F: 501-575-6401
Web site: http://www.uark.edu/depts/hepoinfo/

University of Guelph
Graduate and Doctoral Programs in Family Relations and
Human Development
50 Stone Road East
Guelph, Ontario, N1G 2W1
Canada
P: 519-824-4120 ext. 56321
Web site: http://www.family.uoguelph.ca

University of Hawaii at Manoa, John A. Burns School of Medicine
Department of Anatomy and Reproductive Biology
1951 East-West Road
Honolulu, HI 96822
P: 808-956-7131
F: 808-956-9481
Web site: http://www.jabsom.hawaii.edu/Grad_Physiol

University of Kansas
Women, Gender, and Sexuality Studies
1440 Jayhawk Blvd., Rm. 213
Lawrence, Kansas 66045- 7574
P: 785-864-4012
Web site: http://www.womensstudies.ku.edu/

University of Minnesota Medical School
Postdoctoral fellowships in Human Sexuality and Behavioral Medicine
Department of Family Medicine and Community Health
1300 So. Second St., Suite 180
Minneapolis, MN 55454
P: 612-625-1500
F: 612-626-8311
Director: Eli Coleman, Ph.D.
Web site: http://www.med.umn.edu/fm/phs/home.html

University of Sydney
Graduate Program in Sexual Health
(Distance/Flexible Learning Option)
East Street, PO Box 170
Lidcombe, NSW 1825
Australia
Web site: http://www.usyd.edu.au/sexualhealth/

University of Utah
Doctoral Program in Clinical Psychology with research in Human Sexuality
Department of Psychology
380 S. 1530 E. Room 502
Salt Lake City, Utah 84112
P: 801-581-6123
F: 801-581-5841

University of Washington
Center for AIDS and STD
Training/Graduate Certificate / Research in AIDS and STDs
325 9th Ave, Campus Box 359931
Seattle, WA 98104
P: 206-744-4239
F: 206-744-3693
Web site: http://depts.washington.edu/cfas/training/index.html#2

University of Waterloo
Program in Sexuality, Marriage, and Family
200 University Avenue West
Waterloo, Ontario, Canada N2L 3G1
P: +1 519-884-8110
E-mail: smf@sju.uwaterloo.ca
Web site: http://www.ucalendar.uwaterloo.ca/ARTS/smf.html

Widener University
Graduate Program in Human Sexuality Education
One University Place
Chester, PA 19013–5792
P: 610-499-4372
E-mail: humansexualityprogram@widener.edu
Web site: http://www.widener.edu

University of Wisconsin
Doctoral Training in Sexuality Research
Department of Sociology
University of Wisconsin
1180 Observatory Dr.
Madison, WI 53706–1393
P: 608-262-4357
F: 608-262-8400

## CURRICULA

These training programs offer material to help educators in teaching areas of human sexuality. Such education programs provide full lesson plans and activities that build on sexuality information, interpersonal skills, and decision making, as well as problem solving and life skills.

Abstinence: Pick and Choose Activities for Grades 7–12
Written by Michael Young, PhD, and Tamera Young
ETR Associates, 1996
Santa Cruz, CA
Includes 40 abstinence activities, enhances students' self-esteem, builds interpersonal skills, develops decision-making skills, teaches valuable life-planning skills, and includes background information, step-by-step procedures, and student activity sheets.

Be Proud! Be Responsible!
Select Media
An education program emphasizing HIV prevention that consists of eight one-hour modules that include group discussions, videos, games, brainstorming, experiential exercises, and skill building. The program has been successfully tested among young African American adolescents.
For more information:
P: 1-800-707-6334
Web site: http://www.etr.org/recapp/programs/proud.htm

Becoming A Responsible Teen (BART)
ETR Associates
An education program focusing on HIV prevention that consists of eight 1 1/2- to 2-hour sessions that include group discussions, role plays, and activities focusing on creative problem solving and extending learning beyond the classroom. The program uses an Afro-centric approach.
For more information:
P: 1-800-321-4407
Web site: http://www.etr.org

Carrera Program
Developed by noted sexologist Michael Carrera with the Children's Aid Society. The Adolescent Pregnancy Prevention Program is a nationally recognized teen

model that addresses seven components of life skills. The program has been shown to be highly successful in reducing teen pregnancy and improving teen school performance and is being implemented in school curricula.
For more information:
P: 212-949-4800
Web site: http://www.childrensaidsociety.org/cas/teenpreg.html

¡Cuidate!
This HIV-prevention curriculum is tailored for use with Latino adolescents. Its goals are to (1) influence attitudes, beliefs, and self-efficacy regarding HIV risk reduction, especially abstinence and condom use; (2) highlight cultural values that support safer sex practices; (3) reframe cultural values that might be perceived as barriers to safer sex; and (4) emphasize how cultural values influence attitudes and beliefs in ways that affect sexual risk behaviors. It consists of six one-hour modules delivered over consecutive days. The program is recommended for urban Latino youth ages 13–18.
For More Information:
Antonia M. Villarruel at the University of Michigan School of Nursing
400 N. Ingalls, Suite 4320
Ann Arbor, MI, 48109–0482
P: 734-615-9696
E-mail: avillarr@umich.edu

Educating about Abortion
Peggy Brick & Bill Taverner
Planned Parenthood of Greater Northern New Jersey
A compilation of 9 student-centered lessons. Includes 16 interactive worksheets, plus a special resource for pregnant women: Unsure about pregnancy? A guide to making the right decisions.
Web site for this and other PPGNNJ resources: http://www.ppgnnj.org/edu/index.php?sub=books

F.L.A.S.H.: Family Life and Sexual Health Grades 5–6, 7–8, 9–10, and 11–12
Elizabeth Reis
Seattle-King County Department of Public Health:
Comprehensive sexuality education curriculum addressing such issues as physical development, promotion of sexual health, prevention of disease, affection, interpersonal relationships, body image, and gender roles.
Order online: http://www.metrokc.gov/health/famplan/flash

Focus on Kids
ETR Associates
An education program emphasizing HIV prevention that consists of eight sessions that provide facts about HIV prevention and emphasize skills development with regard to communication, decision making, and condom use. The program uses an Afro-centric approach.
For more information:

P: 1-800-321-4407
Web site: http://www.etr.org

Get Real About AIDS
Sociometrics
An education program with 14 one-hour sessions including group discussions, lectures, public service announcements, role-plays, and videos.
For more information:
P: 650-949-3282
Web site: http://www.socio.com/srch/summary/pasha/paspp01.htm

Making Connections: Identifying the Links Between Body Image and Sexual Health
ETR ReCAPP Web site, 2001
Through small group work, discussion, and brainstorming, participants discuss the connection between negative body image and risky sexual behavior. Ages 12–18.
Web site: http://www.etr.org/recapp/freebies/freebie200111.htm

Making Smart Choices About Sex
Eva S. Goldfarb, PhD, and Elizabeth Schroeder, EdD, MSW
The foundation of this three-session abstinence curriculum for adolescents is that postponing sex is a positive, life-enhancing decision. Topics covered include: reasons for postponing sex, setting goals, making healthy choices, and effective communication. Each kit contains the curriculum, 30 interactive CDs, 30 homework packets, and 30 pre- and post-tests. For grades 7 and 8 (or younger).
Call 877-603-7306 for information on Product Preview and Training.
Web site: http://www.metrix-marketing.com/dbID/90.html

The New Teaching Safer Sex
Peggy Brick and Colleagues
This manual is designed to provide young people with opportunities to acquire the knowledge, attitudes, and skills they need to practice safer sexual behavior. It consists of 21 skill-based lessons targeted to adolescents and young adults. The lessons can also be used for training teachers, counselors, and parents. Lessons cover topics such as abstinence, STDs, communication skills, HIV/AIDS, and condoms.
Planned Parenthood of Greater Northern New Jersey
196 Speedwell Ave.
Morristown, NJ 07960
P: 973-539-9580
F: 973-539-3828
Web site: http://www.ppgnnj.org

Open Minds to Equality: A Sourcebook of Learning Activities to Affirm Diversity and Promote Equality
Editors: Nancy Schniedewind and Ellen Davidson

This is a practical book for teachers for building multicultural, gender-fair classrooms and for teaching students about both discrimination and approaches to equality. Grounded in theory but fully accessible to teachers, the book's first two chapters explain the need for equitable classrooms, and the remaining chapters provide activities with full-size worksheets for use with children. This is a "teacher-friendly" book that opens teachers' and students' eyes, hearts, and minds to equality.

Our Whole Lives: Sexuality Education for Grades K–1
Barbara Sprung
8 sessions, 1 hour each
Unitarian Universalist Association
Supports parents in educating children about birth, babies, bodies and families. Following a Parent Meeting and Parent/Child Orientation, the eight class sessions engage children with stories, songs, and activities and include a weekly HomeLink—a homework project for parents and children to do together. Promotes dialogue between parent and child. Appropriate for use in classroom and home settings.
Web site: http://www.uuabookstore.org

Our Whole Lives: Sexuality Education for Grades 4–6
Elizabeth Casparian, PhD, and Eva Goldfarb, PhD
Unitarian Universalist Association
8 sessions, 1 hour each
Participants learn about and discuss the physical and emotional changes of puberty. Participants will read *It's Perfectly Normal* by Robie Harris and examine topics such as values and sexuality, communication, and decision making. Each session includes a HomeLink—a homework activity for parents and children to complete together. Note: This program is designed for use with either a grades 4–5 group, a grades 5–6 group, or with one of the three grades separately.

Our Whole Lives: Sexuality Education for Grades 7–9
Pamela M. Wilson
Unitarian Universalist Association
25 sessions, 1 1/2 hours each
Presents a comprehensive approach to human sexuality in an age-appropriate manner. Based firmly on the values of respect, responsibility, justice, and inclusivity, this program helps young people apply these values to their behavior and provides them with information and skills they can use throughout life. Includes a comprehensive parent orientation.
Web site: http://www.uuabookstore.org

Our Whole Lives: Sexuality Education for Grades 10–12
Eva S. Goldfarb and Elizabeth M. Casparian
Unitarian Universalist Association
12 sessions, 2 hours each
Using a comprehensive approach, this program helps senior-high youth gain the knowledge, life principles, and skills they need to express their sexuality in

life-enhancing ways. Includes a parent orientation. Adaptable for classroom, after school, or youth group settings.
Web site: http://www.uuabookstore.org

Positive Encounters: Supporting Healthy Contraceptive and Safer Sex Decisions
Amy Vogelaar
These two volumes provide information, values clarification activities, and exercises to help adults have "positive encounters" that support the healthy decision— making of youth. The first volume is a manual on how to provide a training work shop for professionals about having positive encounters with youth. The second is a guidebook that complements what is learned in the workshop and can serve as a desk reference for professionals who work with youth.
Planned Parenthood of Greater Northern New Jersey
196 Speedwell Ave.
Morristown, NJ 07960
P: 973-539-9580
F: 973-539-3828
Web site: http://www.ppgnnj.org

Positive Images: Teaching Abstinence, Contraception, and Sexual Health
Peggy Brick and Bill Taverner
This manual focuses on prevention behaviors as well as the developmental, social, emotional, interpersonal, historical, cultural, and cross-cultural forces that shape healthy behavior change. Intended as a supplement to existing curricula, the manual includes 29 activities for middle school, high school, and college-age groups.
Planned Parenthood of Greater Northern New Jersey
196 Speedwell Ave.
Morristown, NJ 07960
P: 973-539-9580
F: 973-539-3828
Web site: http://www.ppgnnj.org

Project SAFE (Sexual Awareness for Everyone)
This gender- and culture-specific behavioral intervention consists of three sessions, each lasting three to four hours. Designed specifically for young African American and Latina women ages 15 through 24, it actively involves participants in lively and open discussion and games, videos, role plays, and behavior modeling. Discussions cover abstinence, mutual monogamy, correct and consistent condom use, compliance with STI treatment protocols, and reducing the number of one's sex partners. Each participant is encouraged to identify realistic risk reduction strategies that she can use in the context of her own life and values.
For more information or to order, contact:
Sociometrics, Program Archive on Sexuality, Health & Adolescence
P: 1-800-846-3475
F: 650-949-3299
E-mail: pasha@socio.com
Web site: http://www.socio.com

Reducing the Risk (RTR)
A sex education curriculum, including information on abstinence and contraception. In 16, 45-minute sessions, it offers experiential activities to build skills in refusal, negotiation, and communication, including that between parents and their children. Designed for use with high school students, especially those in grades 9 and 10, it is recommended for use with sexually inexperienced, urban, suburban, and rural youth—white, Latino, Asian, and black. For more information or to order, contact:
Sociometrics, Program Archive on Sexuality, Health & Adolescence
Phone: 1-800-846-3475
Fax: 650-949-3299
E-mail: pasha@socio.com
Web site: http://www.socio.com
Or:
ETR Associates
P: 1-800-321-4407
Web site: http://www.etr.org

Streetwise to Sex-Wise: Sexuality Education for High-Risk Youth
Steve Brown and Bill Taverner
This manual is intended as a supplement to a sexuality education curriculum and focuses on issues of particular concern to high-risk teens. It consists of 25 lessons broken up into two series: one for young teenagers ages 9–13 and one for older teenagers ages 14–19. Topics addressed include communication and decision-making skills, contraception, STDs, sexual orientation, and sexual abuse.
Planned Parenthood of Greater Northern New Jersey
196 Speedwell Ave.
Morristown, NJ 07960
P: 973-539-9580
F: 973-539-3828
Web site: http://www.ppgnnj.org

Wise Guys/"Jovenes Sabios" (Spanish Version)
Family Life Council of Greater Greensboro
A 13-session male responsibility curriculum for young adolescent males.
For more information:
P: 1-800-333-6890
Web site: http://www.greensboro.com/family/wiseguys.htm

## BOOKS

This list is a selection of books that provide information as well as storytelling on all aspects of human sexuality. These books allow readers to examine issues pertaining to specific age groups, topics, and cultures. In addition to providing access to understanding human sexuality and its impact, these books provide a way for adults to talk about uncomfortable topics with children and young adults in ways that are informative and easier to talk about.

The Adonis Complex: The Secret Crisis of Male Body Obsession
Harrison G. Pope Jr., Katharine A. Phillips, and Roberto Olivardia
Free Press, 2000
This interesting and provocative book describes a form of obsession in which otherwise healthy men become absorbed by compulsive exercising, eating disorders, body-image distortion, and ultimately, abuse of anabolic steroids.

Beyond Dolls & Guns: 101 Ways to Help Children Avoid Gender Bias
Susan Hoy Crawford
Heinemann, 1996
This easy-to-read guide gives anyone concerned about children practical and simple suggestions to challenge the gender bias pervasive in most communities. Includes a section on current research on girls and boys and a bibliography of nonsexist children's and adult reference books.

Beyond the Big Talk: Every Parent's Guide to Raising Sexually Healthy Teens from Middle School to High School and Beyond
Debra Haffner
New Market Press, 2002
Examining issues ranging from physical development to peer pressure to youth culture, the book is arranged by grade level and explores issues especially relevant to particular age groups and offers solid advice and resources to parents, who will greatly appreciate her candor.

Bodies and Biases: Sexualities in Hispanic Cultures and Literatures
Edited by David William Foster and Roberto Reis
University of Minnesota Press, 1996
Looking at a wide range of cultural practices and artifacts, including television, popular music, and pornography, this book addresses representations of sexual behavior and collective identity, homosexuality, and ideologies of gender in historical and contemporary Hispanic culture. Topics include cross-dressing on the seventeenth-century Spanish stage, gay life in Cuba and Mexico, a butch-femme reading of Peri-Rossi's Solitario de amor, pornography, and queer and lesbian spaces. Reflecting a diversity of sociological, literary, and psychological theoretical underpinnings, *Bodies and Biases* is a fascinating analysis of sexuality in the context of Hispanic literature and culture.

Boys Will Be Men: Raising our Sons for Courage, Caring and Community
Paul Kivel
New Society Publishers, 1999
Drawing on his decades of experience as a social activist and his antiviolence work with men and teens, Kivel challenges the traditional training boys receive and urges

parents to raise sons to be critically thinking, socially invested men and agents of change in a violent world.

"But How'd I Get in There in the First Place?": Talking to Your Young Child about Sex
Deborah Roffman
Perseus Press, 2002
Young children ask questions about sex, sexuality, conception, and birth that can be embarrassing or uncomfortable for parents. This book's guidance can put even the most awkward parents at ease, giving them the skills to talk confidently with young children about these important but delicate issues.

Caution: Do Not Open Until Puberty! An Introduction to Sexuality for Young Adults with Disabilities
Rick Enright
Devinjer House, 1995
This book attempts to break the silence that seems to prevent an open discussion of sexuality with disabled adolescents and their families. Also recommended for professionals and parents looking for a nonthreatening and humorous way to discuss sexuality with children and adolescents.

Changing Bodies, Changing Lives
Ruth Bell
Random House, 1998
Packed with information on sex, the body, sexual harassment, and relationships. Teens' personal stories about these topics are used throughout the book.

The Complete Idiot's Guide to Dating
Dr. Judy Kuriansky
Alpha Books, 3rd edition, 2003
Dating never gets easier. Here's time-tested advice for everyone from first-daters to those who have been around the block. Loaded with information on how to meet interesting people, break the ice, keep conversations going, and find the relationship of your dreams.

The Complete Idiot's Guide to a Healthy Relationship
Dr. Judy Kuriansky
Alpha Books, 2nd edition, 2002
Offers advice that is relevant and useful to anyone in any relationship. Dealing with more than one aspect of relationships, the book covers all the bases: what constitutes a healthy relationship, how to keep the passion alive, and how to overcome obstacles to a long-lasting relationship. New chapters on relationships in the new millennium, including content on managing long-distance relationships and relating in the Internet age, are included in this second edition.

The Complete Idiot's Guide to Tantric Sex
Dr. Judy Kuriansky
Alpha Books, 2nd edition, 2004

Comprehensive guide to the increasingly popular practices of tantric sexuality. Includes all the basics and more advanced practices about sacred loving and enlightenment, as well as unique chapters on adaptations for all ages, stages, and types of relationships and techniques for healing, better health, and peace.

Continuum Complete International Encyclopedia of Sexuality
Robert T. Francoeur, PhD, and Raymond J. Noonan, PhD, Editors
The Continuum International Publishing Group, New York and London, 2004
Written by more than 200 leading sexologists in their respective countries and cultures, each lengthy entry explores such areas as heterosexual relationships, children, adolescents, adults, gender-conflicted persons, unconventional sexual patterns, contraception, sexually transmitted diseases, AIDS, sexual dysfunctions, and therapies. It also includes sexual issues for older persons and physically and mentally challenged individuals.

The Facts of Life . . . and More: Sexuality and Intimacy for People with Intellectual Disabilities
Leslie Walker-Hirsch, M.Ed., FAAMR (editor)
Brookes Publishing Co., 2007
This book gives teachers, caregivers, and direct support professionals the information they need to educate people with disabilities about sexuality and help them make the best possible choices throughout their lives. Also includes interviews that show how couples with disabilities handle the joys and challenges of their relationships. It assists people in managing risks associated with sexual activity and uses behavior interventions to encourage appropriate sexual expression.

Families Like Mine: Children of Gay Parents Tell It Like It Is
Abigail Garner
HarperCollins, 2004
Abigail Garner was five when her parents divorced and her dad came out as gay. Growing up immersed in gay culture, she now calls herself a "culturally queer" heterosexual woman. This is a deeply personal book about gay parenting, from the perspective of grown children raised in these families.

Family Book
Todd Parr
Two Lives Publishing, 2003
Family favorite Todd Parr celebrates all kinds of families, including LGBTQ: "Some families have two moms or two dads . . ." Simple drawings of people, pets, and other animals are perfect for kids ages 2 and up.

Flight of the Stork: What Children Think (and When) About Sex and Family Building
Anne C. Berstein
Perspective Press, 1996
Provides parents with some insight on how children come to understand sex and reproduction. This understanding of child development will help adults

communicate better with children about the origin of families as well as the origin of babies. The revision also deals with such twenty-first-century topics as assisted reproductive technology, donor insemination, and surrogacy.

Free Your Mind
Ellen Bass and Kate Kaufman
Harper Perennial, 1996
A practical resource guide that helps LGBT youth and their allies understand, accept, and celebrate their sexual orientation; overcome obstacles; make healthy choices about relationships and sex; and participate in the gay and lesbian community. Bass and Kaufman weave together their professional experience with the immediate voices of dozens of gay and lesbian youths.

Gay and Lesbian Parenting
Deborah Glazer and Jack Drescher
Haworth Medical Press, 2001
A guide for lesbian and gay parents.

Generation Sex
Dr. Judy Kuriansky
Harper Books, 1996
Unique collection of thousands of questions from young people about sexuality and relationships and the author's advice. Based on questions from teens, college students, and Gen-Exers, who called an extremely popular radio advice show, this extensive collection covers an extremely broad range of topics, including attraction, virginity, body image, fantasy, common concerns, and unusual behaviors, providing an invaluable way to know about the worries, problems, and practices of young people that persist to modern times.

The Go Ask Alice! Book of Answers: A Guide to Good Physical, Sexual, and Emotional Health
Columbia University's Health Education Program
Henry Holt & Company, Inc., 1998
Provides straightforward, nonjudgmental, comprehensive answers to the toughest, most embarrassing questions teens (and adults) have about their sexual, emotional, and physical health. Inspired by Columbia University's award-winning and hugely popular Q&A Web site, this essential book is packed with answers to questions initially posed online. A thorough list of resources is included, providing telephone numbers and Internet addresses for related health organizations, as well as directions for where to look on the Go Ask Alice Web site for more information on the immense variety of subjects.

Growing a Girl: Seven Strategies for Raising a Strong, Spirited Daughter
Barbara Mackoff
Dell Publishing, 1996
Identifies seven specific strategies designed to help parents strengthen their daughter's individuality, self-esteem, and independence. Strong examples and

suggested approaches within these seven strategies give readers the opportunity to employ the strategies immediately.

It's Not the Stork: A Book about Girls, Boys, Babies, Bodies, Families and Friends
Robie H. Harris
Candlewick Press, 2008
From the expert team behind "It's Perfectly Normal" and "It's So Amazing!" this is a book for younger children about their bodies—a resource that parents, teachers, librarians, health care providers, and clergy can use with ease and confidence.

It's Perfectly Normal: Growing Up, Changing Bodies, Sex and Sexual Health
Robie Harris
Candlewick Press, 1996
Providing accurate, unbiased answers to nearly every imaginable question, from conception and puberty to birth control and AIDS, this book offers young people information to make responsible decisions and to stay healthy.

It's So Amazing!: A Book about Eggs, Sperm, Birth, Babies, and Families
Robie H. Harris
Candlewick Press, 1999
This creative book uses bird and bee cartoon characters to present straightforward explanations of topics related to sexual development.

My Body, My Self For Boys (3rd ed.)
Lynda Madaras and Area Madaras
Newmarket Press, 2007
Features detailed coverage, in age-appropriate language, of the body's changing size and shape, the growth spurt, the reproductive organs, voice changes, romantic and sexual feelings, puberty in the opposite sex, and much more. Filled with activities, checklists, illustrations, and plenty of room for journal jottings, plus lots of personal stories in which boys share their concerns and experiences about growing up. For ages 10 and up.

My Body, My Self For Girls (3rd ed.)
Lynda Madaras and Area Madaras
Newmarket Press, 2007
Features detailed coverage, in age-appropriate language, of the body's changing size and shape, the growth spurt, the reproductive organs, menstruation, romantic and sexual feelings, puberty in the opposite sex, and much more. Filled with activities, checklists, illustrations, and plenty of room for journal jottings, plus lots of personal stories in which girls share their concerns and experiences about growing up. For ages 10 and up.

Period
JoAnn Loulan and Bonnie Worthen
Book Peddlers, 2001
Covers questions about puberty and menstruation. The authors emphasize the positive and use diagrams to familiarize readers with the inner workings of their

bodies, including what happens during menstruation. A question-and-answer format in the last three chapters allows girls to locate easily the information they seek. A parent's guide bound into the back suggests how to begin a conversation about puberty and what to cover.

Raising Boys: Why Boys are Different—and How to Help Them Become Happy and Well-Balanced Men
Steve Biddulph
Celestial Arts, 2008
Australia's best-known family therapist and parenting author looks at the most crucial issues that happen in the male's lifetime, from birth to manhood, and offers instruction on the warm, firm guidance that boys need in order to become happy, well-balanced men.

Sexual Etiquette 101 . . . and More
Robert Hatcher, Shannon Colestock, Erika Pluhar, and Christian Thrasher
Bridging the Gap Communications, Inc., 2002
A crash course on sexuality, this book for college students contains stories, resources, ideas, and other valuable tools to help successfully navigate the often confusing world of relationships and sexuality. This book aims to provide information to help prevent the possibly negative and harmful side of sexuality, to be able to enjoy the pleasurable and beautiful side of sexuality, and to make the right decisions.

Sexuality Education: What Adolescents' Rights Require
Nova Publishers, 2007
This book explores adolescent changes and challenges by examining the extent to which we may foster adolescent development in ways that respect and foster adolescents' basic rights to relationships they deem appropriate, fulfilling, and worthy of protection. It also explores those changes and rights from a view that acknowledges the need to respect the rights of others, that recognizes that adolescents' rights are not for them alone.

Sexuality Education Across Cultures: Working with Differences
Janice M. Irvine
Jossey-Bass, 1995
Cultural differences affect sexuality education. This book includes information on approaching the topic with different cultures and gaining an understanding of the diverse perspectives of sexual speech. Examples of how to develop culturally appropriate education programs are also included.

Third Base Ain't What it Used to Be
Logan Levkoff, PhD
New American Library, 2007
Brings parents up to date on the world that their kids are living in: what their slang means, what myths and stereotypes they are learning from friends, and how pop culture is affecting how they make decisions. Arranged by topic, it includes

common questions that children and teens have asked the author and offers tips
and talking points for tackling these issues in your own home.

The "What's Happening to My Body" Book for Boys (rev. 3rd ed.)
Lynda Madaras with Area Madaras
Newmarket Press, 2007
To help boys realize they are not alone in their concerns about masturbation,
body hair, growth spurts (or lack thereof), female puberty, voice changes,
perspiration, shaving, and sexuality, this classic guide is written in a down-to-
earth, nonjudgmental style and filled with answers to the many questions boys
have as their bodies begin the transformation into adulthood. The third edition
has been revised to include more detailed discussion of penis size (the authors
get more questions about penis size than all other topics combined); updated
information on acne treatment; expanded sections on eating right, exercise,
steroid abuse, and weight training; important facts about STDs, AIDS, and birth
control; and more.

The "What's Happening to My Body" Book for Girls (rev. 3rd ed.)
Lynda Madaras with Area Madaras
Newmarket Press, 2007
Straight talk on the menstrual cycle, reproductive organs, breasts, emotional
changes, puberty in boys, body hair, pimples, masturbation, and all the other fun,
scary, and interesting things that go along with growing up. Filled with anecdotes,
illustrations, diagrams, and honest, sensitive, nonjudgmental information for
the young girl, the revised edition also addresses the new scientific facts about
when a girl actually begins puberty (earlier than previously thought), advice on
"female athletic syndrome," eating disorders, unwanted attention because of early
development, and information on eating right, exercise, AIDS, STDs, birth control,
and more.

## NEWSLETTERS

Newsletters are an important resource because they make available relevant
issues and research in a brief manner while offering support to those interested in the field of human sexuality. Newsletters also provide information on
upcoming events and conferences dealing with human sexuality.

Contemporary Sexuality
American Association of Sexuality Educators, Counselors, and Therapists
(AASECT)
P.O. Box 1960
Ashland, Virginia, 23005–1960
P: 804-752-0026
F: 804-752-0056
The monthly voice of the Association. The newsletter discusses contemporary
and relevant issues through lead articles; provides a summary of significant

contemporary issues, legislation, and policy related to the field; and lists AASECT-approved and -sponsored continuing education workshops.
Web site: http://www.aasect.org

The Kinsey Institute Newsletter—Kinsey Today
E-mail: Kinsey@indiania.edu
Web site: http://www.kinseyinstitute.org/newsletter/

The Sexual Health Network (TSHN) Newsletter
3 Mayflower Lane
Shelton, CT 06484
Dedicated to providing easy access to sexuality information, education, support, and other resources.
Web site: http://www.SexualHealth.com

SIECUS Newsletter
Newsletter for the Sexuality Information and Education Council of the United States.
Web site: http://www.siecus.org

## MAGAZINES

These magazines offer useful information about human sexuality to stay up to date with the latest information, research, and issues in the field of human sexuality.

American Sexuality Magazine
National Sexuality Resource Center
San Francisco State University
835 Market St, Suite 517
San Francisco, CA 94103
P: 415-817-4525
F: 415-817-4540
E-mail: nsrcinfo@sfsu.edu
Web site: http://nsrc.sfsu.edu/MagWebpage.cfm

Sex, Etc.
Answer
Rutgers University
41 Gordon Road, Suite C
Piscataway, New Jersey 08854–8067
P: 732-445-7929
F: 732-445-7970
Web site: http://www.sexetc.org

## VIDEOS/DVDS

Videos and DVDs about sexuality provide educators in the field of human sexuality a tool for their own learning, as well as for making learning interesting and visual for others. These visual aides can be useful in various contexts, including in the classroom, and in public and professional presentations. Through documentaries and animated videos those who watch will be able to gain the knowledge they would often find in the pages of books, journals, and textbooks. Information, as well as personal stories and experiences, can help learners relate to issues, and can leave a lasting memory.

Girls: Moving Beyond Myth
Produced by: Susan Macmillan
This documentary focuses on the sexual dilemmas and difficult life choices young girls face as they come of age in contemporary American culture. Challenging long-held myths about girlhood, the film draws on the insights of girls themselves to explore and shed light on their actual lived experience as they navigate our increasingly hypersexualized society.
http://www.mediaed.org/videos/

In Our Own Words: Teens and AIDS
Family Health Productions, Inc., 1995
Boston, MA
P: 978-282-9970
Denial can lead to disease. Teens infected with HIV through unprotected intercourse discuss denial, condoms, postponing sex, and how alcohol affects decision making. With discussion guide. 20 minutes. Available in Spanish. Recommended for grades 5 through 12, parents, and other caregivers.
http://www.abouthealth.com/h_products.htm

The Power of Girls: Inside and Out
Family Health Productions, Inc., 2003
Boston, MA
Strong connections help young people make healthy choices. These girls discuss how they dealt with bullying, eating disorders, early sexual activity, and deep loss by talking with friends, parents, or other caring adults. With discussion guide. 20 minutes. Recommended for grades 5 through 12, parents, and other caregivers.
http://wordscanwork.com/products/productsservices.html

Raising Healthy Kids: Families Talk About Sexual Health
Family Health Productions, Inc., 1997
Boston, MA
P: 978-282-9970
Communication about sexual health begins at birth. These parents and young people tell how they discuss sexual health. Experts offer insight and skills to help families start and continue these conversations. Includes discussion guides. Recommended for parents and other caregivers.
http://www.abouthealth.com/h_products.htm

Speak Up!: Improving the Lives of GLBT Youth
Media rights
Copyright 2001

Gay, lesbian, bisexual, and transgender (GLBT) students and their allies face unique challenges of violence and harassment in schools. *SPEAK UP!* explores what these students and their allies have done to transform their schools into safer and more welcoming environments. Interviews with students, parents, teachers, administrators, and national activists highlight not only the need for transformation, but offer resources and advice for those actively working for change. http://www.mediaed.org/videos/MediaGenderAndDiversity/SpeakUp

Talking About Sex: A Guide for Families
Planned Parenthood Federation of America, 1996
New York
An animated video designed to educate children about the basics of sexual relations, including puberty, relationships, contraception, and abstinence. Includes a guide for parents as well as an activity book for children. For ages 10–14.

Teens & Sex in Europe: A Story of Rights, Respect & Responsibility
Narrated by Mariette Hartley
Advocates for Youth, 1998
Provides a fascinating glimpse into the sexual health attitudes of Dutch, German, and French teens and their parents and into the attitudes of government officials, educators, and health care providers.

## FILM COMPANIES

Some film companies specialize in producing visual aides that can help educators in their own learning and with presentations, as well as help individuals and couples gain knowledge and skills about sexuality. These companies offer a variety of products for these purposes.

Access Instructional Media
1750 N. Sierra Bonita Ave.
Hollywood, CA 90046
P: 1-800-772-0708 (toll free; to order)
Online superstore. Offers couples-friendly instructional erotica videos.
E-mail Dr. Michael Perry: mepsexdoc@aol.com
Web site: http://www.sexualintimacy.com/home.htm

Alexander Institute
15030 Ventura Blvd., Suite 400
Sherman Oaks, CA 91403
P: 888-270-6510 (toll free; to order)
P: 818-508-1296
F: 818-508-9076
Produces the most critically acclaimed sexuality video series for couples and singles who want to enhance their sex life. World-renowned sex therapists, educators, and best-selling authors developed these erotic and informative series.

E-mail: sales@alexander-institute.com
Web site: http://alexander-institute.com

Femme Productions
A unique collection of "female-friendly" films made with a women's perspective, voice, and pleasure in mind, following story lines and fantasies that appeal to women, and also provide positive female role models, but can be enjoyed by men. The company also offers sexuality-related toys and aides. Founded by a woman. Intended for use by individuals 18 or older.
Web site: http://www.candidaroyalle.com/catalog.html

Sinclair Institute Library
402 Millstone Drive
Hillsborough, NC 27278
P: 1-800-865-9165
F: 1-800-794-3318
Sinclair Institute has earned its reputation as a trusted source for couples seeking greater intimacy, variety, or passion in their sex lives. They offer a wide range of videos and DVDs, which have been produced on a vast array of topics about sexuality. In addition, they sell sexual aids designed to enhance sex and intimacy, including adult toys, videos, massagers, educational products, and sexy clothing for both men and women. Sinclair Institute selects only top-quality products to sell in a discreet and comfortable Web environment.
E-mail: cservice@sinclairinstitute.com
Web site: http://www.sinclairinstitute.com

Vivid-Ed
The sex education imprint of Vivid Entertainment produces videos that cover a range of topics in human sexuality, from anal sex and G-spot stimulation to fellatio and bondage. Vivid-Ed videos offer useful information and explicit techniques' taught by experts, demonstrated by enthusiastic performers, and presented with sensuality.
Web site: http://www.vivid-ed.com/index.php

## SEX MUSEUMS

Sex museums provide entertainment and education about the history, development, and cultural significance of human sexuality throughout the world and about the particular culture and country they are set in. Permanent, and sometimes rotating, exhibits include erotic art, artifacts, clothing, and diverse historical and modern-day objects related to sexuality, often in multimedia displays, and that vary in the degree to which they are geared to serious study. Most museums also have a retail boutique or store of items for purchase related to the exhibits, as well as books and various sexuality-related aides and items.

USA, New York: Museum of Sex
233 Fifth Avenue

New York, NY 10016
P: 212-689-6337
Web site: http://www.museumofsex.com

USA, Florida: World Erotic Art Museum
1205 Washington Ave.
Miami Beach, Florida 33139
P: 866-969-WEAM (9326)
Web site: http://www.weam.com

USA, Nevada: Erotic Heritage Museum
3275 Industrial Road
Las Vegas, Nevada 89109
P: 702- 369-6442
Web site: http://www.eroticheritagemuseum.com

USA, California: The Erotic Museum Hollywood
6741 Hollywood Blvd.
Hollywood, CA 90028
P: 323-GO-EROTIC (463-7684)
Web site: http://www.theeroticmuseum.com/them/

Denmark: Erotica Museum
Købmagergade 24
1150 København K, Denmark
P: +45 3312 0311
Web site: http://www.museumerotica.dk

Netherlands: The Sex Museum Amsterdam
Damrak 18, Amsterdam
1012 LH Amsterdam
P: +31 0 20 622 8376
Web site: http://www.sexmuseumamsterdam.nl

France: Musée de l'érotisme de Paris
72, boulevard de Clichy
75018, Paris, France
Web site: http://www.musee-erotisme.com

Spain: Museo de Erotic in Barcelona
Rambla, 96
08002, Barcelona, Spain
P: +34 93 318 98 65
Web site: http://www.erotica-museum.com

England: Amora Academy of Sex and Relationships
13 Coventry St.

London W1D7DH, England
Web site:  http://www.amoralondon.com

Germany: Beate Uhse Erotik–Museum
Joachimstaler Str. 4
10623 Berlin Charlottenburg
P: +49  886 06 66
Web site: www.beate-uhse.ag

Czech Republic: Sex Machines Museum
Melantrichova 18–11000 Prague 1
P: +420 227 186 260
Web site:  http://www.sexmachinesmuseum.com

China: The Chinese Sex Culture Museum
Tongli Town
Jiang Su Province 215217
China
E-Mail: hongxia508@hotmail.com
Web site: http://www2.hu-berlin.de/sexology/CSM/index.htm

Japan: Beppu's Hihōkan Sex Museum
338–3 Shibuyu Kannawa
Beppu City, Oita Prefecture
P: 0977-66-8790
Web site: N/A

## INNOVATIONS

Contemporary times are characterized by technology and new innovations. The following resources represent innovations in the field of human sexuality that allow people to get personalized information, and also to come in touch with others through the Internet and communicate about issues relating to human sexuality.

Internet Sexuality Information Services, Inc. (ISIS)
This nonprofit has been an innovator in the field of sexual health promotion and disease prevention online. Their most well-known project is an e-card service for people to notify their partners of potential exposures to sexually transmitted diseases. Called **inSPOT** (http://www.inspot.org), the site exists in the United States, Romania, and Canada and is being translated into Spanish and French. Recipients of the e-cards can click back to the site to get local testing referrals and disease treatment and prevention information. **SexINFO** (http://www.sextext.org), a short message service (SMS) text-messaging service on mobile phones to inform low-income youth about sexual health and resources. Users type in a code and get a menu of frequently asked questions and answers about HIV, STDs, unintended

pregnancies, and sexual activity, together with one or two local youth-friendly resources.
Web site: http://www.isis-inc.org

Kinsey Confidential Podcast
An opportunity to ask questions and have them answered by experts in sexual health and behavior from the Kinsey Institute at Indiana University.
Web site: http://www.kinseyconfidential.org/podcast/

# INDEX

# ABOUT THE EDITORS AND CONTRIBUTORS

## EDITORS

**Judy Kuriansky, PhD,** is a clinical psychologist and sex therapist and educator, international trainer, author, and journalist. She is on the adjunct faculty in the Department of Counseling and Clinical Psychology at Columbia University Teachers College and Columbia University College of Physicians and Surgeons, visiting professor at Peking University Health Sciences Center and honorary professor in the Department of Psychiatry of the University of Hong Kong. A diplomat of the American Board of Sexology and fellow of the American Academy of Clinical Sexology (AACS) and awarded the AACS Medal of Sexology for Lifetime Achievement, she is a veteran sexuality educator and therapist, working with individuals, couples, and groups across the country and the world. A past board member of the American Association of Sexuality Educators, Counselor and Therapists (AASECT) and a cofounder of the Society for Sex Therapy and Research, she has authored hundreds of articles in professional journals and mass-market publications about sexuality and sexual health.

As a pioneer of Internet advice and radio call-in advice, "Dr. Judy" has given sexuality and relationship advice in many formats and forums to thousands of men and women of all ages for decades. She has led innumerable workshops across the United States and the globe and developed unique approaches to teaching about safer sex and relationship enhancement, integrating Western and Eastern techniques, which have been presented nationally and internationally from China and Japan to India, Israel, Iran, Austria, and Argentina. In the early days of the developing field of sexuality, she served on the committee determining the first sexuality diagnostic criteria for the American Psychiatric Association's *DSM-III* and evaluated the Masters and Johnson techniques. She has also written advice columns for decades in many mass market publications like *Family Circle Magazine, CosmoGirl, Chicago Tribune's Womanews, Single Living, King Features newspapers,* the *South China Morning Post,* the *Singapore Straits Times, China Trends Health Magazine, Bottom Line Women's Health* newsletter, and the *New York Daily News* Web site. Her commentary about sexuality and relationship issues is quoted in many print sources from newswires to Web sites like abc.com to magazines like *In Touch.* She has developed numerous Internet educational Web sites on topics such as women's issues, healthy aging, and overcoming blues in the bedroom. Her own Web site is www.DrJudy.com.

A former feature television reporter for WABC-TV and CBS-TV and host of CNBC'S *Money and Emotions,* she has been a guest commentator on innumerable TV news and talk shows including *Oprah, Larry King,* and *CNN Headline News' Issues* and *Showbiz Tonight;* has hosted TV specials on topics like "Teens and AIDS" and "No Secrets" about child sex abuse; and has been featured in media from *People* magazine to the *New York Times.* A Fellow of the American Psychological Association and board member of the Peace division, cofounder of the Media Division and Committee of International Relations representative for the Society for Humanistic Psychology, she has extended help to individuals' relations and intercultural relations, consistent with her philosophy that "peace within leads to peace between people and then peace between nations."

She collaborates extensively with colleagues worldwide, including in China doing trainings for health professionals and helping develop a family planning and reproductive health hotline. She has presented her work about sexuality at World Association of Sexology conferences in Rio, Hong Kong, and Sydney, Australia, Asia-Oceanic Conferences on Sexology, and for the China Association of Sexology. At the United Nations, she is the main representative for the International Association of Applied Psychology and the World Association for Psychotherapy and serves on the executive committee of the Committee on Mental Health. A former advisory board member of Planned Parenthood, she is currently on the advisory board and the head of psychosocial programs for U.S. Doctors for Africa and is a member of the executive committee of the section on disasters of the World Association of Psychiatry in association with the Iberoamerican Ecobioethics Network for Education, Science and Technology and the UNESCO Chair in Bioethics. Her books on resolving conflict include *Terror in the Holy Land* and *Beyond Bullets and Bombs: Grassroots peace building between Israelis and Palestinians.*

At Smith College she was a Sloan Foundation Science Research Grant awardee and received her EdM in counseling psychology from Boston University and her PhD in clinical psychology from New York University. She was awarded two Maggie awards for her work with adolescents, as well as a Freedoms Foundation award and a STAR award for individual achievement in radio from American Women in Radio and TV (AWRT), and the first AWRT International Outreach Award.

Besides her professional accomplishments, she is in a band called the *Stand Up for Peace Project*, which performs at peace summits around the world, including recently at the International Peace Summit with the Dalai Lama in Hiroshima. Her many books about sex and relationships include *Generation Sex: America's Hottest Sex Therapist Answers the Hottest Questions about Sex*, *The Complete Idiot's Guide to Dating*, *The Complete Idiot's Guide to A Healthy Relationship*, and *The Complete Idiot's Guide to Tantric Sex*, as well as books originally published in Japan and China. She helps others get their work published in her role as a series editor for two Praeger books' series: Practical and Applied Psychology and Sex, Love, and Psychology.

**Elizabeth Schroeder, EdD, MSW,** is an international trainer, consultant, and author in the areas of sexual health and sexuality education, curriculum development, teacher training, and counseling. She has provided trainings as well as conference workshops and keynote addresses throughout the United States and overseas to thousands of youth-serving professionals and young people.

Dr. Schroeder is currently the Executive Director for Answer, a national organization based at Rutgers University that is dedicated to providing and promoting comprehensive sexuality education throughout the United States. Known worldwide for their award-winning Web site, "Sex, Etc." (www.sexetc. org), Answer also provides much-needed professional development for teachers and other youth-serving professionals (http://answer.rutgers.edu).

Dr. Schroeder was the cofounding editor of the *American Journal of Sexuality Education*, a journal that provides not only the most cutting-edge research in sexuality education, but also "lessons from the field" as well as lesson plans. In addition to many articles, she is coauthor of several curricula, including "Making SMART Choices: A Curriculum for Young People," and "Being Out, Staying Safe: An STD Prevention Curriculum for LGBQ Youth," both with Dr. Eva Goldfarb. She has edited the 5th, 6th, and 7th editions of *Taking Sides: Clashing Views in Controversial Issues in Family and Personal Relationships*, and authored chapters in *Health Counseling: Applications and Theory* and *The Continuum Complete International Encyclopedia of Sexuality*. She was also proud to contribute a lesson on lesbian and gay issues and aging for *New*

*Expectations: Sexuality Education for Mid- and Later Life,* coedited by Peggy Brick and Jan Lunquist.

Dr. Schroeder has taught courses on human sexuality, health counseling, curriculum development, and teaching methods at Montclair State University and has been a guest lecturer at other colleges and universities. She also served as the Associate Vice President of Education and Training at Planned Parenthood of New York City, where she worked to establish their training institute for teachers and other youth-serving professionals. Before that, she was the Manager of Education and Special Projects at Planned Parenthood Federation of America, where she coordinated the production of their multiple award-winning video kit for families with adolescent children, *Talking About Sex: A Guide for Families.*

Dr. Schroeder has lent her expertise to Web-based sexuality education initiatives as an expert on the Sex, Etc. Web site, a Web site by teens, for teens. In addition to responding to questions through the "Ask the Experts" section, Dr. Schroeder answered questions and provided counseling during moderated live chats. She has also provided sexuality education for adults by writing articles and responding to e-mails for http://www.sexualhealth.com.

Elizabeth Schroeder has been honored with the Schiller Award by the American Association of Sexuality Educators, Counselors, and Therapists for her approaches to teaching Internet safety to adolescents, and the Mary Lee Tatum Award, given to "the person who most exemplifies the qualities of an ideal sexuality educator." She has been recognized by the Society for the Scientific Study of Sexuality as an "Emerging Professional" in sexuality education and research, and back in 1999, she was given the national Apple Blossom Award, which recognized a Planned Parenthood Education or Training Director who has "risen quickly to the forefront with new ideas, energy, and commitment."

Dr. Schroeder has served as Chairperson of the Sexuality Information and Education Council of the United States (SIECUS) Board of Directors and on numerous local, state, and national task forces and committees. She earned an EdD with a specialization in Human Sexuality Education from Widener University and a Master's Degree in clinical Social Work from New York University.

## CONTRIBUTORS

**Lauren A. Antonecchia, BS,** is currently a second year Psychological Counseling EdM student at Teachers College, Columbia University. Presently is working on a participatory action research project with a New York City public high school and completing a one year internship with the counseling department at a Westchester County high school. She plans to go on to be a high school counselor and is interested in human sexuality education, with a focus on adolescent behavior.

**Patti Britton, PhD** is a nationally board-certified clinical sexologist and author of hundreds of articles and four books. The original sexpert for iVillage. com, she hosts her own Web site and 30 DVDs. She has appeared extensively on television, live talk and news radio shows, and in print media. A President of AASECT, Clinical Fellow of the American Academy of Clinical Sexologists, Diplomate of the American Board of Sexology, and Associate Professor of Sexology at the Institute for the Advanced Study of Human Sexuality, she has a private practice in Los Angeles.

**John P. Elia, PhD,** is associate professor and associate chair in the Department of Health Education at San Francisco State University, where he has taught for over 20 years. Dr. Elia's current research interests include the history of school-based sexuality education in the United States and queer popular culture. He has coedited five books and written scholarly articles, book chapters, encyclopedia entries, and book reviews in the areas of human sexuality studies and LGBT and queer studies. The associate editor of the *Journal of Homosexuality,* he serves on the editorial boards of the *Journal of LGBT Youth, Journal of Popular Culture,* and *The Educational Forum.*

**Mickey J. Eliason, PhD,** is assistant professor of health education at San Francisco State University. Her research interests include substance abuse and treatment, human sexuality studies, LGBT and queer studies, and LGBTQ health. She has published a number of articles in scholarly journals, as well as "Improving Substance Abuse Treatment: An Introduction to the Evidence-Based Practice Movement." She is the coeditor of *Queer Studies: A Lesbian, Gay, Bisexual, and Transgender Anthology* and coauthor of a forthcoming volume on LGBT health.

**Eva S. Goldfarb, PhD,** is Professor of Health Education and chair of the department of Health and Nutrition Sciences at Montclair State University. For nearly 20 years, she has written, taught, and trained professionals, parents, and youth nationwide in the areas of human sexuality and sexual health. She is coauthor of *Our Whole Lives: Sexuality Education for Grades 10–12* and *4–6; Making SMART Choices about Sex;* and *Being Out, Staying Safe* and has contributed to many other publications.

**Barbara Kemp Huberman, BSN, MEd,** is a noted trainer and author on adolescent sexuality. She has been involved in cross-country comparisons of policies, practices, and programs to promote healthy and positive adolescent sexual health for over 40 years. She is a former President of the National Organization on Adolescent Pregnancy and Parenting (now Healthy Teen Network) and one of the founders of the National Campaign to Prevent Teen Pregnancy. She is the Director of Education and Outreach for Advocates for Youth in Washington, DC.

**Leslie M. Kantor, MPH,** is a nationally recognized expert on effective sex education, pregnancy prevention, and adolescent sexual health. She is currently Director of Planning and Special Projects and Assistant Professor of Clinical Population and Family Health for the Heilbrunn Department of Population and Family Health, Mailman School of Public Health, Columbia University. She has received awards from the American Public Health Association recognizing her work.

**Gary F. Kelly, MEd** has been a sexuality educator and author for 40 years. After recently retiring as Headmaster of The Clarkson School and Vice President for Student Affairs at Clarkson University in Potsdam, New York, he continues to teach courses in the Psychology Department, including Human Sexuality. He recently received the Outstanding Teaching Award from Clarkson's student body. He is the author of a popular college textbook *Sexuality Today*.

**Martha E. Kempner, MA,** Vice President for Information and Communications at SIECUS, is responsible for raising the visibility of the importance of sexuality-related issues in the media. She oversees the development of all SIECUS articles, fact sheets, and Web sites and the public relations and media activities at local, state, national, and international levels. She also monitors and analyzes current trends in sexuality education. An adjunct instructor of human sexuality at Marymount Manhattan College, she earned a master's degree in human sexuality from New York University.

**Judy Kuriansky, PhD,** is a clinical psychologist, sex therapist and educator, and international trainer on the adjunct faculty at Columbia University Teachers College and Columbia University College of Physicians and Surgeons. A visiting professor at Peking University Health Sciences Center and honorary professor in the Department of Psychiatry of the University of Hong Kong, she is a Fellow of the American Psychological Association and main United Nations representative for the International Association of Applied Psychology. Past board member of AASECT, she was awarded a Medal of Sexology for Lifetime Achievement from the American Academy of Clinical Sexology.

A veteran radio talk show advice host and TV commentator, and pioneer of "media sexology," she has authored many books, including *Generation Sex* and *The Complete Idiot's Guide to Tantric Sex*. She writes advice for many publications and on her Web site www.DrJudy.com, and helps others get their books published as a Praeger series editor for the Practical and Applied Psychology and Sex, Love, and Psychology series.

**Jean Levitan, PhD,** is a professor in the Department of Public Health at William Paterson University of New Jersey, having joined the faculty in 1978. She is also an affiliated faculty member in the Women's Studies Department. She teaches undergraduate courses in Human Sexuality, Reproductive Rights, Women's Health, Current Health Issues, and First Year Seminar. Levitan co-authored the undergraduate textbook *Healthy Sexuality*.

**Konstance McCaffree, PhD,** is an adjunct professor in Widener University's Program in Human Sexuality. She consults internationally, assisting in the development of sexuality education curriculum and the training of teachers. She has taught sexuality in secondary schools for over 30 years. Dr. McCaffree is the coauthor of the Centers of Disease Control (CDC) award-winning and nationally promoted curricula for minority youth, "Be Proud! Be Responsible!," "Making a Difference," and "Making Proud Choices."

**Sabitha Pillai-Friedman, PhD, LICSW,** is a relationship and certified sex therapist at the Institute for Sex Therapy, Council for Relationships in Philadelphia. She holds a PhD in Social Work from Bryn Mawr College and has over 18 years' experience providing individual, couple, and sex therapy. She is the director of supervision for and an adjunct assistant professor at the Jefferson/CFR Couple and Family Therapy Program. Dr. Pillai-Friedman presents nationally and internationally on various topics related to sexuality and has been interviewed on NBC and NPR.

**Maria D. Ramirez, MA,** is obtaining her masters degree in Psychological Counseling at Teachers College, Columbia University. She has an internship at New Rochelle High School as a school counselor and is involved in Participatory Action Research involving middle school students.

**Elizabeth Schroeder, EdD, MSW,** is the executive director for Answer, a national sexuality education organization housed at Rutgers University in New Jersey (http://answer.rutgers.edu). She is an award-winning sexuality educator, author, and consultant who has worked with thousands of youth-serving professionals and teens throughout the United States and overseas. A regular presenter at national and international conferences, she has written extensively about sexuality, counseling and training issues, and appears frequently in the media as a sexuality expert, with particular expertise in parent-child communication about sexuality and sexual orientation issues. Dr. Schroeder is the cofounding editor of the *American Journal of Sexuality Education,* a past Chairperson of the Sexuality Information and Education Council of the United States' Board of Directors, and has served as an adjunct professor at Montclair State University. Dr. Schroeder earned her Doctorate in human sexuality education from Widener University and her Master's degree in clinical social work from New York University.

**Rose M. Somerville, PhD,** was a faculty member of the Department of Sociology and Section of Child Development and Family Studies at San Diego State University.

**William R. Stayton, ThD, PhD,** is the former Director of the Human Sexuality Graduate Program at Widener University and still serves as Professor and Scholar in Residence. He also served until August 2008 as the Executive Director of the Center for Sexuality and Religion. As of September 2008, he is Professor of Sexuality and Religion at the Morehouse School of Medicine with a joint appointment at the Interdenominational Theological Center in Atlanta.

**Christian J. Thrasher, MA,** is the Director of the Center of Excellence for Sexual Health in the Satcher Health Leadership Institute at the Morehouse School of Medicine in Atlanta, Georgia. The center aims to advance a national dialogue on sexuality, sexual health, and responsible sexual behavior based on the recommendations put forth in the 16th Surgeon General's *Call to Action to Promote Sexual Health and Responsible Sexual Behavior.*

**Michael Young, PhD,** is a professor and the Associate Department Head for Research and Doctoral Studies in the Department of Health Science at New Mexico State University. He is coauthor of the award-winning "Sex Can Wait" abstinence education curriculum series and the training program from which it originated. He has published extensively on abstinence education and other adolescent health issues and received the American Association for Health Education's Scholar Award and the American School Health Association's Research Award.